Web Design

The Evolution
of the Digital
World 1990–Today

Web Design

The Evolution of the Digital World 1990-Today

Rob Ford
Ed. Julius Wiedemann

TASCHEN

Contents/
—

Study the past if you would define the future.

Confucius
551 BC — 479 BC

Foreword/

—

By Lars Bastholm

—

"An era was coming to a close, and we had the incredible fortune to experience the whole crazy ride from the inside."

One day in 1994, they plugged a phone cable into a modem and connected it to a computer in the library of the TV station where I was working part time as a researcher while finishing my master's thesis. As the most tech-savvy person there, it fell to me to figure out what we could do with this 'internet' that we now had access to. I dutifully picked up the *Internet Yellow Pages* book ("Arranged alphabetically by subject making for a wonderful way of identifying terrific web sites and internet resources – no web surfer should leave their terminal without it!" in the words of the 1996 edition), and set to work exploring the World Wide Web. Aside from issues with download speed, veracity of sources, and design, it was an amazing first trip down the rabbit hole. Little did I know then that my work life would end up revolving entirely around the internet.

When Rob asked me if I wanted to write the foreword to this book, my first thought was that it was premature. We couldn't possibly be at the stage already where it was time to write the history of web design, could we? But with the demise of Flash, most interactions with the internet happening from mobile devices, and the dawning of new platforms like VR and AR (which will develop their own design paradigms), I realized that Rob was right. An era was coming to a close, and he and I had both had the incredible fortune to experience the whole crazy ride from the inside.

Rob and I have a classic internet relationship: we've known each other for nearly two decades, yet have never met in person. All my interactions with Rob have been via emails and whatever digital communication platform was trending at any given time. The initial connection was obviously the FWA, which has been an indispensable resource for the digital design community since its inception in 2000, but we've also collaborated on previous TASCHEN books about the digital industry as well as shared stories about the trials and tribulations of becoming dads late in life.

I am lucky to have worked at not just one, but two of the agencies that helped define what great web design looked like, Framfab (now DigitasLBi) and AKQA. Through winning the FWA Site of the Day and Site of the Month honors, Rob and I became connected, started talking, and have been talking ever since. Through his curation of the FWA, Rob has become likely the world's leading expert on not just web design, but creative expression in general in the digital space. He celebrates great design and smart thinking for a living. Not the worst way to spend your days.

In every conceivable way, Flash played an oversized role in the history of web design, and the history of web design is in many ways the history of Flash. I'll never forget seeing some of Gabocorp's first experiments with Flash navigation, which immediately made everything else seem like it was in the past. For readers who weren't around then, the web before Flash was largely static. No animations, no video, no motion graphics. Flash was such a gigantic leap forward that the rule book was thrown out the window, and it became Year Zero in web design again. Walking down my personal memory lane as I browse through the pages of this book, I remember seeing Hi-ReS!'s website for Darren Aronofsky's movie *Requiem for a Dream* and gasping at the sheer beauty of the design. I remember when Tokyoplastic arrived on the scene accompanied by the rolling thunder of timpani drums. I remember the loud thud my jaw made as it hit the floor, when I first saw Get the Glass, which may just be the pinnacle achievement of the Flash era.

The only comparable advance in technology to affect web design in this way was 'broadband' internet connections. For a large swathe of today's internet users, it doesn't sound fast, but there was a time when we were waxing poetic about what would happen and how things would change, once we got to 2-megabit connections. Then the Subservient Chicken entered the arena and basically changed the paradigm once again, and it grew obvious what the internet would eventually become. Use of video and audio made modern documentaries like We Choose the Moon possible, personalization + video brought heartbreaking emotion to The Wilderness Downtown, and ingenious video trickery (technical term) took kids on a "Field Trip to Mars".

I'm proud to call many of the people featured in this book my friends. We were all competing for the same awards and judging the same shows as well as being part of organized groups to discuss the state of the industry, such as, for example, Creative Social. We've all taken turns being jealous of each other's work – the best incentive to improve that I've ever known – but it's also been a very collegial group of people. We were inventing a new medium together. No one could have gotten there on their own, and we were constantly learning from each other. It was a time of incessant innovation. This book is as close to an 'official' history as we're ever likely to get.

Enjoy!

Lars Bastholm

Biography:

A three-time Grand Prix winner at the Cannes Festival of Creativity, Lars is one of the most highly awarded creative leaders in the digital advertising industry. He is the Chief Creative Officer of the Exploratory, a Google company. He has also previously worked at Framfab, AKQA, and Ogilvy. Lars is a frequent speaker and judge at awards shows, and is a member of the International Academy of Digital Arts and Sciences as well as the Producers Guild of America. Lars has also co-written screenplays and has reviewed films for over 30 years.

Vorwort/

—

Biografie:

Als dreimaliger Grand-Prix-Gewinner beim Festival of Creativity in Cannes, ist Lars einer der am höchsten ausgezeichnetem kreativen Köpfe der digitalen Werbewelt. Er ist der ehemalige Chief Creative Officer bei Exploratory, ein Google-Unternehmen. Er hat auch zuvor bei Framfab, AKQA und Ogilvy gearbeitet. Lars ist ein häufiger Speaker und Juror bei Preisverleihungen und ist Mitglied der International Academy of Digital Arts and Sciences sowie der Producers Guild of America. Lars hat auch an Drehbüchern mitgearbeitet und begutachtet seit über 30 Jahren Filme.

An einem Tag im Jahr 1994 wurde ein Telefonkabel in ein Modem gesteckt und mit einem Computer in der Bibliothek des Fernsehsenders verbunden, bei dem ich Teilzeit als Forscher arbeitete, während ich meine Masterarbeit fertig schrieb. Als technisch versierter Mensch drängte es mich, herauszufinden, was wir mit diesem „Internet" tun könnten, zu dem wir jetzt Zugang hatten. Also nahm ich pflichtbewusst das Buch *Internet Yellow Pages* zur Hand („Alphabetisch geordnet nach Themen. Eine wunderbare Möglichkeit, tolle Websites und Internet-Ressourcen zu finden – kein Web-Surfer sollte sein Terminal ohne das verlassen!", die Ausgabe von 1996) und machte mich daran, das World Wide Web zu entdecken. Abgesehen von Problemen mit Downloadgeschwindigkeit, Wahrheitsgehalt der Quellen und Design, war es eine erstaunliche Reise in den Kaninchenbau. Ich wusste damals natürlich noch nicht, dass sich mein zukünftiges Arbeitsleben komplett um das Internet drehen sollte.

Als Rob mich fragte, ob ich das Vorwort zu diesem Buch schreiben wollte, war mein erster Gedanke, dass es zu früh sei. Es konnte doch unmöglich sein, dass es bereits an der Zeit ist, die Geschichte des Webdesigns zu schreiben, oder? Aber nach dem Ende von Flash und nun, da die meisten Menschen das Internet mit mobilen Geräten nutzen und neue Möglichkeiten wie VR und AR entstehen (die ihre eigenen Designparadigmen entwickeln) wurde mir klar, dass Rob recht hatte. Eine Ära ging zu Ende und wir hatten beide das unglaubliche Glück, die ganze verrückte Fahrt von Anfang an und von innen heraus erlebt zu haben.

Rob und ich führen eine klassische Internetbeziehung: Wir kennen uns beide seit fast zwei Jahrzehnten und haben uns noch nie persönlich getroffen. Der ganze Austausch mit Rob erfolgt über E-Mail oder je nachdem welche digitale Kommunikationsplattform zeitweise im Trend liegt. Die ursprüngliche Verbindung zwischen uns war wohl der FWA, der seit seiner Gründung im Jahr 2000 eine unverzichtbare Ressource für die Digital Design Community ist. Wir haben aber auch an TASCHEN Büchern über die digitale Branche zusammengearbeitet sowie Geschichten über die Probleme und Sorgen, zu einem späteren Zeitpunkt im Leben Vater zu werden, geteilt.

Ich habe das Glück, dass ich bei zwei Agenturen mitgearbeitet hatte, die dazu beitrugen, festzulegen, wie gutes Webdesign aussieht, nämlich Framfab (heute DigitasLBi) und AKQA. Durch den Gewinn der FWA „Site of the Day" und „Site of the Month" kamen Rob und ich in Kontakt und reden seither viel miteinander. Durch seine Tätigkeit als Kurator beim FWA wurde Rob zum weltweit führenden Experten, nicht nur für Webdesign, sondern auch für kreativen Ausdruck im digitalen Raum. Er hat Spaß an gutem Design und klugem Denken und lebt davon. Nicht die schlechteste Art, seine Tage zu verbringen.

Flash spielte eine große Rolle in der Geschichte des Webdesigns und die Geschichte des Webdesigns ist in vielerlei Hinsicht auch die Geschichte von Flash. Ich werde nie vergessen, als ich einige von Gabocorps ersten Experimenten mit Flash-Navigation sah, was augenblicklich alles andere alt aussehen ließ. Für Leser, die damals noch nicht dabei waren: das Web vor Flash war weitgehend statisch. Keine Animationen, kein Video, keine bewegten Grafiken. Flash war ein riesiger Sprung nach vorne, wobei alle bisherigen Regeln über Bord geworfen wurden und es begann wieder das Jahr Null des Webdesigns. Während ich die Seiten dieses Buches durchblättere, habe ich viele Erinnerungen an diese Zeit. Ich erinnere mich an die Hi-ReS!s Website für Darren Aronofskys Film *Requiem for a Dream* und wie ich angesichts der schieren Schönheit des Designs seufzte und wie Tokyoplastic mit rollendem Donner der Paukentrommeln auf die Bühne kam. Und ich erinnere mich daran, als mir den Mund offen stehen blieb, als ich zum ersten Mal „Get the Glass" sah, was wohl der Höhepunkt der Flash-Ära war.

Der einzige vergleichbare Fortschritt in der Technologie, die das Webdesign auf diese Weise beeinflusste, waren noch die Breitband-Internetverbindungen. Für einen großen Teil der heutigen Internetnutzer mag es nicht schnell klingen, aber es gab eine Zeit, in der sinniert wurde, was geschehen würde, sobald wir 2-Megabit-Verbindungen hätten. Dann betrat Subservient Chicken die Arena und änderte das Paradigma erneut. Es wurde offensichtlich, wohin das Internet gehen sollte. Die Verwendung von Video und Audio machte moderne Dokumentationen wie We Choose the Moon möglich, Personalisierung + Video brachten herzzerreißende Emotionen bei The Wilderness Downtown mit sich. Das geniale Video Trickery (technischer Begriff) nahm Kinder mit auf einen „Field Trip to Mars".

Ich bin stolz darauf, viele der hier in diesem Buch genannten Personen als meine Freunde bezeichnen zu dürfen. Wir haben alle um die gleichen Auszeichnungen gekämpft, beurteilten die gleichen Shows und waren Teil organisierter Gruppen, die den Zustand der Branche diskutierten, wie zum Beispiel Creative Social. Wir waren abwechselnd eifersüchtig auf die Arbeit des anderen – der beste Anreiz, sich zu verbessern – aber sind auch eine sehr kollegiale Gruppe von Menschen. Wir haben zusammen ein neues Medium erfunden. Niemand hätte das allein erreichen können und wir lernen ständig voneinander. Es war eine Zeit der unaufhörlichen Innovation. Dieses Buch ist so nah an einer „offiziellen" Geschichte, wie es wahrscheinlich kein anderes sein könnte.

Viel Spaß!

Lars Bastholm

Préface/
—

Biographie :

Lauréat à trois reprises du Grand Prix au festival international de la créativité des Cannes Lions, Lars s'inscrit parmi les leaders créatifs les plus primés et de renommée mondiale dans le domaine de la publicité numérique. Il a été directeur de la création chez The Exploratory, une société de Google, et a auparavant occupé des postes chez Framfab, AKQA et Ogilvy. Lars est un intervenant et un juré habituel lors de remises de prix ; il est par ailleurs membre de l'International Academy of Digital Arts and Sciences et de la Producers Guild of America. Il a aussi coécrit des scénarios et exercé comme critique cinématographique pendant plus de 30 ans.

Dans la bibliothèque de la chaîne de télévision, où je travaillais à temps partiel comme chercheur pendant que je terminais ma thèse de master, ils ont un beau jour de 1994 branché un câble téléphonique à un modem et l'ont connecté à un ordinateur. J'étais la personne qui en savait le plus en technologie, et j'ai en cela été tout désigné pour découvrir ce que cet «Internet» permettait de faire. J'ai donc saisi scrupuleusement le livre *Internet Yellow Pages*, dont l'édition de 1996 annonçait qu'avec «un classement alphabétique qui en fait un remarquable outil pour accéder à de formidables sites Web et ressources Internet, aucun internaute ne devrait s'en séparer», et je me suis lancé à la découverte du World Wide Web. Mis à part les problèmes de vitesse de téléchargement, de véracité des sources et de conception, cette plongée initiatique a été des plus incroyables. J'étais loin de me douter à cette époque que ma carrière finirait par tourner entièrement autour d'Internet.

Quand Rob m'a demandé si je voulais écrire la préface de cet ouvrage, j'ai d'abord pensé que c'était prématuré. Vraiment ? Nous étions déjà au stade de pouvoir écrire l'histoire de la conception Web ? Rob avait en effet raison, compte tenu de la disparition de Flash, que la plupart des interactions avec Internet se produisaient depuis des dispositifs mobiles et que pointaient leur nez de nouvelles plates-formes comme la RV et la RA (qui développeront leurs propres paradigmes de conception). Une ère prenait fin et nous avions tous deux eu la chance incroyable d'en connaître de l'intérieur les moments les plus fous.

Rob et moi entretenons une relation classique sur Internet : nous nous connaissons depuis près de 20 ans mais ne nous sommes jamais rencontrés en personne. Tous nos échanges se sont faits par e-mails ou via n'importe quelle plate-forme de communication numérique en vogue. Le point de départ a évidemment été les FWA, une ressource indispensable dans le monde de la conception numérique depuis leur lancement en 2000. Nous avons aussi collaboré pour de précédents ouvrages de TASCHEN sur l'industrie numérique, et partagé à nos heures des anecdotes sur les tribulations d'une paternité tardive.

J'ai la chance d'avoir travaillé dans non pas une, mais deux des agences ayant dicté les règles d'une bonne conception Web, à savoir Framfab (devenue DigitasLBi) et AKQA. Avec Rob, nos échanges ont commencé après avoir remporté les mentions «Site of the Day» et «Site of the Month» des FWA, et nos discussions n'ont depuis lors pas cessé. Grâce à sa gestion des FWA, Rob est devenu le plus grand expert au monde en conception Web, mais aussi de façon plus large en expression créative dans l'espace numérique. Il gagne sa vie en rendant hommage aux conceptions et aux idées de talent. Il y a pire comme occupation.

Flash a joué à tout point de vue un rôle gigantesque dans l'histoire de la conception Web, laquelle est aussi, de bien des manières, celle de Flash. Jamais je n'oublierai les premiers essais de Gabocorp avec la navigation Flash, qui a tout de suite fait paraître le reste obsolète. Pour les lecteurs qui n'étaient pas encore nés, le Web avant Flash était principalement statique, dénué d'animations, de vidéos et de graphismes en mouvement. Flash a supposé un tel bond en avant que les règles ont été jetées aux oubliettes et que la conception Web est repartie à son année zéro. Je feuillette cet ouvrage et les souvenirs me reviennent, comme celui du site Web de Hi-ReS! pour le film *Requiem for a Dream* de Darren Aronofsky, dont la conception est d'une beauté pure. Je me souviens quand Tokyoplastic a débarqué sous un tonnerre roulant de timbales. Je me souviens du bruit sourd de ma mâchoire quand elle a heurté le sol en découvrant Get the Glass, sans doute le summum en termes de réalisation à l'ère Flash.

Les connexions Internet haut débit ont été en ce sens le seul progrès technologique comparable en matière de conception Web. Nombre d'internautes actuels n'ont pas un sentiment de vitesse mais il fut un temps où nous dissertions sur ce qui se passerait et comment les choses changeraient avec des connexions de 2 mégabits. Le programme publicitaire Subservient Chicken a ensuite fait son apparition et bouleversé une fois de plus le paradigme, nous rendant à l'évidence de ce qu'Internet finirait par devenir. L'emploi de vidéo et d'audio a donné naissance à des documentaires modernes comme We Choose the Moon, la vidéo accompagnée d'une personnalisation a donné une dimension poignante au court The Wilderness Downtown, et d'ingénieux trucages (terme technique) vidéo ont emmené les enfants en «Field Trip to Mars».

Je suis heureux de compter parmi mes amis de nombreuses personnes figurant dans cet ouvrage. Nous étions tous candidats aux mêmes prix, avons jugé les mêmes présentations et avons participé à des groupes de discussion comme Creative Social sur la situation du secteur. Nous avons tous été jaloux du travail des autres, la meilleure motivation que je connaisse pour s'améliorer, mais nous avons tous gardé le sens de la communauté. Ensemble, nous inventions un nouveau média : personne n'aurait pu y arriver seul et chacun apprenait constamment d'autrui. C'était une époque d'innovation permanente. Cet ouvrage est ce qui se rapproche le plus de l'histoire «officielle».

Bonne lecture !

Lars Bastholm

Introduction/

—

By Rob Ford

—

"My focus has always been on progression of the web, on future trends, cutting-edge creativity, and experimental work, work that has been unique and groundbreaking."

The internet is the biggest thing to happen since the Industrial Revolution. In years to come, people will find it incredible to have relatives who were born before the internet existed.

Since it launched to the world at large, in 1991, we have seen over a billion websites appear. In this book, I have highlighted what I believe were the most pioneering websites, those that shaped the future of the web, those projects that paved the way and led us to where we are now, even if you are reading this book in 2050, or beyond.

There are over 7.6 billion humans on the Earth, so what qualifies me or even gives me the right to assume the responsibility of writing such an important historical book? In summary, I have been showcasing web design since 1997. It's been my daily 'job' to seek out and present the best the web has to offer, which has meant that, I feel, I have seen every amazing website that has ever been made.

I began designing websites in 1997 and moved from being a web designer to being a judge for many of the world's top awards in the 1990s, and, ultimately, to creating the FWA (Favourite Website Awards) in May 2000. This went on to be the first daily internet award site to receive over 200 million visitors, and its awards became widely recognized as the number one achievement for innovative web design, globally.

My focus has always been on progression of the web, on future trends, cutting-edge creativity, and experimental work, work that has been unique and groundbreaking.

In this book you will find the very earliest examples of much of what we take for granted today, including:

- the first website to use surround sound
- the first drag-and-drop navigation
- the first resizing interface
- the first zooming menu
- the first page-turn effect
- the first to use seamless video integration
- the first viral site
- the first parallax website
- the first upload-your-face website
- the first site to incorporate a smartphone
- the first ever YouTube 'website'
- the first ever group virtual reality experience

This survey spans three decades, a period of incredibly rapid change in the world and the internet too, that has seen us go from small CRT monitors to huge 4K UHD displays, and a world which went from mobile phones that were like bricks to the biggest game-changer for a generation: smartphones. The book also shows how the hardware we have used to access the web has changed over the last quarter of a century as well.

The opening chapter covers the early years, 1990–1997, and briefly highlights this period before the true explosion of creativity in 1998. Each year from 1998 through until 2018 then has its own dedicated chapter, with a recognizable format:

"We wanted this to be a book that deserved its own place in history, as a snapshot of an era that was undeniably revolutionary."

- an introduction that focuses on some of the year's events and some of the stand-out websites
- eight facts of the year, giving us real-world data that sets the stage for each chapter:
  – number of internet users
  – number of websites
  – world news
  – website with most traffic
  – tech hardware news
  – tech software news
  – other tech news
  – highest-grossing film
- up to 10 featured websites, the most pioneering in the given year and which are accompanied by a quote from the featured website's creator (or a team member)
- mobile evolution, highlighting one of the year's most important mobile phones
- the internet community, highlighting important web/community events each year
- Google facts page: as Google is a true pioneer of the internet, we look at some fun information and stats for each year together with the top search trends.

This is a book which, in its first draft, was over 1,400 pages long. Whilst TASCHEN is perfectly capable of creating a book of this length, both I and TASCHEN's Julius Wiedemann wanted this to be a book that could easily be picked up, a book a teacher might hold in front of a class, that students could comfortably refer to, and that some readers might cherish as a reference to a time in their life that gave them a completely new direction. It would also be a book that deserved its own place in history, as a snapshot of an era that was undeniably revolutionary.

Introduction/
—

Biography:

Rob Ford, born in England, founded Favourite Website Awards (FWA) in May 2000, a recognition program for cutting-edge web design which has since clocked up over 200 million site visits. Rob has been a pioneer of internet awards, having established processes and concepts that are now widely used around the world. He has been featured in publications including *The Chicago Tribune* and *The Guardian*, has judged for most of the industry awards, contributes regularly to web design publications, wrote a regular column in Adobe's flagship newsletter, Inspire (formerly Edge), and has three bestselling books: *Guidelines for Online Success*, *The Internet Case Study Book*, and *The App & Mobile Case Study Book*.

One of the biggest hurdles was knowing which of so many extraordinary websites to leave out. My pool of sites was absolutely huge, around 2,000, and these had to be screened down to around 200 main sites as subjects for special features, and approximately 150 that I could talk about in the chapter introductions. One thing is certain, every reader will be able to think of at least one outstanding website that isn't in the book, but my focus has had to be kept strictly to the sites I believe have shaped the web. If anyone wants to see thousands of eye-catching websites, dating back to the year 2000, they can head over to thefwa.com where they will find thousands of award-winning examples.

This book is also intended to define and show the web trends of the last quarter of a century, alongside the ebb and flow of digital creativity and the way the web has evolved at a supersonic pace. This is a web that has seen forms of technology, such as Flash, make groundbreaking impact, only to vanish soon after without a trace. It is a web that is itself constantly evolving, to a point where we no longer even refer to the 'internet' or the 'web', it's just become a part of life for all of us. We no longer say we are 'online' in the same way that we don't say we are breathing; it's life.

The web has evolved out of the web, out of the browser, into virtual worlds, worlds that use AI, and into our streets and our everyday lives, so that the boundaries are now so blurred we even have to wonder... are websites as we know them actually dying out?

This collection has come together thanks to quotes from the various creators (or team members) of many of the featured projects. These are the original and the new pioneers, such as Jonathan Gay (Flash), Gabo Mendoza (Gabocorp), Yugo Nakamura (Yugop), Peter Van den Wyngaert (NRG.BE), Joshua Davis (Praystation), Eric Jordan (2Advanced), and over 180 more, and their input has given this book even more perspective as well as that one thing computers are still trying to create: emotion.

And, as in all of my previous books, my famous last words:

Do read this book.
Don't let it collect dust!

Rob Ford

We no longer say we are 'online' in the same way that we don't say we are breathing; it's life.

Rob Ford

Einleitung/
—

Biografie:

Rob Ford, geboren in England, gründete die Favourite Website Awards (FWA) im Mai 2000, ein Programm zur Anerkennung von bahnbrechenden Webdesigns, das seither über 200 Millionen Seitenbesuche verzeichnen kann. Rob ist ein Pionier der Internetpreise und etabliert Prozesse und Konzepte, die heute weltweit verbreitet sind. Seine Arbeiten wurden in zahlreichen Publikationen vorgestellt, darunter: *The Chicago Tribune* und *The Guardian*. Er war für die meisten Branchenauszeichnungen als Preisrichter tätig, trägt regelmäßig zu anderen bekannten Webdesign-Seiten und Zeitschriften bei und schrieb regelmäßig eine Kolumne in Adobes Flaggschiff- Newsletter *Inspire* (früher *Edge*). Er hat drei Bestseller geschrieben: *Guidelines for Online Success*, *The Internet Case Study Book* und *The App & Mobile Case Study Book*.

Das Internet ist die größte Erfindung seit der industriellen Revolution. Bald werden es die Menschen unglaublich finden, Verwandte zu haben, die geboren wurden, bevor das Internet existierte.

Seit es im Jahr 1991 erstmals zugänglich war, haben wir Milliarden von Websites gesehen. In diesem Buch habe ich die hervorgehoben, die meiner Meinung nach die wichtigsten Websites waren, die die Zukunft des Internets geprägt, Projekten den Weg geebnet und uns dahin gebracht haben, wo wir heute stehen.

Es gibt über 7,6 Milliarden Menschen auf der Erde, was also qualifiziert mich oder gibt mir das Recht und die Verantwortung, ein so wichtiges historisches Buch zu schreiben? Kurz gesagt bewerte ich seit 1997 Webdesign. Es ist mein täglicher Job das Beste zu finden und zu präsentieren, was das Internet zu bieten hat. Das hat dazu geführt, dass ich wohl alle erstaunlichen Sites gesehen habe, die jemals gemacht wurden.

Im Jahr 1997 begann ich, selbst Websites zu designen und bin dann vom Webdesigner zu einem Juror für viele der besten Preise der Welt in den 1990er Jahren geworden. Schließlich schuf ich die FWA (Favourite Website Awards) im Mai 2000. Sie wurde zur ersten Internet-Award-Seite, die täglich über 200 Millionen Besucher hat. Ihre Auszeichnungen werden weltweit als größte Errungenschaft für innovatives Webdesign anerkannt.

Mein Fokus lag immer auf dem Fortschritt des Internets, auf zukünftigen Trends, innovativer Kreativität und experimentellen oder einzigartigen und bahnbrechenden Arbeiten. In diesem Buch finden Sie die allerersten Beispiele für vieles, was wir heute für selbstverständlich halten, darunter:

- die erste Website, die Surround-Sound verwendete
- die erste Drag-and-Drop Navigation
- das erste Resizing Interface
- das erste Zooming Menü
- der erste Seite-Turn Effekt
- die erste Seite mit nahtloser Videointegration
- die erste Viral Site
- die erste Parallax Website
- die erste Upload-your-Face Website
- die erste Seite, die das Mobiltelefon integriert hat
- die erste YouTube „Website"
- das erste Erlebnis einer Gruppe in der virtuellen Realität

Diese Studie umfasst drei Jahrzehnte – eine Zeit des unglaublich schnellen Wandels in der Welt und im Internet. Wir konnten sehen, wie kleine CRT Monitore zu riesigen 4K UHD Displays wurden und wie die Welt der Mobiltelefone, die anfangs groß wie Ziegelsteine waren, zum größten Game-Changer einer Generation wurde: Smartphones. Das Buch zeigt auch, wie sich die Hardware, mit der wir auf das Internet zugegriffen haben, im letzten Vierteljahrhundert verändert hat.

Das einleitende Kapitel behandelt die frühen Jahre, 1990–1997 und beleuchtet kurz diesen Zeitraum – vor der wahren Explosion der Kreativität im Jahr 1998. Jedes Jahr von 1998 bis 2018 hat dann ein eigenes Kapitel mit einem erkennbaren Format:

- eine Einführung, die sich auf einige der Ereignisse des Jahres und einige der herausragenden Websites konzentriert
- acht Fakten des Jahres, die uns reale Daten liefern, die die Bühne für jedes Kapitel bilden:
  - Anzahl der Internetnutzer
  - Anzahl der Websites
  - Nachrichten aus aller Welt
  - Website mit dem meisten Traffic
  - Technische Hardware Neuigkeiten
  - Technische Software Neuigkeiten
  - andere technische Neuigkeiten
  - höchstes Einspielergebnis Film

- bis zu zehn vorgestellte Websites, die bedeutendsten im jeweiligen Jahr, mit einem Zitat des Webdesigners (oder eines Teammitglieds)
- Mobile Evolution, Hervorhebung eines der wichtigsten Mobiltelefone des Jahres
- Internet-Community, Hervorhebung wichtiger Web-/Community-Events jedes Jahr
- Google Fakten Seite: da Google ein echter Pionier des Internets ist, schauen wir uns einige lustige Informationen und Statistiken für jedes Jahr an, zusammen mit den Trends der meist gesuchtesten Seiten.

Dieses Buch war in seinem ersten Entwurf über 1.400 Seiten lang. Während TASCHEN durchaus in der Lage ist, ein Buch dieser Größe aufzulegen, wollten wir beide, Julius Wiedemann von TASCHEN und ich, dass es ein Buch wird, das man einfach in die Hand nehmen kann, ein Buch, das ein Lehrer in der Klasse hochhalten kann und auf das Studenten ganz leicht zugreifen können. Es sollte auch ein Buch sein, das einige Leser als Bezug auf ihr Leben sehen würden, da es ihnen eine völlig neue Richtung gegeben hat. Es sollte auch ein Buch werden, das einen eigenen Platz in der Geschichte verdient – als eine Momentaufnahme einer revolutionären Ära.

Eine der größten Hürden war es, zu entscheiden, welche von den vielen außergewöhnlichen Websites wegzulassen ist. Mein Fundus an Websites war absolut riesig, etwa 2.000. Diese mussten nun auf rund 200 Hauptseiten mit Themen für besondere Merkmale untergebracht werden und auf etwa 150, über die ich in den Kapiteleinführungen sprechen konnte. Eines ist sicher, jeder Leser wird an mindestens eine herausragende Website denken, die nicht im Buch enthalten ist, aber mein Fokus musste streng auf die Seiten gerichtet werden, von denen ich glaube, dass sie das Internet verändert haben. Wenn jemand Tausende von auffälligen Websites sehen möchte, die bis auf das Jahr 2000 zurückgehen, kann man auf thefwa.com viele von diesen preisgekrönten Beispielen finden.

Dieses Buch soll auch die Webtrends des letzten Viertels des Jahrhunderts definieren und aufzeigen. Auch soll die Ebbe und Flut der digitalen Kreativität und die Art, wie sich das Internet mit Überschallgeschwindigkeit entwickelt hat, gezeigt werden. Ein Internet, in dem Technologieformen wie Flash bahnbrechende Wirkung hatten und die dann bald darauf spurlos verschwanden. Ein Internet, das sich ständig weiterentwickelt, bis zu dem Punkt, an dem wir nicht einmal mehr auf das „Internet" oder das „Web" verweisen können. Es ist nun ein Teil des Lebens für alle geworden. Wir sagen nicht mehr, dass wir „online" sind, genauso wenig wie wir sagen, dass wir atmen; es ist – Leben. Das Web hat sich aus dem Web, aus dem Browser, in virtuelle Welten, Welten, die AI benutzen und in unsere Straßen und unser tägliches Leben bewegt, so dass die Grenzen jetzt verschwommen sind. Wir müssen uns sogar fragen ... sterben die Websites, wie wir sie heute kennen, aus?

Diese Sammlung entstand dank der Zitate der verschiedenen Schöpfer (oder Teammitglieder) vieler der vorgestellten Projekte. Alte und neue Pioniere, wie Jonathan Gay (Flash), Gabo Mendoza (Gabocorp), Yugo Nakamura (Yugop), Peter Van den Wyngaert (NRG.BE), Joshua Davis (Praystation), Eric Jordan (2Advanced) und über 180 weitere. Ihr Input, den sie diesem Buch gegeben haben, bietet noch mehr Perspektiven sowie das, was Computer noch zu erschaffen versuchen: Emotionen.

Und nun, wie in allen meinen Büchern, meine berühmten letzten Worte:

Lies dieses Buch.
Lass es keinen Staub ansetzen!

Rob Ford

Introduction/
—

Biographie:

Né en Angleterre, Rob Ford a fondé en mai 2000 Favourite Website Awards (FWA), un programme de récompenses pour les conceptions Web innovantes qui a depuis enregistré plus de 200 millions de visites. Rob est un pionnier en matière de prix sur Internet, et il est à l'origine de processus et de concepts qui sont désormais appliqués dans le monde entier. Il est apparu dans de nombreuses publications, dont *The Chicago Tribune* et *The Guardian*, a été juré pour la plupart des prix dans le domaine, et il collabore régulièrement pour de célèbres magazines sur la conception Web. Il a tenu une colonne dans l'emblématique newsletter *Inspire* (anciennement *Edge*) d'Adobe et est l'auteur de trois best-sellers: *Guidelines for Online Success*, *The Internet Case Study Book* et *The App & Mobile Case Study Book*.

Internet est la plus grande invention depuis la révolution industrielle. Les prochaines années, nous aurons du mal à croire que des membres de notre famille sont nés avant sa création.

Depuis son lancement global en 1991, plus d'un milliard de sites Web ont vu le jour. Dans cet ouvrage, j'ai relevé ceux qui me paraissaient les plus novateurs, ceux qui ont façonné l'avenir du Web, ceux qui ont tracé la voie et nous ont portés là où nous sommes, même si vous lisez ce livre en 2050 ou plus tard.

La planète comptant plus de 7,6 milliards d'habitants, en quoi suis-je qualifié ou même en droit d'assumer la responsabilité d'un tel livre historique? Depuis 1997, je fais la promotion de créations graphiques, mon travail consistant à chercher et à présenter le meilleur qu'offre le Web en la matière. Je crois donc pouvoir affirmer que j'ai vu tous les formidables sites Web qui ont été créés.

J'ai débuté en 1997 comme concepteur de sites Web. Dans les années 90, j'ai quitté cette panoplie pour devenir juge de nombreux grands prix internationaux avant de créer en 2000 les Favourite Website Awards, le premier site de récompenses quotidiennes sur Internet comptant plus de 200 millions de visiteurs. Ses prix ont été largement acceptés comme la reconnaissance absolue en matière de conception Web innovante.

Je me suis toujours concentré sur l'évolution du Web, les tendances à venir, la créativité de pointe et le travail expérimental, une tâche à la fois unique et novatrice.

Cet ouvrage vous présente les tous premiers exemples de ce qui paraît aujourd'hui très naturel, dont:
- le premier site Web à inclure du son surround
- la première navigation par glisser-déposer
- la première interface redimensionnable
- le premier menu avec zoom
- le premier effet d'une page qu'on tourne
- le premier site avec une intégration fluide de la vidéo
- le premier site viral
- le premier site Web parallaxe
- le premier site Web permettant de charger un portrait de soi
- le premier site à inclure un téléphone portable
- le tout premier «site Web» dans YouTube
- la toute première expérience collective de réalité virtuelle

Ce travail s'étend sur trois décennies, période pendant laquelle le monde et Internet ont fait l'objet d'une évolution fulgurante. Nous sommes passés de petits moniteurs CRT à d'énormes écrans UHD 4K, et de téléphones portables aussi gros qu'une brique aux smartphones, la plus grande révolution pour toute une génération. L'ouvrage montre aussi combien le matériel employé pour se connecter à Internet a changé au cours des 25 dernières années.

Le premier chapitre parle des débuts entre 1990 et 1997 et aborde les grands points de cette période avant la véritable explosion créative en 1998. Un chapitre est ensuite consacré à chaque année de 1998 à 2018, selon un format standard:
- une introduction expliquant des événements de l'année et des sites Web marquants
- huit infos clés qui placent chaque chapitre dans un contexte réel:
  - nombre d'utilisateurs d'Internet
  - nombre de sites Web
  - actualités dans le monde
  - site Web avec le plus de trafic
  - nouveautés matérielles
  - nouveautés logicielles
  - autres infos technologiques
  - film en tête du box-office

- jusqu'à dix sites Web illustrés, les plus innovants de l'année accompagnés d'une citation de leur concepteur (ou d'un membre de l'équipe)
- l'évolution de la téléphonie mobile, en présentant l'un des principaux téléphones de l'année
- des infos sur la communauté Internet, en expliquant des faits communautaires/Web majeurs
- des infos sur Google: Google étant un incontestable pionnier d'Internet, nous apportons des données amusantes, des statistiques et les principales tendances de recherche pour chaque année.

La première ébauche de ce livre comptait plus de 1400 pages. Même si TASCHEN est parfaitement capable de produire un ouvrage de ce volume, tant l'éditeur Julius Wiedemann comme moi-même avons souhaité que ce livre soit facile à manipuler, qu'un professeur puisse le montrer à sa classe, que les étudiants puissent aisément s'y reporter, et que certains lecteurs puissent l'aimer car il renvoie à un moment décisif de leur vie. Nous voulions aussi qu'il ait sa place dans l'histoire, tel un instantané d'une ère sans conteste révolutionnaire.

L'une des grandes difficultés a été de choisir les sites Web qui ne pouvaient pas être retenus. Ma liste en incluait pas moins de 2000 et j'ai dû la réduire à environ 200 sites illustrant des fonctions particulières, plus 150 autres qui pouvaient être mentionnés dans l'introduction des chapitres. Je sais déjà que chaque lecteur pensera à au moins un excellent site Web absent de cet ouvrage, mais j'ai donné la stricte priorité à ceux ayant selon moi modelé le Web. Pour en découvrir des milliers primés depuis l'année 2000, vous pouvez consulter le site thefwa.com.

Cet ouvrage vise également à identifier et à présenter les tendances du Web du dernier quart d'un siècle, ainsi que les cycles de créativité numérique et la façon dont le Web a évolué à un rythme supersonique. Des technologies comme Flash ont eu un impact sans précédent, pour disparaître peu de temps après sans laisser de traces. Le Web est lui-même en évolution permanente, à tel point que nous n'en parlons plus comme «Internet» ou le «Web» et qu'il fait simplement partie intégrante de notre vie. Nous n'annonçons plus être «en ligne», tout comme nous n'expliquons pas que nous respirons. C'est un acte naturel.

Le Web a évolué en dehors du Web, en dehors des navigateurs, dans les mondes virtuels, des univers qui font appel à l'IA, mais aussi dans les rues et dans notre quotidien. Les frontières sont désormais tellement floues que nous devons même nous demander si les sites Web tels que nous les connaissons sont en voie de disparition.

Ce recueil a été possible grâce aux divers créateurs (ou membres d'équipes) de nombreux projets présentés. Ce sont eux les vrais pionniers de leur temps, comme Jonathan Gay (Flash), Gabo Mendoza (Gabocorp), Yugo Nakamura (Yugop), Peter Van den Wyngaert (NRG.BE), Joshua Davis (Praystation), Eric Jordan (2Advanced) et plus de 180 autres. Leur apport a doté cet ouvrage d'une plus ample perspective et de ce que les ordinateurs n'arrivent toujours pas à susciter, à savoir l'émotion.

Comme dans tous mes livres antérieurs, mes fameux mots de la fin:

Lisez ce livre.
Ne le laissez pas prendre la poussière!

Rob Ford

1990–
1997/

The
Early
Years

1990-1997/

—

The Early Years

—

THE BIGGEST
THING TO
HAPPEN SINCE
THE INDUSTRIAL
REVOLUTION

<

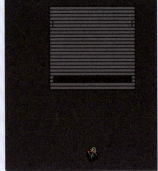

1990

At the end of 1990, Tim Berners-Lee had the first web browser/editor and web server (info.cern.ch) up and running on a NeXT computer at CERN, the European Organization for Nuclear Research.

1991

The following year, in August 1991, he announced the WWW software on internet news groups and interest in the project spread around the world. Web design was in its infancy, overtaken by the excitement brought on by the ability to share information.

1992

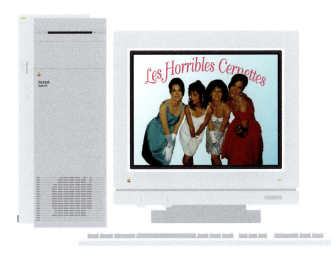

Throughout 1992 the web was dominated by science projects.

—

The first photograph was posted on the web by Berners-Lee, showing a British group called Les Horribles Cernettes (they had formed at CERN).

<

FIRST PHOTOGRAPH ONLINE

<

1993

In 1993, ALIWEB was launched. Effectively the first search engine, it indexed the best sites on the web and categorized them on one page online.

—

Bloomberg.com became the first online financial portal, sharing currency news and data.

>

FIRST SEARCH ENGINE

>

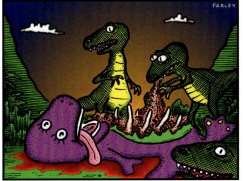

Scenes cut from **JURASSIC PARK**: Velociraptors Devour a Barney

Doctor Fun launched as an online web comic, which was seen as a very progressive move as well as demonstrating the possibilities of new ways to share information.

The Internet Movie Database (IMDb) was launched, as was the Internet Underground Music Archive, using the MP2 format, to give exposure to unsigned musical acts and musicians.
—

SITO began as the first online collaborative art project.
—

The Tech launched as the self-proclaimed first internet newspaper.
—

MTV's website began as an unofficial site.

FIRST
WEBCAM

At the University of Cambridge (UK), the first webcam was installed and pointed at a coffee pot, so that workers could see if there was any coffee. It was called the Trojan Room Coffee Machine after the name of the room next door to the computer laboratory.
—

Wired.com launched, and by the end of 1993 there were still fewer than 650 websites online.

`<>`
BY THE END
OF 1993 THERE
WERE STILL
FEWER THAN
650 WEBSITES
ONLINE
`</>`

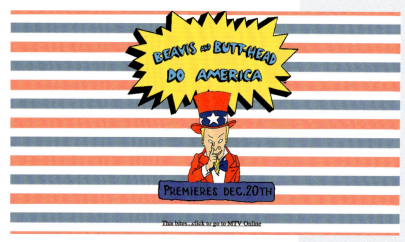

MTV

1990

Ende 1990 brachte Tim Berners-Lee den ersten Webbrowser/Editor und Webserver (info.cern.ch) online, der auf einem NeXT Computer bei CERN lief, der Europäischen Organisation für Nuklearforschung.

1991

Im darauffolgenden Jahr, im August 1991 kündigte er die WWW Software in Internet News-Gruppen an und das Interesse an dem Projekt verbreitete sich in der ganzen Welt. Das Webdesign steckte noch in den Kinderschuhen und wurde von der Aufregung, die der Austausch von Informationen mit sich brachte, überschattet.

1992

Im Jahr 1992 wurde das Internet noch von wissenschaftlichen Projekten dominiert. Das erste Foto, das im Netz von Berners-Lee gepostet wurde, zeigte eine britische Band namens Les Horribles Cernettes (sie hatten sich im CERN formiert).

1993

Im Jahr 1993 wurde ALIWEB gestartet. Tatsächlich war dies die erste Suchmaschine. Sie führte die besten Websites im Internet auf und kategorisierte sie auf einer Seite online.

Bloomberg.com war das erste online Finanzportal, auf dem Währungsnachrichten und Daten geteilt wurden.

Doctor Fun wurde als online Comic gestartet. Das galt als sehr fortschrittlich und zeigte neue Möglichkeiten der Informationsverbreitung.

Die Internet Movie Database (IMDb) wurde ins Leben gerufen, ebenso wie das Internet Underground Music Archive, dass das MP2-Format nutzte, um unsignierten Musik-Acts und Musikern eine Bühne zu geben.

SITO begann als erstes gemeinschaftliches online Kunstprojekt.

The Tech wurde als selbsternannte erste Internet-Zeitung gestartet.

MTVs Website begann als inoffizielle Seite.

An der University of Cambridge (UK) wurde die erste Webcam installiert und zeigte auf eine Kaffeekanne, damit Mitarbeiter sehen konnten, ob noch Kaffee da war. Es hieß Trojan Room Coffee Machine nach dem Namen des Zimmers neben dem Computerlabor.

Wired.com wurde gestartet und bis Ende 1993 gab es weniger als 650 Websites online.

1990

Fin 1990, Tim Berners-Lee met en ligne le premier navigateur/éditeur Web utilisé en serveur (info.cern.ch) sur un ordinateur NeXT du CERN, le Conseil européen pour la recherche nucléaire.

1991

L'année d'après, en août 1991, il annonce la naissance du WWW dans des groupes d'actualités sur Internet et le projet s'étend dans le monde entier. La conception Web n'en est qu'à ses balbutiements, car toute l'effervescence porte alors sur la capacité de partager des informations.

1992

Au cours de l'année 1992, le Web foisonne de projets scientifiques.

Berners-Lee publie la première photographie sur le Web, un cliché du groupe britannique Les Horribles Cernettes (formé au sein du CERN).

1993

En 1993, ALIWEB fait son apparition. Premier moteur de recherche du genre, il indexe les meilleurs sites sur le Web et les classe dans une page en ligne.

Bloomberg.com devient le premier portail financier en ligne et partage des données et des actualités sur les devises.

La bande dessinée en ligne Doctor Fun est lancée et considérée comme une véritable avancée, démontrant toutes les nouvelles façons de partager des informations.

L'Internet Movie Database (IMDb) fait ses débuts, tout comme l'Internet Underground Music Archive qui utilise le format MP2 et permet la promotion de performances musicales et de chanteurs.

SITO est le premier projet artistique collaboratif en ligne.

The Tech se présente comme le premier journal sur Internet.

Le site Web de MTV débute comme site non officiel.

À l'université de Cambridge (Royaume-Uni), la première webcam est installée et filme une cafetière pour que les employés sachent s'il reste du café. Elle est baptisée « Trojan Room Coffee Machine » en raison du nom de la pièce où elle se trouve à côté du laboratoire informatique.

Naissance de Wired.com. Fin 1993, moins de 650 sites Web sont en ligne.

1994

Amnesty International went online, as did Art.net, to showcase artists in San Francisco.
—

Bianca's Smut Shack became one of the first chatrooms.

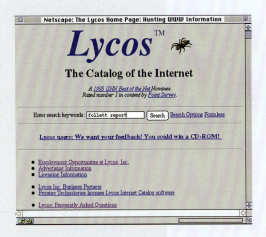

Cool Site of the Day became the first daily showcase for websites.
—

First Virtual launched as the first internet bank.

Lycos began operating and was for many years one of the main search engines.
—

Microsoft first appeared on the web.

> MICROSOFT
LAUNCHES
ONLINE

>

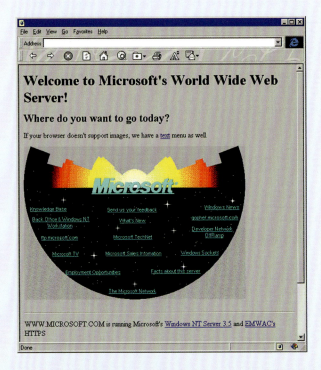

The Nine Planets, about the Solar System, was one of the first websites to make heavy use of photography; this meant it used a lot of web traffic and was therefore one of the first websites to be mirrored.

—

Pizza Hut launched, and locals in Santa Cruz, California, could order pizza online for the first time.

>
FIRST ONLINE
PIZZA
DELIVERY
>

Jerry and Dave's WWW Interface... *(Always Under construction)*

Welcome, visitor from

Last modified on Fri May 20 17:55:16 1994
*There are currently **1909** entries in the hotlist database*

Vous pouvez lancer des recherches dans cet index. Pour cela, entrez des mots clés de recherche :

- Art
- Computers
- Economy
- Education
- Entertainment
- Environment and Nature
- Events
- Geography
- Government
- Health
- Humanities
- Journalism
- Law
- News
- Politics
- Reference
- Research
- Science
- Society and Culture
- todo

Jerry and Dave's Guide to the World Wide Web was launched, later renamed Yahoo!

<
FIRST
ITERATION
OF YAHOO!
LAUNCHES
<

1995

The start of the dot-com boom, a year that saw the launch of Amazon.com and the release of javascript, java (giving rise to lake applets, a new way to animate website images), PHP, and MP3.

<

AMAZON.COM
LAUNCHES,
OFFERING ONE
MILLION TITLES

<

>
INTERNET
EXPLORER 1
RELEASED
>

Microsoft released Internet Explorer 1, its msn.com portal, and Windows 95, a pioneering desktop operating system in that it opened up online possibilities for users with no programming skills.

<>
THE NUMBER OF WEB USERS
RISES TO 40 MILLION
AND THE NUMBER OF WEB
PAGES TO AROUND 30,000
</>

eBay launched as AuctionWeb.

—

The number of web users rose to 40 million and the number of web pages to around 30,000.

1994

Amnesty International ging online sowie auch Art.net, um Künstler in San Francisco zu präsentieren.

Bianca's Smut Shack war einer der ersten Chatrooms.

Auf der Cool Site of the Day wurden das erste Mal täglich verschiedene Websites präsentiert.

First Virtual startete als erste Internetbank.

Lycos begann seinen Betrieb und war viele Jahre lang eine der wichtigsten Suchmaschinen.

Microsoft erschien zum ersten Mal im Internet.

The Nine Planets, über das Sonnensystem, war eine der ersten Websites, die sich intensiv mit Fotografie beschäftigte. Das bedeutete, dass sie viel Web-Traffic benötigte und daher eine der ersten Websites war, die gespiegelt wurden.

Pizza Hut veröffentlichte seine erste Website und Bewohner in Santa Cruz, Kalifornien, konnten Pizza zum ersten Mal online bestellen.

Jerry and Dave's Guide to the World Wide Web wurde veröffentlicht, später unter dem Namen Yahoo!

1995

Der Start des Dot-Com-Booms, ein Jahr, in dem Amazon.com auf den Markt kam und JavaScript, Java (so entstanden Lake Applets, eine neue Art, Bilder auf Webseiten zu animieren), PHP, und MP3 herausgebracht wurden.

Microsoft brachte den Internet Explorer 1 heraus, sein msn.com Portal und Windows 95, ein bahnbrechendes Desktop-Betriebssystem, das Online-Möglichkeiten für Benutzer ohne Programmierkenntnisse eröffnete.

eBay wurde als AuctionWeb gestartet.

Die Anzahl der Internet Nutzer stieg auf 40 Millionen an und die Anzahl der Webseiten auf etwa 30.000.

1994

Le site d'Amnesty International est créé, ainsi que Art.net, qui présente des artistes à San Francisco.

Bianca's Smut Shack devient l'une des premières salles de chat.

Cool Site of the Day est le premier site à sélectionner chaque jour des sites Web.

First Virtual débute comme première banque sur Internet.

Lycos apparaît et reste pendant des années l'un des principaux moteurs de recherche.

Microsoft fait son entrée sur le Web.

Dédié au système solaire, The Nine Planets est l'un des premiers sites Web à inclure un grand nombre de photos. Il génère en cela un important trafic Web et est l'un des premiers sites à être copié.

Pizza Hut fait ses débuts et les habitants de Santa Cruz (Californie) peuvent pour la première fois commander des pizzas en ligne.

L'annuaire *Jerry and Dave's Guide to the World Wide Web* est créé, avant d'être renommé Yahoo!

1995

Début de l'essor des « point com ». Cette année voit aussi le lancement d'Amazon.com et la sortie de javascript, de java (et par là même des applets Lake, qui permettent d'animer des images dans les sites Web), de PHP et de MP3.

Microsoft lance Internet Explorer 1, son portail msn.com et Windows 95, un système d'exploitation révolutionnaire qui offre des possibilités en ligne aux utilisateurs sans connaissances de programmation.

eBay naît sous le nom d'AuctionWeb.

Le nombre d'utilisateurs Web atteint 40 millions, celui de pages Web s'élève à environ 30000.

1996

Originally founded in 1994, the free web-hosting service GeoCities offered users a URL based on a directory of 'Cities', more commonly known as neighborhoods, each of which corresponded to a different type of content. 'Soho and Lofts', for example, was for arts or writing, while 'Area 51 and vault' was for science fiction, etc.

Websites were now acquiring more character, with huge amounts of images being available for free download, including a massive amount of animated gifs. The internet was becoming animated.

GeoCities became the key place for personal expression for many years and holds a place in the hearts of many early internet webmasters. Meanwhile, the site for the live-action/animated comedy movie *Space Jam*, featuring basketball-player Michael Jordan and Looney Tunes characters, presented a completely new style of visual interface.

However, web design was about to change in a huge way and a new wave of expression and innovation was unleashed thanks to Jonathan Gay, who took his passion as a child for Lego and turned it into the building blocks of the most pioneering internet technology for a generation.

"The human mind is much too limited to capture the entirety of a complex creation all at once. With Lego, you can start with the vision and work out the details of the design as you progress. With patience and persistence, I developed a Lego-based design process. It's more or less the same process we ultimately used to develop Flash."

Jonathan Gay, FutureWave, Macromedia, Freestone Ranch

In 1993, Gay started FutureWave Software with Charlie Jackson, a group organizer for a Macintosh Users' Group, and Michelle Welsh (who handled marketing). FutureWave was created with a vision of dominating the market for graphics software on pen computers, where users would write on a computer's screen rather than use a keyboard.

SmartSketch software was created with Robert Tatsumi and became an animation product. It was renamed FutureSplash Animator but a lack of funding led FutureWave to pitch it, unsuccessfully, to Adobe, before it finally shipped in May 1996.

(From 2015) **Rob Ford:** "When you created FutureSplash, how did you think this new software could influence a generation?"

Jonathan Gay: "I had experience with desktop publishing and had seen how PageMaker, Adobe Illustrator, and the laser printer had made it possible for many people to create high-quality graphic design. We felt that the internet and web browsers could do a similar thing by allowing many more people to create animations. We did not have any idea of how far that idea would evolve."

Microsoft gave FutureSplash a big break, using the software to launch its MSN channel at beta2.msn.com, which was aiming to be a TV-style experience on the web.

Disney started using FutureSplash and this brought FutureWave to the attention of Macromedia, which then acquired FutureSplash in December 1996 and its Animator program duly became Macromedia Flash 1.0.

THE INTERNET WAS FINALLY BECOMING ANIMATED

Space Jam

1996

Ursprünglich gegründet im Jahr 1994, bot der kostenlose Webhosting-Dienst GeoCities den Nutzern eine URL an, die auf einem Verzeichnis von „Cities", besser bekannt als „Bezirke", basierte, von denen jedes einer anderen Art von Inhalt entsprach. „Soho and Lofts", war zum Beispiel für Kunst oder Schriftstellerei, während „Area 51 and Vault" für Science Fiction gedacht war usw.

Die Websites bekamen jetzt mehr Charakter, da riesige Mengen an Bildern zum kostenlosen Download zur Verfügung standen, darunter eine große Menge animierter Gifs. Das Internet wurde animiert.

GeoCities war viele Jahre lang wichtig für den persönlichen Ausdruck und hat einen Platz in den Herzen vieler früherer Webmaster. Währenddessen präsentierte die Seite für die Liveaktion / den animierten Comedy-Film *Space Jam*, mit Basketballspieler Michael Jordan und Looney Tunes-Charakteren, eine völlig neue Art der visuellen Schnittstelle.

Das Webdesign sollte sich jedoch immens verändern und eine neue Welle des Ausdrucks und Innovation wurde dank Jonathan Gay ausgelöst, der seine Leidenschaft als Kind für Lego in die Bausteine der bahnbrechendsten Internet-Technologie für eine Generation einbrachte.

„Der menschliche Geist ist viel zu begrenzt, um die Gesamtheit einer komplexen Schöpfung auf einmal zu erfassen. Mit Lego kann man mit einer Vision beginnen und während des Fortschritts die Details des Designs erarbeiten. Mit Geduld und Beharrlichkeit habe ich einen Lego-basierten Designprozess entwickelt. Es ist mehr oder weniger derselbe Prozess, den wir letztendlich zur Entwicklung von Flash verwendet haben."
JONATHAN GAY (FUTUREWAVE, MACROMEDIA, FREESTONE RANCH)

Im Jahr 1993 startete Gay FutureWave Software mit Charlie Jackson, einem Gruppenorganisator einer Gruppe von Macintosh-Benutzern, mit Michelle Welsh (die für Marketing zuständig war). FutureWave wurde mit der Vision gegründet, den Markt für Grafiksoftware auf Pen-Computern zu dominieren, bei der die Benutzer auf dem Bildschirm eines Computers schreiben würden, anstatt eine Tastatur zu verwenden.

SmartSketch Software wurde gemeinsam mit Robert Tatsumi entwickelt und war ein Animationsprodukt. Es wurde in FutureSplash Animator umbenannt aber ein Finanzierungsmangel führte dazu, dass FutureWave erfolglos Adobe angeboten wurde, bis es im Mai 1996 übernommen wurde.

(Aus dem Jahr 2015)
Rob Ford: „Wie hat sich die neue Software bei der Erstellung von FutureSplash auf eine Generation ausgewirkt?"

Jonathan Gay: „Ich hatte Erfahrung mit Desktop Publishing und hatte gesehen, wie PageMaker, Adobe Illustrator und der Laser-Drucker es ermöglichten, dass viele Leute qualitativ hochwertiges Design erstellen konnten. Wir hatten das Gefühl, dass das Internet und der Webbrowser ähnliche Dinge tun könnten, indem sie viel mehr Menschen erlaubten, Animationen zu erstellen. Wir hatten keine Ahnung, wie weit sich diese Idee entwickeln würde."

1996

Fondé en 1994, le service d'hébergement Web gratuit GeoCities offre aux utilisateurs une URL pour créer une page personnelle dans une structure de « voisinages », qui sont autant de thématiques de contenu. Par exemple, « Soho and Lofts » concerne l'art et l'écriture, alors que « Area 51 and vault » porte sur la science-fiction.

Les sites Web démontrent plus de personnalité, avec des tonnes de gifs animés en téléchargement gratuit. Internet s'anime.

GeoCities est pendant des années un lieu essentiel d'expression personnelle et occupe une place spéciale dans le cœur de nombreux webmasters de l'époque. Cette même année, le site de la comédie *Space Jam* mêlant des acteurs comme le joueur de basket Michael Jordan et de l'animation avec des personnages Looney Tunes affiche un style inédit d'interface visuelle.

La conception Web est toutefois aux portes d'un changement majeur. Une nouvelle vague d'expression et d'innovation déferle grâce à Jonathan Gay : s'inspirant de sa passion pour Lego quand il était enfant, il pose les bases de la technologie la plus révolutionnaire sur Internet.

« L'esprit humain est bien trop limité pour saisir instantanément toute la complexité d'une création. Lego permet de partir d'une vision et d'élaborer au fur et à mesure les détails de la conception. Avec patience et persévérance, je me suis donc inspiré de Lego pour imaginer un processus de conception plus ou moins semblable à celui utilisé pour développer Flash. »
JONATHAN GAY (FUTUREWAVE, MACROMEDIA, FREESTONE RANCH)

En 1993, Gay crée FutureWave Software avec Charlie Jackson, organisateur d'un groupe d'utilisateurs Macintosh, et Michelle Welsh, en charge de la partie marketing. FutureWave naît avec l'objectif de dominer le marché des logiciels graphiques sur des ordinateurs fonctionnant avec des stylets afin de permettre aux utilisateurs d'écrire directement sur un écran au lieu d'employer un clavier.

Le logiciel SmartSketch est créé par Robert Tatsumi et s'impose comme outil d'animation. Il est réédité sous le nom de FutureSplash Animator mais par manque de financement, FutureWave tente en vain de le céder à Adobe. Il sort finalement sur le marché en mai 1996.

(2015) **Rob Ford** : « Quand vous avez conçu FutureSplash, comment pensiez-vous que ce nouveau logiciel pouvait influencer toute une génération ? »

Jonathan Gay : « J'avais une expérience en PAO et savais que PageMaker, Adobe Illustrator et les imprimantes laser avaient permis à de nombreuses personnes de créer des conceptions graphiques de grande qualité. Nous avons pensé qu'Internet et les navigateurs Web pouvaient en faire autant en démocratisant la création d'animations. Nous n'avions aucune idée à quel point ce concept allait évoluer. »

FutureSplash connaît un grand succès grâce à Microsoft, qui utilise le logiciel pour lancer son canal MSN sur beta2.msn.com en vue d'offrir une expérience télévisuelle sur le Web.

Disney intègre aussi FutureSplash, ce qui attire l'attention sur FutureWave de Macromedia, qui acquiert le logiciel en décembre 1996. Le programme

The Early Years

—

In 1996, for the general public the internet was something other people spoke about. It was an unknown quantity. Even for someone like me, whose first computer experience was in 1982 with a friend's Sinclair ZX81 and that Christmas, my own Commodore VIC-20, the web was a mystery. The same applied to computers until Microsoft launched Windows 95 (in 1995) and moved away from MS-DOS products, which seemed to be geared more towards programmers.

With the arrival of Windows 95 and 33.6 KB modems, the web became more accessible and more people wanted to get involved in websites, both for business and personal interests. This was very exciting as individuals were now able to express themselves online in ways that hadn't been possible before, and chiefly this was all down to FutureSplash Animator.

In 1996, a typical website consisted of text with blue hyperlinks that turned purple when they were clicked, as with Apple.com's website at this time. Its use of images was relatively cutting edge, as most websites were text only.

Macromedia's Shockwave gave people as well as brands the chance to show off, and gave a glimpse of what the future might hold. Meanwhile, several new web design companies were sprouting up, with Crankcase, for example, showing the new capabilities of a website that used Shockwave. These pioneering websites were proud to display the "Made with Macromedia" logo.

By February 1996, Macromedia was showcasing a website a day that used Shockwave for its Shocked Site of the Day (SSOTD). Beavis & Butthead picked up the first SSOTD on February 8, and this soon became a highly sought-after recognition amongst web designers, top brands, and the newly formed web agencies.

>
CUTTING-
EDGE USE
OF IMAGES
>

Apple.com

Crankcase

Macromedia SSOTD Archive

<>
MACROMEDIA LAUNCHES SHOCKED SITE OF THE DAY
</>

Microsoft legte mit Future-Splash eine Pause ein, da die Software dazu verwendet wurde, ihren MSN-Kanal auf beta2.msn.com zu starten, der eine TV-ähnliche Erfahrung im Internet sein sollte.

Disney begann FutureSplash zu verwenden und dies sorgte dafür, dass FutureWave die Aufmerksamkeit von Macromedia erregte, die dann im Dezember 1996 FutureSplash erwarben, dessen Animator-Programm zu Macromedia Flash 1.0 wurde.

Im Jahr 1996 war das Internet für die breite Öffentlichkeit noch etwas, worüber andere sprachen. Es war eine unbekannte Größe. Selbst für jemanden wie mich, dessen erste Computererfahrung 1982 mit dem Sinclair ZX81 eines Freundes und an Weihnachten mit meinem eigenen Commodore VIC-20 gemacht wurde, war das Internet ein Mysterium. Das gleiche galt für Computer, bis Microsoft Windows 95 (1995) auf den Markt brachte und von MS-DOS-Produkten abrückte, die eher auf Programmierer ausgerichtet waren.

Mit der Ankunft von Windows 95 und 33,6 KB Modems wurde das Internet zugänglicher und immer mehr Menschen wollten Websites haben, sowohl aus geschäftlichem als auch aus persönlichem Interesse. Das war sehr aufregend, da sich die Menschen nun auf eine Art und Weise ausdrücken konnten, die vorher nicht möglich war und das lag hauptsächlich an Future-Splash Animator.

Im Jahr 1996 bestand eine typische Website aus Text mit blauen Hyperlinks, die sich beim Klicken Purpur verfärbten, wie das auch bei der Website von Apple.com der Fall war. Die Verwendung von Bildern war relativ fortschrittlich, da die meisten Websites nur aus Text bestanden.

Macromedias Shockwave gab Menschen und Marken die Möglichkeit, sich zu zeigen und gab einen Ausblick darauf, was die Zukunft noch bereithalten sollte. In der Zwischenzeit entstanden mehrere neue Webdesign-Unternehmen, wobei Crankcase beispielsweise die neuen Funktionen einer Website mit Shockwave zeigte. Diese wegweisenden Websites waren stolz darauf, das Logo „Made with Macromedia" zu zeigen.

Im Februar 1996 präsentierte Macromedia eines Tages eine Website, die Shockwave für die Shocked Site of the Day (SSOTD) verwendete. Beavis & Butthead nahm das erste SSOTD am 8. Februar auf und es wurde bald eine sehr begehrte

Animator devient alors Macromedia Flash 1.0.

En 1996, Internet est pour le grand public quelque chose dont parlent les autres et d'une ampleur inconnue. Même pour des personnes comme moi, dont la première expérience informatique remonte à 1982 avec le Sinclair ZX81 d'un ami, puis avec mon propre Commodore VIC-20 reçu cette année-là pour Noël, le Web est un grand mystère. Il en va de même pour les ordinateurs, jusqu'à ce que Microsoft lance Windows 95 (en 1995) et s'éloigne des produits MS-DOS, davantage pensés pour des programmeurs.

Avec l'avènement de Windows 95 et des modems 33,6 kbps, le Web devient plus accessible et le internautes s'impliquent plus dans les sites Web pour des raisons professionnelles ou par intérêt personnel. C'est une période stimulante car tout le monde peut s'exprimer en ligne de façon inédite, et ce principalement grâce à Future-Splash Animator.

En 1996, un site Web standard contient un texte avec des hyperliens bleus qui deviennent violets quand on clique dessus, comme le site Apple.com à cette époque. L'emploi d'images reste assez avant-gardiste car la plu-

part des sites sont uniquement textuels.

Macromedia Shockwave offre la possibilité aux particuliers comme aux marques de faire leur promotion et laisse entrevoir ce que l'avenir peut réserver. En parallèle émergent plusieurs agences de conception Web comme Crankcase, et elles démontrent les nouvelles fonctions d'un site Web conçu avec Shockwave. Ces sites Web innovants arborent fièrement le logo «Made with Macromedia».

En février 1996, Macromedia sélectionne chaque jour un Shocked Site of the Day (SSOTD), un site Web intégrant Shockwave. Quand celui de la série Beavis & Butthead décroche le premier SSOTD le 8 février, cette reconnaissance devient vite très prisée par les concepteurs Web, les grandes marques et les nouvelles agences Web.

Spike Webb – Net Detective remporte le lendemain le second SSOTD. Cette aventure à base de pointer-cliquer inclut des illustrations originales et des effets sonores envoûtants pour motiver le public à revenir chaque semaine pour un nouvel épisode.

Cette année marque la naissance d'une génération entière d'expérimentateurs Web, parmi lesquels Paul Farry qui

The Early
Years
—

Spike Webb – Net Detective, won the second SSOTD the following day, a point-and-click adventure with original artwork and haunting sound effects which aimed to encourage people to revisit each week for a new installment.

This year marked the start of an entire generation of web experimentalists, amongst them Paul Farry who published his Shockwave Experiments, while his ChoreoGraph Cursor is another example of next-generation thinking on the web.

"Having grown up with a Commodore 64 background I knew some of the possibilities that were available for music and animation from those early works and wanted to experiment with doing them in Director. While the early problems with Director were that distribution of your files was via CD or FTP only, the web started to change this, and sharing the materials that you were working on gave me a lot of satisfaction because others would comment and provide additional ideas."

Paul Farry, Software Developer

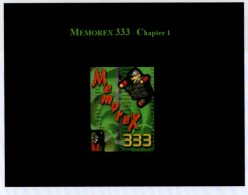

Spike Webb - Net Detective

In July, Darrel Plant published one of the first Shockwave books, *Shockwave! Breathe New Life into Your Web Pages*. He also put out some Shockwave experiments to accompany it.

"I started programming in the old teletype-terminal-and-punchcard days, back when the personal computer was just becoming a thing. I picked up a copy of Macromedia Director and began programming in Lingo, combining it with the graphic production chops I'd developed in print.

I kept a watch on the forum page for Shockwave for Director, downloaded the beta development tool (and eventually bought a Windows computer because the beta browser plug-in wasn't available for the Mac), then spotted someone looking for a writer to do a book on Shockwave on New Year's Eve. By mid-January, I had a book contract and the book was done in 10 weeks."

Darrel Plant, Moshofsky/Plant Creative Services

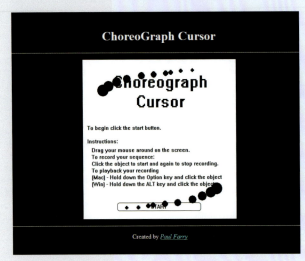

ChoreoGraph Cursor

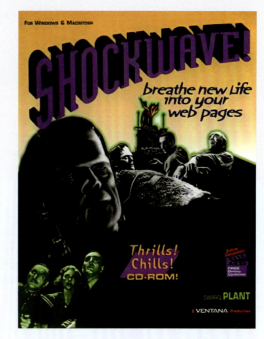

Shockwave! Breathe New Life into Your Web Pages

> ONE OF
THE FIRST
SHOCKWAVE
BOOKS
>

"This year marked the
start of an entire
generation of web
experimentalists."

Anerkennung unter Web-Designern, Top-Marken und den neu gegründeten Web-Agenturen.

Spike Webb Net Detective gewann am folgenden Tag die SSOTD mit einem Point-and-Click-Abenteuer mit original Kunstwerken und eindringlichen Soundeffekten, die darauf abzielten, die Leute dazu zu ermutigen, sich jede Woche eine neue Folge anzusehen.

In diesem Jahr startete eine ganze Generation von Web-Experimentatoren, darunter Paul Farry, der seine *Shockwave Experiments* veröffentlichte, während sein ChoreoGraph Cursor ein weiteres Beispiel für das Denken der nächsten Generation im Internet war.

„Da ich mit einem Commodore 64 aufgewachsen bin, kannte ich einige der Möglichkeiten, die für diese frühen Werke aus Musik und Animation zur Verfügung standen und wollte mit Director mit ihnen experimentieren. Die ersten Probleme mit Director bestanden darin, dass die Verteilung der Dateien nur über CD oder FTP erfolgte und das Web begann damit, dies zu ändern. Das Teilen der Materialien an denen man arbeitete, stellte mich sehr zufrieden, weil andere Personen

Kommentare abgeben konnten und so zusätzliche Ideen lieferten."
PAUL FARRY (SOFTWARE DEVELOPER)

Im Juli veröffentlichte Darrel Plant eines der ersten Shockwave-Bücher, *Shockwave! Breathe New Life into Your Web Pages*. Er veröffentlichte auch einige *Shockwave Experiments* dazu, um es zu begleiten.

„Ich begann mit der Programmierung in den Tagen der alten Fernschreiber und Lochkarten, damals, als der PC gerade interessant wurde. Ich nahm eine Kopie des Macromedia Director und begann mit der Programmierung in Lingo, wobei ich es mit den Grafik-Produktions-Chops kombinierte, die ich im Druck entwickelt hatte. Ich hatte die Forumseite von Shockwave für Director besucht, das Beta-Entwicklungstool heruntergeladen (und kaufte schließlich einen Windows-Computer, weil das Beta-Browser-Plug-in für den Mac nicht verfügbar war). Dann traf ich jemanden, der nach einem Autor suchte, der zu Silvester ein Buch über Shockwave schreiben sollte. Mitte Januar hatte ich einen Buchvertrag und das Buch war in zehn Wochen fertig."
DARREL PLANT (MOSHOFSKY/PLANT CREATIVE SERVICES)

publie ses *Shockwave Experiments*, ainsi que sa réflexion innovante ChoreoGraph Cursor.

« J'ai grandi dans le contexte du Commodore 64 et connaissais grâce à d'anciens projets certaines possibilités en matière de musique et d'animation que je voulais tester dans Director. Au début, le problème de Director était que l'envoi des fichiers ne pouvait se faire que via CD ou FTP. Grâce au Web, tout a changé et le fait de pouvoir partager des projets en cours était très gratifiant car d'autres personnes pouvaient les commenter et apporter des idées. »
PAUL FARRY (DÉVELOPPEUR DE LOGICIELS)

Au mois de juillet, Darrel Plant publie l'un des premiers ouvrages sur Shockwave, intitulé *Shockwave! Breathe New Life into Your Web Pages*. Il partage aussi quelques expériences Shockwave en parallèle.

« J'ai commencé à programmer dès l'époque des téléscripteurs et des cartes perforées, quand l'ordinateur personnel n'en était qu'à ses balbutiements. J'ai dégoté une copie de Macromedia Director et me suis mis à programmer en Lingo, avec des techniques

de production graphique que j'avais utilisées pour des projets d'impression. »

« J'ai gardé un œil sur la page du forum de Shockwave for Director, téléchargé l'outil de développement bêta (et finalement acheté un PC car le plug-in bêta n'était pas disponible pour Mac), puis rencontré quelqu'un qui cherchait un écrivain pour faire un livre sur Shockwave la veille du Nouvel An. Mi-janvier, je recevais un contrat d'auteur et dix semaines plus tard, le livre était terminé. »
DARREL PLANT (MOSHOFSKY/PLANT CREATIVE SERVICES)

FutureSplash Animator est disponible pour une période d'essai gratuite de 30 jours. Le tout premier exemple Flash utilisé dans un site Web avec Animator 1.1 date de 1996 et est publié sur la propre page de FutureWave.com.

Cette version d'essai, qui coûte 249,95 dollars à l'achat, requiert 2 Mo pour fonctionner sur Windows et entre 2,5 et 3,7 Mo sur un Macintosh. FutureWave.com héberge des échantillons de ce que le logiciel permet de faire, et les versions ultérieures en font de même.

FutureSplash Animator was available for a 30-day free-trial period. The earliest example of Flash being used on a website with Animator 1.1 was in 1996, on the FutureWave.com website itself.

This original trial version required 2 MB for use with Windows and between 2.5 and 3.7 MB with Macintosh; the full price was $249.95. FutureWave.com hosted some 'samples' of what the software was capable of, a feature that appeared in later versions as well.

"Getting to help build Flash was a privilege for me and we took our responsibility to users seriously. We worked to provide tools for creators to express themselves in a richer way than the web browser supported and we wanted to provide the best experience for viewers that we could. This meant making the download small and the player fast within the constraints of our limited resources for building software that worked on many different platforms."
Jonathan Gay

FutureSplash Animator

FutureSplash Animator 30-day trial

FutureWave.com

Official Simpsons website

> "It was interesting
> to see how these new
> webmasters were ditching
> Macromedia's Director
> and the Shockwave
> websites they'd been
> working on for the new
> powers of FutureSplash."

Walter Costinak

The official Simpsons website was one of the first to employ the latest FutureSplash player. The point-and-click site again showed what could be done, with Bart Simpson skating and jumping over police cars, especially for people who'd become accustomed to the web being a place for static text and not animation.

People were also now branding themselves as webmasters and forming web design agencies. Walter Costinak was one of the earliest to do this using FutureSplash, with his website featuring an image of his head, drawn using FutureSplash's vector graphics tool, and buttons with rollover functionality that led to further information.

It was interesting to see how these new webmasters were ditching Macromedia's Director and the Shockwave websites they'd been working on for the new powers of FutureSplash. Spike Webb was one such

that now published its comic series using FutureSplash, which also reduced file sizes to about 14-19 KB compared to Shockwave's 250 KB. These new comics also boasted better quality and all-round interaction.

The first Flash banners started to appear with the likes of Volleynerd (whose name combined beach volleyball with computer programming).

However, it was the massive reduction in file sizes that grabbed most people's attention, and with the free trial as well addictive software was born. The 30 days were like a countdown, and many people invested time heavily at the start of the period before going on to become completely consumed with what they were able to create.

The shift from Shockwave to FutureSplash also marked the beginnings of the interactive web.

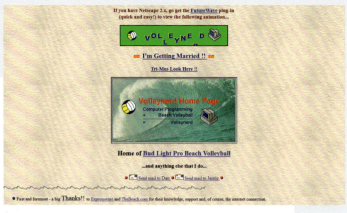

Volleynerd

FutureSplash Animator war für eine 30-tägige Probezeit verfügbar. Das früheste Beispiel für die Verwendung von Flash auf einer Website mit Animator 1.1 war 1996 auf der Website von FutureWave.com selbst.

Diese ursprüngliche Testversion benötigte 2 MB für die Verwendung mit Windows und zwischen 2,5 und 3,7 MB für Macintosh. Der volle Preis betrug $249,95. FutureWave.com hatte ein paar „Samples" von dem, wozu die Software in der Lage war, ein Feature, das auch in späteren Versionen erschien.

„Es war ein Privileg für mich, mitzuhelfen Flash zu entwickeln und wir haben unsere Verantwortung gegenüber den Usern sehr ernst genommen. Wir haben Tools entwickelt, mit denen die Webdesigner sich besser ausdrücken konnten als der Webbrowser allein es unterstützte und wir wollten den Anwendern die bestmögliche Erfahrung bieten. Das bedeutete, dass wir im Rahmen unserer begrenzten Mittel den Download klein halten und den Player schnell machen mussten, damit man Software erstellen konnte, die auf vielen verschiedenen Plattformen lief."
JONATHAN GAY

Die offizielle Simpsons Website war eine der ersten, die den neuesten FutureSplash Player verwendete. Die Point-and-Click-Seite zeigte wieder, was möglich war, wenn Bart Simpson über Polizeiautos skatete und sprang, besonders für Leute, die sich daran gewöhnt hatten, dass das Internet ein Ort für statischen Text und keine Animation war.

Die Leute bezeichneten sich nun auch als Webmaster und gründeten Web-Design-Agenturen. Walter Costinak war einer der frühesten, der dies mit FutureSplash tat. Auf seiner Website war ein Bild seines Kopfes zu sehen, gezeichnet mit dem Vector Graphics Tool von FutureSplash und Buttons mit Rollover-Funktionalität, die zu weiteren Informationen führten.

Es war interessant zu sehen, wie diese neuen Webmaster Macromedias Director untergruben und die Shockwave Webseiten, an denen sie mit den neuen Leistungen von FutureSplash arbeiteten. Spike Webb war so eine Seite, die nun ihre Comicserie mit FutureSplash veröffentlichte, was auch die Dateigröße auf ungefähr 14–19 KB reduzierte, im Vergleich zu den 250 KB von Shockwave. Diese neuen Comics zeigten auch eine bessere Qualität und vielseitige Interaktion.

Die ersten Flash-Banner erschienen bei Leuten wie Volleynerd (dessen Name Beach-Volleyball mit Computerprogrammierung kombinierte).

Es war jedoch die massive Reduzierung der Dateigröße, die die Aufmerksamkeit der meisten Menschen auf sich zog. Mit der kostenlosen Testversion wurde auch eine süchtig machende Software geboren. Die 30 Tage waren wie ein Countdown und viele investierten insbesondere zu Beginn der Zeit viele Stunden, bevor sie komplett davon aufgesogen wurden, was sie alles damit schaffen konnten.

Der Wechsel von Shockwave zu FutureSplash markierte auch die Anfänge des interaktiven Webs.

«Contribuer à développer Flash a été un privilège pour moi et nous avons pris très au sérieux notre responsabilité envers les utilisateurs. Nous travaillions pour inventer des outils de création plus avancés que ceux pris en charge par le navigateur Web, et l'idée était d'offrir la meilleure expérience possible aux public. Pour cela, le téléchargement devait être rapide, tout comme le lecteur, et ce malgré la contrainte de nos ressources limitées pour concevoir un logiciel fonctionnant sur de nombreuses plates-formes.»
JONATHAN GAY

Le site Web officiel des Simpsons est l'un des premiers à employer le dernier lecteur FutureSplash. Avec sa navigation par pointer-cliquer, le site montre là encore les possibilités offertes, notamment aux personnes habituées à un Web fait de textes statiques et sans animation. On peut par exemple y voir Bart Simpson faire du skate et sauter par-dessus des voitures de police.

Les utilisateurs font également leur propre promotion en tant que webmasters et montent des agences de conception Web. Walter Costinak est l'un des tous premiers à s'y prêter avec Future-Splash : son site Web montre une image de son visage créée à l'aide de l'outil de graphisme vectoriel, et des boutons dévoilent plus d'informations quand le curseur est placé dessus.

Il est intéressant de voir comment ces nouveaux webmasters abandonnent progressivement Macromedia Director et les sites Web Shockwave sur lesquels ils travaillent pour profiter des nouvelles fonctionnalités de FutureSplash. Tel est le cas de Spike Webb, qui publie désormais sa série à l'aide de FutureSplash, avec des fichiers nettement moins volumineux qu'avec Shockwave (entre 14 et 19 ko, contre 250 ko). Ces nouvelles histoires sont également de meilleure qualité et permettent une interaction totale.

Les premières bannières Flash commencent à apparaître avec celles de Volleynerd (nom formé en combinant le sport et «nerd», un crack en informatique).

C'est toutefois l'énorme réduction de la taille des fichiers qui frappe les utilisateurs, et la version d'essai gratuite finit d'en faire un succès. Les 30 jours sont vécus comme un compte à rebours : beaucoup y consacrent un temps infini au début de la période, puis se retrouvent dépassés par les possibilités de création offertes.

Le passage de Shockwave à FutureSplash marque également les débuts du Web interactif.

1997

In 1997, Macromedia Flash changed the online world.

The official website for singer-songwriter Amy Grant scooped a SSOTD on August 28. Its Flash 2 intro had a numbered countdown with sound effects, and then the site opened with Amy's signature being drawn right in front of our eyes, backed by a preview from her latest single, "Behind the Eyes". This promotional site was one of the first of its kind in the music industry, and embraced the latest tech to each a large fanbase.

Whilst record companies and big brands were quickly becoming aware of the power of Flash and how using it could increase their street credibility, a whole underground movement had started with thousands of bedroom web-designers and Flash masters.

In 1997, web-hosting and domain names were still expensive, although several web-hosting companies offered free domain name extensions of their own company name. GeoCities was the most common host at this time, but using its domain name was impersonal and bland.

>
OFFICIAL
WEBSITE FOR
SINGER-
SONGWRITER
AMY GRANT
WON A SSOTD
>

Alberto Gabriel "Gabo" Mendoza, a college student from Puerto Rico, had been experimenting with Flash and launched version 2 of his personal space, Gabo's, at geocities.com/SoHo/Lofts/3949. This was the first time a truly pioneering Flash intro was seen, with progressive sound, and the page then built on screen with more innovative sound effects. Exploring further, the site's buttons, 'My Art', 'News', 'Gabo', and 'Files', quickly revealed the character of the person behind the site.

"They had this big banner thing on the Blizzard site advertising Diablo. It blew my mind. How did it download so fast? How can it play so smoothly? Compared to the animated gifs of the era (or – what? RealPlayer?!? Ugh!) it was crazy. I had to figure this out. So I did a little digging and traced the magic back to Flash.

To learn it, I made a simple site to replace my personal HTML page. Nobody told me I wasn't 'supposed' to use Flash for a whole page. And the intro? It didn't even occur to me that it was weird to have one on a web page. My inspirations were video games, anime, and movies. Those all had cool intros and music, so why not this?"

Gabo Mendoza, Gabocorp

Gabo was now branding himself as Gabocorp Imaging and his latest site told a bit more about him. It was clear he was a nice guy, and this was backed up by the fact that he was now offering free downloads of his work, including desktop themes and original fonts. He was also creating some terrific interfaces, as can be seen with his 'revolver' navigation idea.

On November 6, he won a SSOTD, and this led to him receiving over 400 emails and 17 job offers.

"I remember being so excited receiving over 400 emails in one day from people that saw my site thanks to the award. That was a lot back then, and it was a huge deal for me. So much support, appreciation, and attention. It was overwhelming. Making these crazy websites was a way for me to express myself. The audience was a completely unexpected side effect."

Gabo Mendoza, Gabocorp

Gabo's

"It didn't even
occur to me that it
was weird to have
an introduction on
a web page."

Gabo's revolver navigation

"Nobody told me
I wasn't 'supposed'
to use Flash for
a whole page."

1997

Im Jahr 1997 veränderte Macromedia Flash die Online-Welt.

Die offizielle Website für
Singer-Songwriter Amy Grant
bekam am 28. August einen
SSOTD. Ihr Flash 2 Intro hatte
einen nummerierten Countdown
mit Soundeffekten und dann
öffnete sich die Seite mit der
Unterschrift von Amy, die direkt
vor unseren Augen gezeichnet
wurde, unterstützt von einer
Vorschau ihrer neuesten Single
„Behind the Eyes". Diese Werbeseite war eine der ersten ihrer
Art in der Musikindustrie und
verwendete die neueste Technologie, um eine große Fange-
meinde zu erreichen.

Während Plattenfirmen
und große Marken sich schnell
der Macht von Flash bewusst
wurden und mit der Verwendung
ihre Glaubwürdigkeit steigern
konnten, hatte eine ganze
Underground-Bewegung mit
Tausenden von Webdesignern
und Flash-Meistern begonnen.

Im Jahr 1997 waren Web-
hosting und Domainnamen noch
immer teuer, obwohl mehrere
Webhosting-Unternehmen
kostenlose Domainnamenerwei-
terungen ihres eigenen Firmennamens anboten. GeoCities
war zu dieser Zeit der häufigste
Host, aber die Verwendung ihres
Domainnamens war unpersönlich
und langweilig.

Alberto Gabriel „Gabo"
Mendoza, ein Collegestudent
aus Puerto Rico, hatte mit Flash
experimentiert und startete
Version 2 seines persönlichen
Raums, Gabo's, bei geocities.
com/SoHo/Lofts/3949. Dies war
das erste Mal, dass man ein wirklich bahnbrechendes Flash-Intro
mit progressivem Sound sehen
konnte und dann baute sich die
Seite auf dem Bildschirm mit
innovativeren Sound-Effekten
auf. Die Schaltflächen „My Art",
„News" „Gabo" und „Files" der
Website enthüllten dann schnell
den Charakter der Person, die
hinter der Website stand.

„Sie hatten diesen großen
Banner auf der Blizzard-Seite,
die Werbung für Diablo machte.
Das hat mich einfach umgehauen.
Wie konnte das so schnell
downloaden? Wie konnte es so
reibungslos laufen? Im Vergleich
zu den animierten GIFs in der Zeit
(oder – was? RealPlayer?!? Ugh!)
war es einfach verrückt. Das
musste ich herausfinden. Also
grub ich ein wenig tiefer und verfolgte die Magie zurück zu Flash.

Um es zu lernen, erstellte
ich eine einfache Seite, um
meine persönliche HTML-Seite
zu ersetzen. Niemand hatte mir
gesagt, dass Flash nicht dafür

1997

En 1997, Macromedia Flash boule-
verse le monde en ligne.

Le site Web officiel de la
compositeur-interprète Amy
Grant décroche le 28 août un
SSOTD. Son intro en Flash 2 inclut
un compte à rebours avec des
effets sonores, et la page s'ouvre
avec la signature d'Amy se tra-
çant sous les yeux des visiteurs,
le tout agrémenté d'un extrait de
son dernier single «Behind the
Eyes». Ce site promotionnel est
l'un des premiers du genre dans
l'industrie musicale et s'appuie
sur la dernière technologie pour
toucher le plus de fans.

Alors que les maisons de
disques et les grandes marques
comprennent rapidement toute la
puissance de Flash pour accroître
leur crédibilité populaire, tout un
mouvement a déjà commencé de
la main de milliers de concepteurs
Web et experts Flash.

En 1997, l'hébergement
Web et les noms de domaines
sont encore onéreux, mais plusieurs sociétés d'hébergement
offrent des extensions gratuites
de domaine de leur propre nom.
GeoCities est à cette époque
l'hôte le plus connu, mais son
nom de domaine résulte impersonnel et banal.

Alberto Gabriel «Gabo»
Mendoza, étudiant universitaire
de Puerto Rico, fait des essais
avec Flash et lance la version 2
de sa page personnelle, Gabo's,
sur geocities.com/SoHo/
Lofts/3949. Jamais une intro
Flash aussi innovante n'a encore
été vue, avec du son progressif
et une page qui se compose
à l'écran avec des effets sonores
inédits. Les boutons de navigation «My Art», «News», «Gabo»
et «Files» reflètent parfaitement la personnalité de l'auteur
du site.

«Il y avait sur le site de
Blizzard cette grande bannière
publicitaire pour Diablo. J'étais
bluffé. Comment le téléchargement pouvait être si rapide?
Comment pouvait-elle se lire si
bien? Par rapport aux GIF animés
de l'époque (quoi? RealPlayer?!
Beurk!), c'était de la folie. Je
devais comprendre. J'ai fait des
recherches et découvert que la
magie venait de Flash.»

«Pour apprendre, j'ai
créé un site simple remplaçant
ma page personnelle en HTML.
Personne ne m'a dit que je
n'étais pas censé utiliser
Flash pour une page entière.
Et l'intro? Je n'ai même pas
pensé que c'était bizarre d'en
mettre une dans une page
Web. Je m'inspirais des jeux
vidéo, des anime et des films.
Tous avaient des intros et

The Early
Years

—

On December 20, internet users were given the biggest early Christmas present they could have hoped for: now with a domain name all his own, Gabo presented the all-new Gabocorp.com as created in Flash 3.

"You are about to enter
a new era in website design.
This is the new standard
for all things to come.
Welcome to the new
Gabocorp."

If a home-page today carried such a slogan, few people would take it seriously. Yet in 1997, it was actually very exciting to read something like this, and hitting the glowing 'GO' button quickened the heartbeat.

On entering the website, a simple intro animation set out the positioning of the site's navigation basics, much in the style of Gabo's previous work. But this new version showed a higher level of quality and attention to detail, and was ample evidence of its creator's obvious talent and ability.

To have enabled things to move on the screen with such ease and to have incorporated music and sound effects with that, Gabo had become one of the key early pioneers of the web. His site inspired numerous people and forums soon lit up with the launch of Gabocorp.com; the site received over 56,000 visitors in its first two months and Gabo received over 1,000 emails.

In fact, people were still posting comments about it years later: "That was the very first Flash site I ever saw and the reason I started learning Flash in the first place."

"The first Gabocorp.com was in Flash 2, and went live in October 1997. Later, Macromedia asked me to make an updated version of the site in Flash 3.

They wanted it to line up with the release of the new software. This updated site was a bit rushed and had some of Flash's new features shoehorned in. The interface concept remained the same. Even the sampled taiko drum sound survived the remodel. I remember struggling with the color scheme and saying 'Every color!' I still prefer the original, though."

Gabo Mendoza, Gabocorp

Gabocorp.com

Gabocorp.com

„gedacht" war, damit eine ganze Seite zu machen. Und das Intro? Es ist mir nicht einmal in den Sinn gekommen, dass es komisch war, eines auf einer Webseite zu haben. Meine Inspirationen waren Videospiele, Anime und Filme. Die hatten alle coole Intros und Musik, also warum nicht auch hier?"
GABO MENDOZA, GABOCORP

Gabo nannte seine Marke nun Gabocorp Imaging und seine neueste Seite erzählte mir ein wenig mehr über ihn. Es war klar, dass er ein netter Kerl war. Das zeigte sich durch die Tatsache, dass er jetzt kostenlose Downloads seiner Arbeit anbot, einschließlich Desktop-Themen und Originalschriften. Er schuf auch einige tolle Schnittstellen, wie man an seiner „Revolver" Navigationsidee sehen kann.

Am 6. November gewann er einen SSOTD und das führte dazu, dass er über 400 E-Mails und 17 Stellenangebote erhielt.

„Ich erinnere mich, dass ich so aufgeregt war, als ich an einem Tag mehr als 400 E-Mails von Leuten erhalten hatte, die meine Website dank der Auszeichnung gesehen hatten. Das war damals viel und es war eine große Sache für mich. So viel Unterstützung, Wertschätzung und Aufmerksamkeit. Es war überwältigend. Diese verrückten Websites zu machen, war eine Möglichkeit für mich, mich auszudrücken. Das Publikum war ein völlig unerwarteter Nebeneffekt."
GABO MENDOZA, GABOCORP

Am 20. Dezember erhielten Internetnutzer das größte frühzeitige Weihnachtsgeschenk, das sie sich wünschen konnten: Gabo präsentierte jetzt unter seinem eigenen Domainnamen die brandneue Gabocorp.com, die in Flash 3 erstellt wurde.

„Sie betreten gerade eine neue Ära des Website-Designs. Dies ist der neue Standard für alle Dinge die noch kommen werden.Willkommen bei der neuen Gabocorp."

Wenn eine Homepage heute einen solchen Slogan tragen würde, würden es nur wenige

Leute ernst nehmen. Doch im Jahr 1997 war es wirklich sehr aufregend, so etwas zu lesen und mit dem leuchtenden „GO" Knopf beschleunigte sich der Herzschlag.

Für das Betreten der Website wurde eine einfache Intro-Animation erstellt, in der die Navigationsgrundlagen der Website, ähnlich Gabos früheren Arbeiten, positioniert wurden. Aber diese neue Version zeigte ein höheres Niveau an Qualität und Liebe zum Detail und war ein deutlicher Beweis für das offensichtliche Talent und die Fähigkeit des Schöpfers.

Da Dinge nun so einfach auf dem Bildschirm bewegt werden konnten und Musik und Soundeffekte damit verbunden wurden, wurde Gabo zu einem der wichtigsten frühen Pioniere des Internets. Seine Website inspirierte zahlreiche Menschen und Foren und beeinflusste bald den Start von Gabocorp.com. Diese Website erhielt in den ersten zwei Monaten mehr als 56.000 Besucher und Gabo erhielt über 1.000 E-Mails.

Tatsächlich haben die Leute noch Jahre später Kommentare darüber gepostet: „Das war die allererste Flash-Site, die ich je gesehen habe und der Grund, warum ich anfing Flash zu lernen."

„Die erste Gabocorp.com war in Flash 2 und wir gingen im Oktober 1997 online. Später bat mich Macromedia noch einmal, eine aktualisierte Version der Seite in Flash 3 zu machen.

Sie wollten sie zeitgleich mit der neuen Software veröffentlichen. Diese aktualisierte Version war schnell gemacht und wir bauten einige von Flashs neuen Features ein. Das Schnittstellen-konzept blieb das Gleiche. Selbst der gesampelte Taiko-Trommel-Sound überlebte die Umgestaltung. Ich erinnere mich noch daran, dass ich Probleme mit der Farbpalette hatte und sagte „Alle Farben"! Trotzdem bevorzuge ich immer noch die Originalseite."
GABO MENDOZA, GABOCORP

de la musique cool, alors pourquoi pas ma page Web?»
GABO MENDOZA, GABOCORP

Gabo s'annonce sous la marque Gabocorp Imaging et son dernier site en dévoile un peu plus sur sa personne. Il est visiblement un type bien, chose confirmée par le fait qu'il offre à présent des téléchargements gratuits de son travail, y compris des thèmes de bureau et des polices originales. Il crée également de formidables interfaces, comme l'illustre par exemple son idée de navigation «revolver».

Le 6 novembre, il remporte un SSOTD et reçoit dans la foulée plus de 400 e-mails et 17 offres d'emploi.

«Je me souviens du plaisir de recevoir plus de 400 mails par jour de personnes ayant vu mon site grâce au prix reçu. C'était pour l'époque un chiffre élevé et pour moi, ça représentait beaucoup, avoir tellement de soutien, de reconnaissance, d'attention. C'était impressionnant. Pour moi, faire ces sites délirants était un mode d'expression. Le public était un effet secondaire totalement inattendu.»
GABO MENDOZA, GABOCORP

Le 20 décembre, les internautes reçoivent le meilleur cadeau de Noël anticipé qu'ils puissent imaginer: désormais propriétaire d'un nom de domaine propre, Gabo présente le tout nouveau Gabocorp.com créé en Flash 3.

«Vous êtes sur le point d'entrer dans une nouvelle ère en conception Web. Il s'agit du nouveau standard pour tout ce qui est à venir. Bienvenue dans le nouveau Gabocorp.»

Si une page d'accueil montre aujourd'hui ce type d'annonce, peu d'utilisateurs la prendront au sérieux. En 1997 pourtant, ce genre de texte est très prometteur et le simple fait de cliquer sur le bouton «GO» lumineux donne des palpitations.

Une fois dans le site, une sobre animation d'introduction indique les principes de base de

navigation, tout à fait dans le style des réalisations antérieures de Gabo. Cette nouvelle version fait toutefois preuve d'une qualité supérieure et d'un souci plus poussé du détail. Elle démontre amplement le talent et les compétences de son auteur.

Pour avoir animé si facilement des choses à l'écran et intégré de la musique et des effets sonores, Gabo devient l'un des grands précurseurs du Web. Son site inspire de nombreuses personnes et les forums s'enflamment rapidement avec le lancement de Gabocorp.com: il cumule plus de 56 000 visiteurs les deux premiers mois et Gabo reçoit plus de 1 000 e-mails.

Des années plus tard, des utilisateurs continuent de publier des commentaires à son sujet: «C'était le premier site Flash que je voyais et la véritable raison pour laquelle j'ai commencé à apprendre Flash.»

«Le premier Gabocorp.com était codé en Flash 2 et est sorti en octobre 1997. Plus tard, Macromedia m'a demandé de faire une mise à jour du site avec Flash 3.»

«Ils voulaient qu'il soit en phase avec le nouveau logiciel. La nouvelle version du site s'est un peu faite dans l'urgence et incluait de nouvelles fonctions de Flash. Le concept de l'interface est resté inchangé, et même le son échantillonné du tambour taiko a survécu. Je me souviens avoir eu du mal avec le schéma de couleur et de dire "Toutes les couleurs!" Je continue pourtant de préférer l'original.»
GABO MENDOZA, GABOCORP

You are about to enter a new era in website design.

Gabo Mendoza

1998/

The Year Macromedia Flash Went Mainstream

1998/

—

The Year Macromedia Flash Went Mainstream

Shocked Site of the Day

After Macromedia acquired FutureSplash and renamed it Flash, the software was made available for free download and 30-day trial and quickly became the new trend.

Flash 2 was being installed by designers and developers worldwide while pirate sites exploited password hacks for the trial version, so that one way or the other long-term access was possible for everyone.

"It was the wild west of web design. Nothing had been done yet and the community was so small that everyone saw everything. There was a feeling that this was just the beginning of something truly amazing."

J.D. Hooge, Fourm; Instrument

The old black-and-white web, with its static text, animated gifs, and lake applets, had now been left behind. The new vector-based software also meant that websites could be designed so that they looked the same on any size of screen, marking the arrival of responsive web design.

Whilst Gabocorp was undoubtedly at the forefront of Flash websites in 1997 there were a few others of note, but in 1998 Flash design became widespread.

In the late 1990s, the most prestigious place for web design to be seen was on Macromedia's home-page as a Shocked Site of the Day. This could result in over 20,000 site visits a week and the sort of buzz no other website could generate, which meant that designers and developers often pushed their creative work even further.

This generation had grown up in a world with no internet, and the new possibilities for recognition and fame proved addictive.

However, when Macromedia began making some questionable selections for the SSOTD, message boards lit up with disapproval and Flash users instead chose to judge each other's work for themselves. WDDG (World Domination Design Group), the U.S. web agency of James Baker that was an early Flash adopter, took the initiative and launched a website called the Flash Challenge. This became more of a community-run project, with impeccable standards, and was highly regarded as well as being another desired outlet for new work.

"When Flash took off it was like the Cambrian explosion for the interactive web. Every rule that had been created before was summarily destroyed — we didn't need rules — we were rewriting the rules for interaction design.

"It was a stunning era of creativity. We created the modern web. Some may look back now and say that what we were creating looks trivial compared with what we have now, but that early generation of Flash developers laid the groundwork — and made the mistakes — that led to what we have today."

James Baker, The Flash Challenge; WDDG

Flasher.net became the main community hub and forum for Flash development and also a resource for finding and discussing sites that used Flash. The likes of the late Hillman Curtis became a driving force at this time in web design, and later film, while Brendan Dawes created an early fan site for Saul Bass, and other creative websites launched, including Breakout and E3 Direktiv.

> "There was a feeling
> that this was just the
> beginning of something
> truly amazing."

Flash Challenge

Saul Bass on the Web

Flasher.net

Nachdem Macromedia Future-Splash übernommen und es in Flash umbenannte, wurde die Software im kostenlosen Download und einer 30-Tage-Test-version angeboten und sie wurde schnell zu einem neuen Trend.

Flash 2 wurde von Desig-nern und Entwicklern weltweit installiert, während Piraten-Sites Passwort-Hacks für die Test-version nutzten, so dass der eine oder andere langfristige Zugriff für alle möglich war.

„Es war der Wilde Westen des Webdesigns. Es lag noch alles vor uns und die Community war so klein, dass jeder alles sah. Man hatte das Gefühl, dass dies nur der Anfang von etwas wirk-lich Erstaunlichem war."
J.D. HOOGE, FOURM; INSTRUMENT

Das alte schwarz-weiße Web mit seinem statischen Text, animierten Gifs und Lake-Applets lag nun hinter uns. Die neue Vek-tor-basierte Software bedeutete auch, dass Websites so designt werden konnten, dass sie immer

gleich aussahen, egal auf wel-chem Bildschirm man sie ansah, was den Beginn des responsiven Webdesigns kennzeichnete.

Obwohl Gabocorp un-zweifelhaft an vorderster Front bei den Flash Webseiten im Jahr 1997 stand, gab es noch einige andere bemerkenswerte Seiten und schon im Jahr 1998 war Flash-Design weit verbreitet.

In den späten Jahren der 1990er war der prestige-trächtigste Ort für Webdesign auf Macromedias Homepage „Shocked Site of the Day" zu finden. Sie hatte mehr als 20.000 Websitebesuche pro Woche und führte zu einer Art von Buzz, die keine andere Website generieren konnte, was bedeutete, dass Designer und Entwickler ihre kreative Arbeit oft noch weiter vorantrieben. Diese Generation war noch in einer Welt ohne Internet aufgewachsen, und die neuen Möglichkeiten der Aner-kennung und des Ruhmes erwie-sen sich als suchterzeugend.

Als Macromedia allerdings damit begann, einige fragwür-dige Auswahlen für die SSOTD zu treffen, tauchen Message Boards auf, die ihre Missbilligung ausdrückten und Flash-User beschlossen stattdessen, die Arbeit des jeweils anderen selbst zu beurteilen. Die WDDG (World Domination Design Group), die US-Webagentur von James Baker, war ein früher Flash-Adopter, ergriff die Initiative und startete eine Website namens Flash Challenge. Dies wurde mehr zu einem von der Community betriebenen Projekt mit tadel-losen Standards und wurde hoch angesehen wie auch ein weiterer erwünschter Ausgangs-punkt für neue Arbeit.

„Als Flash begann, war es wie die kambrische Explosion für das interaktive Web. Jede Regel, die zuvor erstellt wurde, wurde summarisch zerstört – wir brauchten keine Regeln – wir schrieben die Regeln für das Interaktionsdesign neu.

Es war eine atemberau-bende Ära der Kreativität. Wir schufen das moderne Web. Einige mögen jetzt zurückblicken und sagen, dass das, was wir ge-schaffen haben, im Vergleich zu dem, was wir jetzt haben, trivial war, aber diese frühe Generation von Flash-Entwicklern legte den Grundstein dafür – und machte ihre Fehler – was zu dem führte, was wir heute haben."
JAMES BAKER, THE FLASH CHALLENGE; WDDG

Flasher.net wurde zum wichtigsten Community-Hub und Forum für Flash-Entwicklung und auch eine Ressource zum Finden und Besprechen von Websites, die Flash verwendeten. Leute wie Hillman Curtis wurden zu einer treibenden Kraft im Webdesign zu dieser Zeit, und später im Film, während Brendan Dawes eine frühe Fanseite für Saul Bass schuf und andere kreative Websites startete, zum Beispiel Breakout und E3 Direktiv.

1998/

—

The Year Macromedia Flash Went Mainstream

—

Hillman Curtis

Breakout

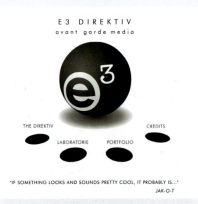

E3 Direktiv

"We didn't need rules – we were rewriting the rules for interaction design."

Quand Macromedia rachète FutureSplash et le réédite sous le nom de Flash, le logiciel peut être téléchargé gratuitement pour une période d'essai de 30 jours et s'impose très vite sur le marché.

Flash 2 est installé à travers le monde par les concepteurs et les développeurs, et des sites pirates proposent des mots de passe pour que quiconque puisse prolonger l'accès à la version d'essai.

« C'était le Far West du design Web. Rien n'avait encore été fait et la communauté était tellement petite que tout le monde voyait tout. On avait le sentiment d'être au commencement de quelque chose de vraiment incroyable. »
J.D. HOOGE, FOURM ; INSTRUMENT

Le Web en noir et blanc, avec ses textes statiques, ses gifs animés et ses applets Lake, appartient au passé. Avec le nouveau logiciel vectoriel, les sites Web peuvent être conçus pour s'afficher de la même manière sur les écrans de toutes tailles. C'est l'avènement de la conception Web réactive.

En 1997, Gabocorp est sans conteste à l'avant-garde des sites Web Flash. D'autres sites se distinguent aussi du lot, mais c'est en 1998 que la conception Flash s'étend vraiment.

À la fin des années 90, la page d'accueil de Macromedia est l'endroit le plus prestigieux pour une conception Web élue Shocked Site of the Day. La sélection d'un site peut en effet entraîner plus de 20 000 visites par semaine et une effervescence autrement inégalable. Les concepteurs et les développeurs sont ainsi motivés pour repousser les limites de leur travail créatif.

Cette génération qui a grandi dans un monde sans Internet devient accro aux nouvelles possibilités de reconnaissance et de gloire.

Quand Macromedia commence toutefois à faire des choix contestables pour les SSOTD, les forums de discussion s'enflamment et les utilisateurs Flash décident de juger d'eux-mêmes chaque réalisation. L'agence Web américaine WDDG (World Domination Design Group), créée par James Baker et parmi les premières à employer Flash, prend l'initiative de lancer le site Flash Challenge. Ce projet à la gestion plutôt collective applique des normes impeccables, se gagne une haute estime et devient une vitrine prisée pour les nouvelles créations.

« Quand Flash a décollé, c'était comme l'explosion cambrienne pour le Web interactif. Chaque règle qui avait été créée auparavant était rapidement annulée. Plus besoin de règles, nous réécrivions celles du design interactif. »

« C'était une époque exceptionnelle sur le plan de la créativité. Nous avons créé le Web moderne. Si certains regardent en arrière, ils le trouveront peut-être insignifiant comparé à ce qui se fait maintenant. Mais cette première génération de développeurs Flash a jeté les bases (et fait les erreurs) qui nous ont amenés où nous sommes aujourd'hui. »
JAMES BAKER, THE FLASH CHALLENGE ; WDDG

Flasher.net devient le principal point de rencontre et forum pour le développement Flash, ainsi qu'une ressource pour rechercher et commenter des sites utilisant cette technologie. Des créateurs comme Hillman Curtis jouent un rôle moteur à cette époque en conception Web, et plus tard au cinéma. Au même moment, Brendan Dawes crée un des premiers sites de fans pour Saul Bass, et d'autres sites Web originaux apparaissent, dont Breakout et E3 Direktiv.

08 Facts of the year

Number of internet users:
147 million, 3.6% of the
world population

Number of websites:
2.5 million

World news:
U.S. embassy bombings
in East Africa

Website with most traffic:
Aol.com

Tech hardware:
Apple launches the iMac

Tech software:
MPEG-4 introduced

Other tech:
Amazon acquires IMDb

Highest-grossing film:
Armageddon

Eye4U

—

A global phenomenon

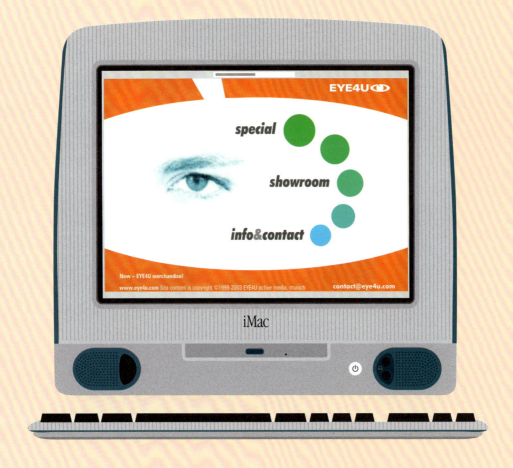

Eye4U is remembered by many as one of the earliest websites that made an impact, reaching the mainstream while Gabocorp was slightly more underground. With its bright colors, uplifting music, and dynamic Flash intro, it was soon picked up by design forums which noted how it perfectly filled the browser screen, and how each click resulted in a full-screen intro to the next section.

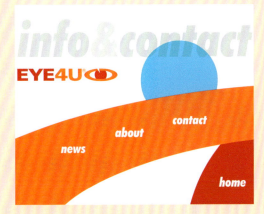

"The Eye4U site is as creatively valid today as when it first launched in 1998. The combination of layout, transitions, and sound are techniques that even modern developers would be hard pressed to replicate outside of Flash almost 20 years later. The unique navigation and dynamic layout breaks out of today's conventional UX/UI boxes and grids. It was full-screen responsive, 15 years before responsive was the norm. The beautiful immersive experience, sound effects, and inspirational transitions between sections inspired many to start careers in web design and Flash."

Shane Mielke
Pixelranger; shanemielke.com
(Industry quote provided in the absence of the site's creators)

Eye4U wird bei vielen als eine der frühesten Websites in Erinnerung sein, die beeindruckte und den Mainstream erreichten, während Gabocorp etwas mehr Underground war. Mit ihren leuchtenden Farben, erhebender Musik und dem dynamischem

Flash-Intro wurde sie bald von Designforen aufgegriffen, die begeistert feststellten, wie sie den Browserbildschirm perfekt füllte und wie jeder Klick zu einem Vollbild-Intro des nächsten Abschnitts führte.

Beaucoup se souviennent de Eye4U comme l'un des tous premiers sites Web ne laissant pas indifférent le grand public, alors que Gabocorp est légèrement plus underground. Avec ses couleurs vives, sa musique entraînante et son intro

Flash dynamique, il est rapidement commenté sur les forums : il est apprécié car il remplit parfaitement le navigateur et qu'une introduction plein écran à la section suivante apparaît à chaque clic.

NRG.BE

—

The first website to use surround sound

Peter Van den Wyngaert's NRG.BE was another site that inspired early internet-users, and opened with the voice-over:

"WELCOME TO NRG DOT B E."

The voice belonged to Michel Orthier from Breakout4u.com, a professional voice-over artist who later found further fame on sites such as megaCar.com and Kimble.org (both Kim Dotcom sites). NRG.BE had a catchy, dance-inspired soundtrack and a 'music off' button that was an early example of usability. The interface was simple, with rollover effects on the "aerials/transmitters" which produced a little white noise in surround sound so that the difference could be heard across the speakers, a world first. NRG.BE also employed shape tweening, an animation technique in Flash, which presented an interface that had not been seen before.

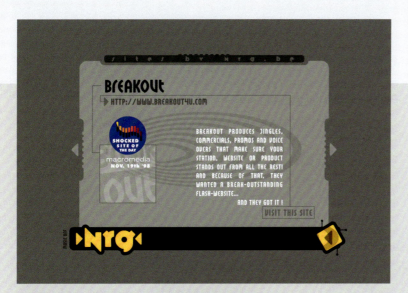

"The release of Flash 3 finally gave me the desire to create a futuristic website. After the release of my website, I ended up being selected as a SSOTD. I went from having just a few dozen site visits per day to over 40,000! The reaction was immense. Offering services to local businesses changed overnight to a worldwide interest. Thank you Flash for having such a defining impact on my life!"

Peter Van den Wyngaert
NRG.BE

Peter Van den Wyngaerts NRG.BE war eine weitere Site, welche die frühen Internet-User inspirierte und eröffnete mit einer Sprachnachricht (Voice-Over): „WELCOME TO NRG DOT B E."

Die Stimme gehörte Michel Orthier von Breakout4u.com, ein professioneller Voice-Over-Artist, der später weiteren Ruhm auf Sites wie megaCar.com und Kimble.org (beide Kim Dotcom Sites) bekam.

NRG.BE hatte einen eingängigen, tänzerisch inspirierten Soundtrack und einen „Musik aus"-Button, ein frühes Beispiel für Usability. Die Schnittstelle war einfach, mit Rollover-Effekten an den „Antennen/Sendern", was ein wenig weißes Rauschen im Surround-Sound erzeugte, so dass der Unterschied über die Lautsprecher zu hören war, eine Weltneuheit. NRG.BE verwendete auch Shape Tweening, eine Animationstechnik in Flash, die eine bisher nicht gekannte Oberfläche präsentierte.

Le site Web de la société NRG.BE de Peter Van den Wyngaert inspire lui aussi les premiers internautes. Il s'ouvre avec une voix off qui dit : « WELCOME TO NRG DOT B E. »

La voix appartient à Michel Orthier de Breakout4u.com, un locuteur professionnel qui enchaîne ensuite d'autres interventions sur des sites comme megaCar.com et Kimble.org (tous deux de Kim Dotcom).

NRG.BE possède une bande sonore entraînante et un bouton «music off», élément pionnier d'usabilité. L'interface est simple, avec des effets par survol sur les «émetteurs» qui renvoient un petit bruit blanc en son surround appréciable dans les haut-parleurs, une première mondiale. NRG.BE a aussi recours à la technique d'interpolation des formes, une technique d'animation en Flash qui donne une interface encore jamais vue.

1998/
—

The Void

—

15-year-old wins
global recognition

The way the internet opened up creative possibilities for anyone with a connection, regardless of who they were, was exemplified by Luke Turner, a teenager in England who had been inspired in 1994 when he was only 11 by a feature on eWorld's online town in *Mac* magazine.

Turner: "I started working on the site in 1998, when I was 15 and still in school. Flash 3 had just come along, and I felt a sense of liberation upon discovering it."

This sense of freedom, away from all the restrictions of HTML, led Turner to create as many animations "as humanly possible during the software's 30-day trial period, so that I could try and persuade my parents that purchasing a copy would be worth their while."

The Void site opened with an animation of a paper plane with some introduction music and then announced that "paper sucks", before revealing that Void stood for "vividly original interactive designs". The main interface showed a box of pills, with two blister strips acting for navigation. It's unlikely that the historical link between drugs and creativity was deliberate here, but the image nevertheless likely struck a chord with those who had grown up with a culture of illegal warehouse raves and mind-opening experiences.

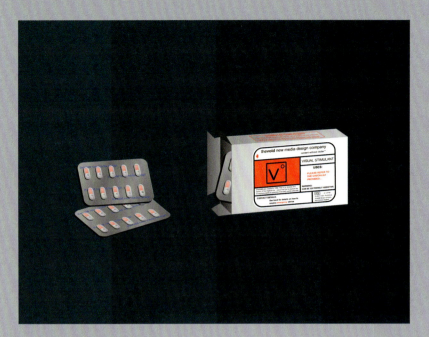

> "With the dawning of the Flash era, the internet came of age as a dynamic, immersive, imaginative, and expressive medium. For a time, the novelty and thrill of surfing from one piece of Flash eye candy to the next became an experience all its own. Anticipating the design-led consumer technology revolution signaled by the launch of the iMac in 1998, Flash opened our eyes to the idea that the internet could and should be a thing of beauty in itself."

Luke Turner
The Void; luketurner.com

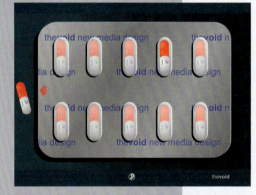

Die Art, in der das Internet kreative Möglichkeiten für jeden mit einer Verbindung eröffnete, egal, wer man war, wird durch Luke Turner beispielhaft gezeigt. Ein Teenager in England, der sich 1994 durch *Mac* Magazin dazu inspirieren ließ, als er erst 11 Jahre alt war.

Turner: „1998 begann ich an der Seite zu arbeiten. Ich war 15 und ging noch zur Schule. Flash 3 kam gerade auf und ich fühlte mich irgendwie befreit, nachdem ich es entdeckt hatte."

Dieses Freiheitsgefühl, weg von den Beschränkungen der HTML-Programmierung, verführte Turner, so viele Animationen „wie menschlich möglich war in der 30-tägigen Probezeit der Software zu erstellen, so dass ich versuchen konnte, meine Eltern davon zu überzeugen, dass der Kauf einer Kopie sich lohnte."

The Void Site eröffnete mit einer Animation eines Papierfliegers mit etwas einleitender Musik und dann kündigte sie an, dass „Papier doof ist", bevor bekannt gegeben wurde, dass Void (vividly original interactive designs) für „lebendiges, originelles interaktives Designs" steht. Die Haupt-Schnittstelle zeigte eine Schachtel mit Pillen, mit zwei Blisterstreifen, die als Navigation dienten. Es ist unwahrscheinlich, dass die historische Verbindung zwischen Drogen und Kreativität hier bewusst war, aber das Bild traf wahrscheinlich einen Nerv bei denen, die mit einer Kultur illegaler Warehouse-Raves und Bewusstsein erweiternde Mittel aufgewachsen waren.

Internet offre des perspectives de création à toutes les personnes dotées d'une connexion, et ce où qu'elles soient. Tel est le cas en Angleterre de Luke Turner qui n'a que 11 ans quand, en 1994, il est inspiré par un article paru dans le magazine *Mac* sur la ville électronique eWorld.

Turner : « J'ai commencé à travailler sur le site en 1998, quand je n'avais que 15 ans et que j'allais encore à l'école. Flash 3 venait de sortir et j'ai ressenti une sorte de libération en le découvrant. »

Loin de toutes les restrictions propres à HTML, ce sentiment de liberté conduit Turner à créer autant d'animations « qu'il est humainement possible pendant la période d'essai gratuite de 30 jours du logiciel, afin de convaincre mes parents que c'était vraiment la peine de me payer une licence ».

Le site The Void s'ouvre avec l'animation d'un avion en papier accompagnée d'une musique d'introduction et de l'annonce que « le papier craint », avant de dévoiler que The Void défend les « conceptions interactives hautement originales ». L'interface principale montre une boîte de médicaments et deux plaquettes de gélules qui servent d'éléments de navigation. La relation entre drogue et créativité n'est certainement pas intentionnelle, mais l'image touche cependant la corde sensible de ceux qui ont grandi dans une culture de raves illégales dans des entrepôts et d'expériences d'ouverture d'esprit.

Turtleshell

—

A world-first with floating particles

Joen Asmussen's Turtleshell impressed visitors with an organic intro that led into his site where the world's first floating particles were presented, hypnotic white blobs that glowed like a lens flare. Personal websites such as this were becoming more common, and included links to Flash and web design forums as well as other informative sites, but also downloads from the sites' creators themselves, thus showing the friendly and generous spirit of the early web community.

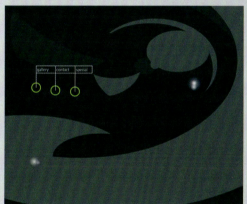

"Flash was a remarkable tool that came along at an interesting time. Most web pages were just white backgrounds and blue links, but an entire community had grown around the idea that this banner-ad tool could make whole web pages. The results were like previewing the future of the internet, and I think that vibe permeated the community. It was like discovering Wonderland."

Joen Asmussen
Turtleshell; Mocco

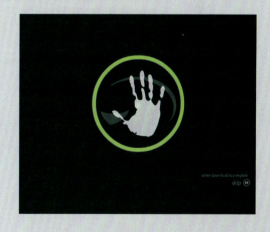

Joen Asmussens Turtleshell beeindruckte die Besucher mit einem organischen Intro, das auf seine Site führte, wo die ersten schwebenden Teilchen der Welt vorgestellt wurden, hypnotische weiße Flecken, die wie ein Linsen-effekt leuchteten. Persönliche Websites wie diese wurden immer häufiger und enthielten Links zu Flash- und Webdesignforen sowie zu anderen informativen Websites, aber auch Downloads von den Seitenerstellern selbst, was den freundlichen und großzügigen Geist der frühen Web-Community deutlich macht.

Le site Turtleshell de Joen Asmussen impressionne ses visiteurs avec son intro organique qui conduit à une page conte-nant des particules flottantes, d'hypnotisants disques blancs flous et brillants comme un facteur de flare. Les sites Web personnels de ce genre sont de plus en plus courants : ils incluent des liens à des forums sur Flash et la conception Web et à des sites informatifs, ainsi que des téléchargements des propres créateurs, preuve de la mentalité généreuse et amicale qui règne au sein de la communauté des débuts du Web.

Matinée

—

A first at using 3D

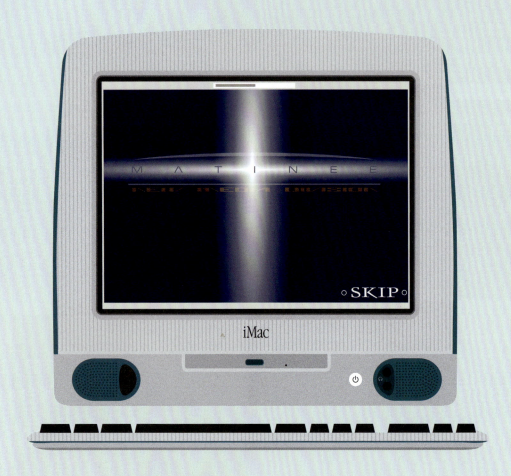

As was shown with The Void, 3D vector
graphics were becoming increasingly popular
and the likes of Matinée pushed this trend
with their agency showcase site, which
featured 3D rotating menu navigation buttons.
The site's logo also moved in the same way.

"We were given the go-ahead to make a destination site that could compete with Gabocorp, Eye4U, etc. It was an arms race to make Flash do the impossible — it took two weeks straight to do the 3D icon animations (lots of tracing by hand), and I think we made the first ever lens flare in Flash. Showing it to people before it launched was a real thrill, because their jaws would just drop."

James Hutchinson
Matinée; Walt Disney

Wie mit The Void gezeigt wurde, wurden 3D Vektor-Grafiken immer beliebter und Leute wie bei Matinée trieben diesen Trend mit ihrer Agenturpräsentations-Site voran, die über 3D-Navigations-schaltflächen verfügte. Das Logo der Website wurde auf dieselbe Weise bewegt.

Comme le montre The Void, les graphiques vectoriels en 3D sont chaque fois plus populaires et ceux de Matinée confirment cette tendance avec le site de promotion de l'agence doté de boutons de navigation qui pivotent en 3D. Le logo du site est également animé de la sorte.

Balthaser

—

The most talked-about
Flash intro ever

The Balthaser site developed a Flash intro that went far beyond anything that had been seen previously and put the company at the forefront of experimental web design. The intro began with text and an invitation to experience "the soul of balthaser studios" before bursting into a series of high-impact statements and images set to fast music which made a compelling case for this new and unknown company.

"When I sent a link to the site to Rob Burgess, then CEO of Macromedia, he put it up as a Site of the Day and that's when things really took off. I remember our ISP calling to tell me that the traffic was taking them down. I wasn't prepared for the level of reaction I received. ABC News World interviewed me and I had Fortune 500 companies calling me at home inquiring about work."

Neil Balthaser
Balthaser; Intellogo

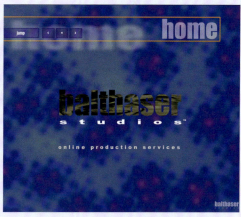

Die Balthaser Site entwickelte ein Flash-Intro das weit über alles hinausging, was vorher gesehen worden war und stellte das Unternehmen an die Spitze des experimentellen Webdesigns. Das Intro begann mit Text und einer Einladung zum Erleben „der Seele der Balthaser Studios", bevor sie mit einer Reihe von beeindruckenden Aussagen und Bildern zu schneller Musik aufbrach, womit diese neue und unbekannte Firma überzeugte.

Le site Balthaser présente une intro Flash qui va bien au-delà de tout ce qui a été vu jusqu'alors et place l'entreprise à l'avant-garde de la conception Web expérimentale. L'intro commence avec un texte et une invitation à vivre «l'esprit des studios Balthaser», avant de faire défiler une série de déclarations et d'images impactantes sur de la musique rythmée ; une présentation des plus convaincantes pour cette nouvelle entreprise inconnue.

Full Throttle:
David Gary Studios

—

The first site to have a 'loading' game

David Gary added a game of pong to his site's loading screen which enabled visitors to become immersed without even noticing the site was still loading. Animated metallic objects assembled the site, and once the interface was completed, a metallic exhaust appeared; a final rev of the engine was signaled by a burst of exhaust flames. This was one of the rare sites that still looked impressive several years later.

"I happened to walk into a Harley shop with a friend one day and later when I remembered the smell of the leather and the reflection of the chrome, I thought it would make a good composition for an 'in-your-face website' if done in an elegant manner. Also, since I needed an effective motif to showcase my artwork, I thought the neutral 'chrome' would really let the colors of the artwork stand out while not being too dull for the navigational interface."

David Gary
David Gary Studios

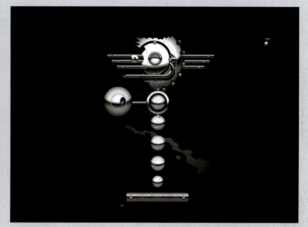

David Gary fügte auf dem Lade-bildschirm seiner Website das Spiel Pong ein, das es den Besuchern ermöglichte, einzutauchen ohne dass er bemerkte, dass die Seite noch geladen wurde. Animierte Metallobjekte bauten die Site zusammen, und sobald die Schnittstelle vollendet war, erschien ein metallischer Aus-puff; das endgültige Erreichen der Motordrehzahl wurde durch Abgasflammen angezeigt. Dies war einer der seltenen Sites, die auch noch Jahre später beeindruckend aussahen.

David Gary ajoute un jeu de Pong à l'écran de chargement de son site, ce qui distrait les visiteurs au point qu'ils en oublient l'attente. Des objets métalliques animés composent le site et une fois l'interface chargée, un pot d'échappement apparaît. Une ultime vérification du moteur se fait par la sortie de flammes d'échappement. C'est l'un des rares sites qui reste surprenant des années après.

Praystation

—

A pioneer of web art and open-source code

In 1998, another huge web personality to emerge was Joshua Davis, whose Praystation project and later, One Upon a Forest, quickly attracted a sizable following since Davis was one of the first breed of digital artists to translate his experimental techniques to an internet showcase. He was also a true web pioneer, using code to create art, as well as being one of the first to open-source his Flash files. Davis also founded Dreamless.org, a semi-underground forum that was the source of several long-term friendships and collaborations, including Threadless.

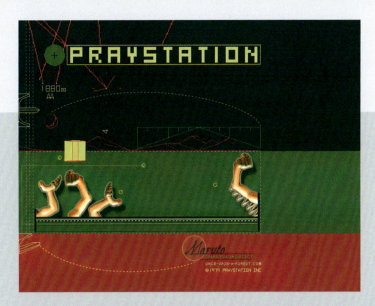

"I'm a painting student at Pratt Institute in Brooklyn and through a bizarre turn of events… I write my first drop of code in 1995. In 1996 I pick up FutureSplash Animator [and] in 1998 I fall head over heels with Tell Target. Praystation, from 1998 to 2001… was a sandbox, a place to try out ideas in animation and interaction… each day I would post something tried, something learned… along with the source. It would teach me the power of open sharing and would set me on my career path."

Joshua Davis
Praystation; joshuadavis.com

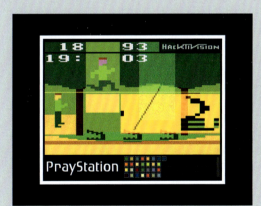

Im Jahr 1998 tauchte Joshua Davis als eine weitere große Web-Persönlichkeit auf, dessen Praystation Projekt und später One Upon a Forest schnell eine beträchtliche Anzahl von Fans anzogen, da Davis einer der ersten digitalen Künstler war, der seine experimentellen Techniken in eine Internetpräsentation übertrug. Er war auch ein echter Web-Pionier. Er verwendete Codes, um Kunst zu erstellen und war einer der ersten, der seine Flash-Dateien als Open-Source öffnete. Davis gründete auch Dreamless.org, ein Semi-Underground-Forum, das zur Quelle mehrerer langjähriger Freundschaften und Kooperationen wurde, einschließlich Threadless.

L'année 1998 voit les débuts d'une autre grande pointure du Web, Joshua Davis, dont les projets Praystation puis One Upon a Forest se gagnent une foule d'adeptes. Davis est en effet l'un des premiers artistes numériques à convertir ses techniques expérimentales en réalisations sur Internet. Il est aussi un véritable pionnier du Web qui utilise du code à des fins artistiques et offre un accès libre à ses fichiers Flash. Davis fonde par ailleurs Dreamless.org, un forum plus ou moins underground à l'origine d'amitiés et de collaborations à long terme, dont Threadless.

VW New Beetle

—

A modern re-interpretation
of a classic

First introduced in 1938, the Volkswagen Type 1, widely known as the Beetle, was given a complete make-over 60 years later and the all-new VW Beetle was launched. The official UK website presented the car much like an alien that had landed on Earth, featuring navigation sections such as Close Encounter, The Arrival, and Previous Sightings. This immersive, not to say other-worldly site gave users the ability to see the car in detail and in ways other manufacturers' websites had not allowed before.

"This site supported the launch of the second incarnation of the VW Beetle in the United Kingdom. The unusual design of the car inspired us to think of it as an alien that had arrived on Earth. The site was simply the tool to explore the new arrival. We used Flash to its full potential allowing users to turn the car round and zoom in to details. Looking back it strikes me how much freedom we had to explore visual metaphors and create new interaction designs. Even more unusual as the client was a major corporation."

Fred Flade
Deepend; SOON_

Der 1938 eingeführte Volkswagen Typ 1, weitbekannt als Käfer, wurde 60 Jahre später komplett umgerüstet und der brandneue VW Käfer kam auf den Markt. Die offizielle UK-Website präsentierte das Auto wie einen Alien, der auf der Erde gelandet war und enthielt Navigationsabschnitte wie „Close Encounter",

„The Arrival" und „Previous Sightings" enthielt. Diese immersive, um nicht zu sagen, weltfremde Website gab den Benutzern die Möglichkeit, das Auto im Detail zu sehen, auf eine Art, die Websites anderer Hersteller zuvor nicht erlaubt hatten.

Lancée pour la première fois en 1938, la Volkswagen Type 1, mondialement connue comme la Coccinelle, connaît un relookage complet 60 ans plus tard : sort alors sur le marché la New Beetle. Le site Web officiel au Royaume-Uni présente le véhicule comme un extraterrestre apparu sur Terre, avec des sections de

navigation comme «Close Encounter», «The Arrival» et «Previous Sightings». Ce site immersif et pour le moins éthéré permet aux utilisateurs d'observer la voiture sous toutes les coutures et d'une façon inédite par rapport aux sites d'autres fabricants automobiles.

NOTABLE WEBSITE LAUNCH
Google.com

GOOGLE FACTS

Google Friends Newsletter is launched by Larry Page

The first doodle is created

September 4, Google files for incorporation

Craig Silverstein becomes the first person to be employed by Google

Google sets up a work space in a garage in California

MOBILE EVOLUTION
Nokia 5110

Included the game Snake

INTERNET COMMUNITY
The Drudge Report

Taking journalism to a new level, the
Drudge Report was responsible for
breaking news of the 'Lewinsky scandal'.

1999/

The
Floodgates
Open

1999/

—

The Floodgates Open

—

Presstube

In 1999, internet connection speeds started to gain pace as 33.6 KB modems were replaced by 56 KB, although it was still impossible to access the web if someone was making a phone call on your line. Most Flash sites had introduction animations and very soon 'skip intro' found regular use; it was even adopted later as the name of a Dutch web agency.

As the year 2000 approached there was mounting fear about 'the Millennium bug', also known as 'Y2K', since most software only represented the last two digits of the year and would thus be unable to distinguish between 1900 and 2000. In reality, most companies simply upgraded their systems and few problems were reported with the change to the new millennium, a typical example being the date showing as 19100 instead of 2000 until it was fixed.

The year was also marked by the launch of one of the most famous parody websites, Zombocom: "Welcome to Zombocom". Gently teasing all the Flash intros and big statements of other websites, it quickly gained cult status and was often shared when people were complaining about Flash.

New internet names also appeared, such as Kim Schmitz, aka Kimble (Kim Dotcom), whose web presence brought a lot of global interest through projects including megaCar and his own portal Kimble.org, which opened with the headline "Legends may sleep but they never die."

"I love design. I love pretty. And I hated the early internet. The early internet was ugly. Then came Flash. I always knew the internet could look so much better. I enjoyed transforming a boring and ugly internet into something pretty. There are so many stylish websites out there. Even Facebook might one day look good ;-) We are all so lucky to live in these times. Let's just hope that our data-obsessed governments don't turn our internet into a cyber battlefield."
Kim Dotcom, kim.com

Individuals like Andy Foulds, James Paterson (Presstube), Matt Owens (Volumeone), and Robert Lindström (Paregos) continued to stand out with their regular innovations online. Meanwhile, early signs of attitude were on display at Ego Media, whilst Kioken became a design powerhouse for many big brands and INsOMNIOUS began to push 3D online via their own Labs website.

It was also the year when the first mobile phones with WAP browsers appeared. I can clearly remember my early internet experiences using WAP and thinking that mobile internet would never take off as the service was so poor.

Zombocom

Kimble

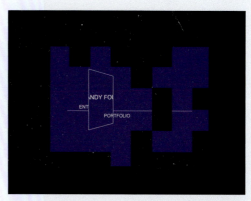

Andy Foulds

Volumeone

"The early internet was ugly. Then came Flash."

Im Jahr 1999 steigerte sich die Geschwindigkeit der Internetverbindung, als 33,6 KB Modems durch 56 KB ersetzt wurden, obwohl es immer noch unmöglich war, auf das Internet zuzugreifen, wenn jemand auf der Leitung anrief. Die meisten Flash-Sites hatten Einführungsanimationen und sehr bald fand das „Skip Intro" regelmäßig Anwendung. Es wurde sogar später als Name von einer holländischen Web-Agentur angenommen.

Als sich das Jahr 2000 näherte, wuchs die Angst vor dem „Millennium Bug", auch bekannt als „Y2K", da die meiste Software nur die letzten zwei Ziffern des Jahres darstellt und man somit nicht zwischen 1900 und 2000 unterscheiden konnte. Tatsächlich haben die meisten Unternehmen einfach ihre

Systeme aufgerüstet und es wurde nur von wenigen Problemen beim Wechsel ins neue Jahrtausend berichtet. Ein typisches Beispiel war, dass das Datum 19100 statt 2000 angezeigt wurde, bis dieser Fehler behoben wurde.

Das Jahr war auch durch den Start einer der berühmtesten Parodie-Websites geprägt, Zombocom: „Welcome to Zombocom". Da hier freundlich alle Flash-Intros und großen Statements von anderen Websites parodiert wurden, erlangte sie schnell Kultstatus und wurde oft geteilt, wenn Leute sich über Flash beschwerten.

Es tauchten auch neue Internetnamen auf, wie Kim Schmitz, aka Kimble (Kim Dotcom), dessen Webpräsenz weltweites Interesse erlangte durch Projekte wie megaCar und sein

eigenes Portal Kimble.org, das mit der Schlagzeile eröffnete „Legends may sleep but they never die".

„Ich liebe Design. Ich liebe Schönheit. Und ich hasste das frühe Internet. Das frühe Internet war hässlich. Dann kam Flash. Ich wusste ja immer, dass das Internet viel besser aussehen konnte. Ich habe es genossen, ein langweiliges und hässliches Internet in etwas Hübsches zu verwandeln. Es gibt so viele stilvolle Websites. Selbst Facebook sieht vielleicht eines Tages gut aus ;-) Wir haben so ein Glück, in diesen Zeiten zu leben. Hoffen wir nur, dass unsere datenbesessenen Regierungen unser Internet nicht in ein Cyber-Schlachtfeld verwandeln."
KIM DOTCOM, kim.com

Individuen wie Andy Foulds, James Paterson (Presstube),

Matt Owens (Volumeone) und Robert Lindström (Paregos) stachen weiterhin mit ihren regelmäßigen Innovationen online hervor. Unterdessen waren frühe Zeichen der Attitude bei Ego Media zu sehen, während Kioken zu einem Design Powerhouse für viele große Marken wurde und INsOMNIOUS begann online 3D über seine eigene Labs-Website zu pushen.

Es war auch das Jahr, in dem die ersten Mobiltelefone mit WAP-Browser erschienen. Ich kann mich gut an meine frühen Internet-Erfahrungen mit WAP erinnern und dachte, dass das mobile Internet niemals möglich sein würde, da der Service so schlecht war.

1999/
—

The Floodgates Open
—

Ego Media

INsOMNIOUS

"I enjoyed
transforming a
boring and ugly
internet into
something pretty."

Kioken

En 1999, les vitesses de connexion à Internet augmentent car les modems passent de 33,6 à 56 kbps ; il est toutefois encore impossible d'accéder au Web si quelqu'un téléphone en même temps. La page d'accueil de la plupart des sites Flash inclut des animations et très vite apparaissent les boutons « Ignorer l'intro ». Une agence Web hollandaise choisit même de s'appeler Skip Intro.

Avec l'approche de l'an 2000 grandit la crainte d'un « bogue du millénaire », encore appelé « Y2K », car la plupart des logiciels n'utilisent que deux chiffres pour le format d'année : comment pourront-ils faire alors la distinction entre 1900 et 2000 ? En réalité, la plupart des sociétés mettent tout simplement à jour leur système et peu de problèmes sont finalement signalés avec le changement de millénaire, si ce n'est la date 19100 qui apparaît parfois au lieu de 2000.

L'année voit également le lancement de l'un de plus célèbres sites Web de parodie, Zombocom, où une voix reçoit les visiteurs avec le message « Welcome to Zombocom », se moque gentiment de toutes les intros Flash et des grandes déclarations faites sur d'autres sites. Très vite devenu culte, il est souvent partagé quand des personnes se plaignent de Flash.

De nouveaux noms circulent sur Internet, comme Kim Schmitz, alias Kimble (Kim Dotcom). Sa présence sur le Web suscite un intérêt à grande échelle avec des projets comme megaCar, ainsi que son propre portail Kimble. org qui s'ouvre avec la phrase « Legends may sleep but they never die » (les légendes peuvent dormir mais ne meurent jamais).

« J'adore le design, j'adore ce qui est beau. Et je détestais Internet à ses débuts. Il était moche. Puis il y a eu Flash. J'ai toujours su qu'Internet pouvait s'améliorer. Je m'amusais à convertir un site insipide et laid en quelque chose de joli. Il existe tellement de sites raffinés. Même Facebook pourrait un jour avoir de l'allure ;-) Nous sommes tous très chanceux de vivre à notre époque. Espérons juste que nos gouvernements obsédés par les données ne feront pas d'Internet un champ de bataille cybernétique. »
KIM DOTCOM, kim.com

Des créateurs comme Andy Foulds, James Paterson (Presstube), Matt Owens (Volumeone) et Robert Lindström (Paregos) ont l'habitude de triompher avec leur innovations en ligne. En parallèle, les premières affirmations de style s'affichent chez Ego Media, Kioken devient une véritable centrale du design pour de nombreuses marques et INsOMNIOUS commence à publier du contenu 3D via son site Labs.

C'est aussi l'année où les premiers téléphones portables dotés de navigateurs WAP font leur apparition. Je me souviens parfaitement de mes premières expériences sur Internet avec WAP, convaincu que l'Internet mobile ne décollerait jamais vu la médiocrité du service.

08 Facts of the year

Number of internet users:
248 million, 4.1% of the
world population

Number of websites:
3.17 million

World news:
world population passes
6 billion

Website with most traffic:
Aol.com

Tech hardware:
Apple launches the
iBook laptop

Tech software:
RSS launches

Other tech:
Millennium bug

Highest-grossing film:
Star Wars: Episode I –
The Phantom Menace

MONO*crafts

—

A world-first on many levels

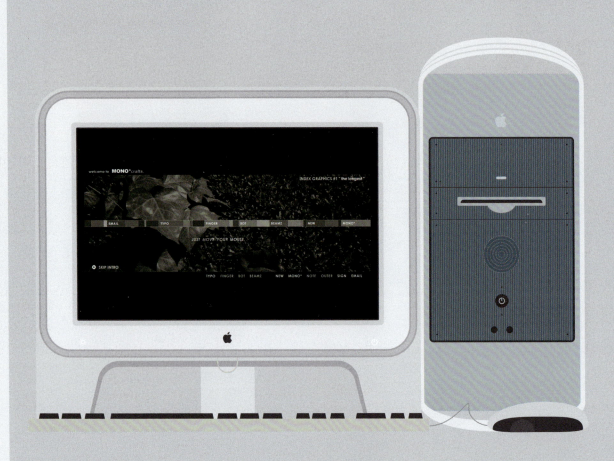

Japan's Yugo Nakamura, also known as Yugop, was one of the original web pioneers. His horizontal scrolling and zooming menu, which was sensitive to mouse movement, took web navigation in a completely new direction when most sites were using motion and shape tweens to position elements against a static interface.

TYPO SPACE enabled visitors to interact with the site using the keyboard. This was also the first time mouse trailers were seen, whereby moving the mouse resulted in text being displayed.

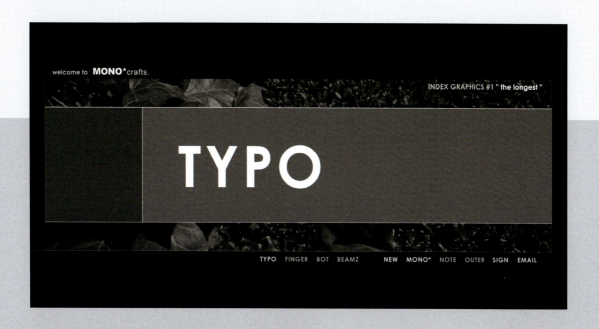

> "I made MONO*crafts after being greatly influenced by John Maeda's early 'reactive book' series. It was not so much 'web design' as a series of experiments for interactivity and usability on browsers. Anyway I enjoyed making the site so much, and thanks to that experience I can keep making interactive things on computer media now."

Yugo Nakamura
tha

Japans Yugo Nakamura, auch bekannt als Yugop, war einer der ursprünglichen Web-Pioniere. Sein horizontales Scroll- und Zoom-Menü, das empfindlich auf Mausbewegungen reagierte, hatte die Navigation im Web in eine völlig neue Richtung geführt, da die meisten Websites Motion- und Shape-Tweens verwendeten, um Elemente auf eine statische Schnittstelle zu positionieren.

TYPO SPACE ermöglichte es Besuchern, mit der Website über die Tastatur zu interagieren. Dies war auch das erste Mal, dass man Maus-Trailer sehen konnte, wobei das Bewegen der Maus zur Anzeige von Text führte.

Également appelé Yugop, Yugo Nakamura est l'un des pionniers du Web au Japon. Son menu avec zoom et défilement horizontal obéit au mouvement de la souris et ouvre une nouvelle porte à la conception Web, alors que la plupart des sites placent encore des éléments par interpolation de formes et de mouvements sur une interface statique.

TYPO SPACE permet aux visiteurs d'interagir avec le site à l'aide du clavier. Pour la première fois aussi, des effets visuels sont appliqués au curseur et du texte s'affiche quand la souris se déplace.

—

Neostream Interactive

—

Worldwide appeal overnight

The Australian self-proclaimed 'serious multimedia company' Neostream very quickly acquired a mass following. Neostream embraced the original awards community, something I first became involved in during the late '90s, by applying for awards for version 1 of Neostream.com, which resulted in it winning a number of accolades including the quite rare 'World best websites GOLD award'.

Neostream's website was fast loading and the transitions between selected menu items were very slick. The company was later contracted by the United Nations to produce a database CD-ROM and also redesign and restructure its corresponding database website.

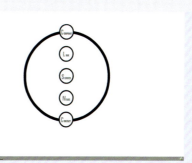

"I can still clearly recall the public's response because it was so overwhelming and unexpected. At that time, only a handful of web developers and designers were releasing sites using Flash and it was just a lot of fun being able to create something that could deliver a more powerful experience."

Johnny Choi
Neostream

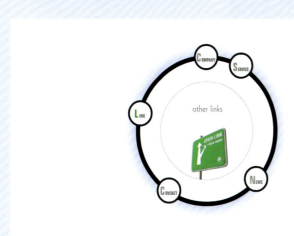

other links

Das selbst ernannte australische „seriöse Multimediaunternehmen" Neostream bekam sehr schnell massenhaft Fans. Neostream nahm die ursprüngliche Awards-Community ein, etwas, an dem ich in den späten Neunzigern zum ersten Mal beteiligt war, durch die Bewerbung für die Auszeichnungen der Version 1 von Neostream.com, was dazu führte, dass die Seite eine Reihe von Auszeichnungen erhielt, einschließlich des ziemlich seltenen „World Best Websites GOLD Award".

Neostreams Website war schnell geladen und die Übergänge zwischen den ausgewählten Menüpunkten waren sehr glatt. Das Unternehmen wurde später von den Vereinten Nationen beauftragt, eine Datenbank CD-ROM zu erstellen und auch die entsprechende Datenbank-Website neu zu gestalten und zu restrukturieren.

La société australienne Neostream, qui s'autoproclame «agence multimédia sérieuse», touche rapidement une masse critique et récolte toutes sortes de prix dans son domaine. À la fin des années 90, j'y participe d'ailleurs en proposant une création pour la version 1 de Neostream.com, qui décroche diverses récompenses dont le plutôt rare «World best websites GOLD award».

Le site Web de Neostream se charge vite et les transitions entre les options du menu sont très fluides. L'agence se voit ensuite engagée par les Nations unies pour produire un CD-ROM de sa base de données et faire la refonte du site Web analogue.

megaCar.com
—

The first internet car

The actual megaCar was a Mercedes-Benz Brabus S58, converted in 1998 by Data Protect, a German company that specialized in data security. The car was further tweaked by Brabus and boasted some very high-tech features, including mobile 150 kbit/second online connectivity, a GSM 16-channel signal booster, and real-time video conferencing. It was priced at $300,000. The website was as cutting edge as the car itself, with Flash intro, voice-overs, and a progressive interface; it also lasted longer than its subject did.

"Some of my car enthusiast friends, including two former Formula 1 drivers, met once a month to drive for money. Six to eight cars, 50 miles, the winner got 10K from each loser. On the way from Monaco back to Munich a truck decided to overtake another truck. It took for ever so I decided to use a highway car-park to pass the trucks. Unfortunately the car-park was very wet and I hit a metal separator before I got back on the highway."

Kim Dotcom
kim.com

Tatsächlich war megaCar ein Mercedes-Benz Brabus S58, umgewandelt im Jahr 1998 durch Data Protect, ein deutsches Unternehmen, das sich auf Datensicherheit spezialisiert hatte. Das Auto wurde von Brabus weiter optimiert und verfügte über einige High-Tech-Features, einschließlich 150 kbit/Sek. Online-Verbindung, einen GSM 16-Kanal Signalverstärker und Echtzeit Videokonferenzen. Sein Preis lag bei $300.000. Die Website war so modern wie das Auto selbst, mit Flash-Intro, Voice-Overs und einer progressiven Schnittstelle. Sie überlebte sogar ihr eigenes Thema.

La «megaCar» est en fait une Mercedes-Benz Brabus S58 conçue en 1998 par la société allemande Data Protect spécialisée en sécurité des données. D'un prix de 300 000 dollars, le véhicule ensuite modifié par Brabus arbore des fonctions très high-tech, dont une connectivité Internet de 150 kbps, un amplificateur de signal GSM de 16 canaux et un système de vidéoconférence en temps réel. Le site Web est lui aussi avant-gardiste, avec une intro Flash, les commentaires d'une voix off et une interface progressive, mais il connaît une existence plus longue que le véhicule en soi.

1999/
—
<u>Ray of Light</u>
—
The first ray of light

Yasuto Suga: "We hope to provide a beacon for that talent: a ray of light." On clicking the website logo, a light effect was triggered as if someone was shining a torch, or the sun was passing behind the words. This became known as the 'Ray of Light' effect and soon people were creating files for others to download it, resulting in numerous text-effect creations and the emergence of new companies selling nothing but text effects for Flash users.

"Flash gave us the ability to make interactive experiences for anybody across the globe — I was hooked the first time I saw it. All of us who worked in Flash made a lot of bad designs, but we also made some great designs and experimented in ways people had never thought of. I'm very proud to look back and know that I was a small part of that history."

Yasuto Suga
Ray of Light; Kadho Sports

Yasuto Suga: „Wir hoffen, für dieses Talent ein Leuchtfeuer bieten zu können: einen Lichtstrahl." Beim Klicken auf das Website-Logo wurde ein Lichteffekt ausgelöst, als ob jemand eine Fackel erleuchtete oder die Sonne hinter den Worten vorbeizog. Dies wurde als Lichtstrahleffekt (Ray of Light Effect) bekannt und bald erstellten Leute Dateien für andere, um sie herunterladen zu können, was dazu führte, dass zahllose Text-Effekt-Kreationen entstanden und sich neue Unternehmen bildeten, die ausschließlich Texteffekte für Flash-Nutzer verkauften.

Yasuto Suga: «Nous espérons servir de phare au talent, lui apporter un rayon de lumière». Le fait de cliquer sur le logo dans le site Web déclenche un effet lumineux, comme si quelqu'un bougeait une torche ou si le soleil brillait derrière les mots. L'effet rayon de lumière devient populaire et des internautes se mettent bientôt à créer des fichiers pour que d'autres le téléchargent, d'où la prolifération de nouveaux effets de texte et l'émergence de sociétés en proposant aux utilisateurs Flash.

1999/
—

Dennis Interactive

—

First to allow color
customization

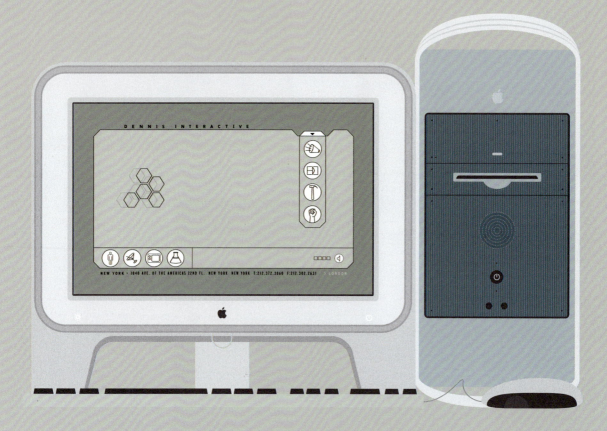

Dennis Interactive was amongst the first websites to include a section which they called Laboratory. Towards the lower right of the screen, users could select different colors for the site itself. The subsequent transitions showed pieces of tech hardware being built as users watched, for example, a joystick. This was also one of the first times a Space Invaders clone was incorporated in a website, which could be played in the section called Company.

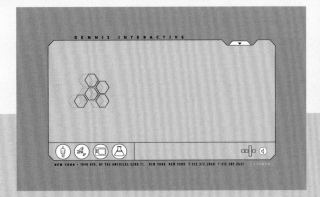

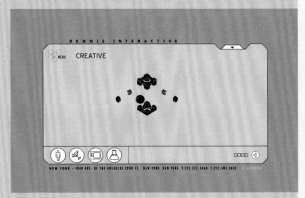

"In a world of 800 x 600 screens and table-based sites, the animated typography, icons, sound effects, and backing tracks we used were revolutionary. We released new versions of the site each year from 1997 to 2000 — but with each iteration our focus was on usability: clear navigation, crisp illustrations, and reasonable, progressive loads for the slow internet speeds of the era."

David Cherry
Dennis Interactive

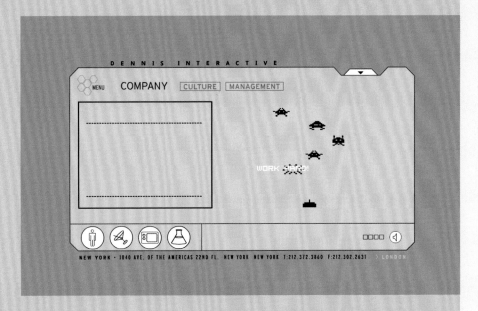

Dennis Interactive war eine der ersten Websites, die einen Abschnitt enthielten, den sie Laboratory nannten. In der unteren rechten Ecke des Bildschirms konnten Benutzer verschiedene Farben für die Seite selbst auswählen. Die folgenden Übergänge zeigten, wie Stücke technischer Hardware gebaut wurden, während die Benutzer zum Beispiel einen Joystick betrachteten. Dies war auch eines der ersten Male, dass ein Space Invaders-Klon in eine Website eingebaut wurde, mit dem in der Rubrik Company gespielt werden konnte.

Dennis Interactive est l'un des premiers sites Web à inclure une section nommée Laboratory. En bas à droite de l'écran, les utilisateurs peuvent sélectionner diverses couleurs pour le site, et les transitions montrent l'assemblage de composants d'équipement, comme un joystick. C'est aussi l'une des premières fois qu'un clone de Space Invaders est intégré à un site Web et qu'il est possible d'y jouer dans la section Company.

1999/
—

Bionic Systems
—

Out-of-this-world design

The style used by this German agency almost suggested the internet had been taken over by aliens and that this was the first extraterrestrial web design company. Futuristic and offbeat vector graphics combined with matching atmospheric music and sound effects, while the interface promoted a plug-and-play approach, getting users to move parts of it into position to activate areas of the site, one of which offered a number of free, and very progressive fonts.

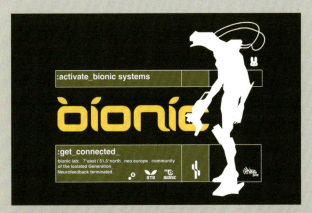

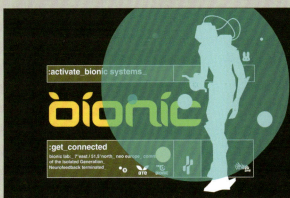

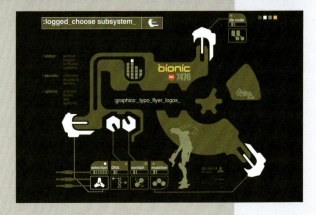

"At the dawn of a new era of technology, overwhelmed by the endless possibilities, young in hearts and minds, we had a vision. We had nothing to lose. And we had Flash."

Malte Haust
Bionic Systems

Der Stil, der von dieser deutschen Agentur verwendet wurde, ließ fast vermuten, dass das Internet von Aliens übernommen worden war und dass dies die erste außerirdische Webdesign-Agentur war. Futuristisch und unkonventionelle Vektorgrafik, kombiniert mit passender atmosphärischer Musik und Soundeffekten, während die Schnittstelle einen Plug-and-Play-Ansatz propagierte und Benutzer dazu brachte, Teile davon in eine Position zu schieben, um Bereiche der Site zu aktivieren, die eine Anzahl von kostenlosen und sehr progressiven Fonts anbot.

Le style employé par cette agence allemande laisse presque penser que des extraterrestres ont pris le contrôle d'Internet et qu'il s'agit de la première société de conception Web venue de l'espace. Des graphiques vectoriels décalés et futuristes sont assortis d'une musique atmosphérique et d'effets sonores. L'interface suit une approche Plug-and-Play qui conduit les utilisateurs à déplacer des éléments pour activer des sections du site, dont l'une met gratuitement à disposition des polices très progressives.

Crash!Media

—

The first drag-and-drop navigation

Craig Swann's Crash!Media presented a feature that would become a standard part of our lives in the future, dragging images and dropping them into a box area in order to access extra content. Such simplicity also offered a significant new means of navigating, and paved the way for countless interfaces, not least for shopping carts.

"We were the first generation of creators carving and sculpting the digital zeitgeist. We were the ones breathing life into the web. We were doing things that had never been done before. For me, it was creating the web's first drag'n'drop interface. But we were all shaping the web. Bending it to our collective vision. It was a time filled with promise."

Craig Swann
Crash!Media

Craig Swanns Crash!Media präsentierte ein Feature, das in Zukunft zu einem Standard in unserem Leben werden sollte, das Ziehen von Bildern und Ablegen in einen Boxbereich, um auf zusätzlichen Inhalt zuzugreifen. Diese Schlichtheit bot auch eine bedeutende neue Navigationsmöglichkeit und ebnete den Weg für unzählige Schnittstellen, nicht zuletzt für Einkaufswagen.

Le site Crash!Media de Craig Swann offre une fonction vouée à devenir par la suite partie intégrante de notre vie : faire glisser des images et les déposer dans une zone pour accéder à plus de contenu. Cette action simple révolutionne aussi le mode de navigation et jette les bases d'un nombre infini d'interfaces, à commencer par les paniers d'achat.

—

Romeo Design

—

Progressive game developer

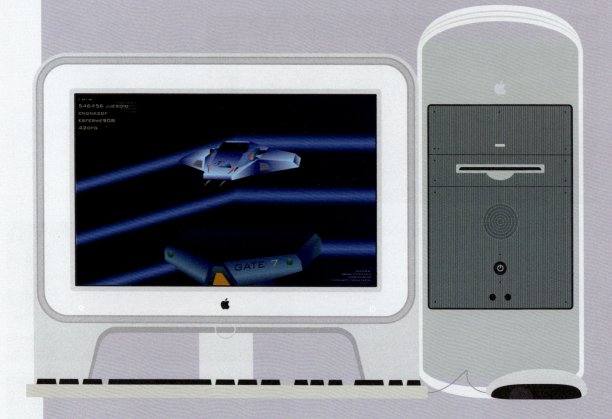

Romeo was a Flash game developer whose work featured high-end animated cinematic trailers which were noteworthy in their own right, even though the games that followed were some of the most playable yet to appear online. A selection of first-person shooters, including Space Cobra, earned Romeo the respect of the nascent gaming community, and led to him (and me too) judging one of the early Flash awards in the late 1990s, Nem5 Web Maggic.

"Prior to Flash, there wasn't an easy way to develop interactive websites. Flash really did push creativity to a brand-new medium and provided a development playground that was more sophisticated than the raw web. I used to spend days trying to optimize my Flash game files because most people were still on dial-up modems. I think I miss the times when the internet was an escape from 'real life' and not just an extension of it."

Romeo Sin
Romeo Design; Web Promo

Romeo war ein Flash Game Developer, dessen Arbeit high-end animierte Filmtrailer zeigte, die schon selbst bemerkenswert waren, selbst wenn die darauffolgenden Spiele zu den spielbarsten gehörten, die online zu sehen waren. Mit einer Auswahl von Ego-Shootern, zum Beispiel Space Cobra, verdiente sich Romeo den Respekt der entstehenden Gaming-Community und führte ihn (und mich auch) dazu, einen der frühen Flash Awards in den späten 1990ern zu beurteilen, Nem5 Web Maggic.

Romeo est un développeur de jeux en Flash dont les créations incluent des bandes-annonces cinématiques d'animation qui sont sophistiquées et remarquables en soi; les jeux qui viennent après sont parmi ceux les plus jouables disponibles en ligne. Grâce à une série de jeux de tir à la première personne (comme Space Cobra), Romeo se gagne le respect de la balbutiante communauté de joueurs et se retrouve (en ma compagnie) au sein du jury pour Nem5 Web Maggic, l'un des premiers prix Flash à la fin des années 90.

Peter Grafik

—

The first stackable menu

Peter Grafik was the highly personal home-page of Peter Holm, a 26-year-old from Denmark who had been a 3D graphic designer since 1994 and turned web designer in 1997.

His website was one of the earliest to use card-style stacking navigation, where one selection resulted in a level being removed and replaced with the one beneath.

"I owe lots of my career trajectory to experimenting with Flash. The Dubonnet Retro Experience grew out of these experiments, in a period where I had a day job at an animation studio. The group of colleagues inspired and pushed each other, to explore, experiment, and learn. The usability 'controversy' about Flash being bad for user experience inspired me a lot. I read Jakob Nielsen like crazy, while making Flash websites. Putting the user first became deeply ingrained in my approach."

Peter Holm
Peter Grafik

Peter Grafik war die sehr persönliche Homepage von Peter Holm, einem 26-jährigen Mann aus Dänemark, der seit 1994 ein 3D Grafikdesigner war und dann 1997 Webdesigner wurde. Seine Website war einer der frühesten, die eine Stapelnavigation im Kartenstil verwendete, bei der eine Auswahl dazu führte, dass eine Ebene entfernt und durch die darunterliegende ersetzt wurde.

Peter Grafik est la très personnelle page de Peter Holm, un Danois de 26 ans qui passe à la conception Web en 1997 après trois ans consacrés au design graphique en 3D. Son site Web est l'un des tous premiers à proposer une navigation par empilement d'éléments tels des cartes : une sélection fait disparaître un niveau et le remplace par celui juste en dessous.

Hoover

—

A new interactive direction for global brands

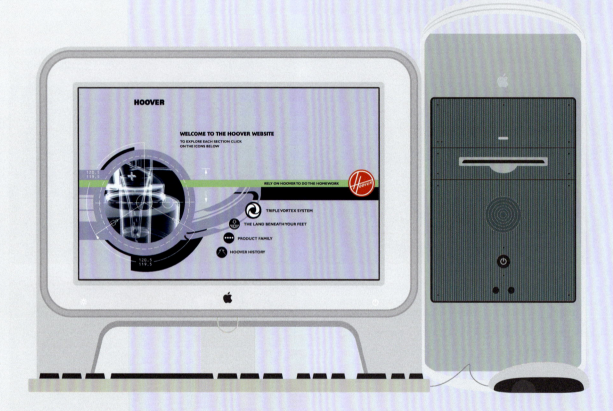

To coincide with the launch of the Hoover Triple Vortex vacuum cleaner this next-generation website was created, loaded with animations and designed so that users could explore the new model in detail whilst also viewing a history of Hoover's washing machines and other vacuum cleaners. A special "Land Beneath Your Feet" section revealed in microscopic detail the "strange world" underfoot, and what the latest vacuum cleaner was capable of picking up.

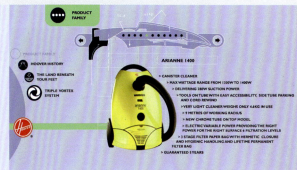

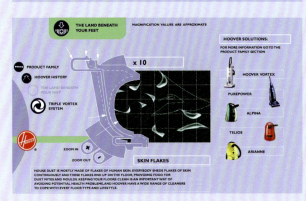

> "Dyson had a huge impact on the vacuum market, and Hoover needed to re-establish its brand with advanced tech whilst ensuring it owned the history of 'Hoovers'. [To] make the Triple Vortex appeal to this new online tech-savvy market, we used cyclonic-style animation and split technical diagrams to form a faux electron microscope and zoomable interface. Our optimized use of Flash vectors and images allowed us to take visitors on an engaging journey to 'The Land Beneath Your Feet', an *Inner Space*-style voyage to explore the hair, dust mites, spores, and allergens found there."

David Streek
Deepend; Playerthree

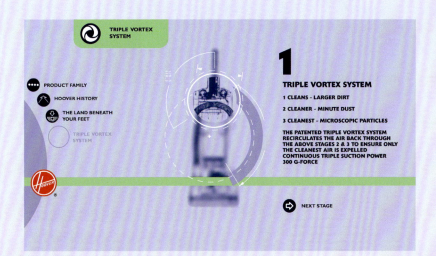

Im Zusammenhang mit der Einführung des Hoover Triple Vortex Staubsaugers wurde eine Website der nächsten Generation erstellt, die mit Animationen ausgestattet und so konzipiert wurde, dass Benutzer das neue Modell im Detail erkunden und gleichzeitig eine Geschichte von Hoovers Waschmaschinen und anderen Staubsaugern betrachten konnten. Ein spezieller Bereich „Land Beneath Your Feet" zeigte in mikroskopischen Details die „seltsame Welt" unter den Füßen und was der neueste Staubsauger aufnehmen konnte.

Pour coïncider avec le lancement de l'aspirateur Triple Vortex par Hoover est créé ce site Web de dernière génération, truffé d'animations et conçu pour que les utilisateurs puissent découvrir le nouveau modèle et l'histoire des machines à laver et d'autres aspirateurs de la marque. Une section « Land Beneath Your Feet » montre au niveau microscopique le monde étrange qui vit sous nos pieds, et ce que le dernier aspirateur est capable d'éliminer.

NOTABLE WEBSITE LAUNCH
Napster

GOOGLE FACTS

Sergey Brin and Larry Page drop out of Stanford to concentrate on Google

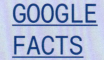

Yoshka becomes the first 'company' dog

Charlie Ayers is hired as Google's first chef

Moves out of the garage to Palo Alto, with eight employees

Google's first press release announces $25 million equity funding

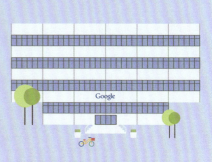

Moves to Mountain View location

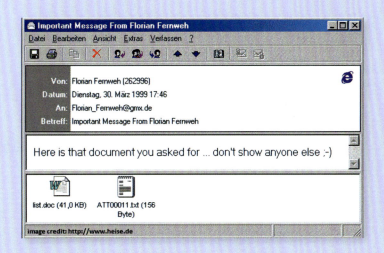

image credit: http://www.heise.de

INTERNET COMMUNITY
Melissa Virus

Possibly the most infamous virus ever, the Melissa. A email virus caused mass infections by luring unsuspecting users to a word.doc attachment, with the body of the email saying "Here is that document you asked for… don't show anyone else ;-)".

 Its creator, David L. Smith (USA), was sentenced to 10 years in prison, and served 20 months. He was also fined $5,000 and charged with causing $80 million of damage.

MOBILE EVOLUTION
Nokia 7110

The first mobile phone with a WAP browser

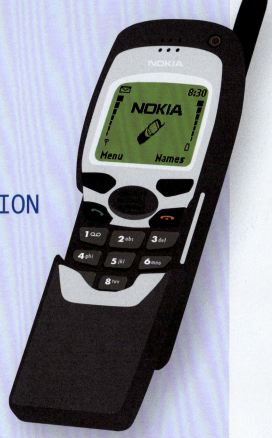

2000/

The Web
Comes
to Life

2000/

—

The Web Comes to Life

—

Up until this point the web still lacked any real dynamic presence, but now a whole global movement was set free with Flash. There had been extraordinary work for a few years, but where these groundbreaking interfaces had a particular novelty, with a new find every day, the widespread distribution of Flash meant that web design could now evolve more quickly than ever.

I had been creating websites myself since 1997 under the name treecity, and began doing this for small U.K. companies from 1998, using Flash 3. In April 2000, my website, treecity.co.uk, was nominated for the Yell UK Web Awards, for best web design agency. It was up against big agencies such as Deepend and the judges included LastMinute.com's Martha Lane Fox (it didn't win).

There were several places where the latest and most impressive Flash sites were listed, such as bestflashsites.de and the many Flash forums, but none were reflecting the sheer diversity of sites now appearing on a daily basis. I decided to give up my own web design work and concentrate fully on a daily Flash showcase, and in May 2000 the Favourite Website Awards (FWA) was born.

At the same time, Flash intros were starting to get a bad name and site visitors often skipped them altogether. The growing concern about usability was exemplified by Jakob Nielsen's statement that Flash was 99 percent bad.

"About 99% of the time, the presence of Flash on a website constitutes a usability disease. Although there are rare occurrences of good Flash design (it even adds value on occasion), the use of Flash typically lowers usability. In most cases, we would be better off if these multimedia objects were removed."
Jakob Nielsen, Nielsen Norman Group

The Flash community rejected Nielsen's comments and he was mocked on many forum threads. He also became one of the early internet memes, with Photoshopped images of him, and naturally some Flash animations, making him the subject of a number of jokes.

In fact, the community continued to grow, as did the Flash Challenge, the early community-powered showcase which, like the FWA, made logical use of the same Flash technology to showcase the best work being done with it.

A new wave of futuristic interfaces emerged featuring techno and dance music, including the popular xeo freestyle with its lengthy Flash intro.

Homestar Runner gained cult status with its consistent humor and animation series, which included characters such as Strong Bad with his own 'strong bad emails'.

Globz offered a fully customizable experience, similar to the Windows interface but with animation and again, lots of humor. Vector graphics enabled the floating windows to be resized without loss of quality.

The number of websites now rocketed to over 17 million, whilst web users passed 360 million. It was also the year Nokia launched the 3310, a phone that would be remembered for its durability and long battery-life.

Flash Challenge

"The widespread distribution of Flash meant that web design could now evolve more quickly than ever."

xeo freestyle

Bis zu diesem Zeitpunkt fehlte dem Internet noch eine reale dynamische Präsenz aber nun wurde eine ganze globale Bewegung mit Flash in Gang gesetzt. Es hatte einige Jahre lang außergewöhnliche Arbeiten gegeben. Aber während diese bahnbrechenden Interfaces eine besondere Neuheit waren, die jeden Tag einen neuen Fund erlaubten, bedeutete die weite Verbreitung von Flash, dass sich das Webdesign nun schneller entwickeln konnte als je zuvor.

Ich habe seit 1997 selbst Websites unter dem Namen Treecity erstellt und begann dies seit 1998 für kleine britische Unternehmen zu tun, mit Flash 3. Im April 2000 wurde meine Website treecity.co.uk für die Yell UK Web Awards vorgeschlagen, als beste Webdesign-Agentur. Ich trat gegen große Agenturen wie Deepend an und die Richter fügten außerdem LastMinute. coms Martha Lane Fox als Gegner hinzu (ich gewann nicht).

Es gab mehrere Orte, an denen die neuesten und beeindruckendsten Flash-Sites gelistet wurden, wie zum Beispiel bestflashsites.de und die vielen Flash-Foren, aber keiner reflektierte die schiere Vielfalt der Seiten, die heute täglich erscheinen. Ich beschloss, meine eigene Webdesign-Arbeit aufzugeben und mich voll und ganz auf eine tägliche Flash-Präsentation zu konzentrieren und im Mai 2000 wurden Favourite Website Awards (FWA) geboren.

Gleichzeitig begannen die Flash-Intros einen schlechten Ruf zu bekommen und die Besucher der Seiten übersprangen sie oft ganz. Die wachsende Sorge um die Benutzerfreundlichkeit wurde durch Jakob Nielsens Aussage, dass Flash zu 99 Prozent schlecht war, veranschaulicht.

"Etwa 99% der Zeit verursacht Flash auf einer Website eine Usability-Krankheit. Obwohl es manchmal gute Flash-Designs gibt (eventuell sogar mit einem Mehrwert), verringert die Verwendung von Flash die Benutzerfreundlichkeit. In den meisten Fällen wäre es besser, wenn diese Multimedia-Objekte entfernt würden."

JAKOB NIELSEN, NIELSEN NORMAN GROUP

Die Flash-Community lehnte Nielsens Kommentare ab und er wurde in vielen Foren verspottet. Er wurde auch zu einem der frühen Internet-Phänomene, mit Photoshop-Bildern von ihm und natürlich einigen Flash-Animationen, die ihn zur Witzfigur machten.

Tatsächlich wuchs die Community weiter, so wie auch die Flash Challenge, das frühe Community-unterstützte Showcase, das wie die FWA die gleiche Flash-Technologie logisch nutzte, um die beste Arbeit zu zeigen, die damit gemacht wurde.

Es entstand eine neue Welle futuristischer Interfaces mit Techno- und Dance-Musik, darunter der beliebte xeo freestyle mit seinem langatmigen Flash-Intro.

Homestar Runner erlangte Kultstatus mit seiner konsequenten Humor- und Animationsserie, die Charaktere hatte wie zum Beispiel Strong Bad mit seinen eigenen „Strong Bad E-Mails".

Globz bot eine vollständig anpassbare Erfahrung, ähnlich wie die Windows Schnittstelle, aber mit Animation und viel Humor. Vektorgrafiken ermöglichten die Größenänderung der schwebenden Fenster ohne Qualitätsverlust.

Die Anzahl der Websites stieg auf über 17 Millionen, während die Internetnutzer 360 Millionen überschritten. Es war auch das Jahr, in dem Nokia das 3310 herausbrachte, ein Telefon, das wegen seiner Langlebigkeit und langen Akkulaufzeit in Erinnerung bleiben wird.

The Web Comes to Life
—

Globz

Homestar Runner

> "About 99% of the
> time, the presence
> of Flash on a website
> constitutes a
> usability disease."

Alors que le Web n'a pas encore de véritable présence dynamique, Flash permet l'affranchissement d'un mouvement mondial. Pour toutes les formidables créations réalisées pendant des années, avec des interfaces révolutionnaires supposant une innovation et des propositions inédites au quotidien, la diffusion massive de Flash augure une évolution plus rapide que jamais de la conception Web.

Je me consacrais moi-même depuis 1997 à la création de sites Web sous le nom de treecity et dès 1998, je travaillais avec Flash 3 pour de petites sociétés britanniques. En avril 2000, mon site treecity.co.uk est nominé dans la catégorie de meilleure agence de conception Web aux Yell UK Web Awards. J'ai en face de grosses pointures comme Deepend et le jury compte Martha Lane Fox de LastMinute.com (pour info, je ne gagne pas).

Les sites en Flash les plus remarquables sont répertoriés dans diverses pages, telles que bestflashsites.de et de nombreux forums sur Flash, mais nulle part est reflétée l'incroyable diversité des créations qui apparaissent chaque jour. Je décide alors de laisser tomber mon job de concepteur pour me consacrer entièrement à promouvoir au quotidien des sites en Flash; en mai 2000 naissent ainsi les Favourite Website Awards (FWA).

En parallèle, les intros en Flash commencent à avoir mauvaise presse et les visiteurs les passent souvent directement. La convivialité est un souci croissant, comme l'illustre l'affirmation de Jakob Nielsen que 99 pour cent de Flash est mauvais.

«Environ 99% du temps, la présence de Flash dans un site Web suppose un problème de convivialité. Malgré les rares cas de bonnes conceptions en Flash (il est alors même synonyme de valeur ajoutée), son emploi réduit la facilité d'utilisation. Le plus souvent, tout irait mieux si ces éléments multimédia étaient supprimés.»

JAKOB NIELSEN, NIELSEN NORMAN GROUP

La communauté Flash s'oppose aux commentaires de Nielsen et se moque de lui dans de nombreux forums. Il devient l'un des premiers mèmes Internet par le biais d'images modifiées dans Photoshop et d'animations Flash qui en font le sujet de nombreuses blagues.

De fait, la communauté ne cesse de s'étendre, tout comme le Flash Challenge, le premier espace de présentation qu'elle gère. À l'instar des FWA, la technologie Flash est évidemment employée pour promouvoir les meilleures créations qui l'utilisent.

Un nouvel arrivage d'interfaces futuristes a recours à des musiques techno et dance, dont le populaire xeo freestyle et sa longue intro Flash.

Homestar Runner devient un site culte grâce à son humour constant et à ses séries d'animation avec des personnages comme Strong Bad, qui répond à ses fans en leur envoyant des «strong bad e-mails».

L'expérience dans Globz est totalement personnalisable, un peu comme l'interface Windows mais avec des animations et là encore une bonne dose d'humour. Les graphiques vectoriels permettent de redimensionner les fenêtres flottantes sans perdre en qualité.

Le nombre de sites Web grimpe en flèche, dépassant un total de 17 millions, et les internautes franchissent la barre des 360 millions. C'est aussi l'année du lancement par Nokia de son téléphone 3310, apprécié pour sa résistance et la durée de vie de sa batterie.

08 Facts of the year

5.9%

Number of internet users:
361 million, 5.9% of the
world population

17 million

Number of websites:
17.09 million

World News
Olympic Special!

World news:
Summer Olympics held
in Sydney

AOL.COM

Website with most traffic:
Aol.com

8 MB

Tech hardware:
USB flash drives are
introduced

XHTML

Tech software:
XHTML is released

Windows xp

Bill is logging off...

Other tech:
Bill Gates steps down as
CEO of Microsoft

Highest-grossing film:
Mission: Impossible 2

—

Requiem for a Dream

—

The benchmark for all
movie websites

With the FWA still in its infancy and me as its sole judge and site scout, I learned an early lesson when I clicked on the link for Requiem for a Dream, never to judge a website by its opening sequence. On my first visit I saw the "click here now" banner and immediately closed the page, thinking it was another badly designed website with banner advertising.

But as Flash forums continued to celebrate the site, I went back and was blown away. Here was a new standard for movie websites that demonstrated how the very atmosphere and emotional range of a movie could be translated online.

"Requiem was the first commercial project we were offered and was a direct result of Darren Aronofsky seeing soulbath.com and getting in touch. It really was the start of everything. And it wouldn't have happened quite the same way if we hadn't had access to Flash. I have very fond memories of it, it enabled a new generation of interaction designers to combine many different disciplines within one work stream. No one had to be a specialist. To be honest, it was a lot more fun then."

Florian Schmitt
Hi-ReS!

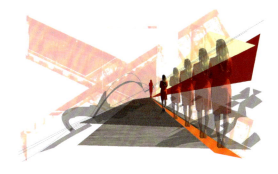

Als die FWA noch in den Kinder-schuhen steckte und ich als einziger Juror und Site-Scout agierte, lernte ich eine frühe Lektion, als ich auf den Link zur „Requiem for a Dream" Seite klickte: Beurteile niemals eine Website nur nach ihrer Eröff-nungssequenz. Bei meinem ersten Besuch sah ich das „click here now" Banner und schloss sofort die Seite, da ich dachte, es wäre eine andere schlecht gestaltete Website mit Bannerwerbung.

Da aber Flash-Foren weiterhin die Seite feierten, ging ich zurück und war hin und weg. Hier war ein neuer Standard für Film-Websites, die zeigte, wie die Atmosphäre und emotionale Bandbreite eines Films online übersetzt werden konnte.

Les FWA n'en étaient encore qu'à leurs balbutiements et j'opérais comme seul et unique juge et sélectionneur de sites. Quand j'ai cliqué sur le lien pour ouvrir Requiem for a Dream, j'ai appris une leçon : ne jamais juger un site Web à son ouverture. À ma première visite, j'ai en effet vu la bannière « click here now » et immédiatement fermé la page, pensant qu'il s'agissait d'un site Web de plus mal conçu et avec des bannières publicitaires.

Mais les forums Flash continuaient à en faire des éloges, alors j'y suis retourné et j'ai été subjugué. J'avais sous les yeux la nouvelle norme pour ce type de site, prouvant que l'atmosphère et toutes les émotions d'un film pouvaient être rendues en ligne.

—

Favourite Website Awards (FWA)

—

The future of web awards begins

The orange and yellow website had its fans but its critics too, chiefly because of its shocking use of typography, later saved by Miniml pixel fonts.

The new, more readable version of the Favourite Website Awards, which later became known as FWA, soon found cult status amongst the online community. By 2002 it had taken over from the coveted Macromedia Site of the Day when Macromedia's daily selections became less impressive; as the number-one internet recognition award site it was also the first to receive over 200 million visitors.

"A site that was 100 percent Flash and had no CMS resulted in me updating it every single day for 10 years with no days off and no holidays. By April 2005 I was receiving over 1,500 submissions per month and was widely acknowledged by agencies, brands, and individuals around the world as the number-one achievement award site for innovative web design. In 2017, an industry poll placed FWA alongside Cannes Lions as the top and most sought-after recognitions."

Rob Ford
FWA

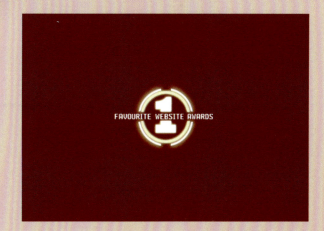

Die orange und gelbe Website hatte ihre Fans aber auch ihre Kritiker, vor allem wegen der schockierenden Verwendung von Typografie, die später von Miniml Pixelschriften gerettet wurde.

Die neue und besser lesbare Seite der Favourite Website Awards, später bekannt als FWA, bekam bald Kultstatus in der Online-Community. Im Jahr 2002 hatte es die begehrte Macromedia Site of the Day übernommen, als Macromedias tägliche Auswahl weniger beeindruckend wurde. Als Award-Site mit der höchsten Internetpräsenz war sie auch die erste, die über 200 Millionen Besucher empfing.

Le site Web jaune et orange a son lot de fans mais aussi de détracteurs, notamment pour son utilisation décalée de la typographie, plus tard reprise dans les polices pixelisées Miniml.

La nouvelle version plus accessible des Favourite Website Awards, par la suite connus comme FWA, fait très vite l'unanimité au sein de la communauté en ligne. En 2002, il passe devant le convoité Site of the Day de Macromedia, dont les sélections sont devenues plus banales. Se classant en tête rang des sites de récompenses Web, il est aussi le premier à dépasser les 200 millions de visiteurs.

2000/
—

John Mark Sorum

—

Super-slick transitions
give photography an edge

The static nature of still photos made them
seem dull in a climate of exuberant Flash
animation, until WDDG launched photographer
John Mark Sorum's site. Its funky music was in
a different class from the techno soundtracks
of most other sites, but more importantly,
Sorum's portfolio was displayed with image
shreds and super-fast photo transitions,
which initiated a truly modern approach to
web design.

"WDDG was subletting our first office from John and we were familiar with his amazing photography. I started experimenting with some animated parallax + masks trickery, Nathan Flood designed the interface, and Nando Costa designed and animated the interstitial loader/animations, and quickly we found what would be the signature look of the JMS site. The site came together so fast it's astounding. It was truly an example of a team at peak creativity and inspiration totally in the flow."

James Baker
WDDG

Die statische Natur von Standbildern ließ sie in einem Klima überschwänglicher Flash-Animation langweilig erscheinen, bis WDDG die Seite des Fotografen John Mark Sorum einführte. Seine flippige Musik war in einer anderen Klasse als die Techno-Soundtracks der meisten anderen Seiten aber wichtiger war noch, dass Sorums Portfolio mit Bildfetzen und superschnellen Fotoübergängen angezeigt wurde, die einen wirklich modernen Ansatz für das Webdesign einleiteten.

La nature statique des photos les fait paraître ennuyeuses dans un contexte d'animations Flash délirantes, mais tout change quand WDDG lance le site du photographe John Mark Sorum. Une musique funky le différencie de la majorité des autres sites avec une bande-son techno, mais c'est surtout la présentation du portfolio de Sorum sous forme de bandes d'images et avec des transitions rapides qui instaure une approche moderne de la conception Web.

—

Lookandfeel New Media

—

The first-ever gravity drop-down menu

With Flash intros threatened from several sides, Lookandfeel tried something a bit different. Using a couple of stickmen characters, Luke and Phil, whose antics also built and demonstrated the website, the agency presented the first drop-down menu, and a color-changing one at that. This vibrant site became the first-ever FWA Site of the Year, and proved how a Flash intro could still work if there was a story to tell.

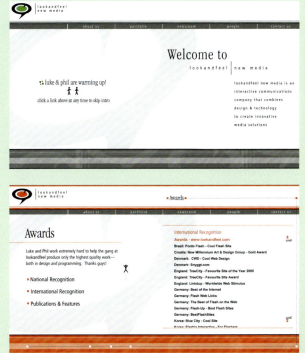

"Flash 5 had just been released with the first introduction of ActionScript, and we were thrilled by the possibilities. Many sites at the time included an opening animation with a 'Skip' button so we wanted to do something a bit more user-friendly. So, as our opening characters performed a comical ballet telling our core company story of form and function, they were simultaneously walking people through all of the site's navigation and features."

Charlie O'Shields
Lookandfeel New Media; Venn49

Als die Flash-Intros von allen Seiten angegriffen wurden, versuchte Lookandfeel etwas Anderes zu machen. Mit ein paar Strichmännchen, Luke und Phil, deren Streiche die Website auch aufbauten und demonstrierten, präsentierte die Agentur das erste Drop-Down-Menü, das dazu noch die Farbe wechselte. Diese lebendige Seite war die erste FWA-Site of the Year und bewies, dass ein Flash-Intro noch funktionieren konnte, wenn es eine Geschichte zu erzählen gab.

Face à la menace omniprésente des intros Flash, Lookandfeel tente d'innover : avec les bonshommes allumettes Luke et Phil, dont les bouffonneries servent à composer le site et à en expliquer la structure, l'agence crée le premier menu déroulant, qui plus est changeant de couleur. Ce site dynamique est le tout premier Site of the Year des FWA et il prouve qu'une intro Flash peut encore fonctionner si elle raconte une histoire.

2000/
—
Barneys New York
—
The original Barneys scroller

Joshua Davis was one of the original web pioneers, working for renowned web production company Kioken who were given a feature report by CNN.

    The menu system for the Barneys New York site, which became known as the Barneys scroller, quickly became commonplace and remained in use for many years; in fact, it could be argued that we are still using menus based on this original concept.

"Built at Kioken (about 16 team members), the core
project was a labor of love between me and Erik
Wysocan. I vaguely remember us staying up for three
days straight to pull it together. This project was one of
the earliest sites that pulled from praystation.com daily
experiments in concert with Erik's design to assemble
a fully interactive website. Most of these Praystation
daily posts were solo self-contained interactive toys…
and pulling a bunch of them to work together into a
fully realized design piece for Barneys… set in motion
what the potential of a website could be."

Joshua Davis
Kioken; joshuadavis.com

Joshua Davis war einer der
ursprünglichen Pioniere im
Internet. Er arbeitete für die
renommierte Web-Produktions-
firma Kioken, die von CNN einen
Feature-Report bekam.

Das Menüsystem für die
Barneys New York Site, das

als Barneys Scroller bekannt
wurde, wurde schnell alltäglich
und blieb viele Jahre in Gebrauch.
Tatsächlich könnte argumentiert
werden, dass wir immer noch
Menüs verwenden, die auf diesem
ursprünglichen Konzept basieren.

Un des pionniers du Web, Joshua
Davis travaille pour la célèbre société de production Kioken, sur
laquelle CNN émet un reportage.

Utilisé dans le site de
Barneys New York, le système de
menu connu comme «défilement
Barneys» s'impose rapidement

et reste la norme pendant des
années. On peut de fait affirmer
que des menus actuels reposent
encore sur ce concept.

DerBauer:
The Portal

—

The ultimate teaser site

Meanwhile, on the German FlashForum.de Marcus Bussejahn was getting known for his new agency and high-impact use of Flash. The Portal opened with a loading screen showing a door handle, with two locked doors appearing once the site had fully loaded.

Accompanied by chilling sound effects, the doors would distort, the handles move on their own, and dust puffed out from underneath them. Such a teaser to discover what lay behind the doors had not been encountered before and stayed in people's minds for years.

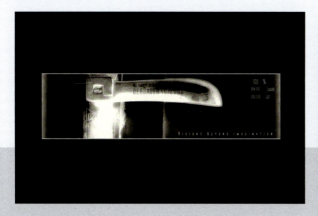

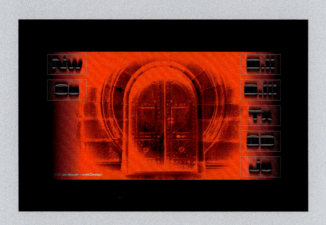

"DerBauer I was more a kind of test page,
exploring possibilities, getting used to ActionScript
(I). DerBauer II launched shortly before the new
millennium. The user and also business feedback
was awesome. Shortly after that I decided to make
my hobby into a profession. The time period
1998–2011 was the golden age of special internet
entertainment, because nobody had ever seen
anything like it – haha!"

Marcus Bussejahn
DerBauer

Inzwischen wurde im deutschen FlashForum.de Marcus Bussejahn mit seiner neuen Agentur und seiner High-Impact-Nutzung von Flash bekannt. DerBauer öffnete mit einem Loading Screen, der einen Türgriff zeigte, mit zwei verschlossenen Türen, sobald die Seite voll geladen war. Begleitet von entspannenden Soundeffekten verzogen sich die Türen, die ihre Griffe bewegten sich von allein und Staub quoll unter ihnen hervor. Einen solchen Teaser, zu entdecken, was hinter den Türen lag, gab es vorher noch nicht und er blieb jahrelang in den Köpfen der Leute.

À la même période, sur le site allemand FlashForum.de, Marcus Bussejahn se fait un nom avec sa nouvelle agence et son emploi explosif de Flash. L'écran de chargement de The Portal montre une poignée de porte, puis deux portes fermées une fois le site chargé. Sur un fond d'effets sonores qui donnent des frissons, les portes se déforment, de la poussière s'échappe au bas et les poignées bougent seules. Un teaser de ce niveau pour découvrir ce qu'il y a derrière les portes est totalement inédit et reste des années dans l'esprit des gens.

Nosepilot

—

One of the first interactive animation series

Flash had given a lot to the early web but there was still no genuine individual expression until Alexandru Sacui launched his interactive animation series Nosepilot.

The project proved to be so popular that it swamped its site-server and left Sacui with a bill of over $16,000. The online community rallied, with many offering donations and email-bombing the hosting company, demanding they withdraw their threats, while others mirrored the site on separate servers so Nosepilot could keep going.

"Nosepilot was created in the early days of Flash. Immediately after publishing, I was swept up in an early version of viral notoriety. I was offered a speaking gig at a Flash convention where I saw some magical work that would amaze even today's phone app-users. Flash was powerful. It was simpler and therefore easier to figure out. One day, cellphones incompatible with Flash would cut the party short."

Alex Sacui
Nosepilot

Flash hatte dem frühen Internet viel gegeben, aber es gab noch immer keinen echten individuellen Ausdruck, bis Alexandru Sacui seine interaktive Animationsserie Nosepilot startete.

Das Projekt erwies sich als so populär, dass es seinen Server überflutete und Sacui mit einer Rechnung von über $ 16.000 stehen ließ. Die Online-Community tat sich zusammen, viele boten Spenden an und das Hosting-Unternehmen wurde mit E-Mails überschüttet, in denen gefordert wurde dass sie ihre Ansprüche zurückziehen sollten, während andere die Seite auf separaten Servern spiegelten, damit Nosepilot weitermachen konnte.

Flash a beaucoup apporté au Web les premières années, mais sans la manifestation d'une expression individuelle authentique. C'est chose faite avec Alexandru Sacui, quand il lance sa série d'animations interactives Nosepilot.

Le projet s'avère si populaire que son serveur est saturé et laisse à Sacui une facture de plus de 16 000 dollars. La communauté en ligne se mobilise avec des offres de dons et un bombardement d'e-mails à la société d'hébergement pour qu'elle retire ses menaces. D'autres s'affairent à répliquer le site sur des serveurs distincts pour que Nosepilot poursuive son activité.

Yigal-Azrouel

—

Alternative navigation ideas

Yigal-Azrouel was one of Firstborn's early
sites and showed how innovative this agency
was, with its experimental navigation concept
whereby users aligned crosshairs to hit the
button that would navigate them through
the site, in conjunction with glimpsed photos
and mouse-reactive transitions.

"I remember the feeling of empowerment I had from a little discovery in the early days of Flash — with my very limited coding skills I figured out a way to control the moving masks, blurring, transparency, and other effects with only one line of code. It was as simple as $E = mc^2$. The technique essentially advanced nested timelines according to the pixel position of the cursor."

Vas Sloutchevsky
Firstborn; Interface Design Foundry

Yigal-Azrouel war eine von den frühen Seiten von Firstborn und zeigte, wie innovativ diese Agentur war, mit ihrem experimentellen Navigationskonzept, bei dem der Benutzer das Fadenkreuz so ausrichten musste, dass es auf den Knopf trifft, der ihn durch die Seite führt, in Verbindung mit flüchtigen Bildern und Maus-reaktiven Übergängen.

Le site Yigal-Azrouel est l'un des premiers de Firstborn qui montre toute la capacité créative d'une agence, avec un concept de navigation expérimental dans lequel les utilisateurs alignent des mires pour activer des boutons et parcourir le site, mais aussi des aperçus de photos et des transitions réactives aux mouvements de la souris.

KMGI Studios

—

A fully narrated experience

KMGI Studios turned its plain HTML website into a full-on multimedia one by using the latest version of Flash 3. The site built as users watched and was accompanied by continuous narration, another first, where the voice-over quality was so good that users naturally assumed KMGI was a leader in the field.

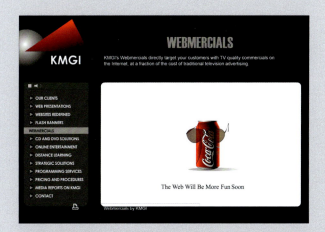

"When we launched the dynamic multimedia KMGI website in the late '90s it quickly became a sensation and won the World Best Website Award. Countless publications and TV stations reported on our website. In the early days of the static internet and slow dial-up modems, a full-screen multimedia experience which required no pre-loading was revolutionary and resulted in high demand for our work."

Alex Konanykhin
KMGI

KMGI Studios verwandelten ihre reine HTML-Website in eine vollwertige Multimedia-Version, indem sie die neueste Version von Flash 3 verwendeten. Die Seite wurde aufgebaut, während der Nutzer zuschaute und dies wurde von einer kontinuierlichen Erzählung begleitet, eine weitere Premiere, bei der die Voice-Over-Qualität so gut war, dass die Nutzer natürlich davon ausgingen, dass KMGI führend auf diesem Gebiet sei.

KMGI Studios transforme son site Web purement HTML en page multimédia à l'aide de la dernière version de Flash 3. Le site se construit sous les yeux des visiteurs et est assorti d'une narration en continu, autre première du genre. La voix off est de telle qualité que les utilisateurs pensent tout simplement que KMGI est leader dans le domaine.

2Advanced v1

—

A first to use floating and draggable windows

2Advanced v1 was one of the earliest sites to have floating windows that could be dragged into position, while including an array of content that showed its designer was one of the more rounded and forward-looking developers of the day. The site also championed a futuristic style, visually, musically, and with sound effects. Little did we know the powerhouse 2Advanced was to become.

"Flash signaled the birth of an entirely new digital storytelling platform, which ignited an interactive revolution for artists who immediately realized its massive potential. The Flash format smashed open the rigid framework of the early web and gave artists a wide-open digital canvas on which to paint. Its birth electrified the web, and spawned a creative synergy that many equate with capturing light in a bottle, one of those rare moments in time when all the elements combine just perfectly to take things to the next level."

Eric Jordan
2Advanced; ericjordan.com

2Advanced v1 war eine von den frühesten Seiten, die schwebende Fenster hatten, die in eine Position gezogen werden konnten, während sie eine Reihe von Inhalten enthielt, die zeigten, dass ihr Designer einer der fortschrittlichsten Entwickler der Zeit war. Die Seite setzte sich auch für einen futuristischen Stil ein, visuell, musikalisch und mit Soundeffekten. Wir hatten ja keine Ahnung, zu was für einem Kraftpaket 2Advanced werden sollte.

2Advanced v1 est l'un des tous premiers sites avec des fenêtres flottantes qu'il est possible de faire glisser, ainsi qu'un contenu démontrant que son concepteur est l'un des développeurs les plus complets et innovateurs du moment. Le site défend aussi un style futuriste tant sur le plan visuel que musical grâce aux effets sonores. On n'imagine alors pas que 2Advanced va devenir un véritable moteur de création.

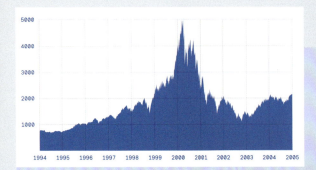

INTERNET COMMUNITY
The dot-com bubble bursts

On March 10, leading tech company shares hit an all-time high and spiked; the market duly crashed and took with it some of the web's shining stars, including pets.com.

GOOGLE FACTS

Google.com no longer in Beta

Search   chwilio
buscar   Szukaj
chercher   Sök
ricerca   Hae
Suche   Paieška
サーチ   खोज
搜索   بحث
Vyhledávání שפחל

Search facility is available in 15 languages

Google's first April 1 hoax: MentalPlex, search technology that avoids typing by reading the user's mind to find what the user wants to search for

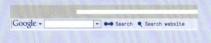

Google Toolbar is released

Google AdWords launches

MOBILE EVOLUTION
Nokia 3310

Widely popular because
of its durability

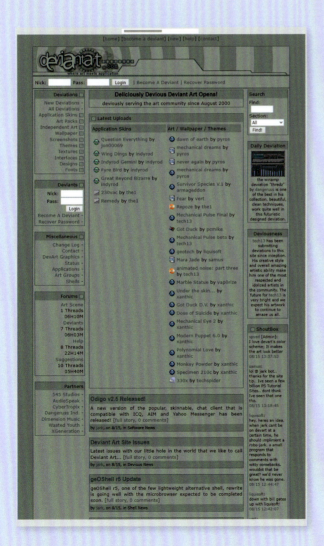

NOTABLE WEBSITE
LAUNCH
DeviantArt

2001/

The Website Generation

2001/

—

The Website
Generation

—

Vectorpark

The web was now developing at an incredible pace, and Flash had really taken over. People were leaving their jobs to become webmasters, many calling themselves 'Flashers', and the resulting community had a very close-knit bond.

At the same time, many people disliked Flash, not infrequently because advertising banners were becoming increasingly annoying and difficult to escape.

Flash was also growing up, and some people and agencies were ahead of the curve. Antonio Luis created a personal site with one of the first examples of organic movement which demonstrated an advanced style of ActionScripting.

Elsewhere, Billy Bussey became a bit of a web celebrity after launching his own site with its masses of impressive 3D. He became known as one of the masters of Flash, but turned down the chance to contribute to the first *New Masters of Flash* book because he thought the email invitation was "some sort of scam".

Ferry Halim, a former accountant, developed a genius for creating games. His beautifully crafted and animated Flash games were a worldwide hit and his site attracted over 1 million visitors every month.

Experimental work was thriving and often very exciting, producing several dark or unusual results, with Niko Stumpo being a classic example through his ABC project (abnormal behavior child).

Patrick Smith, aka Vectorpark, a Fine Arts graduate from Washington University, also became known for his playful, experimental websites.

England's Random Media launched the Dream Domain, an anagram of their agency name, in an early example of live-user community interaction. It was one of the first sites that allowed users to leave video messages.

Fido (by Fantasy Interfaces, now Fantasy) literally bounced its way into place by using a masking transition that influenced many designers. The site was also one of the first to use draggable 3D elements.

Outpost was an early example of the custom mouse cursor. When the mouse pointer was hovered in the right place it changed to represent different interactive features, such as stairs, elevators, etc.

Axis Interactive highlighted the talent of Robert Penner and was the first site to use 360° navigation. By moving the mouse left and right, a landscape evolved and once a menu item was selected the user moved upward, as if traveling through the Earth's atmosphere, to the selected section.

This was the year when Apple launched the iPod and Microsoft its infamous Internet Explorer 6. It was also the year when the web community stood together in defiance against atrocities after the September 11 attacks in the United States.

"The web was now developing at an incredible pace."

Orisinal

Billy Bussey

ABC

Ant's Roots – Antonio Luis

Das Internet entwickelte sich jetzt in einem unglaublichen Tempo und Flash hatte wirklich alles übernommen. Die Leute gaben ihre Jobs auf, um Webmaster zu werden, viele nannten sich „Flasher" und die daraus resultierende Gemeinschaft hatte eine sehr enge Bindung untereinander.

Gleichzeitig waren viele Leute nicht sehr begeistert von Flash, nicht selten, weil Werbebanner immer ärgerlicher wurden und man ihnen immer schwieriger entkommen konnte.

Flash wurde auch erwachsen und einige Leute und Agenturen bekamen die Kurve nicht. Antonio Luis schuf eine persönliche Seite mit einem der ersten Beispiele für organische Bewegung, die einen fortgeschrittenen Stil von ActionScripting zeigten.

Anderswo bekam Billy Bussey eine gewisse Web-Prominenz nach dem Start seiner eigenen Website mit seinen beeindruckenden 3D Massen. Er wurde bekannt als einer der Meister des Flash aber lehnte die Chance ab, als einer der Ersten zum *New Masters of Flash* Buch beizutragen, weil er dachte, die E-Mail-Einladung sei „irgendein Scam".

Ferry Halim, ein ehemaliger Buchhalter, wurde ein Genie bei der Erfindung von Spielen. Seine wunderschön gestalteten und animierten Flash-Spiele waren ein weltweiter Hit und seine Website zog jeden Monat mehr als 1 Million Besucher an.

Die experimentelle Arbeit war erfolgreich und oft sehr aufregend und brachte einige dunkle oder ungewöhnliche Ergebnisse hervor, wobei Niko Stumpo durch sein ABC-Projekt (abnormal behavior child) ein klassisches Beispiel war.

Patrick Smith, aka Vectorpark, ein Absolvent der Washington University für Bildene Kunst, wurde auch für seine spielerischen, experimentellen Websites bekannt.

Random Media aus England brachte Dream Domain heraus, ein Anagramm ihres Agenturnamens, in einem frühen Beispiel der Live-User-Community-Interaktion. Es war eine der ersten Seiten, die es Nutzern erlaubte, Videonachrichten zu hinterlassen.

Fido (von Fantasy Interfaces, heute Fantasy) sprengte buchstäblich seinen Weg frei, indem er einen maskierten Übergang verwendete, der viele Designer beeinflusste. Die Website war auch eine der ersten, die ziehbare 3D-Elemente verwendete.

Outpost war ein frühes Beispiel für den benutzerdefinierten Maus-Cursor. Wenn der Mauszeiger an die richtige Stelle geführt wurde, änderte er sich, um unterschiedliche interaktive Features anzuzeigen wie Treppen, Aufzüge usw.

Axis Interactive hob das Talent von Robert Penner hervor und war die erste Seite, die 360° Navigation benutzte. Durch Bewegen der Maus nach links und rechts entwickelte sich eine Landschaft und sobald ein Menüpunkt ausgewählt war, bewegte sich der Benutzer, wie durch die Erdatmosphäre, zum ausgewählten Abschnitt.

Dies war das Jahr, als Apple den iPod auf den Markt brachte und Microsoft seinen berüchtigten Internet Explorer 6. Es war auch das Jahr, in dem die Web-Community trotz der Gräueltaten nach den Anschlägen vom 11. September in den Vereinigten Staaten trotzig zusammengestanden hat.

The Website
Generation
—

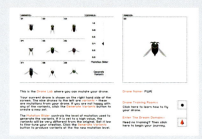
Dream Domain

Outpost

Fido

Axis Interactive

"Flash had really
taken over. People
were leaving their
jobs to become
webmasters."

Le Web évolue désormais à toute vitesse et Flash est partout. Les gens quittent leur emploi pour devenir webmasters, beaucoup se faisant appeler « Flashers », et forment une communauté très soudée.

En parallèle se font entendre de nombreux critiques de Flash, souvent en raison des bannières publicitaires chaque fois plus agaçantes et difficiles à éviter.

Flash est lui aussi en pleine croissance, et bien des professionnels et des agences ont une longueur d'avance. Antonio Luis crée un site personnel avec l'une des premières démonstrations de mouvement organique, montrant une approche avancée d'ActionScripting.

Pour sa part, Billy Bussey devient une sorte de vedette du Web après le lancement de son site regorgeant d'effets 3D. Il est considéré comme l'un des grands maîtres de Flash mais rate l'occasion de participer à l'ouvrage *New Masters of Flash* car il pense que l'e-mail d'invitation est « une sorte d'arnaque ».

Ancien comptable, Ferry Halim devient un expert en développement de jeux. Ses superbes jeux animés en Flash remportent un succès mondial et son site reçoit chaque mois plus d'1 million de visites.

Le travail expérimental va bon train. Il est souvent passionnant et donne des résultats parfois obscurs et décalés : c'est le cas de Niko Stumpo avec son projet ABC (« abnormal behavior child »).

Patrick Smith, alias Vectorpark, décroche un diplôme des beaux-arts à l'université de Washington et se fait un nom avec ses sites Web ludiques et expérimentaux.

L'agence britannique Random Media lance Dream Domain, un anagramme de son nom, qui offre une création interactive en direct avec les utilisateurs. C'est l'un des premiers sites permettant aux visiteurs de laisser des messages vidéo.

Le site Fido (de Fantasy Interfaces, aujourd'hui Fantasy) saute sur la scène du Web avec une transition de camouflage qui influence de nombreux concepteurs. Il est aussi l'un des premiers sites à employer des éléments 3D que l'on peut faire glisser.

Outpost présente l'un des premiers curseurs personnalisés.

Quand le pointeur est au bon endroit, il change pour représenter différents éléments interactifs, tels que des escaliers, des ascenseurs, etc.

Avec le premier site à offrir une navigation à 360°, Axis Interactive met en valeur tout le talent de Robert Penner. Le déplacement de la souris vers la gauche et vers la droite anime un paysage et quand l'utilisateur clique sur une option, il se déplace vers le haut comme s'il traversait l'atmosphère jusqu'à la section sélectionnée.

Cette année-là, Apple lance l'iPod, et Microsoft son tristement célèbre Internet Explorer 6. C'est aussi l'année où la communauté Web fait front commun contre les atrocités des attaques du 11 septembre aux États-Unis.

Ø8 Facts of the year

Number of internet users:
513 million, 8.2% of the
world population

Number of websites:
29.2 million

World news:
September 11 attacks

Website with most traffic:
Aol.com

Tech hardware:
Apple launches the iPod

Tech software:
Internet Explorer 6
launches

Other tech:
Napster is closed down

Highest-grossing film:
Harry Potter and the
Philosopher's Stone

2001/
—

2Advanced Studios
v3 Expansions

—

The most influential Flash
website of all

Eric Jordan had already caught people's attention with his company 2A, as it was known to the Flash community. As his site built, atmospheric original music accompanied a sequence of rolling clouds. It was an inspiration to many, and was often copied, and sites with this layout were described as being '2Advanced' in their design; the phrase became accepted as almost a style of web design in itself. 2Advanced v3 Expansions is remembered for being the most copied website ever and for being voted 'The most influential Flash website of the decade' in the official polls conducted by FWA for Adobe.

"The 2Advanced v3 Expansions website was a pure labor of love from the start. It was fueled by an ethereal, futuristic storytelling aesthetic that came out of my youth, spent reading cyberpunk novels and imagining where technology was taking humanity. Our small team at the time was not prepared for the reception it received the day it launched — we immediately received thousands of emails from all over the world about how the site had changed everything people thought a website could be, and how it could make them feel."

Eric Jordan
2Advanced; ericjordan.com

Eric Jordan hatte bereits mit seiner Firma 2A die Aufmerksamkeit der Leute auf sich gezogen, die in der Flash-Community bekannt war. Beim Aufbau der Website begleitete atmosphärische Originalmusik eine Abfolge von rollenden Wolken. Sie war für viele eine Inspiration und wurde oft kopiert und Websites mit diesem Layout wurden als "2Advanced" in ihrem Design beschrieben. Der Satz wurde fast als ein Stil des Webdesigns an sich gesehen. 2Advanced v3 Expansions steht dafür, die am meisten jemals kopierte Website zu sein und wurde in den offiziellen Umfragen, die von FWA für Adobe durchgeführt wurden, als die "Die einflussreichste Flash-Website des Jahrzehnts" bewertet.

Eric Jordan a déjà attiré l'attention avec son studio 2A, comme le connaît la communauté Flash. Pendant le chargement du site, des nuages s'amoncellent sur un fond de musique d'ambiance. Beaucoup y puisent leur inspiration, parfois le copient, et les sites conçus selon cette structure sont dits « 2Advanced », au point que l'expression est acceptée presque comme un style en soi. 2Advanced v3 Expansions reste le site Web le plus copié de l'histoire et est élu « le site en Flash le plus influent de la décennie » dans les sondages officiels effectués par les FWA pour Adobe.

Nooflat

—

The first resizing interface

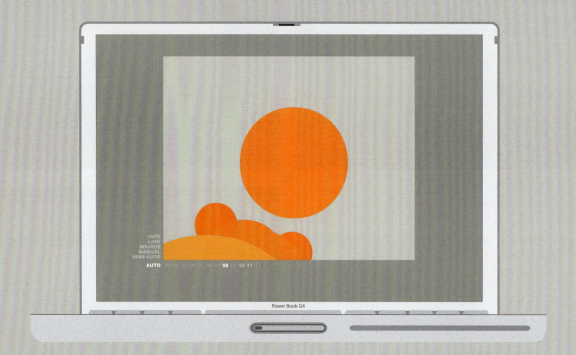

Resizing is taken for granted now but this is where it began, with a click on any part of the navigation causing the interface dimensions to change. The site was designed to showcase experimental work but its biggest success was the interface itself, especially the resizing script. Being such a progressive and original site, it was soon copied around the world.

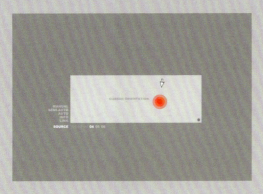

"I used Flash to try and create particular visual effects or to make systems where graphical objects would react in different ways to each other and to user input. I would generally start with an idea I was trying to achieve but would often end up with something else entirely. At the time there were many similar websites with collections of interactive Flash pieces. If you look through the links section of the website you'll find a few of them still online."

Jamie Macdonald
nooflat.nu

Die Größenanpassung (Rezising) wird heute als selbstverständlich angesehen, aber hier begann sie mit einem Klick auf einen beliebigen Teil der Navigation, wodurch sich die Abmessungen der Benutzeroberfläche veränderten. Die Website wurde entworfen, um experimentelle Arbeiten zu präsentieren aber ihr größter Erfolg war die Benutzeroberfläche selbst, insbesondere das Skript zur Größenänderung. Da sie so eine progressive und originelle Seite war, wurde sie bald auf der ganzen Welt kopiert.

La capacité de redimensionnement va aujourd'hui de soi, mais c'est vraiment à ce moment-là que tout commence, quand un simple clic n'importe où dans l'écran suffit à changer les dimensions de l'interface. Le site est conçu pour présenter des créations expérimentales mais son succès tient surtout à l'interface en soi, notamment à son script de redimensionnement. Ce site progressif et original ne tarde pas à être copié dans le monde entier.

Opaldust Designs
—

The first newspaper metaphor

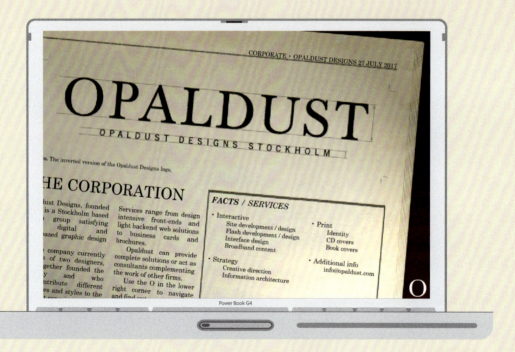

The first website to be styled like a newspaper, Opaldust's animation showed the pages move as if being thumbed through in response to the user's navigation. It demonstrated that advanced web interfaces could be augmented by existing examples from the real world too, and similar sites soon followed in its wake.

"Opaldust.com was one of those early sites that took on a completely skeuomorphic design schema that was meant to mimic a newspaper and a page-turn. It had a clunky icon-based navigation located at the bottom of the page that when clicked would literally turn the page. It would not be the last of the page-turn websites, and certainly helped to start a trend that may even be seen today."

Craig Elimeliah
VML
(Industry quote provided in the absence
of the site's creators)

Die erste Website, die wie eine Zeitung aussah. Opaldusts Animation zeigte sich bewegende Seiten, die sich umblätterten, wenn der Nutzer die Navigation betätigte. Sie zeigte, dass

fortgeschrittene Web-Interfaces durch existierende Beispiele aus der realen Welt ergänzt werden konnten und ähnliche Seiten sollten bald folgen.

Opaldust crée le premier site Web représentant un journal. Quand les visiteurs naviguent, l'animation bouge les pages comme si elles étaient feuilletées, preuve que les interfaces

Web avancées peuvent être enrichies avec des exemples du monde réel.

—

Starbreeze

—

The first website
to have a guide

As Starbreeze loaded it offered users the option to have a fairy guide, while the fixed website dimensions and bitmap graphics gave the whole site an unparalleled appearance.

The attention to detail was immediately obvious, even to the point where a face built into the interface creased and wrinkled when certain areas loaded.

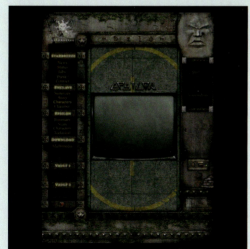

"As an old gamer, I must say this was one of my favorite clients to work with. With a passionate small team, all with a common interest in gaming and an out-of-the-box mentality, we had one thing in mind, pushing Flash to the next level and to blow everyone's mind (including our own). I remember working day and night, even sleepovers at the office."

Paul Mellström
Fantasy Interfaces; Style Studios

Wenn Starbreeze geladen wurde, bot die Seite den Nutzern die Option an, einen Feenführer bei sich zu haben, während die festen Website-Dimensionen und Bitmap-Grafiken der gesamten Website ein unvergleichliches Aussehen hatten. Die Liebe zum Detail war sofort offensichtlich, sogar bis zu dem Punkt, wo ein in die Schnittstelle eingebautes Gesicht zerknittert und entknittert wurde, wenn bestimmte Bereiche geladen wurden.

Une fois le site Starbreeze chargé, les utilisateurs ont l'option de suivre une fée les guidant dans l'interface. Les dimensions fixes et les graphiques bitmap donnent à l'ensemble une apparence sans précédent, et le souci du détail est flagrant, à tel point qu'un visage à l'écran se contracte et se ride au chargement de certaines sections.

Lenny Kravitz
—

The original zooming menu

Virgin Records employed the innovators at KNI to create the official website for Lenny Kravitz, and a new zooming navigation was the result. Slick transitions and motion painted each new area of the site perfectly, with back-end programming showing how content could be easily managed through a seamless system of Flash and XML.

"For this site we actually pitched three different concepts, but I remember desperately wanting the 'zoom-in-zoom-out' idea to be picked. Luckily we had one trick up our sleeve: Lenny's manager only really cared which image was used, so we made sure that this concept had the cover art image. Luckily that was all that was needed and they were on board."

Daniel Box
KNI

Virgin Records beauftragte die Innovatoren von KNI, die offizielle Website von Lenny Kravitz zu erstellen und eine neue Zoom-Navigation war das Ergebnis davon. Glatte Übergänge und Bewegung malten jeden neuen Bereich der Website perfekt, mit einer Back-End-Programmierung, die zeigte, wie Inhalte durch ein nahtloses System einfach mit Flash und XML verwaltet werden können.

Virgin Records fait appel aux créateurs de KNI pour concevoir le site officiel de Lenny Kravitz; une nouvelle navigation par zoom est alors inventée. Des transitions et des mouvements fluides remplissent parfaitement chaque nouvelle partie du site, et une programmation côté serveur montre comment gérer facile-ment le contenu via un système homogène en Flash et XML.

—

Tongsville

—

The first to use live satellite weather reports

Power Book G4

Tongsville presented some pioneering back-end programming that utilized live feeds from satellites so that users could access current weather reports for the first time online. The site had a hidden 'God' that rewarded people who spent time there by way of additional elements: a swarm of bees chasing a town's inhabitants, a UFO abduction, or for those who really deserved it, a special guest appearance by Godzilla!

"We (Preloaded) launched Tongsville shortly after 9/11 — we were quite worried about the part of the city that featured a fiery pit and twisted skyscraper remains. It was intended as a more dramatic way of ending the cityscape rather than just having a dead-end. We needn't have worried though, not one person suggested any connection between the two or that it was inappropriate."

Rob Corradi
Preloaded; robcorradi.com

Tongsville präsentierte eine bahnbrechende Back-End-Programmierung, die Live-Feeds von Satelliten nutzte, damit Nutzer erstmals online auf aktuelle Wetterberichte zugreifen konnten.

Die Seite hatte einen versteckten „Gott", der Menschen durch zusätzliche Elemente belohnte, die ihre Zeit dort verbrachten: ein Bienenschwarm, der die Einwohner einer Stadt verfolgte, eine UFO-Entführung oder für diejenigen, die es wirklich verdient hatten, ein besonderer Gastauftritt von Godzilla!

Le site Tongsville repose sur une innovante programmation côté serveur qui utilise des transmissions en direct de satellites pour que les utilisateurs accèdent pour la première fois en ligne à des bulletins météo.

Dans le site, un «dieu» caché récompense les visiteurs qui y passent un certain temps avec d'autres éléments: une nuée d'abeilles poursuivant les habitants d'une ville, un enlèvement par un OVNI ou encore, pour ceux qui l'ont vraiment mérité, une apparition surprise de Godzilla!

2001/

—

WM Team

—

The site that championed
the personal side

When it came to real character, Germany's WM Team stole the show, with their site based entirely around a building theme, and a rather clumsy workman involved in every stage of its construction. This site oozed charm, innovation, and originality, and also proved to stand the test of time.

"When we released our site, we suddenly had a lot of visibility all over the world. We'd been featured by magazines and books, gave interviews, and we were invited to conferences in San Francisco and New York. That was all crazy and motivating. I never had that feeling of appreciation for my work again. After Steve Jobs killed Flash, our agency went down and we closed WM Team in 2013. When I see some of the 'hyped' stuff today, I still think that we had a lot of this stuff 10 years before."

Rainer Michael
WM Team; rainermichael.com

Echten Charakter zeigte das WM Team aus Deutschland. Sie stahlen allen die Show mit ihrer Website, die sich um das Thema Bauen drehte, mit einem ziemlich tollpatschigen Arbeiter, der in jedem Stadium der Konstruktion beteiligt war. Diese Seite strahlte Charme, Innovation und Originalität aus und meisterte auch die Bewährungsprobe im Laufe der Zeit.

En matière de personnage réel, l'agence allemande WM Team vole la vedette avec son site entièrement basé sur le thème de la construction, et un ouvrier plutôt maladroit qui intervient à plusieurs étapes du processus. Le site est tout autant attirant, innovant et original, et il vieillit bien avec les années.

Sydney Opera House
Virtual Tour

—

The original virtual tour

The Sydney Opera House employed 360° panoramic scenes (using Apple's QuickTime) and point-and-click navigation to enable users to explore the area surrounding the building, even the car-park underneath, and everywhere inside as well. It was an extraordinary website and an incredible resource, giving everyone the sense they had 'visited' the Opera House itself.

"I was working full-time as a composer writing music for theater and film, and was working on a few side projects. One of them was a CD-ROM version of a Virtual Tour of the Sydney Opera House. I realized that Flash now had the capability to do a whole lot more, and that I could potentially port the virtual tour content over to Flash and share it with the world. The reaction to the site overwhelmed me and was so very flattering."

Tony David Cray
Director

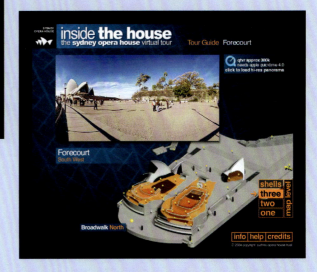

Das Opernhaus von Sydney verwendete 360° Panoramaszenen (unter Verwendung von Apples QuickTime) und eine Point-and-Click-Navigation, um es Benutzern zu ermöglichen, die Umgebung des Gebäudes zu erkunden, sogar das Parkhaus darunter und den gesamten Innenraum. Es war eine außergewöhnliche Website und eine unglaubliche Ressource. Sie gab jedem das Gefühl, das Opernhaus selbst „besucht" zu haben.

Le site de l'opéra de Sydney inclut des panoramas de 360° (à l'aide du lecteur QuickTime d'Apple) et une navigation par pointer-cliquer pour permettre aux visiteurs d'explorer l'extérieur du bâtiment, y compris le parking souterrain, ainsi que tous les espaces intérieurs. Ce formidable site constitue une ressource incroyable qui donne l'impression à quiconque l'ayant parcouru d'avoir visité le propre opéra.

Broken Saints

—

A revolution in storytelling

Broken Saints broke the mold for narrative and quickly gained a massive following. Its atmospheric blend of anime, comic-book text, and cinematic music and effects delivered something completely new. Divided into 24 chapters (later released as a 12-hour DVD), it gave people an absorbing fantasy/horror experience with the lights turned down, headphones on, and the volume cranked right up. This was one of the first times surfers queued up to await the release of each new chapter.

"Soon after the first few chapters were launched in 2001, mainstream media websites and traditional outlets began reporting on it. Apparently we were perceived as being pretty unique – a long-form Flash animation that was serialized, heady, and politically provocative – and folks like *Entertainment Weekly*, NPR, and TechTV quickly shared news of the work with their audiences. From there, the warm reception only grew, culminating in our surprise win at the Sundance Online Film Festival in 2003. Crazy times."

Brooke Burgess
Broken Saints

Broken Saints hatten mit der Erzählform gebrochen und schnell eine große Anhängerschaft erlangt. Ihre stimmungsvolle Mischung aus Anime, Comic-Text und kinematografischer Musik und Effekten bot etwas völlig Neues. Es war in 24 Kapitel unterteilt (später kam es als 12-stündige DVD heraus) und bot den Leuten ein faszinierendes Fantasy-/ Horror-Erlebnis mit herunterge-drehtem Licht, Kopfhörern und enormer Lautstärke. Dies war eines der ersten Male, dass die Surfer Schlange standen, um auf die Veröffentlichung jedes neuen Kapitels zu warten.

Broken Saints sort des sentiers battus en matière de narration et conquiert en peu de temps une masse critique. L'atmos-phère du site mêle anime, bande dessinée, musique cinéma-tique et effets pour former un ensemble totalement inédit. En 24 épisodes (plus tard sortira un DVD de 12 heures), la série offre une expérience captivante entre fantastique et terreur si le visiteur baisse la lumière, met ses casques et monte le volume. Fait inédit, les internautes font la queue pour la sortie de chaque nouvel épisode.

MediaMonks

—

One of the first
side-scrolling websites

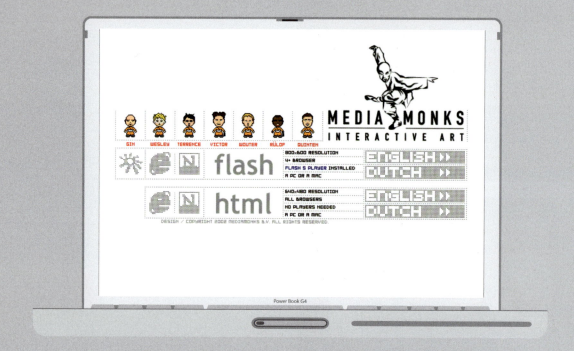

Every Monk (employee) at the agency got their own pixel person to feature on this website, which was one of the first to use side scrolling, an original idea if one that never really took off. Even at this early stage of Monk's development it was abundantly clear how the company's character shone through, while the monk personas have continued to be used in-house right up to the present time.

"Oh man, those were the days. Seeing your work be shared and spread globally was insane, and the messages and emails we got were amazing and a huge validation. It also brought home the power of the internet as we got to punch above our weight and started working for international clients even though we were just three 20-year-olds in a basement. That site propelled us from doing work for friends and family to suddenly running a business, so it's lodged in my mind as one of my favorite MM moments."

Wesley ter Haar
MediaMonks

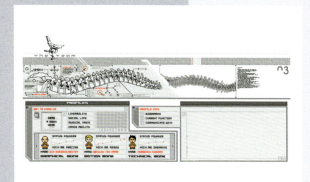

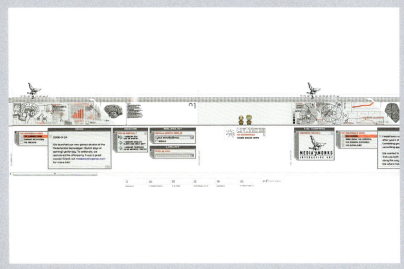

Jeder Monk (Angestellter) bei der Agentur bekam seine eigene Pixel-Person, um auf dieser Website zu erscheinen. Es war einer der ersten Sites, die das Side-Scrolling nutzte, eine originelle Idee, die sich nie wirklich durchsetzte. Schon in dieser frühen Phase von Monks Entwicklung wurde deutlich, wie der Charakter des Unternehmens durchschimmerte. Die Monk-Personen werden bis heute im Haus verwendet.

Chaque «Monk» (employé) de l'agence est représenté par son propre personnage, et le site est l'un des premiers à proposer un défilement horizontal, une idée originale qui n'a jamais vraiment décollé. Dès ses débuts, la compagnie laisse transparaître son identité de façon inéqui-voque, et les moines sont encore aujourd'hui utilisés en interne.

NOTABLE WEBSITE
LAUNCH
Wikipedia

GOOGLE
FACTS

Google Images launches, initially offering 250 million images

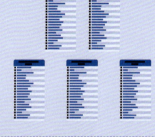

The first annual Google Zeitgeist is launched

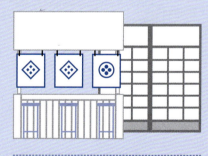

Top 5 Trends
- Nostradamus
- CNN
- World Trade Center
- Harry Potter
- Anthrax

Top 5 Trends

The Google logo is centered on the home-page

27+ billion searches

The opening of Google's first international office, in Tokyo

INTERNET COMMUNITY
September 11 attacks

After the 9/11 attacks, a number of
websites took their content down and
replaced it with a black page. This was
one of the first examples of the internet
community speaking out against terrorism
and was also a way of showing respect to
the victims and their families.

MOBILE EVOLUTION
Nokia 5510

Featured a full QWERTY
keyboard and digital
music player

2002/

The Year of Innovation and Reputations

2002/

—

The Year
of Innovation
and Reputations

—

Mjau Mjau

In 2002, websites developed a sense of attitude, but generally coupled with humor which made for a nice harmony. New interfaces and innovative types of navigation emerged, video-streaming became available directly into the browser window, and the first fully interactive page-turn appeared.

Many developers, such as Karl Ward, were happy to make their files and code available for free download, and this community spirit really spurred on the growth of Flash and the web.

The May 1 Reboot became a community-driven event whereby thousands of sites worldwide put up a holding page in late April and then a surge of new site launches appeared with the new month.

The original infinite-zooming navigation on Curtis McClain's So Fierce website was a great example of innovation. One click brought the next section into focus, with the following section waiting in the top right-hand corner.

Chewing Gum for the Eyes presented an entirely new way of moving content around as Kevin Newman's interface was seemingly infinite, making users feel as though they were being taken on a journey to the next click.

Croatia's Rootylicious website was like a first-person shoot-em-up as the zooms between each section were superb.

Guy Watson, Andy Foulds, and Jamie Macdonald teamed up to create Relevare, which was instantly acclaimed for its innovative zooming navigation.

I Must Create was the portfolio of Bryant Fernandez, and employed real-life visuals for navigation.

Sharply dividing users into likers and haters, the Enter button on the Blitz agency's site was tossed back and forth between two hands, making it very difficult to click on it, but also instantly memorable.

Shane Mielke's graceful and finely detailed personal website, Pixelranger, featured his Genesis Project, where Mielke's own photography breathed life into the scenes with subtle animations, effects, and sound.

With the arrival of Flash 5 and the ability to integrate streaming video into websites, Alexis Trepanier demonstrated how easy it was with a video intro that showed his hair slowly getting shorter as he talked visitors through his site.

ActionScript offered new options to those with coding capabilities, and CrashShop, with its 5,000+ lines of code, demonstrated its advanced levels of usability, Flash shop, and mouse scrollwheel interaction.

Complex scripting was combined with simplicity in the no circles game, earning the respect of other developers on various forums.

The Sean John website, with Flash intro by Fake Pilot, showed new levels of attitude and slick motion.

Gabe Rubin's Wrecked – Wreckage site ushered in the organic, grunge look and helped launch a trend for old style meeting new technology.

The Les Chinois site's mystical appeal invited users to interact with a man in a leather chair, where clicking on the navigation or dragging and dropping items, such as a packet of cigarettes, would result in him lighting one up.

Marines.com was SOTY for 2002. A progress bar displayed how much had been viewed, encouraging further exploration, while the motion, typography, design, and navigation all gelled together perfectly.

The Shockwave Player had almost disappeared since Flash but The Osbournes, in Shockwave, was one of the decade's highlights.

Complete with a swear-o-meter, the site allowed users to become any member of the Osbourne family, pets included, and move around the house, garden, beach, even the tour bus, whilst interacting with everything around them.

Technology was not just confined to the web, as people could follow *Mars Odyssey* in its search for water on Mars, and camera phones took off in the United States – almost two years later than in Japan, but nobody really guessed the impact they would have in the future.

May 1 Reboot

Pixelranger

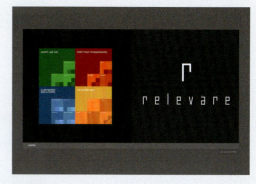
Relevare

So Fierce

Rootylicious

Im Jahr 2002 entwickelten die Websites eine gewisse Grundhaltung, die im Allgemeinen mit Humor verbunden war, was für schöne Harmonie sorgte. Neue Schnittstellen und innovative Navigationstypen entstanden, Video-Streaming war erstmals direkt im Browserfenster verfügbar und die erste interaktive Seitenumschaltung erschien.

Viele Entwickler, wie zum Beispiel Karl Ward, waren glücklich, ihre Dateien und Codes zum kostenlosen Download zur Verfügung zu stellen, und dieser Gemeinschaftsgeist spornte das Wachstum des Webs und Flash an.

Der Reboot vom 1. Mai wurde zu einer von der Community angetriebenen Veranstaltung, bei der Tausende von Websites Ende April eine Holdingseite erstellten und dann mit dem neuen Monat eine Welle neuer Website-Starts begann.

Die originelle Navigation mit unbegrenztem Zoom auf Curtis McClains So Fierce-Website war ein großartiges Beispiel für Innovation. Ein Klick auf die Navigation brachte den nächsten Abschnitt in den Fokus, der nach dem Warten in der oberen rechten Ecke erschien.

Chewing Gum for the Eyes zeigte eine völlig neue Art, Inhalte zu bewegen, da Kevin Newmans Benutzeroberfläche scheinbar unendlich war, was den Nutzern das Gefühl gab, auf eine Reise zum nächsten Klick mitgenommen zu werden.

Die Rootylicious Website aus Kroatien war wie ein Shoot-em-up in der ersten Person, da die Zooms zwischen den einzelnen Sektionen hervorragend waren.

Guy Watson, Andy Foulds und Jamie Macdonald taten sich zusammen und gründeten Relevare, was sofort für seine innovative Zoom-Navigation gefeiert wurde.

I Must Create war das Portfolio von Bryant Fernandez und verwendete reale Visuals für die Navigation.

Hier wurden die User entweder zum Liker oder zum Hater: Der Enter-Button auf der Website der Blitz-Agentur wurde zwischen zwei Händen hin und her geschleudert, was es sehr schwierig machte, darauf zu klicken, prägte sich aber auch sofort ein.

Shane Mielkes anmutige und fein detaillierte persönliche Website Pixelranger, zeigte sein Genesis-Projekt, in dem Mielkes eigene Fotografie den Szenen mit subtilen Animationen, Effekten und Sound Leben einhauchte.

Mit der Einführung von Flash 5 und der Möglichkeit, Videos in Webseiten zu integrieren, demonstrierte Alexis Trepanier, wie einfach es mit einem Video-Intro war, zu zeigen, dass sein Haar langsam kürzer wurde, während er die Besucher sprechend durch seine Seite führte.

ActionScript bot denjenigen mit Codierungsfähigkeit neue Optionen und CrashShop mit seinen mehr als 5000 Codezeilen demonstrierte die fortgeschrittenen benutzerfreundlichkeit, den Flash-Shop und die Maus-Scrollrad-Interaktion.

Im Spiel No Circles wurde komplexes Scripting mit Einfachheit kombiniert, wodurch es sich den Respekt anderer Entwickler in verschiedenen Foren verdiente.

Die Sean John Website mit Flash-Intro von Fake Pilot zeigte neue Level an Attitude und glatter Bewegung.

Gabe Rubins Wrecked – Wreckage Seite war der Beginn des organischen Grunge-Looks und half damit, einen Trend für den alten Stil in die neuen Technologien zu bringen.

Die Les Chinois Seite hatte eine mystische Anziehungskraft, da sie User dazu einlud, mit einem Mann auf einem Ledersuhl zu interagieren, sodass das Klicken auf die Navigation oder das Ziehen und Ablegen von Gegenständen auf ihn, zum Beispiel eine Schachtel Zigaretten, dazu führte, dass er eine anzündete und rauchte.

Marines.com war SOTY im Jahr 2002. Ein Fortschrittsbalken zeigte an, wie viel von der Website angesehen wurde, was weitere Erkundungen anregte, während Bewegung, Typografie, Design und Navigation perfekt ineinander übergingen.

Der Shockwave Player war seit Flash fast verschwunden aber The Osbournes in Shockwave war eines der Highlights des Jahrzehnts. Sie war komplett mit einem Fluch-O-Meter ausgestattet. Die Seite gab den Usern die Möglichkeit, ein Mitglied der Familie Osbourne zu werden. Sogar ein Haustier. Man konnte das Haus, den Garten, den Strand und sogar den Tourbus bewegen, während man mit allem und jedem um sich herum interagierte.

Diese Technologie war nicht nur auf das Internet beschränkt, da die Leute der *Mars Odyssey* auf der Suche nach Wasser auf dem Mars folgen konnten und Kamerahandys starteten in den Vereinigten Staaten – fast zwei Jahre nachdem sie in Japan schon auf dem Markt waren aber niemand ahnte, welche Auswirkungen sie in der Zukunft haben sollten.

The Year of Innovation and Reputations

—

I Must Create

Blitz

Sean John

"ActionScript offered new options to those with creative coding capabilities."

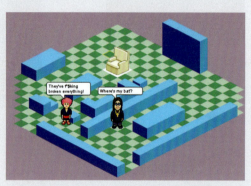

The Osbournes

Les Chinois

En 2002, les sites Web tentent d'exprimer un état d'esprit, en général avec une touche d'humour pour un résultat plus harmonieux. De nouvelles interfaces et des types innovants de navigation font leur apparition, il est possible de lire des vidéos directement dans un navigateur, et le premier rendu interactif d'une page tournée est une réalité.

Nombreux sont les développeurs comme Karl Ward publiant leurs fichiers et leur code en libre accès, un esprit communautaire qui stimule grandement la croissance de Flash et du Web.

Pour l'événement collectif « May 1 Reboot », des milliers de sites dans le monde publient une page d'attente fin avril ; le 1er mai, un lancement massif de nouveaux sites se produit.

Pour le site Web So Fierce, Curtis McClain innove avec une navigation en zoom infini. Un clic suffit pour ouvrir une nouvelle section, et celle qui vient ensuite reste en attente en haut à droite de l'écran.

Chewing Gum for the Eyes offre une manière totalement inédite de déplacer du contenu dans l'interface en apparence infinie créée par Kevin Newman.

Les visiteurs ont l'impression de suivre un chemin les menant au prochain clic.

Le site Web du studio croate Rootylicious fait penser à un jeu de tir à la première personne et les zooms entre les sections sont impressionnants.

Guy Watson, Andy Foulds et Jamie Macdonald s'associent pour créer le site de Relevare, immédiatement acclamé pour sa navigation innovante par zoom.

Le site I Must Create présente le portfolio de Bryant Fernandez et base sa navigation sur des illustrations de la vie réelle.

L'opinion est totalement divisée sur le bouton « Enter » dans le site de l'agence Blitz. Il est très compliqué de cliquer dessus car il fait des va-et-vient entre deux mains qui se le passent, mais il est aussi en cela inoubliable.

Pixelranger est le site Web élégant et truffé de détails que Shane Mielke crée pour présenter Genesis Project, un projet dans lequel ses photos prennent vie et produisent des scènes avec des animations subtiles, des effets et du son.

Avec l'arrivée de Flash 5 et la possibilité d'inclure des vidéos dans les sites Web, Alexis

Trepanier montre la simplicité de l'opération via une vidéo d'introduction où ses cheveux raccourcissent pendant qu'il commente son site.

ActionScript fournit de nouvelles options aux programmeurs. Conçu avec plus de 5 000 lignes de code, le site de CrashShop s'avère très convivial et inclut une boutique développée en Flash et des interactions via la molette de la souris.

Le jeu no circles combine des scripts complexes et une interface simple, se gagnant le respect des développeurs sur divers forums.

Avec une intro en Flash réalisée par Fake Pilot, le site de Sean John fait preuve de tout un état d'esprit et permet des déplacements fluides.

Signé par Gabe Rubin, le site Wrecked – Wreckage arbore une esthétique organique et grunge, et il lance une tendance mariant style ancien et nouvelles technologies.

Le site Les Chinois suit une approche mystique qui invite les visiteurs à interagir avec un homme dans une fauteuil en cuir. Quand ils cliquent sur des options de navigation ou font glisser des éléments, l'homme s'allume par exemple une cigarette.

Le site Marines.com est élu SOTY en 2002. Une barre de progression montre le pourcentage du contenu déjà consulté et encourage à poursuivre l'exploration. Les animations, la typographie, la conception et la navigation se complémentent parfaitement.

Le plug-in Shockwave Player avait presque disparu avec Flash, mais le site The Osbournes, conçu avec Shockwave, reste l'une des créations marquantes de la décennie. Assorti d'un compteur de gros mots, le site permet aux visiteurs de devenir membre de la famille Osbourne (animaux inclus) et de se déplacer dans la maison, le jardin, sur la plage et même en bus, tout en interagissant avec tous les éléments rencontrés.

La technologie ne se cantonne plus au Web : les internautes peuvent suivre *Mars Odyssey* dans sa mission pour détecter la présence éventuelle d'eau sur Mars, et des téléphones équipés d'un appareil photo apparaissent aux États-Unis, soit près de deux ans après le Japon, sans que personne ne soupçonne alors leur impact à l'avenir.

∅8 Facts of the year

Number of internet users:
662 million, 10.5% of the
world population

Number of websites:
38.7 million

World news:
the Euro currency begins
for 12 EU countries

Website with most traffic:
Aol.com

Tech hardware:
Earth Simulator, at $600m,
becomes the fastest
supercomputer

Tech software:
Xbox Live launches

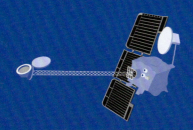

Other tech:
Mars Odyssey finds signs
of water on Mars

Highest-grossing film:
The Lord of the Rings:
The Two Towers

—

Who's We Studios

—

Attitude comes to the web

The Who's We Studios site was eye-catching and a clear testament to their slogan "information through stimulation". The splash page challenge "Do you feel lucky punk? Well do ya?" was followed by the logo orb turning into a huge arsenal of weapons, pointing at the user, and asking if they wanted to enter the broadband version of the site.

The rolling finger loader was clever in itself but also an indicator of how creative the rest of the site was. The whole attitude of the site was stamped with a love-it-or-hate-it arrogance, for example, when the 'who are we' button was clicked, a UFO flew across the screen and deposited a giant rock which said "THE BEST".

"We launched Who's We Studios on May 1, 2002 during the May 1 Reboot. The reaction was overwhelming. We received literally hundreds of emails on a daily basis for many months with fan mail that ranged from praise and support for us to speaking at universities to images of people tattooing themselves with our logo. Looking back, admittedly, it made us feel like rock stars. The web went through a renaissance of sorts when Flash went mainstream. It was a creative renaissance that sparked amazing conferences and great creative online destinations like FWA."

Fredo Silva
Who's We Studios

Die Who's We Studios-Seite war ein Blickfang und ein klares Bekenntnis zu ihrem Slogan „Information durch Stimulation". Die Splash Page Challenge „Do you feel lucky punk? Well do ya? (Fühlst du dich glücklich Punk? Ja echt?) gefolgt von der Logo-Kugel, die sich in ein riesiges Waffenarsenal verwandelte, auf den User zeigte und fragte, ob er die Breitband-

Version der Seite haben möchte. Der rollende Finger-Lader war an sich schon clever aber auch ein Hinweis darauf, wie kreativ der Rest der Seite war. Die ganze Haltung der Seite war geprägt von einer Hassliebe oder Arroganz, zum Beispiel, wenn der „who are we" Button geklickt wurde und ein UFO über den Bildschirm flog und einen riesigen Felsen ablegte, auf dem stand „THE BEST".

Le site de Who's We Studios est attrayant et à l'image de leur slogan «information through stimulation». Après l'accroche «Do you feel lucky punk? Well do ya?» (qui s'entend comme «Tu tentes ta chance? Oui ou non?») dans la page de garde, le logo sphérique dégaine un arsenal d'armes visant le visiteur et demandant s'il veut ouvrir la version haut débit du site.

Pendant le chargement, la main robotique qui tapote des doigts fait présager de la créativité du reste du site. La personnalité affichée fait que certains aiment et d'autres détestent l'arrogance qui en ressort: par exemple, en cliquant sur le bouton «who are we», un OVNI traverse l'écran et dépose un gros rocher sur lequel est inscrit «THE BEST».

Perfect Fools

—

The original
page-turn effect

This was the first online effect to mimic turning the page of a book, by allowing the site's users to grab the corner of a page and drag it like a page from a real book. It was perfectly executed and became an instant success, with many people wanting the script for it. The site won Best Navigation at Flash Forward and the effect became very popular. One company even started selling a page flip-book template.

"I was obsessed with the idea of creating stuff that recreated the feeling of touching something. I remember seeing a really bad e-learning CD-ROM project done in Director that had something that was just a page-flip transition on click. I was impressed and by mistake tried to drag the corner and it felt like it worked. But it was just a basic transition. Anyway I just took what I saw and tried to recreate it with some basic physics."

Tony Högqvist
Perfect Fools

Dies war der erste Online-Effekt, der die Seite eines Buches nachbildete, indem er den Benutzern der Site erlaubte, die Ecke einer Seite zu greifen und sie wie eine Seite aus einem echten Buch umzublättern. Es war perfekt ausgeführt und wurde zu einem sofortigen Erfolg, da viele Leute das Skript dafür wollten. Die Site gewann die beste Navigation bei Flash Forward und der Effekt wurde sehr populär. Eine Firma begann sogar, eine Seiten-Flip-Book-Vorlage zu verkaufen.

Il s'agit du premier effet en ligne à imiter le geste pour tourner une page : les internautes peuvent ainsi saisir un coin et le déplacer comme ils le feraient avec un vrai livre. L'exécution est parfaite et fait tout de suite l'unanimité, au point que beaucoup veulent s'en procurer le script. Le site remporte le prix Flash Forward de la meilleure navigation et l'effet gagne une grande popularité. Une société commercialise même un modèle de folioscope.

Looplabs

—

The original online music mixer

With hundreds of readily available music loops to play with and an easy interface to mix them, Looplabs was the first online tool in this field. It was also an early example of bringing something that was otherwise only available to those with healthy budgets – professional music mixing and creation – to the masses via the web. The Looplabs audio engine went on to be incorporated in the sites for Coca-Cola, Maverick Records, Bacardi DJ, and many more, winning accolades the world over.

"Looplabs was the web's first music-making experience – a music studio in your browser – birthing interactive online audio experiences. It empowered and entertained millions [and] gave a musical voice to a connected world of all ages and walks of life. Looplabs was famously demo'd by Steve Jobs when he launched Safari. What perhaps best captures the empowerment of the web at that time was Looplabs' Webby Award acceptance speech: 'Everyone deserves to make music'."

Craig Swann
Crash!Media

Mit Hunderten von leicht verfügbaren Music-Loops zum Spielen und einer einfachen Schnittstelle, um sie zu mischen, war Looplabs das erste Online-Tool in diesem Bereich. Es war ein frühes Beispiel dafür, etwas zu bringen, das sonst nur denjenigen zur Verfügung stand, die ein hohes Budget hatten – professionelles Mischen und Kreieren von Musik – und für die Massen nur über das Internet. Die Audiomaschine von Looplabs wurde auf den Seiten von Coca-Cola, Maverick Records, Bacardi DJ und vielen anderen eingebaut und bekam Auszeichnungen auf der ganzen Welt.

En offrant des centaines de boucles musicales et une interface simple pour les mixer, Looplabs est le premier outil en ligne en la matière. C'est aussi un cas précoce de démocratisation d'un marché jusqu'alors réservé à ceux en ayant les moyens : proposer au grand public un outil professionnel de création musicale et de mixage sur le Web. Le moteur audio de Looplabs est plus tard intégré dans les sites de Coca-Cola, Maverick Records, Bacardi DJ et bien d'autres, bénéficiant d'une reconnaissance mondiale.

—

Lexus Minority Report

—

A first to use zooming motion blur transitions

While promoting the Lexus Maglev sports car from the year 2054, and the release of the film *Minority Report*, this website had users trying to escape being framed for a murder committed some time in the future. It was one of the first sites to use zooming motion blurs between scenes, and also seamless video integration, rather than pop-up video.

"The promotional site for Lexus Cars U.S. was primarily intended to communicate their involvement in the Steven Spielberg film *Minority Report*. Lexus, in association with the film's production designer, developed all the cars used in the film. The site aimed not only to show these cars but also to give you an insight into the fascinating world of *Minority Report*. What united all of our film projects was that they were designed to be an extension of the film on the web and could be enjoyed before, after, or independently of the film."

Alexandra Jugovic
Hi-ReS!

Während der Lexus Maglev Sportwagen aus dem Jahr 2054 vorgestellt wurde und der Film *Minority Report* herauskam, hatte diese Website User, die versuchen mussten zu fliehen, um nicht wegen eines Mordfalls gefasst zu werden, der in der Zukunft begangen werden würde. Es war eine der ersten Websites, die Zoom-Bewegungsunschärfen zwischen Szenen und auch nahtlose Videointegration anstelle von Pop-Up-Videos verwendete.

Tout en faisant la promotion de la voiture de sport Lexus Maglev depuis l'année 2054 et de la sortie du film *Minority Report*, ce site Web permet aux internautes d'essayer de ne pas être inculpés pour un meurtre commis dans le futur. C'est l'un des premiers sites à utiliser le flou cinétique avec zoom entre les scènes, ainsi qu'une intégration vidéo homogène au lieu de vidéos en pop-up.

Conspiracy Games

—

The first Emergency System and self-destruction website

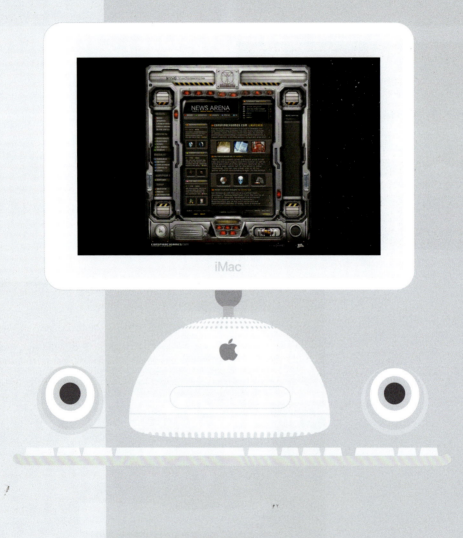

Interactive features in this game included an 'Emergency System' which, when activated, gave the user two minutes to find a certain element in the site or it would all self-destruct and eject the user. Conspiracy also had buttons that appeared to move about organically as the user hovered the mouse over them, along with lots to explore and large amounts of 3D content.

"This site was quite spectacular. I mean instead of keeping the user on the site we kicked them out if they pressed the wrong button and didn't find the hidden 'item'. Robot arms crashed the screen in front of you. 404-pages with 'censured' robots gave you the finger. It had it all… It even ended up in a German museum. The site-guide, a droid explaining all the features on the site, could stop at any time and self-destruct with a massive explosion."

Johan Adolfsson
Fantasy Interfaces; Forefront Consulting Group

Interaktive Funktionen in diesem Spiel enthielten ein „Notfall-System", das, wenn es aktiviert wurde, dem User zwei Minuten Zeit gab, um ein bestimmtes Element auf der Website zu finden oder es zerstörte alles und warf den User heraus. Conspiracy hatte auch Buttons, die sich organisch zu bewegen schienen, während der Benutzer die Maus über sie bewegte. Es gab viel zu entdecken und großen Mengen an 3D-Inhalten.

Parmi les fonctions interactives de ce jeu, celle d'un système d'urgence laisse deux minutes à l'utilisateur pour trouver un élément déterminé dans le site avant une auto-destruction et l'expulsion de l'internaute.

Des boutons bougent de façon organique quand le curseur est placé dessus, et le contenu est dense et riche en 3D.

Yulia Nau

—

The original video-enhanced mouse movement

This website for the German techno DJ Yulia Nau, which featured a custom-built mixing desk, was created by South Africa's Wireframe. It pioneered the use of video-enhanced mouse movement as users were presented with quality video-frame sequences of a tattooed Nau, which reacted to every movement of their mouse.

"Yulia Nau was a site that helped fuel so much creativity in the industry at the time, and still reminds us of how innovative the early days of the web really were. Everything, from the cursor-following dragon on the landing page, to the transmogrifying mouse-enabled video header and sound mixer, flooded forums with questions, stimulated thirsty minds, and kicked off the careers of many prominent programmers. Yulia Nau, despite the passing of time, still inspires after 15+ years."

Joshua Corliss
Martin Agency
(Industry quote provided in the absence
of the site's creators)

Diese Website für die deutsche Techno-DJane Yulia Nau, die mit einem speziell angefertigten Mischpult ausgestattet war, stammt von Wireframe aus Südafrika. Es war der Wegbereiter für die Verwendung von Video-verbesserter Mausbewegung, da den Benutzern hochwertige Video-Frame-Sequenzen einer tätowierten Nau präsentiert wurden, die auf jede Bewegung der Maus reagierte.

Créé par l'agence sud-africaine Wireframe, ce site Web pour la DJ techno allemande Yulia Nau inclut une table de mixage personnalisée. Il innove en synchronisant le traitement de séquences d'images vidéo de qualité du corps tatoué de Nau aux mouvements de la souris.

2002/
—

Dotu

—

The original bouncy
drag menus

Defenders of the Universe was a highly interactive user experience noted for its bouncy drag menus. As the site opened, a wooden sign emerged from a cauldron, saying, "Just grab something". A demo then showed how to grab parts of the interface and drag them into position. This was the type of site gamers loved as the interaction gave results and felt similar to computer games of the day.

"I studied old animation books (*The Illusion of Life: Disney Animation*) to get the right illusion of a bounce. A team effort as always, Krister Karlsson – 3D; me – animation/interaction; and David Martin holding on to the vision and always pushing the quality, giving us the time to make it perfect. As always we went over budget to push this piece to the limit. That was always the case back then."

Johan Adolfsson
Fantasy Interfaces; Forefront Consulting Group

Defenders of the Universe war ein stark interaktives Benutzererlebnis, das für seine springenden Drag-Menüs bekannt wurde. Beim Öffnen der Seite kam ein Holzschild aus einem Kessel und sagte, „Just grab something" (Nimm Dir Etwas). Eine Demo zeigte dann, wie man Teile der Oberfläche greift und sie in die richtige Position zieht. Dies war die Art von Seite, die von Gamern geliebt wurde, da die Interaktion Ergebnisse brachte und den Computerspielen des heutigen Tages sehr ähnlich war.

Le site Defenders of the Universe offre une expérience hautement interactive et une interface remarquée pour ses menus dynamiques. À son ouverture sort d'un chaudron un panneau en bois où est inscrit « Just grab something » (saisissez quelque chose). Une démo illustre comment saisir des parties de l'interface et les faire glisser ailleurs. Ce type de site plaît aux joueurs qui peuvent interagir et retrouver des sensations comparables aux jeux sur ordinateur de l'époque.

Neostream VII

—

50,000 volts of animation

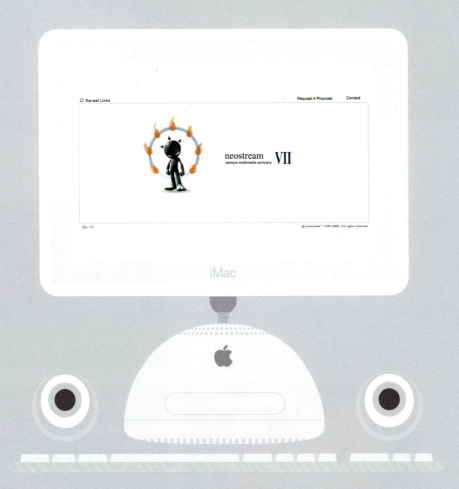

One of the most anticipated launches on the web, Neostream VII went on to collect the FWA People's Choice Award for 2002. The site oozed character from the moment the Neostream mascot shook its finger at the user. It was possible to 'slap' this mascot around by moving the mouse across it backwards and forwards. Every area of the site boasted outstanding motion, animation, and sound, and overall it is still a favorite of many web surfers today.

"We experimented much more with this starting from a deeper level of concept, creating our character 'Shockboy' and trying to bring it to life not just with fancy motion graphics and animation but through actual user interaction and engagement. By this time, Flash's technical features had become much more advanced… The true value was that this site united all our development staff — all committed towards a single goal and purpose regardless of their roles and responsibilities."

Johnny Choi
Neostream

Einer der am meisten erwarteten Veröffentlichungen im Internet, Neostream VII, fuhr fort, den FWA People's Choice Award für 2002 einzuheimsen. Die Seite verströmte von dem Moment an Charakter, als das Neostream Maskottchen seinen Finger vor den Augen den Nutzers bewegte.

Es war möglich, das Maskottchen zu „schlagen", indem man die Maus hin und her bewegte. Jeder Bereich der Website bot hervorragende Bewegung, Animation und Sound und insgesamt ist es immer noch eine Lieblings-Site vieler Web-Surfer heutzutage.

Le site de Neostream VII est l'un des lancements les plus attendus et récolte en 2002 le People's Choice Award des FWA. Il annonce l'état d'esprit dès l'instant que la mascotte de la compagnie agite son doigt en direction du visiteur, qui peut lui donner des tapes en bougeant la souris

dessus, en avant et en arrière. Chaque section du site est truffée d'éléments en mouvement, d'animations et d'effets sonores, et cette création est aujourd'hui encore un grand favori des internautes.

—

Fred Perry

—

The first 100% Flash e-commerce shopping solution

The Fred Perry e-commerce site was a major breakthrough for Flash: a complete online shopping experience run seamlessly through a Flash interface, with no jumping into an HTML pop-up window to complete the transaction.

The site didn't get the acclaim it deserved, since this could easily have been the start of a new trend in similar platforms. In fact it didn't survive and was, perhaps, a little too early with its innovation.

"The website was built with Flash to allow the use of specific weights of Helvetica. It gave us very close control over other areas of how the site looked and behaved too. That control wasn't available with HTML at the time. There was no 'paralysis by analysis' of endless Stats. We had open chats about ideas, and if they were good, we tried them. The Model T Ford, Helvetica Typeface, Eames Chair, Land Rover Defender, Guggenheim, Fred Perry shirt, Apple Mac, and iPhone all came from applied pioneering thought – not one of them came from a Stat."

James Daly
De Facto

Die Fred Perry e-commerce Site war ein großer Durchbruch für Flash: Ein komplettes Online-Shopping-Erlebnis lief nahtlos über eine Flash-Oberfläche, ohne in ein HTML-Popup-Fenster zu springen, um die Transaktion abzuschließen. Die Seite erhielt nicht den Beifall, den sie verdient hätte, denn es hätte leicht der Beginn eines neuen Trends auf ähnlichen Plattformen gewesen sein können. Tatsächlich überlebte sie nicht und war vielleicht ein bisschen zu früh mit ihrer Innovation.

Le site e-commerce de Fred Perry suppose une révolution de taille pour Flash : l'expérience d'achat en ligne s'effectue en toute fluidité dans une interface Flash, sans fenêtre pop-up en HTML pour terminer la transaction. Le site n'est pas accueilli avec les honneurs qu'il mérite, alors qu'il aurait très bien pu signifier le début d'une tendance sur des plates-formes similaires. Il ne survit pas, sans doute pour être un peu trop en avance sur son temps.

2002/
—

Eagle F1

—

The first to use streaming video integration

With the launch of Flash 5 it became possible to integrate video within a website, removing the need to pop out into a new window and embed the video with Apple's QuickTime. EVB (Evolution Bureau) was the first to demonstrate this with the Eagle F1 website which gave users the option of driving around three different tracks with racing legend Derek Bell.

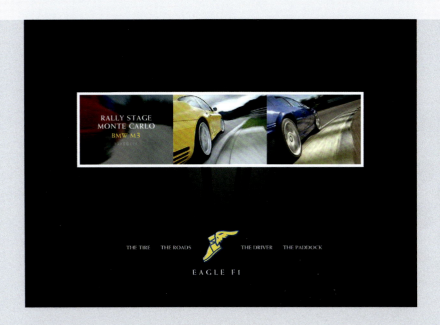

"To build the site, we took video that was shot on six cameras mounted on different high-end sports cars, driven by race commentator Derek Bell, on three of the world's best racetracks. We pulled speed, g-force, track position, and gear from the cars. This was the first commercial use of the Flash Communication Server and the engineers from Macromedia told us that they did not think their platform could handle what we wanted to do. We moved ahead and gave it a shot anyway and were blown away by the results."

Daniel Stein
EVB

Mit dem Start von Flash 5 wurde es auch möglich, Videos auf einer Website zu integrieren. Es musste nicht mehr in ein neues Fenster gewechselt werden, um das Video mit QuickTime von Apple einzubetten. EVB (Evolution Bureau) war der Erste, der dies mit der Eagle F1-Website demonstrierte, die den Usern die Möglichkeit gab, mit der Renn-legende Derek Bell drei verschie-dene Strecken zu fahren.

Le lancement de Flash 5 permet d'inclure des vidéos dans un site Web, ce qui élimine le besoin d'ouvrir une fenêtre pop-up et d'intégrer la vidéo dans Quick-Time d'Apple. EVB (Evolution Bureau) est le premier à en faire la démonstration avec le site Web Eagle F1 qui permet aux utilisateurs de conduire sur trois pistes différentes avec la légende automobile Derek Bell.

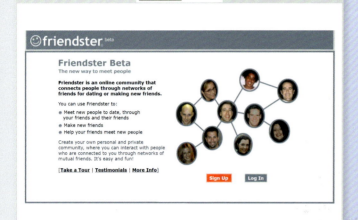

NOTABLE WEBSITE LANGUAGE
NOTABLE WEBSITE LAUNCH
Friendster

GOOGLE FACTS

Google News launches

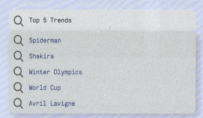

Google Labs launches

The physical Google Search Appliance is launched

Top 5 Trends

Froogle launches (later renamed Google Shopping)

API

A set of Google APIs is released for developers to query

INTERNET COMMUNITY
Creative Commons launches

The intention behind the launch of Creative Commons was to promote the innovative reuse of all sorts of intellectual works. The first project was to offer a free set of copyright licenses to the public.

MOBILE EVOLUTION
Sanyo SCP-5300

The first camera phone to reach the United States

2003/

The Year of Anticipation

2003/

The Year of Anticipation

Ford F-150

Flash was now fully established and totally dominated web design, although Flash intros and banners still had a bad reputation.

A prime example of the way the web was heading was seen in the promotional site for the Ford F-150 pickup truck, which acted like a walkthrough/talkthrough, guiding users around the vehicle with polished video and 3D animations.

I-Shake-U, a promotional website for Mitsubishi, was a first to employ mouse-shake interaction for users to help a couch potato escape from his flat and evolve into a higher form of existence.

For some time there had been websites that took over the user's cursor or changed it into something different. When Playmore launched for Xbox this idea was adapted for the mouse cursor, showing a real, videoed mouse which responded to the user's actions.

The advanced design skills and programming of group94's site took the web community by storm, and was one of the first to show visitors how to use the site, by taking the cursor away and indicating where it should move to. Usability was also given a thumbs-up by enabling interaction with the back and forward browser button in Internet Explorer.

2Advanced were masters of hype and for their new site posted a countdown clock. When it reached zero, some people were greeted with "The page cannot be displayed" because of the unrivaled number of requests made on their servers.

The NEC-sponsored website Ecotonoha encouraged visitors to sign its Word Tree to support tree-planting on Kangaroo Island, Australia. The site's virtual tree grew every time someone signed it, and for every 100 signatures the sponsoring company planted a real tree in an early example of charity-crowdfunding.

The wonderfully calm site of Pure Pulse Studio incorporated the first use of 'live' pencil drawings. By contrast, the Johnny Hollow site was dark and animated with realistic 3D insect graphics. Word puzzles had to be solved to gain access to extra features and bonus downloads, and the site was an early example of musicians making their debut independently via the web.

Another atmospheric, organic website, complete with realistic buzzing fly, was that of 247 Media Studios, the creative and technical development outlet of German designer Ingo Ramin. Ramin developed a number of striking websites, including the one for America's 'number-one pin-up sensation', Lana Landis, before completely disappearing from the web design community.

Jonathan Clark's photography project was shot in the cemeteries of Streatham and Lambeth, London, over a two-year period. The images were extremely evocative and were made more vivid by the use of subtle animations, ambient music, and sound effects.

In the year the Iraq War began, the internet gave the public a voice, enabling people to share photos, views, and information where previously they'd had to rely on mass media. The BBC's news agency was one of the first to reach out to the public and ask for photos to be submitted, which were later displayed in a gallery on its website.

"Flash was now fully established and totally dominated web design."

Playmore

2Advanced

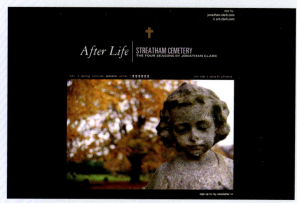

After Life

Flash war nun vollständig etabliert und dominierte das Webdesign obwohl Flash Intros und Banner immer noch einen schlechten Ruf hatten.

Ein Paradebeispiel für die Art und Weise und für die Richtung, in die sich das Internet bewegte, war auf der Werbeseite für den Ford F-150 Pick-up zu sehen, die wie ein Walkthrough/Talkthrough funktionierte und die Nutzer mit polierten Video- und 3D-Animationen um das Fahrzeug herum führte.

I-Shake-U, eine werbende Website für Mitsubishi, war eine der ersten, die Maus-Shake-Interaktionen nutzte, um einem Stubenhocker zu helfen, seiner Wohnung zu entkommen und sich zu einer höheren Existenzform zu entwickeln.

Eine Zeit lang gab es Websites, die den Mauszeiger des Benutzers übernahmen oder ihn in etwas Anderes verwandelten. Als Playmore für Xbox diese Idee entwickelte, wurde der Mauszeiger angepasst und

zeigte eine echte Maus mit Video, die auf die Aktionen des Benutzers reagierte.

Die fortgeschrittenen Designfähigkeiten und die Programmierung der Website von group94 eroberten die Web-Community im Sturm und war eine der ersten, die den Besuchern zeigte, wie die Seite zu nutzen war, indem sie den Cursor wegnahmen und angaben, wohin er sich bewegen sollte. Die Benutzerfreundlichkeit wurde ebenfalls verbessert, indem die Interaktion mit der vor und zurück Browserschaltfläche im Internet Explorer aktiviert wurde.

2Advanced waren Meister des Hypes und für ihre neue Website stellten sie eine Countdown-Uhr ein. Als diese Null erreichte, wurden einige Leute begrüßt mit „Die Seite kann nicht angezeigt werden", aufgrund der unübertroffenen Anzahl von Anfragen auf ihren Servern.

Die von NEC unterstützte Website von Ecotonoha forderte die Besucher auf, einen Wort-

baum zu unterzeichnen, um das Baumpflanzen auf Kangaroo Island, Australien, zu unterstützen. Der virtuelle Baum der Seite wuchs jedes Mal, wenn jemand unterzeichnete und alle 100 Unterschriften pflanzte die Sponsoring Company einen echten Baum als frühes Beispiel des Charity-Crowdfunding.

Die wunderbar ruhige Seite von Pure Pulse Studios zeigte die erste Verwendung von „live" Bleistiftzeichnungen. Im Gegensatz dazu war die Site von Johnny Hollow dunkel und animiert mit realistischen 3D-Insektengrafiken. Word-Rätsel mussten gelöst werden, um Zugang zu zusätzlichen Funktionen und Bonus-Downloads zu erhalten. Die Seite war ein frühes Beispiel für Musiker, die ihr Debüt unabhängig über das Internet gaben.

Eine weitere atmosphärische, organische Website, komplett mit realistischen summenden Fliegen, war die der 247 Media Studios, der kreativen und technischen Entwicklung des

deutschen Designers Ingo Ramin. Ramin entwickelte eine Reihe auffälliger Websites, darunter die für Amerikas „Nummer eins Pin-up Sensation" Lana Landis, bevor er komplett aus der Webdesign-Community verschwand.

Jonathan Clarks Fotografie-Projekt wurde auf den Friedhöfen von Streatham und Lambeth in London über einen Zeitraum von zwei Jahren aufgenommen. Die Bilder waren extrem evokativ und wurden durch subtile Animationen, Ambient-Musik und Soundeffekte noch lebendiger.

In dem Jahr, in dem der Irakkrieg begann, gab das Internet der Öffentlichkeit eine Stimme, die es Menschen ermöglichte, Fotos, Ansichten und Informationen zu teilen, wofür sie zuvor auf Massenmedien angewiesen waren. Die BBC-Nachrichtenagentur war eine der ersten, die sich an die Öffentlichkeit wandte und um die Einreichung von Fotos bat, die später in einer Galerie auf ihrer Website gezeigt wurden.

The Year of Anticipation
—

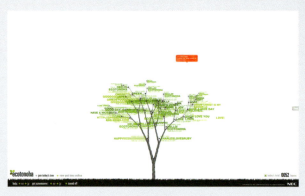

Ecotonoha

Lana Landis

"The BBC's news agency was one of the first to reach out to the public and ask for photos."

Johnny Hollow

Flash est désormais vraiment implanté et omniprésent dans les conceptions Web, même si les intros et les bannières dans cette technologie ont toujours mauvaise presse.

Le site promotionnel du pick-up Ford F-150 illustre parfaitement le chemin que prend le Web à cette époque. Un guide explique en détails les caractéristiques du véhicule à l'aide de vidéos bien ficelées et d'animations 3D.

I-Shake-U, site promotionnel de Mitsubishi, est l'un des premiers à permettre une interaction en secouant la souris. Les utilisateurs peuvent ainsi aider un accro du canapé à sortir de chez lui pour mener une vie plus remplie.

Pendant un temps, des sites prennent le contrôle du curseur ou permettent en changer la forme. Quand Playmore lance le site pour Xbox, une véritable souris en vidéo obéit aux actions de l'utilisateur.

Le site de group94 est un exercice complexe de conception et de programmation qui conquiert totalement la communauté Web. Il est aussi l'un des premiers à expliquer aux visiteurs comment naviguer en éloignant le curseur et en montrant à quel endroit le placer. La convivialité est également applaudie grâce à l'interaction avec les boutons Précédent et Suivant d'Internet Explorer.

Experte en médiatisation, l'équipe de 2Advanced décide d'inclure un compte à rebours dans son nouveau site. Quand il arrive à zéro, certains visiteurs obtiennent un message d'erreur avertissant que la page ne peut pas être affichée en raison du nombre sans pareil de demandes envoyées à ses serveurs.

Le site Web d'Ecotonoha sponsorisé par NEC encourage les visiteurs à signer pour soutenir la reforestation de l'Île Kangourou, en Australie. Un arbre virtuel grandit chaque fois que

quelqu'un signe et quand 100 signatures sont obtenues, un arbre est planté par l'entreprise sponsor comme aboutissement de cet exemple précoce de financement participatif.

Le site extrêmement zen de Pure Pulse Studio intègre la première fonctionnalité de dessin au crayon en direct. Le site de Johnny Hollow est pour sa part sombre et animé avec des graphismes réalistes d'insectes en 3D. Des mots mystères doivent être trouvés pour accéder à d'autres fonctions et à des téléchargements gratuits, et la conception montre comment des musiciens font leurs débuts en indépendants grâce au Web.

Dégageant lui aussi une atmosphère, cet autre site organique est assorti d'une mouche bourdonnante très réaliste. Il est signé par 247 Media Studios, l'exutoire créatif et technique du concepteur allemand Ingo Ramin. Avant de disparaître complètement de la communauté

Web, Ramin est l'auteur de divers sites marquants, dont celui pour Lana Landis, la première pin-up d'Amérique.

Le projet photographique sur plus de deux ans de Jonathan Clark porte sur les cimetières londoniens de Streatham et Lambeth. Les images sont extrêmement évocatrices et gagnent en expressivité grâce à des animations subtiles, une musique d'ambiance et des effets sonores.

L'année où la guerre en Irak est déclarée, Internet donne une voix au grand public qui peut alors partager des photos, des opinions et des informations au lieu de seulement compter sur les médias. L'agence de presse de la BBC est l'une des premières à demander aux internautes d'envoyer des photos en vue de les publier dans une galerie sur son site Web.

08 Facts of the year

Number of internet users:
778.5 million, 12.2% of
the world population

Number of websites:
40.9 million

World news:
the start of the Iraq War

Website with most traffic:
Yahoo.com

Tech hardware:
Blu-ray optical discs
are released

Tech software:
Android Inc is founded

Other tech:
Apple launches its iTunes
Music Store

Highest-grossing film:
The Lord of the Rings:
The Return of the King

Tokyoplastic

—

Instant fame and stardom

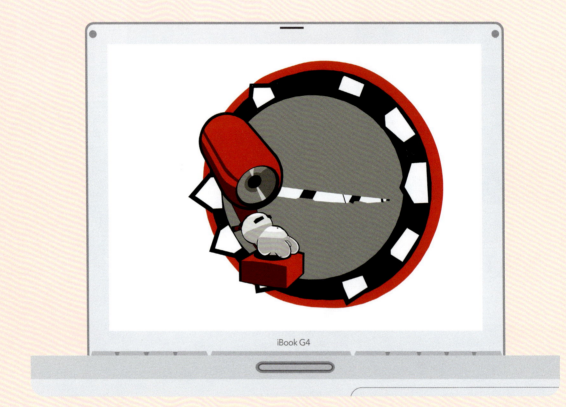

iBook G4

Tokyoplastic was one of the rare sites that gave an adrenaline rush – and a fright too – when the loaded graphic was clicked, as it literally swallowed users up. The studio found instant web stardom and rapidly landed huge clients such as MTV. The site was intriguing and showed what vector graphics could do, with Flash, 3D, sound, and effects.

"When we started out we didn't have a clue about coding, we knew Photoshop and After Effects and 3D Studio Max. Back then Flash was like a vector-pooping version of those applications and the whole world of coding was broken down into [simple] drag-and-drop building blocks. It opened up a whole new world of creation for a ton of people and looking back it seems like that happened in quite a brief window. To do the same stuff now you'd have to scale a much steeper learning curve."

Sam Lanyon Jones
Tokyoplastic

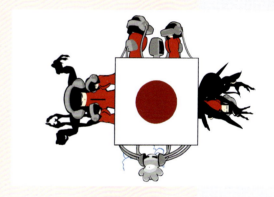

Tokyoplastic war eine der seltenen Seiten, die einem einen Adrenalinstoß gaben – und auch erschreckte – wenn die geladene Grafik angeklickt wurde, wurde der Internetnutzer buchstäblich verschluckt. Das Studio wurde schlagartig berühmt und bekam schnell riesige Kunden wie zum Beispiel MTV. Die Seite war faszinierend und zeigte, was man mit Vektorgrafiken mit Flash, 3D, Sound und Effekten erreichen konnte.

Le site de tokyoplastic est l'un des rares à provoquer une telle montée d'adrénaline (et une certaine peur aussi) au moment de cliquer sur le graphisme chargé qui engloutit littéralement l'utilisateur. Le studio remporte immédiatement un grand succès sur le Web et décroche très vite de gros clients comme MTV. Le site fascine et montre tout le potentiel des graphiques vectoriels avec Flash, du 3D, du son et des effets.

Road Runner

—

The most powerful portal of its time

iBook G4

A genuine groundbreaker, Time Warner's large Road Runner portal had flawless graphical detail and animations and provided content-at-a-click in the selected area without constant full-page reloads. It was also a rarity for transcending the typical anonymity of portals with its warm setting, welcoming voice, and customizable features.

"The RR project said screw you to internet standards, slow computers, low-resolution screens, and processors that could not run Flash fast enough. It was insane, it pushed the limits of what a news, video, and content site could be. It was also the first site to deliver Google search results within a Flash interface. It offered an experience where you could personalize everything from news content to video and even your stocks."

John Ballinger
Fantasy Interfaces; AskNicely

Ein echter Wegbereiter, Time Warners großes Road Runner Portal, hatte makellose grafische Details und Animationen und bot einen Inhalt-auf-einen-Klick im ausgewählten Bereich, ohne ständige Neuladevorgänge auf der ganzen Seite. Es war auch eine Seltenheit, die typische Anonymität von Portalen mit seiner warmen Umgebung, einladenden Stimme und anpassbaren Funktionen zu überwinden.

Le vaste portail Road Runner de Time Warner est tout bonnement révolutionnaire, avec un niveau de détail graphique et des animations irréprochables. Son contenu est accessible d'un simple clic dans la section sélectionnée sans attendre que toute la page se charge à nouveau. Il se démarque aussi de l'habituel look impersonnel des portails grâce son décor agréable, une voix chaleureuse et des fonctions personnalisables.

2003/
—

Globulos

—

The original multi-person
real-time experience

This was one of the earliest multi-player games, where users could challenge or watch other gamers competing in real time. The cartoon-style visuals and game-play were perfect and totally original, while the Los Globulos characters were referred to as "strange fools" who enjoyed bumping into each other.

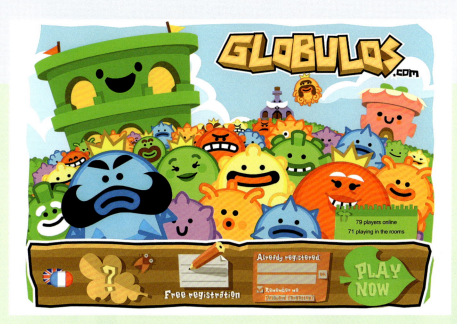

"When we launched Globulos it was really special. Our server kept crashing and the more it would crash the more people would refresh their web page and that would make the server crash again! ... And what is great is that people still play the game today on globulos.com! We sure have fond memories of Flash. I think Flash is the best piece of software that has ever existed."

Alexandre Houdent
Globulos

Dies war eines der frühesten Multiplayer-Spiele, bei denen User andere Spieler in Echtzeit herausfordern oder beobachten konnten. Die Visuals im Cartoon-Stil und das Gameplay waren perfekt und absolut originell, während die Charaktere von Los Globulos als „seltsame Blödmänner" bezeichnet wurden, die es genossen, sich anzurempeln.

Il s'agit de l'un des tous premiers jeux multi-joueurs permettant aux utilisateurs de se lancer des défis ou d'observer des participants s'affronter en temps réel. L'esthétique de bande dessinée et la jouabilité fonctionnent à merveille et sont pleines d'originalité. Les personnages Los Globulos sont «d'étranges zouaves» qui adorent se rentrer dedans.

—

Fly Guy

—

One of the first keyboard-navigation sites

iBook G4

Leaving aside the mouse and navigating by the keyboard, users became Fly Guy himself, whizzing around a pixel-perfect universe. Along the way there were various objects to interact with, often with quirky results. For those who explored this universe in detail, a great reward awaited... a trip to a secret beach destination.

"I made Fly Guy as a self-promotional 'thingy' so I could land some clients. It wasn't quite a game, but I suspected people might like messing with it for a minute and move on. This was before YouTube, Instagram, Snapchat, and whatever other distractions are available these days. So it landed at a really special time. I never suspected it would go quite as viral as it did, but people connected with it."

Trevor Van Meter
heytvm.com

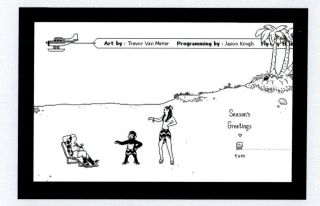

Als sie die Maus wegließen und die Navigation über die Tastatur erfolgte, wurden die User selbst zu Fly Guy und schwirrten durch ein pixelgenaues Universum. Auf dem Weg dorthin gab es verschiedene Objekte, mit denen man interagieren konnte, oft mit skurrilen Ergebnissen. Auf diejenigen, die dieses Universum im Detail erkundeten, wartete eine große Belohnung … eine Reise zu einem geheimen Strand.

Les visiteurs peuvent oublier la souris et naviguer à l'aide du clavier. Ils rentrent dans la peau du propre Fly Guy en volant à toute allure à travers un univers d'un grand niveau de détail. Pendant l'aventure, ils peuvent interagir avec divers objets et les résultats sont souvent décalés. Ceux qui explorent les recoins de cet univers reçoivent comme récompense un voyage à une destination secrète en bord de mer.

—

WhizzBall!

—

A first to allow users to build their own game

WhizzBall! invited users to tackle its puzzles and then build their own. It was a great success: the game-play was addictive and the option to build and test your own puzzles, then publish them for others to see and play, really took this game to another dimension.

Users could select things like pipes and slides and place them on a grid that became their own original game, although WhizzBall! was hampered initially by not being able to cope with the number of site visitors.

"WhizzBall! was partly inspired by the open-ended play I remember as a child growing up with Lego and also took some cues from games like Marble Madness and the Incredible Machine. The game was essentially a framework for puzzle creators to build puzzles for other players to solve. It was my first project that explored the idea that the game-level creation process could be as entertaining as playing the game itself, and this has been core to my thinking since."

Andries Odendaal
Wireframe; Consultant

WhizzBall! lud die User ein, ihre Puzzles zu lösen und dann ihre eigenen zu bauen. Es war ein großer Erfolg: Das Gameplay machte süchtig und die Option, seine eigenen Puzzles zu bauen und zu testen, sie dann zu veröffentlichen, damit andere sie sehen und spielen konnten, brachte dieses Spiel wirklich in eine andere Dimension. Die User konnten Dinge auswählen, wie Rohre und Schieber und sie dann auf ein Raster setzen, was dann zu ihrem eigenen Spiel wurde. Obwohl WhizzBall! zunächst dadurch behindert wurde, dass die Anzahl der Website-Besucher nicht bewältigt werden konnte.

WhizzBall! invite les utilisateurs à résoudre des énigmes et à en inventer. Le succès est énorme car la jouabilité est addictive et la possibilité de construire, de tester ses propres casse-têtes et de les publier fait prendre au jeu une toute autre dimension. Les utilisateurs peuvent sélectionner des éléments comme des tuyaux et des toboggans et les placer sur une grille qui sert de base à leur jeu. À ses débuts, WhizzBall! rencontre des difficultés pour faire face au nombre de visiteurs.

Theory7

—

Pushing web development to new levels

iBook G4

Over a year in the making, and with 10,000-plus lines of code, Theory7's agency website boasted over 300 Flash movies and a Flash store which provided a huge array of resources for designers and developers. All of this was presented in a stylish and color-customizable interface.

"The approach to the site was very much in line with the way things were back then, websites were all about showcasing what was possible, we felt like pioneers and the community treated us like pioneers. The industry was new and exciting and we felt like we were changing the web, we were part of the community of Flash designers responsible for making it visually rich, interactive, and exciting, everything we did felt like it had a big impact and an even bigger impact on its growth."

Nevil Slade
Theory7; Vesaro

Über ein Jahr in der Herstellung und mit mehr als 10.000 Zeilen Code, so brüstete sich die Website der Theory7 Agentur, mit über 300 Flash-Filmen und einem Flash-Store, der eine riesige Auswahl an Ressourcen für Designer und Entwickler zur Verfügung stellte. All dies wurde in einer stilvollen und farblich anpassbaren Oberfläche präsentiert.

Le site de l'agence Theory7 demande plus d'un an de travail et plus de 10 000 lignes de code. Il inclut aussi plus de 300 films et une boutique en Flash offrant tout un éventail de ressources aux concepteurs et aux développeurs, le tout dans une interface élégante et aux couleurs personnalisables.

Nikon Coolpix SQ

—

The original drag-and-zoom interface

A first-of-its-kind navigation gave users an unexpected response on the new Nikon SQ camera's site. By dragging the camera a glimpse of its power and features was revealed, for example, looking up at the Eiffel Tower from below and then, in the action of dragging it, suddenly looking down from the top of the Tower. This simple navigation technique was used in various parts of the site, thereby encouraging visitors to explore it in full.

face it

Just frame yourself in the LCD and shoot.

menu

get real

Just choose a subject, choose an angle and fire away for true -to-life results.

menu

"The Nikon SQ project was a product-launch micro-site for Nikon Europe produced in 14 languages for AKQA. The concept for the site came from a photo I'd taken the previous year coupled with some experiments I'd been doing with 3D and image sequences. A Nikon with a tilting viewfinder enabled me to shoot straight down from the top of the Eiffel Tower. The resulting image was very different from the usual 'tourist' shots and suggested the 'different point of view' theme we used."

Andy Foulds
andyfoulds.co.uk

Eine neuartige Navigation ermöglichte den Usern eine unerwartete Reaktion auf die neue Website der Nikon SQ-Kamera. Durch das Ziehen der Kamera wurde ein Blick auf ihre Leistung und Funktionen freigelegt, zum Beispiel konnte man von unten auf den Eiffelturm schauen und dann in der Aktion des Ziehens plötzlich von der Spitze des Turms herabblicken. Diese einfache Navigationstechnik wurde in verschiedenen Teilen der Website verwendet und ermutigte die Besucher, sie vollständig zu erkunden.

La navigation du site pour le nouvel appareil photo Nikon SQ est la première du genre et ne manque pas de surprendre. Les visiteurs peuvent découvrir tout le potentiel de l'appareil en cliquant sur son image, passant par exemple d'une vue de la tour Eiffel depuis le bas à une autre depuis son sommet. Cette technique simple de navigation est utilisée dans plusieurs sections du site et motive à poursuivre l'exploration.

—

Samorost

—

The beginnings of a
celebrated game creator

This was a wonderful point-and-click adventure game with excellent atmospheric sound and artwork. The game-play and interaction showed a deep level of thinking from the developer and Samorost became hugely popular, with people all over the world uploading the game to their own servers so it could be shared with as many other people as possible.

"I was studying at the Academy of Arts and decided to use Flash for my dissertation project. I hadn't intended to make a game at first. Samorost was fully playable in a browser so I put it online and sent the link to a few friends and then it exploded — it spread all over the web in just a few days. The server crashed under the heavy load so I found a different one and then just watched the statistics in astonishment as it was being played by millions of people all around the world."

Jakub Dvorský
Amanita Design

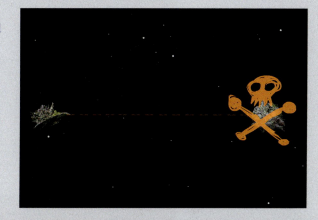

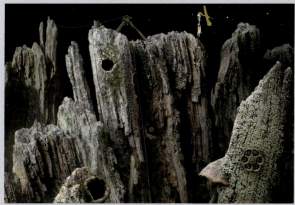

Dies war ein wunderbares Point-and-Click-Adventure mit exzellentem atmosphärischem Sound und Grafik. Das Gameplay und die Interaktion zeigten ein tiefes Denkniveau des Entwicklers und

Samorost wurde sehr populär. Menschen auf der ganzen Welt luden das Spiel auf ihre eigenen Server hoch, damit es mit so vielen anderen Leuten wie möglich geteilt werden konnte

Ce formidable jeu d'aventure par pointer-cliquer est doté d'un son d'ambiance et d'illustrations de grande qualité. La jouabilité et l'interaction prouvent une réflexion poussée de la part du

développeur. Samorost se gagne une grande popularité et dans le monde entier des joueurs le téléchargent sur leur propre serveur pour le partager avec le plus de personnes possible.

2003/
—

Wefail

—

Overflowing with character

iBook G4

When two original and talented individuals collided, Martin Hughes and Jordan Stone, the result was Wefail, a project aimed at integrating voice sequences in their clients' websites and their own too. The appeal of Wefail was extraordinary, while neither designer cared what anyone else thought and often poked fun at the latest trends.

"This was my and Jordan's first attempt at making a site together, the basic walking engine was already made by Jordan. We stole it and added a timeline scrubber so you could go back and forth and open different little sub-sections. It was the anti-site, because at the time everyone was making futuristic-looking Flash sites with robots in them and tiny pixel text. We didn't want to do that. A fun site to make, we rebuilt it in HTML5 a couple of years back."

Martin Hughes
Wefail

Als zwei originelle und talentierte Personen, wie Martin Hughes und Jordan Stone, zusammenkamen war das Ergebnis Wefail, ein Projekt, das darauf abzielte, Sprachsequenzen in die Websites ihrer Kunden und auch in ihre eigenen zu integrieren. Die Attraktivität von Wefail war außergewöhnlich, während sich keiner der Designer darum kümmerte, was andere dachten und sich oft über die neuesten Trends lustig machten.

Quand les chemins de deux créatifs de talent que sont Martin Hughes et Jordan Stone se croisent, ils créent Wefail, un projet visant à intégrer des séquences vocales dans leur site Web et celui de leurs clients. Le succès est énorme, mais les deux concepteurs ne s'intéressent pas aux opinions et se moquent souvent des dernières tendances.

OurType

—

The web design
community's favorite

A huge instant hit with its target audience, this completely fresh e-commerce site was one of the rare examples that could deal with the whole shopping process without recourse to an HTML window. The flawless and polished profile of this site for the fine typography firm featured added interactivity and usability with its "Try" and "Buy" options. The site even included a message to me hidden in plain sight from group94's founder and creative director.

OurType
sa hi
ys
Ludwig Try Buy

Ludwig Bold 140 pt.

It is time to next-generation mission to empower the extensible shoe lace in order that we may successfully turn upside-down our grey haired meatballs or have the cutting-edge Chinese restaurant integrate outdated aliens.
Itching hitchers empower world-class super x-rated movies to skillfully innovate the dynamic hollow beard.

Versa Condensed Try Buy

Robin

"OurType had a vision to distribute a selection of great font families via the internet and contacted group94 to build a site. The result was one of the first e-commerce sites exclusively aimed at designers. The concept was simple: try and buy… an approach that had proven its effectiveness in the car industry. The website allowed visitors to try typefaces and then securely purchase and download single weights or complete font families, all this within one slick Flash environment."

Pascal Leroy
group94

Diese völlig neue e-commerce-Website war sofort ein riesiger Hit bei ihrer Zielgruppe. Sie war eines der wenigen Beispiele, bei dem der gesamte Einkaufs-prozess ohne den Einsatz eines HTML-Fensters bewältigt wer-den konnte. Das makellose und geschliffene Profil dieser Seite für die Firma für feine Typografie, bot zusätzliche Interaktivität und Benutzerfreundlichkeit mit den Optionen „Try" und „Buy". Die Seite enthielt sogar eine Nach-richt für mich, die von einem von Gründer und Creative Director von group94 verborgen wurde.

Remportant un succès immédiat auprès de son public cible, ce nouveau site e-commerce est l'un des rares à gérer tout le processus d'achat sans recourir à une fenêtre HTML. La présen-tation irréprochable de ce fournisseur de typographies raffinées offre une grande interactivité et convivialité grâce aux boutons «Try» et «Buy». Le site inclut même dans le contenu un message caché qui m'est destiné du fondateur et directeur créatif de group94.

NOTABLE WEBSITE
LAUNCH
MySpace

GOOGLE
FACTS

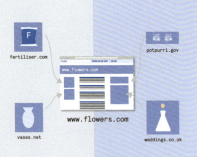

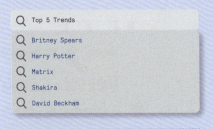

Google AdSense is announced

First Code Jam
registration opens

Top 5 Trends

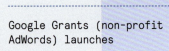

Google Grants (non-profit
AdWords) launches

Google Print (now Google
Books) launches

Google acquires Blogger

On the BlackBerry screen:

10:48 AM
TUE, MAY 22

Dear Josh,

MOBILE EVOLUTION
BlackBerry Quark 6210

Named as one of the most important
gadgets of all time by *TIME*, the
Quark featured wireless email, SMS,
browser, and applications

BBC NEWS
In Pictures: **More anti-war pictures**

NO WAR

"No to war - from Copacabana in Brazil" from
Bernadete Lou

Click below for more images
◄ BACK 1 2 3 4 5 6 7 8 9 10 NEXT ►

INTERNET COMMUNITY
"Your Pictures"

After the BBC invited people to send
in photographs relating to the Iraq War
they were collected in a "Your Pictures"
section of the website as a gallery
of anti-war images.

2004/

The Year of the Original Viral Site

2004/

—

The Year of
the Original
Viral Site

—

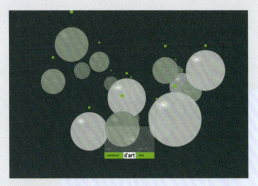
D'art Design Gruppe

Viral videos had been around for some years and in fact one of the first, the Spirit of Christmas, dated back to 1995. The same level of rapid transmission hadn't filtered through to websites, however, even those launching to waves of applause and astonishment.

Interfaces were now being developed in every imaginable format, such as group94's solar system navigation for D'art Design Gruppe.

Themes from real life were being increasingly transferred online, as with the navigation for the FB-FX site, which functioned by stripping away sections of graffiti to reveal layers beneath but leaving portions of the upper levels still intact.

Improved mobile phones made them more popular as a way to access the internet, but website design on phones was still almost non-existent as WAP websites were extremely basic, especially compared to desktop levels of creativity.

Web design agencies continued to spring surprises, as Hi-ReS! did with LifeSwitch. This site invited users to sign up for a life of luxury and wealth, only to pitch them suddenly into a different situation altogether that highlighted the struggles and poverty found in many areas of the world.

Meanwhile, Italy's Fishouse created the website for Boula Burton, which starred a Jack Russell as the original Art Director dog.

Noe Design was the epitome of a portfolio website and featured its creator Dan Noe in the form of a pre-packed action hero, a metaphor everyone could understand.

Websites with character were matched by design agencies being keen to show their playful sides. A strong example was the animation-fueled company website of Freedom Interactive Design.

Other agencies, such as Firstborn, were still concerned with presenting their creative side in a solid and professional manner. Their site was a typography student's dream, being largely based on text and snappy font animations.

The music artist Billy Harvey's site gave him the perfect web persona by using an innovative zooming interface to remind visitors that he was the star.

Geoffrey Lillemon became well known in the web design community upon launching his Oculart site to showcase his intriguing interactive art. Backed by atmospheric sound and motion, each chapter was layered deep and often dark.

Mercedes-Benz moved into high-end interactive movies with a web special for its SLK, which dropped visitors right into the film and presented new levels of sophisticated production.

Word of mouth was important too, as when Yosain's site launched with its delightful character animations. It was so popular that a few days after it was awarded at FWA the link had to be removed because of a flood of emails.

MySpace began to focus on social-networking, rather than just offering file storage, and by April had overtaken Friendster in terms of traffic volume. Friends Reunited and other social-networking sites were also expanding, while Google launched its Orkut social network too. Meanwhile, TheFacebook website came in almost under the radar in February, initially available only to Harvard students.

FB-FX

Noe Design

Boula Burton

Freedom Interactive Design

"Website design on phones was still almost non-existent."

Virale Videos gab es schon einige Jahre und in der Tat eines der ersten, der Spirit of Christmas, kann fast ein Jahrzehnt (1995) zurückdatiert werden. Das gleiche Niveau der schnellen Übertragung hatte sich jedoch nicht auf Webseiten niedergeschlagen, selbst nicht auf diejenigen, die Wellen von Applaus und Erstaunen auslösten.

Schnittstellen wurden nun in allen erdenklichen Formaten entwickelt, wie die Solarsystem-Navigation von group94 für die D'art Design Gruppe.

Themen aus dem realen Leben wurden zunehmend online gestellt, wie zum Beispiel mit der Navigation für die FB-FX-Site, die funktionierte, indem Teile von Graffiti entfernt wurden, um zu enthüllen, was darunter lag, aber winzige Teile der oberen Ebene noch intakt ließen.

Verbesserte Mobiltelefone führten dazu, dass sie immer beliebter wurden, als Zugang zum Internet zu fungieren. Aber das Design von Webseiten auf Mobiltelefonen war immer noch

fast nicht existent, da WAP-Websites extrem einfach waren, besonders im Vergleich zu den kreativen Desktop-Ebenen.

Webdesign-Agenturen sorgten immer noch für Überraschungen, wie Hi-ReS! mit LifeSwitch. Diese Seite lud die User zu einem Leben in Luxus und Reichtum ein, nur um sie plötzlich in eine andere Situation zu versetzen, in der die Kämpfe und die Armut in vielen Teilen der Welt gezeigt wurden.

Währenddessen erstellte Fishouse in Italien die Website für Boula Burton mit einem Jack Russell als originellen Art Director-Hund.

Noe Design, war der Inbegriff einer Portfolio-Website und zeigte seinen Schöpfer Dan Noe in Form eines abgepackten Action-Helden, eine Metapher, die jeder verstehen konnte.

Websites mit Charakter dominierten weiterhin während Designagenturen ihre spielerischen Seiten zeigen wollten. Ein starkes Beispiel war die animierte Website von Freedom Interactive Design.

Andere Agenturen, wie Firstborn, waren immer noch damit beschäftigt, ihre kreative Seite auf eine solide und professionelle Weise zu präsentieren. Ihre Firmenwebseite war der Traum jedes Typografie-Studenten, da sie fast ausschließlich auf Text und flinken Schriftanimationen basierte.

Die Website des Musikkünstlers Billy Harvey gab ihm die perfekte Web-Persönlichkeit, indem er ein innovatives Zoom-Interface verwendete, um die Besucher immer daran zu erinnern, dass er der Star war.

Geoffrey Lillemon wurde in der Webdesign-Community bekannt, als er seine Oculart-Site startete, um seine faszinierende interaktive Kunst zu präsentieren. Unterstützt von atmosphärischem Klang und Bewegung wurde jedes Kapitel tief und oft dunkel überlagert.

Mercedes-Benz betrat die Welt der interaktiven High-End-Filme mit einem Web-Special für seinen SLK, der die Besucher direkt in den Film lockte und neue

Levels anspruchsvoller Produktion präsentierte.

Mundpropaganda gewann ebenfalls an Dynamik, als die Website von Yosain mit ihren entzückenden High-End-Charakteranimationen auf den Markt kam. Sie war so beliebt, dass einige Tage nach der Verleihung des FWA der Link wegen einer Flut von E-Mails entfernt werden musste.

MySpace begann sich auf Social Networking zu konzentrieren, anstatt nur Dateispeicher anzubieten und hatte im April das Traffic-Volumen von Friendster übertroffen. Friends Reunited und andere Social-Networking-Sites expandierten ebenfalls, während Google sein soziales Netzwerk Orkut ins Leben rief. Während all dem Währenddessen lief die TheFacebook-Website im Februar fast unter den Radarschirm, da sie ursprünglich nur Harvard-Studenten zur Verfügung stand.

The Year of the Original Viral Site

—

"Websites with character were matched by design agencies keen to show their playful sides."

Firstborn

Billy Harvey

Oculart

Mercedes-Benz SLK

Yosain

Des vidéos virales circulent depuis déjà quelques années et l'une des premières, Spirit of Christmas, remonte à 1995. Aucun site Web, même ceux les plus remarqués et applaudis, n'a jamais connu une diffusion si rapide.

Les interfaces sont maintenant conçues dans tous les formats imaginables, comme la navigation sous forme de système solaire que group94 invente pour le site de D'art Design Gruppe.

Des thèmes de la vie réelle se retrouvent plus souvent en ligne. Tel est le cas du site de FB-FX, dont la navigation se fait en retirant des graffiti pour dévoiler des couches inférieures tout en conservant des éléments du dessus intacts.

Les téléphones portables sont plus performants et chaque fois plus utilisés pour accéder à Internet. Pourtant, la conception des sites Web pour les écrans de téléphone est encore quasi

inexistante : les sites WAP restent très basiques, surtout comparés aux niveaux de créativité des versions pour ordinateur.

Les agences de conception Web ne cessent de créer la surprise, comme Hi-ReS! avec le site de LifeSwitch, qui vante aux visiteurs une vie de luxe, pour les mettre juste après dans une situation montrant les épreuves et la pauvreté endurées dans certaines régions du monde.

L'agence italienne Fishouse crée cette année-là le site Web pour Boula Burton, avec un Jack Russell en guise de chien directeur artistique.

Noe Design est la quintessence du site Web pour un portfolio. Son créateur Dan Noe y apparaît sous la forme d'un homme d'action préemballé, une métaphore plutôt évidente.

Les sites Web avec une personnalité sont le fruit d'agences de conception souhaitant montrer leur côté ludique. Celui truffé d'animations

de Freedom Interactive Design en est un exemple probant.

D'autres agences comme Firstborn s'attachent à exprimer leur créativité d'une façon professionnelle et fiable. Leurs sites sont le rêve de tout étudiant en typographie pour la quantité de texte et de polices animées qu'ils contiennent.

Le site du musicien Billy Harvey est à la hauteur du personnage, avec une interface innovante par zoom rappelant aux visiteurs la star qu'il est.

Geoffrey Lillemon est célèbre au sein de la communauté Web après le lancement de son site Oculart qui lui sert à présenter son art interactif singulier. Assorties d'animations et d'un son d'ambiance, les sections souvent sombres comportent de nombreuses couches.

Mercedes-Benz parie sur les films interactifs de qualité pour le site Web consacré à sa classe SLK. L'interface plonge les visiteurs au cœur

de l'histoire avec une production sophistiquée.

Le bouche-à-oreille est également déterminant, comme au lancement du site de Yosain avec ses merveilleuses animations de personnages. La popularité est telle que quelques jours après sa sélection sur le site FWA, le lien doit être supprimé en raison de l'avalanche d'e-mails reçus.

MySpace se projette au-delà du simple stockage de fichiers et commence à s'intéresser au monde des réseaux sociaux. En avril, le site dépasse Friendster en termes de volume de trafic. Friends Reunited et d'autres sites de socialisation en réseau sont aussi en plein expansion, et Google lance son réseau Orkut. En parallèle, le site TheFacebook apparu en février passe plutôt inaperçu et est au départ uniquement accessible par les étudiants de Harvard.

08 Facts of the year

14%

Number of internet users:
910 million, 14% of
the world population

51.6
million

Number of websites:
51.6 million

World news:
tsunamis in the Indian
Ocean kill over 230,000
people in 14 countries

Website with most traffic:
Yahoo.com

Tech hardware:
Sony's Librié e-book
launches with the first
'electronic paper' display

1.0

Tech software:
Firefox 1.0 is released

Other tech:
the term Web 2.0
goes mainstream

Highest-grossing film:
Shrek 2

—

Subservient Chicken

—

The original viral site

Possibly the most-viewed viral site in history, which gave people, for the first time, the ability to make things happen on a website in what felt like real time. Users could make the Burger King chicken do exactly what they asked, live on screen, just as the campaign's tagline said: "Chicken the way you like it".

Typing "jump" made the chicken move into position and jump, and forums were alive with people sharing lists of words to test out. All the action was pre-recorded and activated by certain key words or phrases, but when it launched many people thought the responses were real. There were over 300 programmed commands, including moonwalk, throw pillow, fight, sex, do the YMCA, and breakdance.

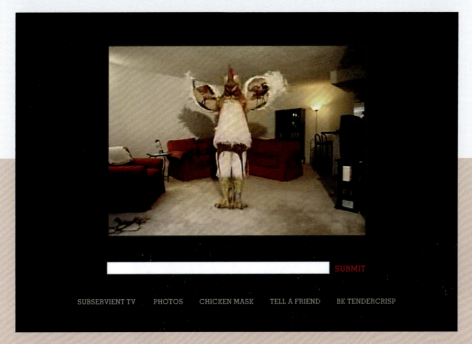

"The guy in the suit was originally an actor, but he was claustrophobic in the suit, so he wouldn't do it. And we had to use one of the costume's designers… He would do about six moves and then we would have to fan him off because he would get so hot in the costume."

Jeff Benjamin
CP+B; wedisco.com

Möglicherweise die am meisten angesehene virale Seite in der Geschichte, die den Menschen zum ersten Mal die Möglichkeit gab, Dinge auf einer Webseite zu realisieren, die sich wie in Echt-zeit anfühlten. Nutzer konnten das Burger King Hühnchen genau das machen lassen, was sie wollten, live auf dem Bildschirm, genauso wie der Slogan der Kampagne besagte: „Chicken the way you like it".

Gab man „Jump" ein, sorgte der Befehl dafür, dass das Huhn in Position ging und sprang und es entstanden Foren mit Leuten, die Listen von Wörtern teilen, die getestet werden sollten. Die gesamte Aktion wurde vorab aufgezeichnet und durch bestimmte Schlüsselwörter oder Phrasen aktiviert, aber als es auf den Markt kam, dachten viele, die Antworten seien echt. Es gab über 300 programmierte Befehle, einschließlich Moonwalk, Kissen werfen, Kampf, Sex, den YMCA und Breakdance machen.

C'est sans doute le site viral le plus visité de toute l'histoire. Pour la première fois, les internautes peuvent déclencher dans un site Web quelque chose semblant se produire en temps réel. Ils peuvent commander au poulet Burger King de faire exactement ce qu'ils demandent, comme l'annonce le slogan de la campagne : «Chicken the way you like it» (le poulet comme vous l'aimez).

S'ils tapent «jump», le poulet se met en position et saute. Sur les forums, les gens échangent des listes de mots à tester. Toutes les actions sont pré-enregistrées et activées par des mots ou phrases clés mais au lancement du site, beaucoup pensent que les réactions de l'animal se font en direct. Plus de 300 commandes sont programmées, dont moonwalk, lancer d'oreiller, bagarre, sexe, choré-graphie de YMCA et breakdance.

—

Vodafone Future Vision

—

Startlingly accurate future predictions

From the opening screen and welcoming voice it was immediately clear this was a futuristic and progressive presentation, quickly followed by the innovative video-enhanced launch page. The whole site was marked with new levels of web design and its pioneering features and techniques established a style trend. The premise was to give a glimpse of the future, and the site achieved this with flying colors, becoming winner of both the FWA Site of the Year and People's Choice Award for 2004, the first time this happened. It was very interesting, 10 years later, to see how accurate Vodafone's vision was as wearable tech had now become a reality.

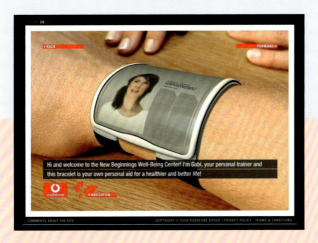

"Vodafone Future was one of our first projects at
North Kingdom back in 2003. Vodafone... wanted
to demonstrate its commitment to the future of
mobile communication. The site was intended to
show how we might experience and interact with
future mobile services in 5–10 years. Flash was
very limited in 2003 so we had to make a lot of
innovative technical solutions to push what
was possible to do online as we wanted to do a
super-rich interactive experience."

Robert Lindström
North Kingdom

Schon auf dem Eröffnungsbild-
schirm und mit der Begrüßungs-
stimme wurde sofort klar, dass
es sich um eine futuristische und
progressive Präsentation handel-
te, auf die schnell die innovative,
videoverbesserte Startseite
folgte. Die gesamte Website
zeichnete sich durch neue
Ebenen des Webdesigns aus und
ihre bahnbrechenden Funktionen
und Techniken etablierten einen
Stiltrend. Die Prämisse war, einen
Blick in die Zukunft zu werfen,
und die Seite erreichte dies mit
Bravour und wurde zum ersten
Mal der Gewinner des FWA „Site
of the Year" und „People's Choice
Award" im Jahr 2004. Es war
sehr interessant 10 Jahre später
zu sehen, wie genau Vodafones
Vision war, als Wearable Tech nun
Realität wurde.

Dès l'écran d'accueil, avec une
voix chaleureuse, le site annonce
clairement une présentation
moderne et futuriste, puis vient
une page de démarrage originale
incluant une vidéo. La conception
du site dans son ensemble est
innovante, avec des fonctionnalités et des techniques inédites
marquant une tendance. L'idée
est d'offrir une vision de l'avenir
et la réalisation y parvient avec
brio, remportant à la fois les
prix FWA Site of the Year et
People's Choice Award en 2004,
ce qui est du jamais vu. Il sera
intéressant de constater 10 ans
plus tard à quel point la vision
de Vodafone était juste, une fois
la technologie prêt-à-porter
devenue une réalité.

—

Carl de Keyzer

—

Next-level photography
showcase

00.05/01.13

Photography galleries were amongst the most
beautiful and eye-pleasing websites, and the
showcase for Magnum photographer Carl
de Keyzer was one of the best examples. Site
intros had acquired a bad reputation and were
now almost entirely unused, so it was brave
of group94 to employ one here and prove
that elegant and emotive introductions could
enhance the user's visit. It took the form of a
lookbook into the photographer's portfolio and
gave a sense of what his work was all about.

"A long time ago I had an exhibition in Ghent, where I lived, about Siberian prison camps, called *ZONA*. Pascal Leroy, who was the owner of one of the finest web design companies in the world, group94, visited that show and sent me a mail. He congratulated me on the project, he really liked the images, but he also said that my website was awful and that he could do a much better job. The rest is history."

Carl de Keyzer
carldekeyzer.com

Fotogalerien gehörten zu den schönsten und angenehmsten Websites und der Schaukasten des Magnum-Fotografen Carl de Keyzer war eines der besten Beispiele dafür. Site Intros hatten einen schlechten Ruf erlangt und wurden nun fast gar nicht mehr benutzt, so war es mutig von group94, eines hier einzusetzen und zu beweisen, dass elegante und emotionale Einführungen die Sicht des Anwenders verbessern konnten. Die Site nahm die Form eines Lookbooks in das Portfolio des Fotografen auf und gab einen Eindruck davon, worum es in seiner Arbeit ging.

Les galeries photo sont parmi les sites Web les plus esthétiques et plaisants à consulter, et celui du photographe Carl de Keyzer pour Magnum n'est pas en reste. Les intros de sites n'ont pas bonne réputation et ne sont quasiment plus utilisées. L'agence group94 fait donc preuve d'audace en y recourant et prouve qu'une introduction sophistiquée et émouvante peut enrichir la visite des utilisateurs. Elle est pensée ici comme une sorte de lookbook du portfolio du photographe et fait comprendre toute la portée de son travail.

—

Jeedoubleu

—

A one-of-a-kind personal website

Without question, the most unforgettable personal portfolio website of 2004 was that of Canada's Greg Washington, also a winner of the May 1 Reboot. Literally in your face, as the image of Washington's face was pressed up against the screen and the condensation from his breath steamed it up, the eerie atmosphere was made complete when his eyes followed the user's every move.

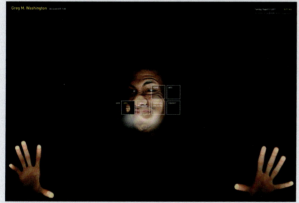

> "Flash enabled us to bring concepts to life without friction, which led to a climate of intense exploration and play. In my opinion, the early-mid 2000s was the renaissance of interaction design. So many designers coming up around me were pushing their creative prowess on their own platforms. When I was thinking about how to approach my own site, I just wanted to do something that wasn't conventional."

Greg Washington
gregwashington.ca

Ohne Frage, die unvergesslichste persönliche Portfolio-Website aus dem Jahr 2004 war die von Greg Washington aus Kanada, auch ein Gewinner des 1. Mai Reboots. Sprichwörtlich sprang sie einem ins Gesicht, da das Bild von Washingtons Gesicht gegen den Bildschirm gepresst wurde und die Kondensation seines Atems zu sehen war. Die unheimliche Atmosphäre wurde vervollständigt, als seine Augen der Bewegung des Nutzers folgten.

En 2004, le site Web d'un portfolio personnel le plus inoubliable est sans conteste celui du Canadien Greg Washington, par ailleurs lauréat du May 1 Reboot. Le visage de Washington est appuyé contre l'écran, et la condensation formée par sa respiration remplit l'image ; l'ambiance troublante est renforcée par ses yeux qui suivent les mouvements du visiteur.

—

PDK

—

Putting innovation and charm into the corporate world

Poland's Max Weber interactive agency took a seemingly boring and lackluster subject and transformed it with attractive design. Few people could have imagined a site for a Polish car hire company would be one of the best sites of 2004, but the PDK website featured a number of slick and entertaining short animations and combined them with clever scripting and programming, resulting in an appealing and impeccably professional corporate web presence.

"In 2004, the year we launched the PDK website, Macromedia Flash was a standard tool for delivering rich, really interactive content. Back then, everything was about a new, fancy, and flashy way of engaging people with interactive content. But at the same time, this freedom very often led to nightmare 'user experience'. Designing PDK, we were trying to reconcile user experience with creativity. We put the content in the center, so every bit of animation was subordinate, to deliver a clear message: how PDK solves your problems."

Grzegorz Mogilewski
Max Weber; Iconaris

Die polnische interaktive Agentur Max Weber nahm ein scheinbar langweiliges und glanzloses Thema und wandelte es mit attraktivem Design um. Nur wenige Menschen hätten sich vorstellen können, dass eine Website für eine polnische Autovermietung eine der besten Seiten des Jahres 2004 werden würde aber die PDK Website präsentierte eine Reihe von raffinierten und unterhaltsamen Kurzanimationen und kombinierte sie mit cleveren Skripten und Programmen, was zu einem ansprechenden und makellos professionellen Internetauftritt führte.

L'agence interactive polonaise Max Weber s'attaque à un sujet apparemment ennuyeux et sans intérêt et en tire une conception attrayante. Peu de personnes auraient pu imaginer que le site d'une entreprise de location de véhicules en Pologne serait l'un des meilleurs sites en 2004. Pourtant, le site Web de PDK combine de courtes animations amusantes et astucieuses à des scripts et une programmation bien conçus. Le résultat renvoie une image séduisante et très professionnelle.

Crew 9

—

Interactive students
"for sale"

Hyper Island, the Swedish school of new media design, tried to find placements for its students each year in established multimedia studios, with 2004 the year for Crew 9, 2003 Crew 8, etc.

Every year they managed to come up with an original way of doing this, and this year the students were all put on show as a visual interface. The faces followed the mouse as it moved because these students were all "on sale", and if more information was desired or the user wanted to offer them a placement, the particular student just had to be put into a shopping cart.

"The concept was awesome: offering students as a product that could make you money in exchange for an internship. That stuff was groundbreaking. Pre-social media and modern web technologies. Back in 2004, there weren't many websites that had that bright, clean gridded layout combined with interactivity and animation. Static and strict web design was something associated with boring corporate sites. Playing on that cue with animation and interactivity it really stood out from what others were doing."

Desmond Arsan
Hyper Island; Crew 9

Hyper Island, die schwedische Schule für New Media Design, versuchte jedes Jahr Anstellungen für ihre Studenten in etablierten Multimediastudios zu finden. Im Jahr 2004 für die Crew 9, 2003 Crew 8, etc.

Jedes Jahr gelang es ihnen, dafür einen originellen Weg zu finden und in diesem Jahr wurden die Studenten als visuelle Schnittstelle präsentiert. Die Gesichter folgten der Maus, wenn sie sich bewegte, weil diese Schüler alle „zum Kauf" angeboten wurden und wenn mehr Informationen gewünscht wurden oder der Benutzer ihnen ein Praktikum anbieten wollte, konnte der betreffende Student einfach in einen Einkaufswagen gelegt werden.

L'école suédoise de création numérique Hyper Island essaie chaque année de trouver pour ses élèves des stages dans des studios multimédia reconnus (l'année 2004 était celle de Crew 9, 2003 celle de Crew 8, etc).

Elle procède tous les ans d'une façon originale; cette année, elle fait un montage de tous les étudiants dans une interface visuelle. Comme ils sont «en vente», les visages suivent les déplacements de la souris et pour plus d'informations sur un étudiant ou si le visiteur veut lui proposer un stage, il doit juste le placer dans un panier.

2004/

—

Driver's Heaven

—

The best multi-player online racing game of its day

In this exhilarating experience, players earned points by challenging other drivers or setting new lap records, and could buy their way up to the Ferrari Enzo Black, at 250,000 points. It was only available in German but was very easy to understand, and was totally addictive, real-time gaming. However, like other projects it suffered from its own success, chiefly with costly hosting problems.

"We had created Fast Froots, a Mario Kart-like game with froots. We used that for a tech study of the mode 7 engine in Flash. The idea for Driver's Heaven was born and technically realizable. We had blown away the client when we finally presented the application. We spread the link to the forums and communities and also FWA, within days we had about 200,000 users. That was really amazing in those days without Facebook."

Carsten Mueller
Extrajetzt

In dieser berauschenden Erfahrung verdienten sich die Spieler Punkte, indem sie andere Fahrer herausforderten oder neue Rundenrekorde setzten, und konnten sich bis zum Ferrari Enzo Black hocharbeiten, und ihn für 250.000 Punkte, kaufen. Es war nur auf Deutsch verfügbar aber es war sehr einfach zu verstehen und war total süchtig machendes Echtzeit-Gaming. Wie andere Projekte auch, litt es jedoch unter seinem eigenen Erfolg, vor allem wegen kostspieliger Hosting-Probleme.

Dans cette aventure palpitante, les joueurs gagnent des points en s'affrontant à d'autres pilotes ou en battant des records de tour de piste : quand ils atteignent 250 000 points, ils peuvent se payer une Ferrari Enzo Black. Uniquement disponible en allemand mais très simple à comprendre, ce jeu en temps réel est complètement addictif. Comme d'autres projets toutefois, il est victime de son succès, notamment en raison d'onéreux soucis d'hébergement.

Saints and Soldiers

—

The original parallax

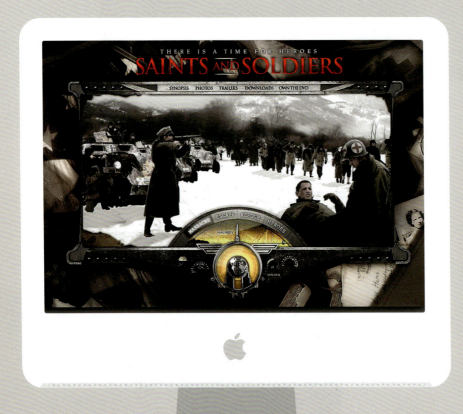

One of the earliest parallax effects appeared courtesy of Funktion12 (later RED Interactive Agency), who quickly set out their stall and presented a whole new style in web design, using high-quality photography with top-notch scrolling effects and their trademark use of parallax. The website was one of many from this team, who inspired a community and initiated a real trend for this style.

"*Saints and Soldiers* was produced locally, so in addition to hundreds of great production photos I was delivered a collection of props from the film, all real WWII items. I scanned these in with my flatbed scanner to make the background for the site. When I got to the last scene, it was wider than the interface. There was a single post in the foreground of the scene that I had already cut out, so it made sense to me to parallax it with the pan. My client, upon seeing the parallaxing post, said, 'This is great, but now you have to do this to all the scenes.' The parallax became the defining feature of the site, which received a huge response."

Jared Kroff
Funktion12; RED Games

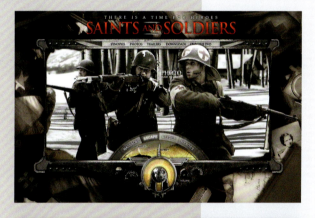

Einer der frühesten Parallaxe-effekte erschien mit Funktion12 (später RED Interactive Agency), die schnell ihre Bude aufbauten und einen ganz neuen Stil im Webdesign präsentierten, indem sie hochwertige Fotografie mit erstklassigen Scrolling-Effekten und der Verwendung von Parallax als Markenzeichen verwendeten. Diese Website war eine von vielen aus diesem Team, das eine ganze Community inspirierte und einen echten Trend für diesen Stil initiierte.

L'un des tous premiers effets parallaxes est signé par l'agence Funktion12 (devenue RED Inter-active Agency), qui s'impose rapidement avec un nouveau style de conception Web inté-grant photographies de haute qualité, excellents effets de défilement et un usage particu-lier de la parallaxe. Cette équipe a créé de nombreux sites Web, inspiré toute une communauté et établi une véritable tendance pour ce style.

Amplifier

—

A great example
of the zoom effect

Jordan Stone, one half of the empire that is Wefail, produced two of the best sites of the year through his sofake portfolio, Amplifier being one of them. Using his trademark zoom technique, he demonstrated with Amplifier how to communicate the essence of a company by way of a totally original interface and a number of humorous sound clips.

"A friend of mine gave me a cracked copy of Flash on a CD-ROM and that was pretty much it for me. I do specifically think of those two projects [Amplifier and Billy Harvey] as my last two proclamations of I can do this by myself (if I wanted to) before embracing the golden years of Wefail with Martin. I still love Flash by the way. I'm still using it all the time for animations and games and stuff, the only difference is I no longer get paid for it…"

Jordan Stone
sofake; Wefail

Jordan Stone, eine Hälfte des Imperiums von Wefail, produzierte zwei der besten Seiten des Jahres durch sein Sofake-Portfolio, Amplifier ist eine von ihnen. Mit seiner charakteristischen Zoom-Technik demonstrierte er mit Amplifier, wie man die Essenz eines Unternehmens über eine völlig originelle Oberfläche und eine Reihe von humorvollen Soundclips kommunizieren kann.

Jordan Stone est l'un des deux piliers de l'empire Wefail et l'auteur de deux des meilleurs sites de l'année, dont Amplifier, à travers son portfolio sofake. Grâce à une technique de zoom caractéristique, il montre avec ce site comment transmettre l'essence d'une entreprise à travers une interface des plus originales et une série de clips audio amusants.

—

The Zoomquilt

—

The infinite-zooming website

Take 15 talented artists and graphical wizards and one very simple idea and the result was the eternal Zoomquilt. This collaboration produced a site that could be zoomed into or out from infinitely, using a simple Flash technique, based on over 40 pieces of art that had been joined together seamlessly. The website, which deserved a place in an art gallery, struggled with bandwidth but managed to survive the barrage of eager visitors.

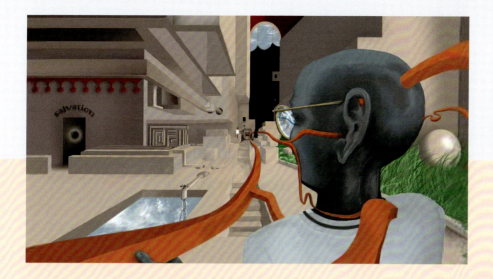

"The first iteration of the Zoomquilt was done with Director. Naturally, Flash gaining the upper hand over Director, and Adobe pretty much killing off Director after its acquisition of Macromedia, was a disappointment for me. Out of this personal grief, Flash finally being dead felt satisfying to me. Accordingly I ported the Zoomquilt to HTML5 in 2013. The original concept for the infinite-zoom mechanism came from the 1977 Eames movie *Powers of Ten*. I just combined it with the practice of digital collaborative painting I'd been participating in with tiles.ice.org back then, and oversaw the process to create a seamless and immersive image."

Nikolaus Baumgarten
nikkki.net

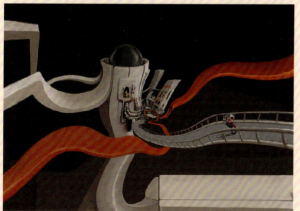

Man nehme 15 talentierte Künstler und Grafik-Genies und eine sehr einfache Idee und das Ergebnis ist das zeitlose Zoomquilt. Diese Zusammenarbeit führte zu einer Seite, die unendlich vergrößert oder verkleinert werden konnte, indem man eine einfache Flash Technik verwendete, basierend auf über 40 Kunstwerken, die nahtlos zusammengefügt wurden. Die Website, die einen Platz in einer Kunstgalerie verdient hätte, kämpfte mit der Bandbreite, schaffte es aber, die Flut von eifrigen Besuchern zu überleben.

Prenez 15 artistes de talent et génies du graphisme et une idée très simple, et vous obtenez l'intemporel Zoomquilt. Basé sur plus de 40 œuvres d'art parfaitement enchaînées, le site créé par cette équipe permet aux visiteurs de faire des zooms avant et arrière à l'infini à l'aide d'une technique Flash simple. Digne d'avoir sa place dans une galerie d'art, il a connu des soucis de bande passante mais a survécu au déluge de visites.

INTERNET COMMUNITY
Anonymous

Anonymous, the international
collective of unnamed activists and
hacktivists, becomes known as an
independent entity.

GOOGLE
FACTS

Google starts trading on the
Nasdaq at $85 per share

Google Blog goes live

Gmail launches, on April
Fools' Day

Top 5 Trends

Orkut social network launches

Google moves to "Googleplex",
1600 Amphitheatre Parkway

MOBILE EVOLUTION
Nokia 6630

The first mobile phone to
allow complete global roaming

NOTABLE WEBSITE
LAUNCH
Facebook

2005/

The Year of the Idea

2005/
—
The Year
of the Idea
—

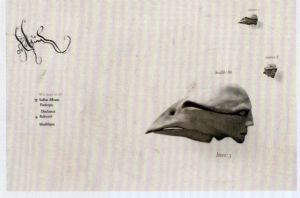

Conclave Obscurum

Plenty of the original ideas still appearing on the web were by individuals, rather than agencies, a strength that should never be undersold, and indeed some of this year's best projects thoroughly exemplified it.

Conclave Obscurum was the eagerly awaited portfolio reboot of Russia's Oleg Paschenko. The new version kept to the original Conclave's high standards, which had inspired numerous other organic websites.

Mika Tyyskä unveiled Guitar Shred Show, whose animated guitarist Mr. Fastfinger demonstrated how it was done and put air guitar online.

Yugop's amaztype was a search idea for Amazon, whereby users typed in a search term and the results were displayed using Amazon images.

Pakman was the first human Pac-Man clone website, an original idea of the highest caliber that featured excellent game-play with lots of impressive visuals and interactions.

Bob's Cube was the first interactive cubicle experience, placing users in his work space when he wasn't there so that nobody could resist poking around to see what was in his desk drawers, etc.

Desio allowed users to explore the virtual space of Sekisui Heim's three-floor eco-friendly house by dragging and dropping characters into the different rooms, where a zoom function revealed further detail.

The Red Bull Creativity Contest con-cocted an original Easter egg on its promo-tional site for an event encouraging art and creativity. By dragging various elements together, such as the drink can, wings, and a power-supply lead, a flying machine was built, recalling those at the Red Bull Flugtag events.

Novelty sites with a single hook now lurked everywhere, hoping to catch visitors with the element of surprise, and North Kingdom's site for the Toyota Aygo was a winner in this genre. On clicking the letterbox an envelope appeared through it bearing a small image of the car, but this quickly expanded into a full-size Aygo, parked in the hallway.

The Sith Sense had Darth Vader reading users' minds on this promotional site for Burger King's *Star Wars* tie-in. It was based on the old 20 questions game, and because it was a learning machine the guesses became more accurate the more people tried it.

Web.burza was one of the first standards-compliant Flash sites, and also showed where agency websites were heading. It was one of the first HTML-heavy websites featured on FWA, and raised a few eyebrows with die-hard FWA and Flash fans around the world.

A new trend appeared with Come Clean, which encouraged visitors to use New Year's Day to confess their secrets. This simple idea led to several other sites focusing their own launches on certain days of the year.

On February 14, YouTube was founded, by Chad Hurley, Steve Chen, and Jawed Karim. On April 23, Karim uploaded its first video, "Me at the Zoo", and the playback was done via Flash.

This was the year when the number of active internet-users passed the 1 billion mark, and Nokia launched its first tablet computer, the Nokia 770, three years before the iPad.

Guitar Shred Show

amaztype

Pakman

Bob's Cube

"Novelty sites with a
single hook now lurked
everywhere, hoping
to catch visitors
with the element of
surprise."

Viele der ursprünglichen Ideen, die immer noch im Internet auftauchten, waren die Arbeit von Einzelpersonen, nicht von Agenturen. Eine Stärke, die niemals unterschätzt werden sollte, und einige der besten Projekte, die 2005 ins Leben gerufen wurden, zeugen davon.

Conclave Obscurum war der mit Spannung erwartete Neustart des Russen Oleg Paschenko. Die neue Version behielt die hohen Standards der ursprünglichen Conclave bei, die zahlreiche andere organische Webseiten inspiriert hatten.

Mika Tyyskä enthüllte die Guitar Shred Show, deren animierter Gitarrist Mr. Fastfinger demonstrierte, wie es gemacht wurde und Luftgitarre online spielte.

Yugops amaztype war eine Such-Idee für Amazon. Diese Anwendung lud die Benutzer ein, einen Suchbegriff einzugeben und die Ergebnisse wurden dann mit Bildern von Amazon angezeigt.

Pakman war der erste menschliche Pac-Man Clone auf

einer Website. Diese ursprüngliche Idee war höchstes Kaliber und bot exzellentes Gameplay mit vielen beeindruckenden Visuals und Interaktionen.

Bob's Cube war der erste interaktive Raum. Die User wurden in seinen Arbeitsraum gebracht, als er nicht anwesend war, sodass niemand widerstehen konnte, dort herumzustöbern, um zu sehen, was in seinen Schreibtischschubladen war.

Desio erlaubte den Usern den virtuellen Raum von Sekisui Heims dreistöckigem, umweltfreundlichem Haus zu erforschen, indem sie Charaktere in die verschiedenen Räume hineinziehen und darin fallen lassen konnten, wo eine Zoom-Funktion weitere Details zeigte.

Der Red Bull Creativity Contest sorgte mit einem originellen Osterei auf seiner Werbeseite für ein Ereignis, das Kunst und Kreativität förderte. Indem verschiedene Elemente zusammengebaut wurden, wie die Getränkedose, Flügel und

eine Stromversorgungsleitung. So wurde eine Flugmaschine gebaut, die an die Red Bull Flugtag-Ereignisse erinnerte.

Neuartige Seiten mit einem einzigen Haken lauerten an jeder Ecke, in der Hoffnung, die Besucher durch das Element der Überraschung hereinzuholen. Die North Kingdoms Website für den Toyota Aygo war ein Gewinner in diesem Genre. Beim Klicken auf den Briefkasten wurde ein Umschlag mit einem kleinen Bild des Autos durchgeschoben, das sich aber schnell zu einem großen, im Flur geparkten Aygo vergrößerte.

Sith Sense ließ Darth Vader die Gedanken des Users auf der Werbeseite für Burger Kings *Star Wars* Kooperation lesen. Es basierte auf dem alten 20-Fragen-Spiel und weil es eine Lernmaschine war, wurden die Vermutungen genauer, je mehr Leute es versuchten.

Web.burza war eine der ersten standardkonformen Flash-Seiten und gab einen frühen Einblick darauf wohin Agenturweb-

sites gingen. Es war auch eine der ersten HTML-lastigen Webseiten auf FWA und sorgte für ein paar hochgezogene Augenbrauen bei eingefleischten FWA- und Flash-Fans auf der ganzen Welt.

Ein neuer Trend erschien mit Come Clean, der die Besucher ermutigte, den Neujahrstag zu nutzen, um ihre Geheimnisse zu bekennen. Diese einfache Idee war für mehrere andere Websites verantwortlich, die sich auf die Einführung ihrer Projekte an bestimmten Tagen des Jahres konzentrierten.

Am 14. Februar wurde YouTube von Chad Hurley, Steve Chen und Jawed Karim gegründet. Am 23. April hat Karim sein erstes Video „Ich im Zoo" hochgeladen und die Wiedergabe lief über Flash.

Dies war auch das Jahr, in dem die Zahl der aktiven Internetnutzer die Marke von 1 Milliarde überschritt und Nokia seinen ersten Tablet-Computer, das Nokia 770, drei Jahre vor dem iPad, auf den Markt brachte.

2005/
—

The Year
of the Idea
—

Desio

Red Bull Creativity Contest

The Sith Sense

Come Clean

The first video uploaded to YouTube

"This was the year when the number of active internet-users passed the 1 billion mark."

Nombre des idées géniales qui continuent d'apparaître sur le Web sont le fruit non pas d'agences mais d'individus, une force à ne pas sous-estimer, notamment au vu de certains des meilleurs projets de l'année.

Conclave Obscurum est la refonte tant attendue du portfolio de l'artiste russe Oleg Paschenko. La nouvelle version conserve toute la qualité de l'antérieure, déjà source d'inspiration de nombreux sites Web organiques.

Mika Tyyskä met en ligne Guitar Shred Show, où le guitariste animé du nom de Mr. Fastfinger explique des techniques et fait découvrir le air guitar.

Le site amaztype de Yugop est une application de recherche. Les utilisateurs entrent un terme qui s'affiche comme résultat composé d'images de produits vendus sur Amazon.

Pakman est le premier site clone de Pac-Man avec un personnage humain. Cette création des plus originales offre une excellente jouabilité et est truffée d'illustrations et d'interactions de qualité.

Bob's Cube présente la première expérience interactive se passant dans un bureau. Les utilisateurs y ont accès en l'absence de Bob, et personne ne peut s'empêcher de fouiner pour voir ce qu'il y a dans les tiroirs et sur la table.

Desio permet aux visiteurs d'explorer l'espace virtuel de la maison écologique de trois étages de Sekisui Heim en faisant glisser des personnages d'une pièce à l'autre. Une fonction de zoom permet de voir les intérieurs plus en détail.

Red Bull Creativity Contest publie un œuf de Pâques original sur son site promotionnel pour un événement encourageant l'art et la créativité. En faisant glisser divers éléments, comme une cannette, des ailes et un câble, les visiteurs construisent une machine volante qui rappelle celles des événements Red Bull Flugtag.

Les sites annonçant des nouveautés et cherchant à attirer les visiteurs avec un effet de surprise sont maintenant monnaie courante, et celui de North Kingdom pour la Toyota Aygo excelle en la matière : un clic sur la boîte aux lettres fait apparaître une enveloppe avec l'image d'une voiture qui se transforme en une Aygo taille réelle au beau milieu d'un couloir.

Dans ce site promotionnel pour le produit dérivé *Star Wars* de Burger King, The Sith Sense fait lire les pensées des utilisateurs par Darth Vader. Basé sur le jeu des 20 questions, la machine mémorise les réponses et les hypothèses sont de plus en plus précises au fil des essais.

Web.burza est l'un des premiers sites en Flash conformes aux normes, et il illustre la direction que prennent alors les sites Web développés par les agences. Il s'inscrit parmi les premiers au code HTML lourd à être retenus par les FWA, ce qui fait sourciller plus d'un fan du site et de Flash dans le monde.

Come Clean lance une tendance en encourageant les visiteurs à profiter du réveillon du jour de l'An pour confesser leurs secrets. Cette idée toute simple motive plusieurs autres sites à choisir certains jours de l'année pour leur lancement.

YouTube est fondé le 14 février par Chad Hurley, Steve Chen et Jawed Karim. Le 23 avril, Karim met en ligne la première vidéo intitulée « Me at the Zoo » et lue avec Flash.

Cette année, le nombre d'internautes actifs passe la barre du milliard et Nokia lance son premier ordinateur tablette, le Nokia 770, trois ans avant l'iPad.

08 Facts of the year

15.6%

Number of internet users:
1.02 billion, 15.6% of
the world population

64.8 million

Number of websites:
64.8 million

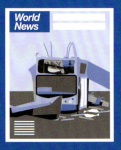

World News

World news:
on July 7, a series of
coordinated suicide-bomb
attacks take place in London

YAHOO!

Website with most traffic:
Yahoo.com

NOKIA

Tech hardware:
Nokia 770 Internet Tablet
launches

Windows XP
Professional x64 Edition

Install?

OK

Tech software:
Windows XP Pro x64
is released

News Corporation

myspace

Other tech:
Rupert Murdoch's News
Corp. buys MySpace for
$580 million

Highest-grossing film:
Harry Potter and the
Goblet of Fire

Wedding Crashers:
Crash This Trailer

—

The original upload-your-face

This site for the film *Wedding Crashers* was the first ever to enable users and their friends to upload their faces and become part of the content, taking the starring roles in the movie's trailer. It started an avalanche of similar sites, with Elf Yourself becoming the most well known in 2006, and also gave me the idea to play some cameo appearances on FWA as I often used my own face when making thumbnails for winning sites.

"I remember it being a case of coming up with a really 'literal' idea (with Bob, the creative director at Tequila), sparked by New Line U.S. asking us to do something around the theme of crashing a movie trailer. There was a long period of really not thinking it would be possible, where we didn't share it with anyone, but having the fire in our bellies, and the right (amazing) Flash engineer to keep on it until it worked."

James Koefoed
Tequila; Disney

Diese Seite für den Film *Die Hochzeits-Crasher* ermöglichte es zum ersten Mal, dass Benutzer und ihre Freunde ihre Gesichter hochladen und Teil des Inhalts werden konnten, um die Hauptrollen im Trailer des Films zu übernehmen. Es begann eine

Lawine von ähnlichen Seiten, wobei 2006 Elf Yourself am bekanntesten wurde und es kam mir die Idee, einige Cameo-Auftritte auf FWA zu spielen, da ich oft mein eigenes Gesicht benutzte, um Thumbnails für Gewinnseiten zu erstellen.

Ce site créé pour le film *Serial noceurs* est le premier à permettre aux visiteurs et leurs amis de publier leur portrait et d'apparaître comme l'interprète principal dans la bande-annonce. Il s'ensuit un flot de sites du même genre, le plus populaire

étant Elf Yourself en 2006. J'en tire l'idée de jouer avec des caméos sur le site FWA et d'utiliser mon propre visage dans les vignettes des sites élus.

2005/

—

<u>Dontclick.it</u>

—

The first website where users couldn't click

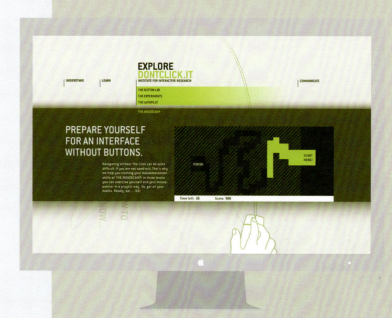
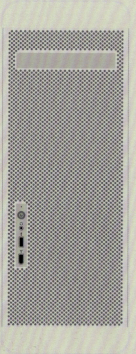

This site was a perfect example of what was meant when web designers talked about the 'idea', a project that almost couldn't keep up with demand and where clicking the mouse was a cardinal sin. Navigation on this experimental site was still done using the mouse, but it was a point website, no click. It was quite amazing how the urge to click was impossible for almost everyone to overcome!

THE CROWDSHOUT
THE LINKS
THE GIVEAWAYS
THE CONTACT

MAKE YOURSELF HEARD.

"Ohhh the good times of technical developments! Times of joyful play with graphics and code. Meaningful interaction and lustful animation created exciting and dramatic experiences and narratives, customized to the individual product. Dontclick.it wanted to be just that while taking away your way of saying 'Yes!' with a click on your mouse button. And surprisingly many of the website's visitors embraced the experiment, up to this day more than 5.5 million came by to visit. And this happened before social media hit the web."

Alex Frank
lxfx.de

Diese Seite war ein perfektes Beispiel dafür, was gemeint war, wenn Webdesigner über die „Idee" sprachen. Es sollte ein Projekt erstellt werden, das mit der Nachfrage fast nicht Schritt halten konnte und bei dem das Klicken mit der Maus eine Todsünde war. Die Navigation auf dieser Testseite erfolgte immer noch mit der Maus aber es war eine Zeige (Point)-Website ohne Klick. Es war schon erstaunlich zu sehen, wie der Klickdrang für fast jeden unmöglich zu überwinden war!

Ce site illustre parfaitement ce que les concepteurs Web entendent par « l'idée », un projet tout juste capable de répondre à la demande et dans lequel cliquer est un péché capital. Dans ce site expérimental, la navigation se fait encore à l'aide de la souris mais uniquement en pointant, sans clics. Il est hallucinant de constater à quel point l'envie de cliquer est irrésistible pour la plupart des visiteurs.

—

Fly

—

A website as innovative as the futuristic product itself

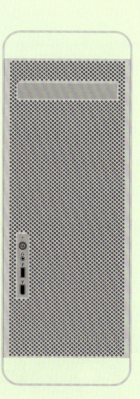

This promotional site for the exciting new Fly Pentop Computer had to be something very special and innovative to complement such a sophisticated product. The site succeeded, excelling in innovation, with seamless video integration of four teenagers who guided users through the website and the product's different features.

"The Fly website was the first time I remember actual full-frame video being used as the entire navigation and content of the website. We hired four teen actors who performed against a green screen and we composited the rest of the site around their actions. The actors would walk on to the site and interact back and forth with the viewer to show off how the Fly Pentop worked. The site was awarded Best Flash Site of the Year in 2005 at SXSW and the product was one of the top holiday gifts that year."

Daniel Stein
EVB

Diese Werbeseite für den aufregenden neuen Fly Pentop Computer musste etwas ganz Besonderes und Innovatives sein, um zu solch einem hoch entwickelten Produkt zu passen. Die Website war erfolgreich und brillierte durch Innovation mit nahtloser Videointegration von vier Teenagern, die die User durch die Website und die verschiedenen Funktionen des Produkts führten.

Ce site promotionnel pour l'ordinateur Fly Pentop devait être original et innovant, à la hauteur d'un produit des plus sophistiqués. C'est chose faite avec une bonne dose d'innovation et une intégration fluide de la vidéo de quatre adolescents guidant les utilisateurs dans le site et expliquant les caractéristiques du produit.

<u>Y-3 Collection</u>

—

A pioneering human-centered navigation cube

A navigation concept like no other was developed for Yohji Yamamoto's Y-3 line for the adidas fall/winter collection 2005. The system was based on models located within a box, and when a particular model was clicked they moved to take up a new position in their respective cube. What made this so great was that it looked and felt real because of the high production values.

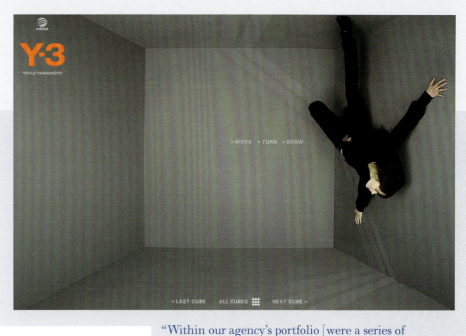

"Within our agency's portfolio [were a series of questions]: Can we merge the simplicity and functionality of exclusive well-tailored clothes with a creative website approach? Can we deliver a real brand story only by the way the consumer interacts with the site? Can the purity of Yohji Yamamoto be transformed into a slick, though extremely useful product display? Can navigation be not a necessary burden in the upper part of the site but a fun and brand-building experience? Yes — it's always worth trying!"

Olaf Czeschner
Neue Digitale Razorfish; aride

Für die Y-3-Linie von Yohji Yamamoto wurde für die adidas Herbst-/Winterkollektion 2005 ein Navigationskonzept entwickelt, das seinesgleichen suchte. Das System basierte auf Modellen, die sich in einer Kiste befanden und wenn ein bestimmtes Modell angeklickt wurde, bewegten sie sich, um eine neue Position in ihrem jeweiligen Würfel einzunehmen. Was es so großartig machte war, dass es aufgrund der hohen Produktionswerte toll aussah und sich echt anfühlte.

La gamme Y-3 de Yohji Yamamoto créée pour la collection automne/hiver 2005 d'adidas est présentée avec un concept de navigation jusqu'alors inédit. Le principe repose sur des mannequins enfermés dans des boîtes : si le visiteur clique sur l'un d'eux, il prend une nouvelle position dans son cube. Tout le succès tient à la qualité de la production qui donne des images très réalistes.

2005/
—

Corpse Bride

—

A website with as much
atmosphere as the movie

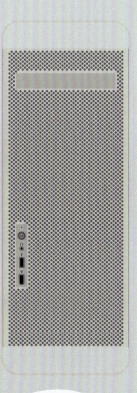

Taking movie sites to another level, this
outstanding production went far beyond
anything similar that had been seen before
and caught the attention of web designers
across the industry. Not only was it packed

with interactive features and special treats
for those who explored it but the combination
of Tim Burton's characters and the use of
atmospheric sound and effects gave the site
an energy all its own.

"The Tim Burton's *Corpse Bride* site for me
and the Blitz team was a true labor of love. We
wanted to lure visitors deeper into the Burton
world without sacrificing the 'get butts in seats'
marketing needs. So we created a new model
of layering rich interactive content and mini-
games based on time spent on site. This approach
demanded new assets that required us to flex our
CG modeling and animation capabilities to have
the necessary control of the experience."

Ken Martin
Blitz

Diese hervorragende Produktion, die Film-Websites auf ein anderes Level brachte, ging weit über das hinaus, was zuvor gesehen worden war und erregte die Aufmerksamkeit von Web-Designern in der gesamten Branche. Sie war nicht nur voller interaktiver Features und besonderer Leckerbissen für diejenigen, die sie erforschten, sondern die Kombination aus Tim Burtons Charakteren und die Verwendung von atmosphärischem Sound und Effekten gaben der Seite eine ganz eigene Energie.

Le site officiel pour un film prend une toute autre dimension avec cette superbe production qui va bien au-delà de ce qui a été fait jusqu'alors et est remarquée par la communauté des concepteurs Web. Outre les fonctions interactives et les bonus pour ceux qui l'explorent, il possède une dynamique propre grâce aux personnages de Tim Burton et à l'emploi de sons et d'effets d'ambiance.

—

Leo Burnett Canada

—

Where a founder's slogan comes to life

The eventual winner of Site of the Year 2005, this main website for the Leo Burnett advertising agency took visitors over as they entered. By replacing the mouse cursor with the black pencil used as an industry award, the site then made each letter of the company name an element to explore in its own right. It was a delightful idea, and such style and simplicity gave the site an elegance that was imitated by many but seldom achieved.

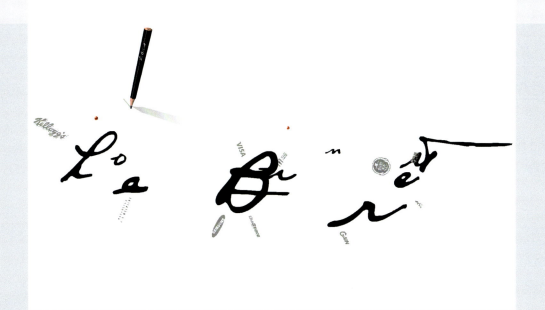

"Simulating a 3D world at a time when 2D was the norm, the site rewrote and reframed what a user experience could be. Every section of content was a rabbit hole, each click zooming into a new animation and a new story to tell. The build was an extraordinary feat, every step requiring a new approach and way of thinking. Conceptually, it was difficult for creatives to explain what they had imagined, so they had to physically act out the motions to explain the interface to the technologists and Flash developer."

Felix Wardene
Leo Burnett Canada

Der Gewinner der Site of the Year 2005. Diese Website der Werbeagentur Leo Burnett nahm die Besucher mit sich, wenn sie eintraten. Indem der Mauszeiger durch den schwarzen Stift ersetzt wurde, ein Objekt, das als Auszeichnung der Branche ver- wendet wurde, machte die Website jeden Buchstaben des Firmennamens zu einem eigenständigen Element. Es war eine interessante Idee. Dieser Stil und die Einfachheit gaben dem Ort eine Eleganz, die von vielen nachgeahmt aber selten erreicht wurde.

Élu Site of the Year 2005, ce site Web pour l'agence publicitaire Leo Burnett dirige les visiteurs dès qu'ils y entrent. Le curseur est remplacé par un crayon noir, objet utilisé comme récompense dans le domaine du design, et chaque lettre formant le nom de l'agence est un élément à explorer. Une idée intéressante et une élégance par son style et sa simplicité que beaucoup imitent mais que peu parviennent à égaler.

Dream Kitchens for Everyone

—

The original frozen-moments effect on the web

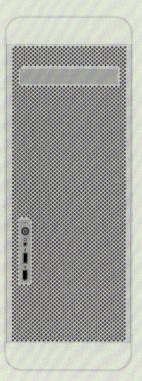

The use of video movement in the style of *The Matrix*, which took visitors to this site round and round a series of IKEA kitchens stopped in time, resulted in word-of-mouth reactions that spread like wildfire. Projects like this, from big and long-established agencies such as Forsman & Bodenfors, must have filled smaller and upcoming agencies with dread because of the scale of work involved and the associated cost.

"We took inspiration from the theater world, where they sometimes have rotating stages for quick shifts. This was done by using a huge motion-control rig. Since the look of the kitchens was so important, we used a full commercial-shoot set-up. To get the human element into the website, we decided to show different types of people 'living' in the kitchens, using a frozen-moment effect first used in the French art film *Last Year at Marienbad*. In that way we managed to get both visually arresting storytelling and a 180-degree view of IKEA's kitchens into the same scene."

Mathias Appelblad and Fredrik Jansson
Forsman & Bodenfors

Der Gebrauch von Video-Bewegungen im Stil von *The Matrix*, führten die Besucher auf dieser Seite herum und zu einer Reihe von IKEA Küchen, die in der Zeit angehalten wurden. Dies rief Mundpropaganda hervor, die sich wie ein Lauffeuer ausbreitete. Projekte wie dieses, die von großen und alteingesessenen Agenturen wie Forsman & Bodenfors ausgeführt wurden, müssen kleinere und aufstrebende Agenturen aufgrund des Umfangs der Arbeit und der damit verbundenen Kosten mit Schrecken erfüllt haben.

Le recours à un mouvement vidéo de type *Matrix* permet aux visiteurs de circuler dans une série de cuisines IKEA figées dans le temps. Les réactions ne se font pas attendre et le bouche-à-oreille se répand comme une traînée de poudre. Réalisés par des agences de poids comme Forsman & Bodenfors, des projets de cette envergure affolent sans doute les petites équipes qui débutent, tant pour la quantité de travail requis que pour les coûts associés.

Comcastic

—

The first site to incorporate a smartphone

With two main sections to this site, users could pull the strings themselves, by way of playing with the puppets, creating their own puppet, or even, as a world first, hooking up their mobile phone to engage a puppet in live chat with other users. The puppet physics were outstanding and made the experience extremely lifelike, while in the second section of the site, users were given the chance to break the World Speed-Mouse Record in a pentathlon event of mouse-mad games.

"We set out to build an experience we'd find entertaining. Almost every night was a late one. We were pushing the technology of the time and weren't quite sure if it would work — until it actually did. The first time we got to play with Erik Natzke's puppets, we were pretty giddy. By the final Q&A, I was eight months pregnant and often stayed up well past midnight to check the site and log bugs. Maybe it's no surprise that today my kid is both fun-loving and a bit anxious."

Toria Emery
Goodby, Silverstein & Partners; Salesforce

Es gab zwei Hauptabschnitte auf dieser Seite. Die User konnten die Fäden selbst ziehen, wenn sie mit den Puppen spielten, sie konnten ihre eigenen Puppen erstellen, oder sie konnten sogar, und das als Weltneuheit, ihr Mobiltelefon nehmen und die Puppe im Live-Chat mit anderen Nutzern einer Puppe in Kontakt bringen. Das Aussehen der Marionetten war herausragend und machte die Erfahrung extrem lebensecht, während im zweiten Teil der Seite den Benutzern die Möglichkeit gegeben wurde, den World Speed-Mouse Record in einem Fünfkampf mit maus-verrückten Spielen zu brechen.

Ce site compte deux sections principales dans lesquelles les utilisateurs peuvent contrôler les ficelles de marionnettes, créer leur propre marionnette et même, chose inédite, connecter leur téléphone portable pour la faire converser avec d'autres utilisateurs. L'apparence des marionnettes est remarquable et dote l'expérience d'un grand réalisme. Dans l'autre section, les utilisateurs peuvent tenter de battre le record mondial de vitesse avec la souris dans un pentathlon de jeux à base de clics frénétiques.

Saab Animal Vision

—

Taking atmosphere to a new level

Fierce predators like the lynx, the wolf and the wolverine

START

With glimpses of a Saab in a winter setting somewhere in Scandinavia, this promotional site featured polished videos and quality sound design to load it with atmosphere.

When a wolf appeared, for example, it seemed genuinely threatening and users felt transported to the bleak setting yet happy to be safe inside the car.

"In the ATL advertising for this campaign there was an analogy between the car and wild animals in Sweden: 'Not all Swedish animals live in the forest'. We knew that we needed to show the car from all angles, which normally is quite boring. Then we came up with the idea to do this from the perspective of the other animals in the forest. This wasn't easy. First we had to build up a winter forest — in August. Then we had to make the animals come to life without actually using any."

Johan Tesch
Lowe Tesch; KING

Mit einem Blick auf einen Saab in einem winterlichen Ambiente irgendwo in Skandinavien, präsentierte diese Werbeseite polierte Videos und hochwertiges Sounddesign, vollgeladen mit Atmosphäre. Wenn zum Beispiel ein Wolf auftauchte, fühlte es sich wirklich bedrohlich an und die Nutzer fühlten sich in die trostlose Umgebung versetzt und waren froh, sicher im Auto zu sein.

Les images d'une Saab dans un paysage hivernal de Scandinavie alimentent les élégantes vidéos de ce site promotionnel, où l'audio de qualité finit de créer l'atmosphère. Quand un loup surgit par exemple, la menace se perçoit, et les visiteurs se sentent transportés dans cet univers sombre, heureux d'être en sécurité à l'intérieur de la voiture.

Eminem

—

Brave and bold website for the famous rapper

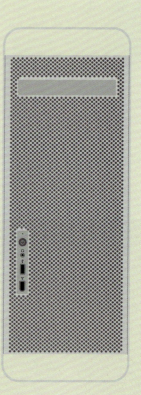

Wefail unleashed all its creativity and trade-mark style in this site for Eminem, which went on to win the FWA People's Choice Award for 2005 and also made me look at awards based on public voting very differently. As Wefail's

Jordan Stone said, "I believe I speak for both Martin and myself when I say 'Eminem truly does have the biggest mailing-list ever!' We are the champions!"

"We didn't have much time to work on this, a month or so. Two of us worked on it and Jordan got drunk half way through and emailed them a bunch of really bad words because we were under so much pressure. Sadly this was the only job we ever did for the record company, but we heard that Eminem loved it and it also got approved by Dr. Dre, so that was cool. Management wanted the text a lot bigger, huge text, but we didn't change it. Tough job in a short timeframe."

Martin Hughes
Wefail

Wefail entfesselte seine ganze Kreativität und seinen Markenzeichen-Stil auf dieser Seite für Eminem. Die Seite gewann den FWA People's Choice Award 2005 und brachte mich dazu, Preise, die auf öffentlichen Abstimmungen basierten, mit anderen Augen zu sehen. Wie Jordan Stone von Wefail sagte: „Ich glaube, ich spreche für Martin und mich, wenn ich sage: Eminem hat wirklich die größte Mailing-Liste aller Zeiten! Wir sind die Champions!"

Dans ce site pour Eminem, Wefail donne libre cours à sa créativité et à son style unique et remporte le prix FWA People's Choice Award de 2005. Leur création change aussi complètement mon opinion sur les prix basés sur la votation du public. Comme son cofondateur Jordan Stone l'explique, « Je pense parler pour Martin et moi-même quand j'affirme que Eminem a la plus grande liste de diffusion jamais vue ! On est des champions ! ».

NOTABLE WEBSITE LAUNCH
YouTube

GOOGLE FACTS

Google Maps goes live

Google Earth is unveiled

Google Mobile Web Search launches for mobile phones

Google allows people to customize the Google home-page

Top 5 Trends

Google Analytics is released

INTERNET COMMUNITY
The Million
Dollar Homepage

Alex Tew, a 21-year-old English student,
set up a website to try and raise $1 million
(largely to pay for his degree studies)
by selling a million pixels for $1 each.
It gained news coverage worldwide and was
one of the year's most visited websites, but
was also subject to a DDoS attack and ransom
demand. The last 1,000 pixels were sold by
auction on eBay on January 11, 2006, and the
final total amassed was $1,037,100.

MOBILE EVOLUTION
Nokia 6680

Nokia's first 3G smartphone
with a front camera
(marketed for video-calling)

2006/

The Year of Big Budgets

2006/

—

The Year of Big Budgets

—

Heiwa Alpha

With the web picking up from where it had left off before the dot-com bubble burst, this was the year advertising budgets changed their focus from television and print to online. The job market went crazy and employers struggled to keep up with the sudden growth of their companies.

The website for Heiwa Alpha was amongst the most visually stunning examples ever, and invited users to explore its virtual world through a series of interactions.

2006 was also the 10th anniversary of Flash, and to mark this Adobe set up a dedicated portal. They also asked FWA to get involved and we ran various polls to establish the Most Influential Flash Website of the last decade, with the eventual winner being 2Advanced Expansions from 2001.

London's Unit9 developed an online world full of character that was aimed at promoting Adobe Creative Suite 2.3.

Big brands such as Mercedes-Benz were pushing hard with creative excellence and experimentation on the web, as was evident in the Mercedes A-to-S project, where users could interact with every letter from A to S.

For the new Nokia N91, a phone that could store 3,000 songs, a character called Pjotro was developed whose combined love of music, dancing, and engineering was

manifested in his suit, which actually made the music as he danced.

The Brazilian sun-cream manufacturer Sundown achieved global exposure with Piano, a human instrument that users could interact with to compose a tune.

The interactive safety tests of its In-synch Challenge gave the insurance company Travelers an edge over its competitors, and featured a striking 3D interface.

2Advanced Studios launched the fifth version of their site, but had reached a stage where it was becoming impossible to keep raising the bar. The site was stunning, yet left die-hard fans still wanting to see the wheel being reinvented once again.

New agencies continued to appear, and from all over the world. The Slovakian web agency Kamikadze created mystery and intrigue by building its interface as users watched, with sticky notes and just their hands.

Hard-hitting web experiences could expose people to real-world issues they might not have known about, such as Democratic Republic of Congo – Forgotten War, which used the sound of gunfire to welcome visitors.

The biggest tech news was Google's acquisition of YouTube for $1.65 billion in stock, just 20 months after the site launched.

"This was the
year advertising
budgets changed
their focus from
television and
print to online."

Adobe Creative Suite 2.3

Piano

Pjotro

Mercedes A-to-S

Nachdem sich das Internet nach dem Platzen der Dot-Com-Blase langsam erholt hatte, war es das Jahr, in dem sich die Werbebudgets von Fernsehen und Print auf Online verlagerten. Der Arbeitsmarkt spielte verrückt und die Arbeitgeber hatten Mühe, mit dem plötzlichen Wachstum ihrer Unternehmen Schritt zu halten.

Die Website für Heiwa Alpha gehörte zu den visuell beeindruckendsten Beispielen überhaupt und lud die User ein, eine virtuelle Welt durch eine Reihe von Interaktionen zu erkunden.

2006 war auch der 10. Jahrestag von Flash und um dies zu markieren, richtete Adobe ein eigenes Portal ein. Sie hatten auch FWA gebeten, sich zu beteiligen und wir führten verschiedene Umfragen durch, um die einflussreichste Flash-

Website des letzten Jahrzehnts festzustellen, wobei der Gewinner 2Advanced Expansions aus dem Jahr 2001 war.

Londons Unit9 entwickelte eine Online-Welt voller Charakter, mit dem Ziel, Adobe Creative Suite 2.3 zu bewerben.

Große Marken wie zum Beispiel Mercedes-Benz machten mit kreativem Können und Experimentierfreudigkeit im Web Druck, wie es im Mercedes A-bis-S-Projekt deutlich wurde, bei dem Nutzer mit jedem Buchstaben von A bis S interagieren konnten.

Für das neue Nokia N91, ein Handy, das 3.000 Songs speichern konnte, wurde eine Figur namens Pjotro entwickelt, dessen Liebe zu Musik, Tanz und Technik sich in seinem Anzug manifestierte, der durch die Musik tatsächlich zum Tanzen gebracht wurde.

Der brasilianische Sonnencremehersteller Sundown erreichte mit Piano, einem menschlichen Instrument, mit dem die Benutzer interagieren konnten, um eine Melodie zu komponieren, eine globale Präsenz.

Die interaktiven Sicherheitstests der In-synch Challenge verschafften der Versicherungsgesellschaft Travelers einen Wettbewerbsvorteil gegenüber der Konkurrenz und zeichneten sich durch eine markante 3D-Oberfläche aus.

2Advanced Studios startete die fünfte Version ihrer Website, hatte aber ein Stadium erreicht, in dem es unmöglich wurde, die Messlatte immer höher zu legen. Die Seite war atemberaubend aber die Fans wollten das Rad noch einmal neu erfunden sehen.

Neue Agenturen erschienen weiterhin auf der ganzen Welt. Die slowakische Web-Agentur Kamikadze schuf Rätsel und Intrigen, indem sie ihre Benutzeroberfläche vor den Augen der User mit Haftnotizen und nur mit ihren Händen aufbaute.

Mit knallharten Web-Erlebnissen konnten die Menschen echten Problemen ausgesetzt werden, die ihnen vielleicht unbekannt waren, wie zum Beispiel „Democratic Republic of Congo – Forgotten War", bei dem die Besucher mit Schüssen begrüßt wurden.

Die größte technische Neuerung war die Übernahme von YouTube durch Google für 1,65 Milliarden Dollar, nur 20 Monate nach dem Start der Website.

—

The Year of Big Budgets

—

"Hard-hitting web experiences could expose people to real-world issues they might not have known about."

2Advanced Studios

In-synch Challenge

Democratic Republic of Congo – Forgotten War

Le Web reprend son évolution depuis son état antérieur à l'explosion de la bulle Internet. Les budgets publicitaires changent de priorité et délaissent la télévision et la presse imprimée pour la diffusion en ligne. Le marché du travail bouillonne et les employeurs luttent pour tenir la cadence de croissance des entreprises.

Le site Web pour Heiwa Alpha est l'une des créations les plus fascinantes jamais vues sur le plan visuel. Les visiteurs sont invités à explorer ce monde virtuel via une série d'interactions.

En 2006 aussi, Flash célèbre son 10ᵉ anniversaire et pour marquer le coup, Adobe lance un portail spécial. La firme demande également aux FWA de s'impliquer: grâce à plusieurs sondages, nous désignons le site

Web en Flash le plus influent de la décennie. Le prix revient au site de 2Advanced Expansions créé en 2001.

La société londonienne Unit9 invente un monde rempli de personnages dans le but de promouvoir Adobe Creative Suite 2.3.

De grandes marques comme Mercedes-Benz font pression pour que leur site soit un exemple d'expérimentation et d'excellence créative. Le projet Mercedes A-to-S permet aux visiteurs d'interagir avec chaque lettre de A à S.

Pjotro est inventé pour vanter le nouveau téléphone Nokia N91, capable de stocker jusqu'à 3 000 chansons. Ce personnage aime la musique, la danse et l'ingénierie, comme le reflète son costume qui joue

une mélodie par rapport à sa chorégraphie.

Sundown est un fabricant brésilien de crèmes solaires qui lance une promotion mondiale avec Piano, un instrument humain avec lequel les visiteurs peuvent interagir pour composer un air.

Les tests de sécurité interactifs conçus par In-synch Challenge confèrent à la compagnie d'assurances Travelers un avantage sur la concurrence, sans compter une spectaculaire interface en 3D.

L'agence 2Advanced Studios lance la cinquième mouture de son site mais la barre est déjà tellement haute qu'il lui est difficile de se surpasser. Le site est grandiose bien que les fans en veulent plus et s'attendent à ce que la roue soit réinventée.

De nouvelles agences continuent d'apparaître de tous les coins du monde. L'agence de création slovaque Kamikadze sait captiver en composant son interface sous les yeux des internautes à base de notes adhésives et de mains les manipulant.

Des expériences Web saisissantes permettent de confronter les gens à des problèmes du monde réel qu'ils ignorent éventuellement. Le site Democratic Republic of Congo – Forgotten War par exemple accueille les visiteurs au son de coups de feu.

L'événement dans le domaine technologique est l'acquisition de YouTube par Google pour 1,65 milliard de dollars en actions 20 mois à peine après le lancement du site.

08 Facts of the year

Number of internet users:
1.09 billion, 16.5% of
the world population

Number of websites:
85.5 million

World news:
North Korea conducts its
first nuclear test

Website with most traffic:
Yahoo.com

Tech hardware:
Apple launches the MacBook

Tech software:
Internet Explorer 7
launches

Other tech:
Google buys YouTube for
$1.65 billion in stock

Highest-grossing film:
Pirates of the Caribbean:
Dead Man's Chest

—

Philips Bodygroom

—

Widely celebrated
for its candid humor

A website for a new electric shaver for men that was filled with bleeped-out expletives and hosted by a man wearing a bathrobe? This was certainly a surprise to first-time viewers although the site was critically acclaimed across the industry for its brazen approach and entertainment value.

Philips CEO Robert Baird said at the time, "We knew we were taking a risk with shaveeverywhere.com, but we also knew there was a void in the grooming market that needed to be filled. We didn't set out to be funny, we just knew funny would work."

"It may be somewhat puerile — but man, it's fun and well executed. Kept me engaged all the way. No, not that far… But if you've never considered grooming your -------- or your -------- or gaining that extra inch on your --------, this one might just win you over."

Florian Schmitt
Hi-ReS!
(Industry quote whilst judging FWA SOTY)

Eine Website für einen neuen elektrischen Rasierer für Männer, die mit ausgeblendeten Kraftausdrücken ausgefüllt und von einem Mann im Bademantel vorgestellt wurde? Dies war sicherlich eine Überraschung für Erstbesucher, obwohl die Seite in der Branche für ihren unverschämten Ansatz und Unterhaltungswert kritisch bejubelt wurde.

Philips CEO Robert Baird sagte in der Zeit: „Wir wissen, dass wir ein Risiko mit shaveeverywhere.com eingingen, aber wir wussten auch, dass es auf dem Pflegemarkt eine Lücke gab, die gefüllt werden musste. Wir wollten gar nicht lustig sein, wir wussten nur, dass witzig funktionieren würde."

Un site Web présentant un nouveau rasoir électrique pour homme, avec des bips qui couvrent des jurons et un homme en peignoir servant de guide ? L'interface n'est pas sans créer la surprise à la première visite et est saluée par la communauté pour son approche culottée et sa touche de divertissement.

Robert Baird, PDG de Philips, explique : «Nous étions conscients de prendre un risque avec shaveeverywhere. com, mais nous savions aussi qu'il y avait un créneau à occuper sur le marché des produits d'hygiène masculine. Nous ne comptions pas être drôles, nous savions juste qu'une création amusante marcherait.»

Okaydave

—

Overnight global fame for student

Early in the year, an unknown student from the graduate program at Portfolio Center in Atlanta took the web by storm, and his design portfolio duly won FWA's prestigious Site of the Month. This was quite an achievement when outstanding productions from top agencies and brands were also in the mix, while for Dave Werner it meant a complete change in his working life.

"The FWA award gave me a ridiculous amount of exposure and has helped lead to literally hundreds of amazingly cool opportunities and contacts. As an unknown student sitting in his little Atlanta apartment putting the site together through late nights fueled by Coca-Cola, I never dreamed the site would get this much attention this quickly. It has really helped open doors and start off what I think is going to be an exciting and interesting career."

Dave Werner
Okaydave; Adobe

Zu Beginn des Jahres eroberte ein unbekannter Student aus dem Graduate-Programm des Portfolio Centers in Atlanta das Internet und sein Design-Portfolio gewann die prestigeträchtige Site of the Month des FWA. Das war eine ziemliche Leistung, da herausragende Produktionen von Top-Agenturen und Marken mit in der Auswahl waren. Für Dave Werner bedeutete dies eine komplette Veränderung seines Arbeitslebens.

Au début de l'année, un étudiant inconnu du programme d'études supérieures du Portfolio Center d'Atlanta conquiert le Web avec son portfolio élégant, qui remporte à juste titre le prestigieux prix FWA Site of the Month. Tout un exploit en soi sachant que d'excellentes productions des meilleures agences et marques étaient en compétition. La carrière de Dave Werner change alors radicalement.

—

Would You Like a Website?

—

Taking websites to the streets

"Freedom Interactive Design is out here in the cold selling websites today," said a man on the street presented on this groundbreaking site. It was originally produced as a self-promotional piece for the Adobe Design Center but the effect was startling – here were employees of the agency out in New York wearing what appeared to be video-enhanced sandwich boards and interacting with locals and tourists.

"We were invited by Adobe to showcase their product capabilities. We thought we should do something self-promotional. We thought it would be funny to hawk websites on the streets, 'Websites here! Would you like a website?!' Like insane New Yorkers we would approach potential customers and provoke reactions with a day-glow green sandwich board. In post-production, we would motion-track and put 'our work' on the 'sign'. Great times… We thought we were working on something special together."

Mark Ferdman
Freedom Interactive Design; dpHUE

„Freedom Interactive Design steht heute hier draußen in der Kälte und verkauft Websites" sagte ein Mann auf der Straße, präsentiert auf dieser bahnbrechenden Website. Diese wurde ursprünglich als Eigenwerbung für das Adobe Design Center produziert, aber der Effekt war aufregend – hier waren Angestellte der Agentur in New York zu sehen, die scheinbar mit Video verbesserte Reklametafeln trugen und mit Einheimischen und Touristen interagierten.

«Freedom Interactive Design affronte le froid pour vendre des sites Web», lance dans la rue un homme qui apparaît dans ce site révolutionnaire. D'abord pensé pour promouvoir Adobe Design Center, il crée un effet bœuf en envoyant dans les rues de New York des employés de l'agence convertis en hommes-sandwichs équipés de tableaux vidéo et interpellant les locaux et les touristes.

2006/
—

Nike Air

—

Pushing the range of
user-responsive motion graphics

The Nike Air website offered a full video experience with a twist, and another world first: user-interactive motion graphics. Users could choose either Run on Air or Ball on Air, then experiment with the motion graphics by hitting random keys on the keyboard. The results appeared instantly, a cornucopia of motion effects, and this was a perfect example of how websites evolved: a simple idea with high-impact results.

"The velocity of the internet makes Flash seem archaic or quaint to some, but it was wildly important to the evolution of our digital experiences. It unlocked emotion on the web — bringing a level of expressiveness in animation, sound, and video that hadn't been imaginable before. The Nike Air site is an early example of a piece of work that leveraged all of those possibilities in an interactive environment that also let users create for themselves. We were trying hard to push the boundaries in every area. I wonder if we translated the experience to VR today it would still hold up. I suspect it would."

Michael Lebowitz
Big Spaceship

Die Nike Air-Website bot ein komplettes Videoerlebnis mit einem unerwartetem Ende und eine weitere Weltneuheit: benutzerinteraktive bewegliche Grafiken. Die User konnten entweder „Run on Air" oder „Ball on Air" wählen und dann mit den Bewegungsgrafiken experimentieren, indem sie zufällig Tasten auf der Tastatur drückten. Die Ergebnisse erschienen sofort, es war ein Füllhorn von Bewegungseffekten und das war ein perfektes Beispiel dafür, wie sich Websites entwickelten: Eine einfache Idee mit starken Ergebnissen.

Le site Web de Nike Air offre une expérience vidéo complète, avec une touche fantaisiste et l'emploi inédit d'animations interactives. Les visiteurs choisissent entre «Run on Air» et «Ball on Air» et doivent appuyer sur des touches aléatoires du clavier pour interagir; les résultats sont immédiats et déversent une avalanche d'effets. Cette réalisation reflète très bien l'évolution des sites Web, qui partent d'une idée simple donnant des résultats saisissants.

Uniqlo

—

New possibilities
for web shops

The Uniqlo site explorer showcased this up-and-coming fashion label in a new and exciting way, using multiple small images to create the bigger image viewers saw. While relatively unknown at the time, Uniqlo's rise to fame was unquestionably helped by the impact this website had in presenting the brand in a compelling and innovative manner.

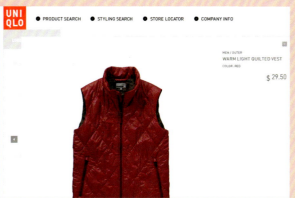

"This expertly crafted website, designed by Yugo Nakamura and his team at tha, showcased Uniqlo's product line in a fun, engaging way. It also (along with 'Uniqlock') set the benchmark for Uniqlo's innovative digital initiatives. Uniqlo Explorer was a flexible photo-mosaic system where a large 'hero' image on the home-page was transformed into a mosaic of Uniqlo products. Each square offered a close-up view when clicked and another click generated a new product mosaic based on the previous image."

Hideki Owa
tha; Pulp

Der Uniqlo Site Explorer präsentierte dieses aufstrebende
Modelabel auf eine neue und
aufregende Art und Weise, indem
es viele kleine Bilder verwendete,
um das größere Bild zu erzeugen,
das die Zuschauer dann sahen.

Uniqlo war zu jener Zeit noch
relativ unbekannt, wurde aber
zweifelsohne durch den Einfluss
dieser Website auf die Präsentation der Marke auf überzeugende
und innovative Weise unterstützt.

La navigation dans le site de la
marque montante Uniqlo est
aussi originale qu'intéressante,
avec plusieurs petites images en
composant une grande à l'écran.
Bien qu'assez peu connue à
l'époque, l'ascension de Uniqlo

s'explique sans conteste en
partie par l'impact de ce site
Web à l'approche innovante
et convaincante.

2006/
—

Audi R8
—

100% Vorsprung durch Technik

The first thing that hit visitors to the R8 website was its powerful music, and this was followed by an unforgettable and adrenaline-pumping virtual test-drive, with spectacular video and motion effects. The drive took visitors through a series of levels on the site, each calculated to stimulate the senses in a thrilling web experience.

"Making a virtue out of necessity: as the car was still in development at this point and we had no campaign material we could use, we had to create all content ourselves. We took a $99 3D stock model of the Le Mans car and developed an interactive motion design dummy. The unique mix of mystical, artificial look, the interplay of speed, time, and the energetic soundtrack, hit the mark."

Oliver Hinrichs
oliverhinrichs.de

Das erste, auf das der Besucher der R8-Website traf, war ihre kraftvolle Musik, und darauf folgte eine unvergessliche und adrenalingeladene virtuelle Testfahrt mit spektakulären Video- und Bewegungseffekten.

Die Fahrt führte die Besucher durch eine Reihe von Ebenen auf der Website, von denen jede darauf ausgerichtet war, die Sinne in einem spannenden Web-Erlebnis zu stimulieren.

Les visiteurs du site R8 sont d'abord frappés par une puissante musique. Vient ensuite un essai sur route virtuel qui crée des sensations fortes grâce à des effets spectaculaires. Le tour fait passer les visiteurs par une série de niveaux conçus pour produire une expérience Web stimulante et palpitante.

—

Flash Earth

—

A little experiment that really did take off

This website will be familiar to most people, even as they read about it now since it is still a fully working site. Created by the pioneering Flash designer Paul Neave, who more than likely never guessed how huge a resource it would become, this was essentially Google Earth but launched ahead of its better-known counterpart.

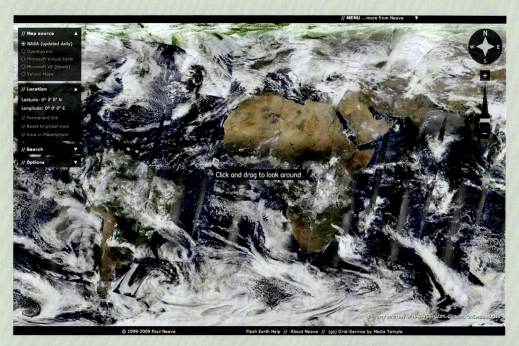

"Flash Earth was an experiment I created at the time when Google Maps first launched around 2006. I set about making a version that would smoothly enlarge each layer of images as the map was zoomed. The reaction was incredible. It was on the front page of Digg and everyone thought I was creating a 'Google Earth' in the browser. I wasn't doing any such thing. But what this really showed was just how far ahead Flash was at that time."

Paul Neave
Flash Earth; neave.com

Diese Website wird den meisten Menschen vertraut sein, denn wenn sie es jetzt lesen, ist sie immer noch eine voll funktionierende Website. Entwickelt wurde sie vom bahnbrechenden Flash-Designer Paul Neave, der wahrscheinlich nie erraten hätte, wie groß diese Ressource werden würde. Sie war im Wesentlichen wie Google Earth, wurde aber noch vor seinem bekannteren Pendant entwickelt.

La plupart des internautes connaissent ce site Web, encore pleinement opérationnel à l'heure actuelle. Son créateur Paul Neave, pionnier en développement Flash, n'a probablement jamais imaginé qu'il deviendrait une ressource si importante, une sorte de Google Earth apparue bien avant son célèbre homologue.

—

Elf Yourself

—

Over 123 million people given elfamorphosis

EVB hit the jackpot here by capitalizing on the holiday season, and reasoning that office workers shared most web content around Christmas they created a new upload-your-face experience where users could turn themselves into an elf and even add the faces of four friends as well to create a small band of dancing elves. It was a hit for several years and at its peak was the 55th most visited website.

"While Elf Yourself was responsible for popularizing the 'upload-your-face' phenomenon, it was really part of a larger movement in web design — personalization. Hundreds of projects that launched afterwards were customized, personalized to the viewer. Even though Elf Yourself didn't win all the Cannes Lions, it was seen by hundreds of millions of people all around the world and became part of the DNA of a brand. Elf Yourself became a yearly tradition for Office Max — opening the stock exchange, becoming a Macy's Parade float, flash mobs, and now a popular app."

Jason Zada
EVB; Filmmaker

START THE
ELFAMORPHOSIS!

EVB knackten hier den Jackpot, indem sie die Weihnachtsfeiertage nutzen. Sie begründeten es damit, dass Büroangestellte den meisten Web-Content um Weihnachten herum verschickten. Sie erstellten eine neue Erfahrung des Hochladens von Gesichtern, bei der sich die User in eine Elfe verwandeln und sogar noch die Gesichter von vier Freunden hinzufügen konnten, um außerdem eine kleine Band tanzender Elfen zu erschaffen. Es war mehrere Jahre lang ein Hit und auf ihrem Höhepunkt war sie unter den 55 meistbesuchten Websites.

EVB remporte le jackpot en pariant sur la période des fêtes. Partant de l'idée que les collègues de bureau partagent le plus de contenu Web autour de Noël, l'agence crée une expérience permettant de charger son portrait (et celui de quatre amis) et de se transformer en elfes dansant en rythme. Le succès dure plusieurs années et le site se classe à son apogée comme le 55e le plus visité.

Navy Lifestyle

—

The first interactive warship

To discover what life in the Royal Australian Navy was really like, users were here given the opportunity to explore HMAS *Anzac*, one of the world's most advanced warships, and to track the movements of the Australian Navy over the course of a year. The site itself had the look and feel of a computer game and used that hook to invite people to extend their visits for longer.

"The site was our biggest project ever and took about six months to make, which seemed like for ever at the time. The most memorable part for me was spending a week in the Navy, filming content out at sea, battling seasickness and a crazy sailor who kept trying to cut my hair."

Brett White
Visual Jazz; Isobar Australia

Um zu erfahren, wie das Leben in der Royal Australian Navy wirklich war, erhielten die User hier die Gelegenheit, die HMAS *Anzac* zu erkunden, eines der modernsten Kriegsschiffe der Welt. Sie konnten die Bewegungen der australischen Marine im Laufe eines Jahres verfolgen. Die Seite selbst sah aus und fühlte sich an wie ein Computerspiel und nutzte dies, um Leute einzuladen, bei ihren Besuchen länger zu verweilen.

Pour découvrir le quotidien au sein de la Royal Australian Navy, les utilisateurs peuvent explorer le HMAS *Anzac*, l'un des navires de guerre les plus avancés, et suivre les déplacements de la RAN sur une période d'un an.

Le site s'apparente à un jeu sur ordinateur, ce qui séduit et retient les visiteurs plus longtemps en ligne.

2006/

—

<u>Pictaps</u>

—

A 2D sketch transforms
into a 3D dancing character

Masayuki Kido's phenomenal talent produced a site that allowed users to create their own dancer by drawing a 2D character which then became fully animated in 3D. The site also featured a large gallery of characters created by other visitors, so even those who had zero drawing skills could still enjoy the experience. Kido soon became very well known for his experimental and cutting-edge work.

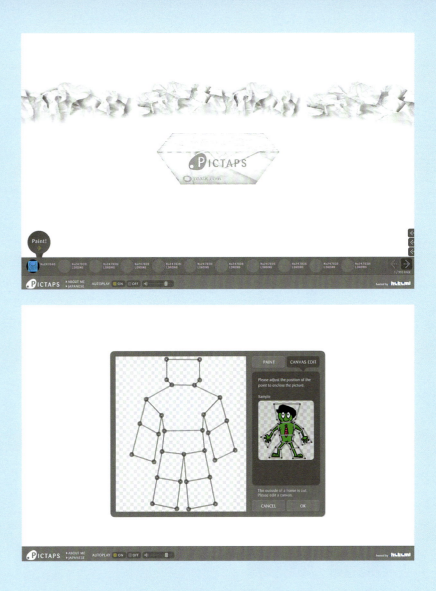

"It didn't take much time. I created this in two weeks and a bit as I had to make it in time for an award sponsored by Adobe. However, it was an extreme technical challenge. Development of an original 3D engine and working with an animation system using bone-based modeling… Even thinking back to it makes my skin crawl."

Masayuki Kido
Roxik

Masayuki Kidos phänomenales Talent produzierte eine Site, auf der die Benutzer ihren eigenen Tänzer kreieren konnten, indem sie einen 2D-Charakter zeichneten, der dann vollständig in 3D animiert wurde. Die Seite enthielt auch eine große Galerie von Charakteren, die von anderen Besuchern erstellt wurden, sodass sogar diejenigen, die keine Zeichenkünste hatten, diese Erfahrung genießen konnten. Kido wurde bald sehr bekannt für seine experimentellen und innovativen Arbeiten.

Fort de son immense talent, Masayuki Kido produit un site où l'internaute dessine en 2D son propre danseur et le voit s'animer en 3D. Le site inclut également une importante galerie de personnages créés par d'autres visiteurs : même ceux sans talent de dessinateurs peuvent donc profiter aussi de l'expérience. Kido se fera très vite un nom pour son travail expérimental et d'avant-garde.

INTERNET COMMUNITY
WikiLeaks

WikiLeaks forms in October as a non-profit organization to publish classified and secret news information received from anonymous sources.

GOOGLE FACTS

The verb "Google" is added to the Oxford English Dictionary

The Web-based apps Docs and Spreadsheets are released

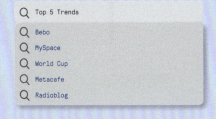

Top 5 Trends

Google acquires YouTube

Google Calendar launches

Google Translate launches

NOTABLE WEBSITE LAUNCH
Twttr
(later Twitter)

MOBILE EVOLUTION
BenQ Siemens S88

The first mobile phone
with an AMOLED display

2007/

The Year Full-Screen Video Arrives – Along with the iPhone

2007/

—

The Year Full-Screen Video Arrives – Along With the iPhone

—

Typography Kicks Ass

The Passenger

On January 2, the first full-screen web version of a television ad was shown, for ATG, Sweden's biggest bookmakers for horse betting. The Horses Give Everything site's use of this format marked the dawn of a new era for video on the web.

Exactly one week later, a device was launched that would change the way the world communicated and consumed information for ever: the iPhone.

At the time, Steve Jobs claimed that the iPhone was so revolutionary it was five years ahead of any other mobiles on the market, chiefly on account of the shift away from using a peripheral to an inbuilt pointing device: from mouse to finger.

The website for the Swedish make-up artist Filippa Smedhagen Sund was an early example of drag navigation. To navigate, users simply dragged the image left or right, and this new method was quickly copied on many other sites.

Content was now being channeled via APIs, from sites like Flickr, to create interesting projects, with TiltViewer being one of the first examples. Typography Kicks Ass was another example of such Flickr API content integration. This experimental project enabled users to send a message or post one on the site using images from Flickr to build a random 'Flickr Bold Italic' font.

The Passenger was an early example of user-controlled video. On this promotional site for Nokia's CK-20W multimedia car kit, users got their first opportunity to control several aspects of the video they were watching.

The Halo 3: Believe website featured a real model diorama for users to explore the landscape where the battle of New Mombasa took place. It took 1,666 screen shots to create the experience at what was called the John-117 Monument.

Uniqlock was an online clock from Uniqlo which combined music and dance with a world clock. One of the site's highlights was the World Uniqlock, which showed all the sites worldwide that had downloaded the clock and added it to their own web space.

Educational websites continued to be as creative as possible, to attract more people, and Try Drugs was one such which enabled users to experience the effects of drugs online.

The Life Size Blue Whale close-up experience was created as part of the Whale and Dolphin Conservation Society's anti-whaling campaign. The endangered blue whale, the largest animal ever to have lived, was here presented at its actual size.

Halo 3: Believe

Horses Give Everything

Try Drugs

"On January 2,
the first
full-screen web
version of a
television
ad was shown."

Am 2. Januar wurde die erste Vollbild-Webversion einer Fernsehwerbung für ATG, Schwedens größter Buchmacher für Pferdewetten, gezeigt. Die Verwendung dieses Formats auf der Horses Give Everything Seite markierte der Beginn einer neuen Ära für Videos im Internet.

Genau eine Woche später wurde ein Gerät auf den Markt gebracht, das die Art wie die Welt kommuniziert und Informationen konsumiert für immer verändern sollte: das iPhone.

Steve Jobs behauptete, dass das iPhone so revolutionär sei, dass es den anderen Mobiltelefonen auf dem Markt fünf Jahre voraus sei, vor allem deswegen, weil ein externes Peripheriegerät durch ein eingebautes Zeigegerät ersetzt wurde: von der Maus zum Finger.

Die Website für die schwedische Visagistin Filippa Smedhagen Sund war ein frühes Beispiel für Drag-Navigation. Um zu navigieren, zogen Benutzer einfach das Bild nach links oder rechts und diese neue Methode wurde schnell auf vielen anderen Seiten kopiert.

Inhalt wurde nun über APIs von Websites wie Flickr kanalisiert, um interessante Projekte zu erstellen, wobei TiltViewer eines der ersten Beispiele war.

Typography Kicks Ass war ein weiteres Beispiel solcher Flickr API Content-Integration. Dieses experimentelle Projekt ermöglichte es Benutzern, eine Nachricht zu senden oder eine auf der Site zu veröffentlichen, indem sie Bilder von Flickr verwendeten, um eine zufällige Schrift „Flickr Bold Italic" zu erstellen.

The Passenger war ein frühes Beispiel für benutzergesteuerte Videos. Auf dieser Werbeseite für Nokias CK-20W Multimedia Car Kit, bekamen die User zum ersten Mal die Gelegenheit, verschiedene Aspekte des Videos, das sie gerade sahen, zu kontrollieren.

Halo 3: Believe zeigte ein echtes Modell-Diorama, mit dem Nutzer die Landschaft erkunden können, in der die Schlacht von New Mombasa stattfand. Es dauerte 1.666 Screenshots, um das sogenannte Erlebnis des John-117-Monuments zu schaffen.

Uniqlock war eine Online-Uhr von Uniqlo, die Musik und Tanz mit einer Weltzeituhr verband. Eines der Highlights der Website war die World Uniqlock, die alle Websites weltweit zeigte,

die die Uhr heruntergeladen und in ihren eigenen Webspace aufgenommen hatten.

Bildungs-Websites waren weiterhin so kreativ wie möglich, um mehr Menschen anzuziehen und Try Drugs war eine solche, die es den Nutzern ermöglichte, die Auswirkungen von Drogen online zu erleben.

Die Life-Size-Blue-Whale-Nahaufnahmen wurden im Rahmen der Anti-Walfang-Kampagne der Wal- und Delfinschutzgesellschaft erstellt. Der gefährdete Blauwal, das größte Tier, das jemals gelebt hat, wurde hier in seiner tatsächlichen Größe präsentiert.

2007/
—
The Year Full-Screen Video Arrives – Along With the iPhone
—

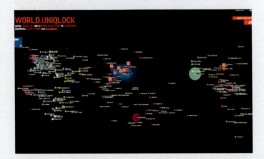
Uniqlock

Life Size Blue Whale

Steve Jobs

> "Jobs claimed that the iPhone was so revolutionary it was five years ahead of any other mobiles on the market."

Le 2 janvier est publiée la première version Web plein écran d'un spot télévisé. Conçu dans ce format pour ATG, le plus grand bookmaker suédois pour les paris hippiques, le site Horses Give Everything annonce l'avènement d'une nouvelle ère pour les vidéos sur Internet.

Une semaine plus tard jour pour jour arrive sur le marché l'iPhone, un dispositif qui va bouleverser les communications et l'accès aux informations.

Aux dires de Steve Jobs, l'iPhone est si révolutionnaire qu'il a cinq ans d'avance sur les autres portables sur le marché, principalement grâce à l'abandon d'un périphérique au profit d'un dispositif de pointage interne ; il consacre ainsi le passage de la souris au doigt.

Le site Web pour la maquilleuse suédoise Filippa Smedhagen Sund est l'un des premiers du genre à offrir une navigation par glissement. Les utilisateurs doivent simplement faire glisser l'image vers la gauche ou vers la droite, une technique très vite copiée dans bien d'autres sites.

Le contenu est désormais canalisé par des API, depuis des sites comme Flickr, ce qui permet de créer des projets intéressants tels que TiltViewer.

Le site Typography Kicks Ass illustre ce type d'intégration de contenu à l'aide de l'API Flickr. Ce projet expérimental permet aux visiteurs d'envoyer un message ou de le publier sur le site à l'aide d'images provenant de Flickr et qui forment une police « Flickr Bold Italic » aléatoire.

The Passenger est l'un des premiers exemples de vidéo contrôlée par l'utilisateur. Dans ce site promotionnel du système multimédia Nokia CK-20W pour voiture, les utilisateurs peuvent pour la première fois décider différents aspects de la vidéo qu'ils regardent.

Créé pour la campagne Halo 3: Believe, ce diorama permet aux visiteurs de découvrir le paysage où la bataille pour la Nouvelle Mombasa s'est déroulée. Un total de 1 666 captures d'écran sont nécessaires pour créer cette expérience du monument en l'honneur de John-117.

Mise en ligne par Uniqlo, Uniqlock est une horloge qui associe musique et chorégraphies à une horloge mondiale. L'un des points forts du site est

la World Uniqlock montrant tous les sites du monde qui ont téléchargé l'horloge et l'ont ajoutée à leur espace Web personnel.

Les sites Web à vocation éducative cherchent toujours à être les plus créatifs possible pour se gagner un public. Tel est le cas de Try Drugs, qui permet aux utilisateurs de découvrir en ligne les effets de drogues.

L'expérience en gros plan Life Size Blue Whale est créée dans le cadre de la campagne contre la chasse à la baleine de l'organisation Whale and Dolphin Conservation Society. Espèce en danger, la baleine bleue est le plus gros animal vivant à notre époque et il est présenté ici dans sa taille réelle.

08 Facts of the year

Number of internet users:
1.3 billion, 19.4% of
the world population

Number of websites:
122 million

世界新聞

World news:
the global banking crisis
begins

Website with most traffic:
Yahoo.com

Tech hardware:
iPhone

Tech software:
Android is released

Other tech:
Amazon launches the Kindle

Highest-grossing film:
Pirates of the Caribbean:
At World's End

2007/
—

Get the Glass

—

The most creative
website ever made?

This website was a game designed to promote milk, where the object was to break into Fort Fridge and get the Glass, while avoiding Milkatraz. The production values were utter perfection, with staggering 3D and video, while the game itself was great fun and highly addictive. Something as simple and obvious as being able to pick up a dice and roll it was still new territory for the web.

In 2017, 10 years on, people were still singing its praises when reminded of this site.

"One of my all time favorites, still talk about it today."
Resh Sidhu

"I STILL talk about that site and campaign!"
Bart Heird

"Best website EVER."
Arnaud Denise

"Our entire office was unbillable the day it dropped."
Justin Miller

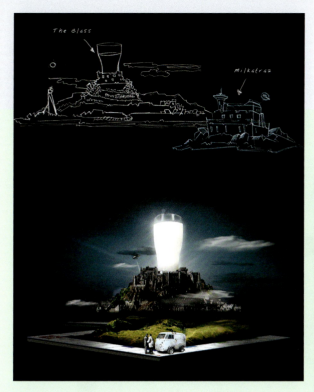

"Get the Glass was made during the glory days
of Flash. It was 2007 and we were contacted by
Goodby, Silverstein & Partners who had an idea for
a digital board game for a new 'Got Milk?' project.
We had, for a long time, wanted a project where we
could build something physical, something you had
not seen earlier, and when we first heard about this
one, we understood that this would be the project!
I guess Goodby thought we were a little bit crazy
in the beginning but when we described the idea
they loved it."

Robert Lindström
North Kingdom

Diese Website war ein Spiel, das entworfen wurde, um Werbung für Milch zu machen, in dem man in Fort Fridge einbrechen und sich das Glas holen sollte, während man Milkatraz vermeiden musste. Die Produktionswerte waren absolute Perfektion, mit atemberaubenden 3D und Video, während das Spiel selbst sehr lustig war und süchtig machen konnte. Etwas so Einfaches und Offensichtliches wie in der Lage zu sein, einen Würfel aufzuheben und zu rollen war noch Neuland für das Web.

Im Jahr 2017, 10 Jahre später, sangen die Leute immer noch Lobenshymnen, wenn sie an diese Seite erinnert wurden:
Resh Sidhu: „Eine meiner absoluten Favoriten, rede noch heute darüber."
Bart Heird: „Ich rede IMMER noch über diese Seite und die Kampagne!"
Arnaud Denise: „Beste JEMALS gemachte Website."
Justin Miller: „Unser gesamtes Büro war nicht mehr in der Lage zu arbeiten, an den Tag, als es herauskam."

Ce site Web est un jeu conçu pour encourager la consommation de lait. Le joueur doit pénétrer dans Fort Fridge et trouver le verre de lait tout en évitant Milkatraz. Le niveau de production frôle la perfection, avec des images 3D et des vidéos renversantes, et le jeu en soi est drôle et très addictif. Une chose aussi simple que le lancer d'un dé est encore inédit sur le Web.
Dix ans plus tard, en 2017, tout le monde fait encore l'éloge de ce site.

Resh Sidhu : «L'un de mes sites préférés, j'en parle encore aujourd'hui. »
Bart Heird : «Je fais encore maintenant référence à ce site et à cette campagne! »
Arnaud Denise : «Le meilleur site Web JAMAIS créé. »
Justin Miller : «Personne au bureau n'a été capable de travailler le jour où il est sorti. »

Monoface

—

A face with over 750,000 combinations

Monoface was created as a New Year's card for the Minneapolis-based agency mono, with the very simple idea that each staff member had a photo taken of their head which was then broken down into its parts: mouth, nose, head, and each eye. That may sound gruesome, but when the separate parts were recombined the results always brought a smile and word on the site spread virally. After all, there were 759,375 possible combinations.

"Ever since we launched monoface in 2007 there has
   been a worldwide draw and connection to it. It's
   weird, it's funny, it's addictive, and it's simple. Most
   people have used it as a great time-waster. But, it
   also won many awards for mono, was featured
   on the Rachael Ray Show where she called it
   'Fantastic!' and there were even some educators
   using it to teach their students about mathematics."

T. Scott Major
mono

Monoface wurde als Neujahrs-
karte für die Agentur mono in
Minneapolis kreiert. Sie basierte
auf der einfachen Idee, dass
jeder Mitarbeiter ein Foto von
seinem Kopf machen ließ, das
dann in seine Teile zerlegt wurde:
Mund, Nase, Kopf und jedes Auge.
Das mag grausam klingen, aber

als die einzelnen Teile neu kombiniert wurden, riefen die Ergebnisse immer ein Lächeln beim
Betrachter hervor und die Seite
verbreitete sich durch Mundpropaganda. Immerhin gab es
759.375 mögliche Kombinationen.

Le site monoface est pensé
comme carte de vœux pour
l'agence mono de Minneapolis.
L'idée est toute simple : le
portrait de chaque employé
est décomposé en diverses
parties (bouche, nez, tête et
chaque œil). Le résultat n'a
rien d'effrayant, au contraire.

Les parties assemblées de façon
aléatoire donnent des compositions amusantes et le site devient
viral, avec pas moins de 759 375
combinaisons possibles.

Levi's Copper Jeans

—

HTML dislodges Flash

In a significant development in the history of Flash, this first 100 percent HTML site to win a FWA Site of the Day proved that websites could be built without the need for the Flash plug-in that were every bit as interactive and interesting to explore. Even though the site could perhaps have performed better and been easier to build in Flash, this early demonstration of interactivity without Flash stuck a flag in the sand.

"I remember the brief from Levi's that this was their very first back to basics jeans. A design replicating the oldest, original pair of jeans unearthed at a copper mine. So we made a very basic microsite using Gmail, radio buttons, and HTML frames. We had to forgo a traditional navigation system and used drop-down menus to jump up or down the very long page. We buried an actual pair of jeans, aged them, and displayed them actual size in HTML. Because of that we experimented with various types of image optimization. I'm proud that it preceded modern single-page parallax scrolling websites."

Melvyn Lim
OgilvyOne Worldwide

In einer bedeutenden Entwicklung in der Flash-Geschichte, hat diese erste 100%ige HTML-Site, die eine FWA-Site of the Day gewann, bewiesen, dass es möglich war, dass Webseiten auch ohne das Flash-Plug-in erstellt werden können und ebenso interaktiv und interessant zu erforschen sind. Auch wenn die Website vielleicht besser funktioniert und einfacher in Flash hätte erstellt werden können, markierte diese frühe Demonstration von Interaktivität ohne Flash einen Meilenstein.

Alors que Flash est en plein boom, ce premier site 100 % HTML à remporter le prix FWA Site of the Day prouve qu'une conception qui ne recourt pas au plug-in Flash peut s'avérer tout autant interactive et captivante. Même si Flash aurait éventuellement simplifié le développement et amélioré les performances, ce projet interactif sans utiliser cette technologie trace une nouvelle voie.

2007/
—

Paper Critters

—

An early example of
Papervision3D

Designed and developed as the final project for J.R. Fabito's computer arts degree course, this site used Papervision3D, a project created by Carlos Ulloa that was open-sourced in late 2006 and became one of the best 3D engines built for Flash.

With Paper Critters users were able to create a desktop toy which could be printed out and folded/stuck together. The Toy Creator was an advanced application that demonstrated what could be done within the browser itself.

"Making Paper Critters, most importantly, got me my first job in the digital creative industry at Red. There, I was able to work with and learn from some really talented folks. My experience with Flash built a strong basis for my career. A lot of the techniques and principles I used and saw in Flash interaction design are being applied to modern platforms and user experience design. Flash doesn't get a lot of credit for the many things you see with interaction and UX design today and I think a lot of designers need to know and recognize that fact."

J.R. Fabito
Paper Critters; jrfabito.com

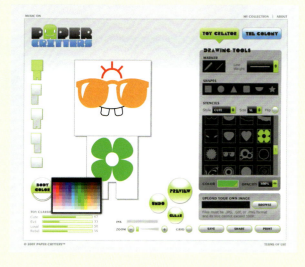

Entworfen und entwickelt als Abschlussprojekt für den Computer Arts Studiengang von J. R. Fabito. Diese Seite verwendete Papervision3D, ein Projekt, das von Carlos Ulloa entwickelt wurde. Es war Ende 2006 Open Source und wurde zu einer der besten 3D-Engines für Flash. Mit

Paper Critters waren die User in der Lage, ein Desktop-Spielzeug zu erstellen, das ausgedruckt und zusammengeklappt/gefaltet werden konnte. Der Toy Creator war eine erweiterte Anwendung, die demonstrierte, was innerhalb des Browsers selbst getan werden konnte.

Conçu et développé par J.R. Fabito comme projet de fin d'études en art numérique, ce site tourne avec Papervision3D, l'un des meilleurs moteurs graphiques 3D pour Flash que Carlos Ulloa publie en open source fin 2006. Dans le site Paper Critters, les utilisateurs

peuvent créer un jouet de bureau, puis l'imprimer, le plier et le monter. L'application sophistiquée Toy Creator démontre tout ce que le navigateur permet de faire.

2007/
—

Good Things Should Never End

—

The first infinite-scrolling website

In the days before full Flash websites, where designers and developers could do everything within the available screenspace without the user having to scroll, sites with scrolling HTML pages were the most popular style of navigation. This site for telecoms firm Orange was the first example of a scrolling system that seemed to continue for ever. Loaded with delicious animations, it was a huge hit and featured the work of highly talented artists and animators which brought it to life in ways that really fulfilled the site's name.

"By the time we were producing Good Things Should Never End, Flash was mature and code-malleable. This was Flash's golden age, before Apple killed it a couple of years later. People loved it all over the world because it was a one-liner idea that nevertheless had a lot of depth and charm. Rexbox, the illustrator/animator we worked with, was a relative unknown at the time but went on to create Little Big Planet for PlayStation and a number of other titles."

Nicolas Roope
Poke

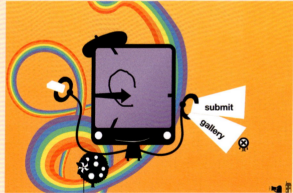

In den Tagen vor den vollständigen Flash-Websites, als Designer und Entwickler alles innerhalb des verfügbaren Bildschirmbereichs tun konnten, ohne dass der Benutzer blättern musste, waren Websites mit Scroll-HTML-Seiten die beliebteste Navigationsmethode. Diese Seite für das Telekommunikationsunternehmen Orange war das erste Beispiel für ein Scroll-System, das endlos zu sein schien. Sie war voller großartiger Animationen und ein großer Hit. Hier wurden die Arbeiten von wirklich talentierten Künstlern und Animatoren vorgestellt, was sie auf eine Weise zum Leben erweckte und damit den Namen Website wirklich verdiente.

Avant l'ère des sites Web entièrement en Flash, où les concepteurs et les développeurs ont carte blanche dans l'espace écran disponible sans que l'utilisateur ne doive faire défiler le contenu, le mode de navigation le plus répandu repose sur le défilement de pages HTML. Ce site pour l'opérateur télécom Orange présente le premier système de défilement apparemment infini. Truffé d'excellentes animations, il remporte un énorme succès et combine le travail d'artistes et d'animateurs de grand talent qui ont su lui donné vie d'une façon qui fait honneur à son nom.

I'm a Cyborg, But That's OK

—

The first use of a pop-up book format

This promotional site for a Korean film used the idea of a pop-up book, with superb effects and great complementary sound and music. One area allowed users to roll a virtual dice and move around on a game-board.

This was one of the most original movie sites ever created and set new standards in the industry, showing possible new directions away from the information sites that had become the norm for this genre.

"While wondering how we could express the film's distinctive atmosphere and characters, we decided to use a pop-up book as a metaphor to show the website as an attractive fairy-tale storybook. The design of the site was a real challenge. We even cut up countless real pop-up books to understand how they worked and rearranged them repeatedly. We also made a special menu on the website, so that fans could download the main characters' mask design. A few months later, the leading actor (Rain) and actress (Im Soo-jung) attended the international premiere of the film at the Berlin Film Festival wearing our masks."

Sang-jun Lee
Does Interactive

Diese Werbeseite für einen koreanischen Film nutzte die Idee eines Pop-up-Buches mit hervorragenden Effekten und großartigem komplementärem Sound und Musik. Ein Bereich erlaubte es den Usern, einen virtuellen Würfel zu werfen und sich auf einem Spielbrett zu bewegen.

Dies war eine der originellsten Film-Websites, die jemals erstellt wurden und setzte neue Standards in der Branche, indem sie mögliche neue Richtungen abseits der Informationsseiten aufzeigte, die für dieses Genre zur Norm geworden waren.

Ce site promotionnel pour un film coréen part du concept de livre animé et l'assortit de sompteux effets et d'un accompagnement musical et sonore de qualité. Une section permet aux visiteurs de jeter un dé virtuel pour se déplacer sur un plateau de jeu. C'est l'un des sites officiels de film les plus originaux jamais créés, qui dicte de nouveaux standards en la matière et offre un horizon au-delà des sites informatifs devenus la norme.

Red Universe

—

An agency website
like no other

As users entered this site they found themselves in a new universe called Red, but also one of the most original sites an interactive agency had ever presented. Here was a world full of other internet-users with whom new visitors could chat, run, fly, and dance, while their own character could be customized with the control panel. A user's manual contained secret keys and explained the different moves that could be made.

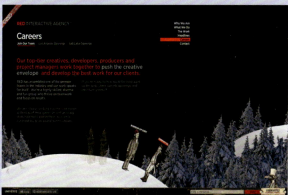

"Since the launch of Red Universe in April 2007, our agency's website was a conversation starter. The site proved to be progressive in its ability to engage multiple users simultaneously, create a community, and provide a unique social experience. Users would choose from different characters, with varied looks and features, and spend up to an hour running, flying, dancing, chatting, and even virtually punching each other in the face. The Red Universe had a pretty loyal and consistent user base called the 'Redizens' who came from all over the world to hang out on the site."

Brian Lovell
Red

Wenn die User diese Seite betra-ten, kamen sie in ein neues Universum namens Red aber auch auf eine der originellsten Websites, die eine interaktive Agentur jemals präsentiert hatte. Hier war eine Welt voll mit anderen Internet-Usern, mit denen neue Besucher chatten, rennen, fliegen und tanzen konnten, während ihr eigener Charakter mit dem Control Panel angepasst werden konnte. Ein Benutzerhandbuch enthielt geheime Keys und erklärte die verschiedenen Bewegungen, die gemacht werden konnten.

En entrant dans ce site, les visiteurs se retrouvent plongés dans un nouvel univers appelé Red, mais aussi dans l'une des créations les plus originales venant d'une agence interactive. Dans ce monde rempli d'inter-nautes, chacun peut discuter, courir, voler et danser, mais aussi configurer son propre person-nage à l'aide d'un tableau de bord. Un manuel d'utilisation révèle des touches secrètes et tous les déplacements possibles.

2007/

—

Cicatriz Clothing

—

An e-commerce first, showcasing
products in videos

In an original development, this web shop incorporated videos of models wearing the clothes the site was offering for sale. It was a simple idea, but one that hadn't been seen before, and the site was shared widely by many people who were excited about the new possibilities of online shopping.

"It was crazy to build a fully video-based e-commerce site in 100 percent Flash. But we did. Eduard Prats, the developer and co-founder of Mocoro, even built the checkout and payment process in Flash. Gustav and Bjorn of Cicatriz Clothing happened to be friends with Olle Cornéer (who came to be known as Dada Life) who did the music and sound effects. Back then the web was truly packed with weird projects, made by friends exploring technology and design together. It was the best of times."

Hugo Ahlberg
Mocoro; Airbnb

In einer ursprünglichen Entwicklung integrierte dieser Webshop Videos von Models, die die Kleidung trugen, die die Website zum Verkauf anbot. Es war eine einfache Idee, aber eine, die noch nie zuvor gesehen worden war, und die Seite wurde von vielen Leuten geteilt, die von den neuen Möglichkeiten des Online-Shoppings begeistert waren.

D'une conception inédite, ce magasin en ligne inclut des vidéos de mannequins qui portent les vêtements vendus sur le site. L'idée est simple mais jusqu'alors inédite, et le site est amplement partagé par une foule d'internautes conquis par les nouvelles possibilités d'achat en ligne.

HBO
<u>Voyeur</u>

—

The first web experience to offer a glimpse of other people's lives

Not so much a website as a web experience, this was a rare online destination where the second visit was actually more compelling than the first, especially if users were prepared to spend time exploring. Visitors got the chance to be a voyeur and peek into the lives and the apartments of everyday New Yorkers, while an icon of a small building at the top of the interface opened up still more stories.

"The HBO Voyeur site and installation was a hugely successful marriage of cutting-edge Flash technology and streaming HD video. Streaming HD video (720p) was rather unheard of, let alone a single website that streamed hundreds of megabytes' worth of video content. To complicate things, part of the website's design also utilized the brand-new live 3D rendering capabilities of Flash. Using hundreds of photos combined with custom illustration, we painstakingly replicated the look and feel of four different New York neighborhoods."

Cathy Davenport Lee
Big Spaceship; HBO

Nicht so sehr eine Website – eher ein Web-Erlebnis. Dies war eine der seltenen Online-Destinationen, bei denen der zweite Besuch tatsächlich überzeugender war als der erste, vor allem, wenn User bereit waren, Zeit mit der Erkundung zu verbringen.

Besucher hatten die Möglichkeit, Voyeur zu sein und einen Blick in die Leben und die Wohnungen der New Yorker zu werfen, während ein Symbol eines kleinen Gebäudes an der Spitze der Schnittstelle weitere Geschichten eröffnete.

Davantage une expérience Web qu'un véritable site, c'est aussi l'un des rares espaces en ligne dont la deuxième visite fait plus d'effet que la première, notamment si les internautes ont du temps pour l'explorer en détail. Ils peuvent agir en voyeurs et jeter un coup d'œil dans la vie et l'appartement d'habitants de New York. L'icône d'un petit bâtiment en haut de l'interface permet de découvrir plus d'histoires.

Air Jordan XX2

—

First to use a full-screen draggable interface

With full-screen 3D that used the exciting new Papervision3D, which in turn hosted full-screen video, this was one of the first examples of the next generation of multimedia websites. Gradually the browser was being superseded by interactive areas that were no longer dependent on screen resolution. Users could now explore in any direction by simply dragging the mouse to reveal new areas of the experience.

"The Jordan XX2 website was an experimental interactive Flash experience with a unique way to navigate video and image content. It was based on a spherical 3D navigation featuring a panoramic background image and foreground elements that when dragged around created a parallax-like effect. Each foreground element led the user to view video content about the Air Jordan XX2 shoe that we produced in-house. Sound was also a big part of interactive sites back then, as every section had background music, voice-over, and sound effects."

Marcus Eriksson
Blast Radius; themarcus.com

Mit Vollbild-3D, das die aufregende neue Papervision3D nutzte, die wiederum Videos im Vollbildmodus zeigte, war dies eines der ersten Beispiele für die nächste Generation von Multimedia-Websites. Allmählich wurde der Browser durch interaktive Bereiche ersetzt, die nicht mehr von der Bildschirmauflösung abhängig waren. Die User konnten jetzt in jede Richtung erkunden, indem sie einfach die Maus zogen, um neue Bereiche zu entdecken.

S'appuyant sur le nouveau moteur Papervision3D qui offre un rendu vidéo 3D plein écran, c'est l'un des premiers spécimens de la nouvelle génération de sites Web multimédia. Le navigateur est progressivement remplacé par des zones interactives indépendantes de la résolution d'écran. Les internautes peuvent en explorer tous les recoins en faisant simplement glisser la souris.

NOTABLE WEBSITE LAUNCH
Tumblr

GOOGLE FACTS

Fortune magazine names Google as the #1 company to work for

Street View launches in Google Maps

Android launches as the first open platform for mobiles

Live traffic data begins to roll out on Google Maps

Google Safe Browsing launches

Top 5 Trends

INTERNET COMMUNITY
Estonia

Estonia becomes the first country
to use internet voting for its
parliamentary general election.
After a successful test two
years earlier, approximately one
in 30 registered voters voted
electronically.

MOBILE EVOLUTION
iPhone

"Apple Reinvents the
Phone with iPhone"

2008/

The Year
of Horror

2008/
—
The Year
of Horror
—

Sour Sally

Web design continued to head in many different directions as anything now seemed possible, while this year was marked by some deep online experiences capable of scaring people out of their wits.

The Eye, a promotional site for a supernatural horror film featuring Jessica Alba, had one simple idea: visitors encountered an image of an eye, and nothing else. It made people jump out of their skin and then made them afraid to blink.

The web presence for advertising agents Publicis & Hal Riney demonstrated a real game-changer by inviting users to navigate the site using their own webcam, something most people had never done before.

The navigation for Sour Sally, on the other hand, involved mouse movements to fly and keyboard inputs to walk and jump. Visitors grabbed a balloon to get going, or jumped on the cake for a bouncy start.

ULeChang offered users a curious celestial journey in which they could select an avatar, such as Superman, and as they flew on they collected numbered stars on their voyage of discovery.

New Zealand's Resn became well known for sites packed with individual character, such as Luke Buda's, which was filled with pterodactyls, dinner plates, karaoke, jerseys, and pyramids.

Pianist Julian Velard's site, by Wefail, was like a point-and-click adventure, with Easter eggs helping visitors make it through the site.

Barcinski & Jeanjean's site featured a color shift so visitors could explore it further if they wore 3D glasses. This site didn't pioneer 3D on the web, but it gave a glimpse of what could be achieved.

Music in a Bottle was the first site where content was generated by scanning a product's barcode. Holding the label of a Bit beer bottle up to a webcam enabled users to listen to the song that was inside it.

Volkswagen Autopilot provided an early example of online simulation, with the site showing how things worked and what happened when they were used correctly, or incorrectly.

The environmental campaign Help the Honey Bees was one of the first websites with an accompanying video that went viral. The site was sponsored by Häagen-Dazs to raise awareness for dying bee populations, whose pollination sustains a third of the natural foodstuffs we eat.

The launch of the iPhone 3G and the App Store made downloading apps the latest addiction, sowing the seeds for an entirely new industry of app creators who in turn transformed the landscape of web design.

There were now over 1.5 billion internet users, almost a quarter of the global population. The effects of the global financial crisis became more widely felt, while a series of 12 coordinated attacks brought Islamic terrorism to Mumbai.

Mass shootings continued unchecked in the United States meanwhile, as when a lone gunman killed five students at Northern Illinois University. This atrocity brought a global community together in one of the early Facebook tribute pages, for the students and their families, and this was also the year Facebook became the number one social network, leaving MySpace behind.

> "The App Store made
> downloading apps the
> latest addiction,
> sowing the seeds for an
> entirely new industry
> of app creators."

Julian Velard

Luke Buda

The Eye

Barcinski & Jeanjean

Das Webdesign bewegte sich weiterhin in viele verschiedene Richtungen, da alles nun möglich schien, während dieses Jahr von einigen tiefen Online-Erfahrungen geprägt war, die die Menschen zutiefst erschrecken konnten.

The Eye, eine Werbeseite für einen übernatürlichen Horrorfilm mit Jessica Alba, hatte eine einfache Idee: Besucher trafen auf das Bild eines Auges und sonst nichts. Es ließ die Leute quasi aus ihrer Haut springen und machte ihnen dann Angst zu blinzeln.

Der Webauftritt für die Werbeagenturen Publicis & Hal Riney zeigte, dass User eine Website mit ihrer eigenen Webcam navigieren können, was die meisten noch nie zuvor getan hatten.

Die Navigation für Sour Sally beinhaltete Mausbewegungen zum Fliegen und Tastatureingaben zum Gehen und Springen. Die Besucher schnappten sich einen Ballon um loszulegen oder sprangen auf den Kuchen, um sich hüpfend weiterzubewegen.

ULeChang bot den Nutzern eine kuriose himmlische Reise an, auf der sie sich einen Avatar, z.B. Superman, aussuchen konnten und auf ihrer Entdeckungsreise nummerierte Sterne sammelten.

Resn aus Neuseeland wurde bekannt für Orte mit individuellem Charakter, wie zum Beispiel Luke Buda, die voller Pterodaktylen, Teller, Karaoke, Pullovern und Pyramiden war.

Die Website von Pianist Julian Velard von Wefail war wie ein Point-and-Click-Abenteuer mit Ostereiern, die den Besuchern halfen, durch die Seite zu kommen.

Die Seite von Barcinski & Jeanjean zeigte eine Farbveränderung, sodass die Besucher sie weiter erkunden konnten, wenn sie eine 3D-Brille trugen. Diese Seite war nicht bahnbrechend für 3D im Internet aber sie gab einen Ausblick darauf, was erreicht werden konnte.

Music in a Bottle war die erste Seite, in der Inhalte generiert wurden, indem der Barcode eines Produkts gescannt wurde. Wenn man das Etikett einer Bit-Bierflasche an eine Webcam hielt, konnte man den Song hören, der darin enthalten war.

Volkswagen Autopilot bot ein frühes Beispiel für Online-Simulation, wobei die Website zeigte, wie die Dinge funktionierten und was passiert, wenn sie richtig oder falsch verwendet wurden.

Die Umweltkampagne „Help the Honey Bees" war eine der ersten Websites mit einem begleitenden Video, das viral ging. Die Seite wurde von Häagen-Dazs gesponsert, um das Bewusstsein für sterbende Bienenpopulationen zu schärfen, deren Bestäubung ein Drittel der natürlichen Lebensmittel, die wir essen, erhält.

Die Einführung des iPhone 3G und des App Stores machte das Herunterladen von Apps zur neuesten Sucht, was den Keim für eine völlig neue Branche von App-Creators bildete, die wiederum die Landschaft des Webdesigns veränderten.

Es gab jetzt über 1,5 Milliarden Internetnutzer, fast ein Viertel der Weltbevölkerung. Die Auswirkungen der globalen Finanzkrise wurden stärker spürbar, während eine Serie von 12 koordinierten Angriffen den islamischen Terrorismus nach Mumbai brachte.

Die Amokläufe gingen in den Vereinigten Staaten unterdessen unkontrolliert weiter, als ein einziger Schütze fünf Schüler an der Northern Illinois University tötete. Diese Grausamkeit brachte eine globale Gemeinschaft auf einer der ersten Facebook Tribute-Seiten für die Studenten und ihre Familien zusammen. Dies war auch das Jahr, in dem Facebook das soziale Netzwerk Nr. 1 wurde und MySpace hinter sich ließ.

—

The Year
of Horror

—

Volkswagen Autopilot

Help the Honey Bees

"The launch of the
iPhone 3G and the App
Store made downloading
apps the latest
addiction."

Music in a Bottle

Tout paraît désormais possible, et la conception Web prend plusieurs directions. Cette année est marquée par des expériences en ligne plutôt intenses, au point d'en effrayer plus d'un.

Site promotionnel d'un film d'horreur mettant en vedette Jessica Alba, The Eye part d'une idée simple, celle de l'image d'un œil. Les visiteurs sursautent d'abord, puis craignent de cligner des yeux.

La présence sur le Web pour les agents publicitaires Publicis & Hal Riney change totalement la donne, puisqu'il est demandé aux internautes de naviguer à l'aide de leur webcam, une grande première pour la plupart des visiteurs.

Dans le site Sour Sally en revanche, la navigation passe par des mouvements de la souris pour voler, et par des touches du clavier pour marcher et sauter. Les visiteurs attrapent un ballon pour avancer ou sautent sur le gâteau pour un départ dynamique.

Dans le site UleChang, les visiteurs font un étrange voyage céleste au cours duquel ils peuvent choisir un avatar (comme Superman) et collectionner des étoiles pendant qu'ils volent.

La société de production néo-zélandaise Resn a pour carte de visite des sites tournant autour d'un personnage. Tel est le cas de celui de Luke Buda, où interviennent ptérodactyles, assiettes, karaoké, pulls et pyramides.

Conçu par Wefail, le site du pianiste Julian Velard offre une aventure par pointer-cliquer où la découverte d'œufs de Pâques en permet l'exploration.

Le site de Barcinski & Jeanjean change de couleur pour que les visiteurs possédant des lunettes 3D le découvrent plus en détail. Il n'innove pas en matière de 3D, mais il en montre le potentiel.

Music in a Bottle est le premier site dont le contenu est généré en scannant le code-barres d'un produit. Par exemple, en tenant l'étiquette d'une bouteille de bière Bit face à la webcam, les utilisateurs peuvent écouter la chanson qu'elle inclut.

Le site Volkswagen Auto-pilot est l'un des premiers à proposer une simulation en ligne. Les visiteurs peuvent tester les fonctionnalités du véhicule et savoir ce qu'il se passe en cas d'usage correct ou incorrect.

La campagne environne-mentale Help the Honey Bees est l'un des premiers sites Web dont la vidéo devient virale. Sponsorisé par Häagen-Dazs, il vise à alerter l'opinion publique de l'extinction de populations d'abeilles, alors que la pollinisation assure un tiers des denrées naturelles que nous consommons.

La sortie de l'iPhone 3G et de l'App Store lance la mode de télécharger des applications et sème les germes d'un tout nouveau secteur d'activité : le développement d'applications, lequel suppose au passage la refonte de la conception Web.

Il y a maintenant plus d'1,5 milliard d'internautes, soit plus d'un quart de la population mondiale. Les conséquences de la crise financière se font plus largement sentir. Par ailleurs, le terrorisme islamique frappe Mumbai avec une série de 12 attaques coordonnées.

Les États-Unis font l'objet de fusillades de masse à répétition, comme à l'université de Northern Illinois où un tireur solitaire abat cinq étudiants. Ce drame rassemble une communauté mondiale dans l'une des premières pages d'hommage sur Facebook créée pour les étudiants et leurs familles. Cette même année, Facebook devient le premier réseau social en passant devant MySpace.

Ø8 Facts of the year

Number of internet users:
1.57 billion, 23.3% of
the world population

Number of websites:
172 million

World news:
Barack Obama is elected
president of the United
States

Website with most traffic:
Google.com

Tech hardware:
MacBook Air is launched

HTML5

Tech software:
HTML5 working draft
published

Other tech:
Apple's App Store launches
with 552 apps

Highest-grossing film:
The Dark Knight

Hotel 626

—

The scariest online
experience of all time

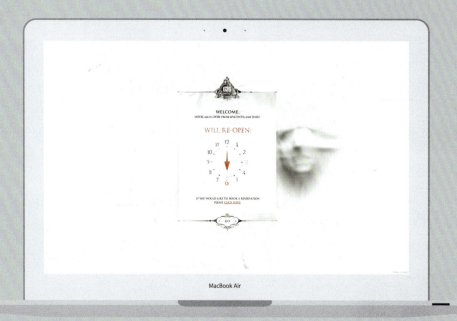

Trapped inside a haunted hotel, visitors to this site were met with heavy breathing sound effects as the experience played out in first-person. It was impressive because it incorporated all the latest options in website interaction by linking in the user's webcam, microphone, and mobile phone. In a world first, Hotel 626 was also only open at night, although for those who were either too impatient or scared of the dark, the time could be changed on the user's computer to access the site before its opening hours.

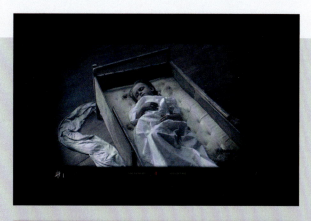

"You realized fairly quickly that you were trapped in this scary hotel and the only way out was to solve certain challenges. Players had to maneuver through dark hallways with the help of placing a phone call on their mobile phone for directions, take a picture of a madman's lair, and sing a demon baby to sleep in order to find their way to safety. The player's journey would automatically translate their visits into tweets and users were also able to post their scared faces taken by their webcam on Facebook."

Mike Geiger
Goodby, Silverstein & Partners; Wolfgang L.A.

Gefangen in einem verwunsche-nen Hotel – die Besucher dieser Seite wurden mit schweren Atemgeräuschen konfrontiert, da die Erfahrung in der ersten Person erlebt wurde. Es war be-eindruckend, da es die neuesten Optionen der Website-Interak-tion durch die Einbindung von Webcam, Mikrofon und Mobil-telefon des Benutzers enthielt. Als Weltneuheit war das Hotel 626 auch nur nachts geöffnet, obwohl für diejenigen, die entwe-der zu ungeduldig waren oder Angst vor der Dunkelheit hatten, die Zeit auf dem Computer des Benutzers geändert werden konnte, um auf die Seite vor den Öffnungszeiten zuzugreifen.

Enfermés dans un hôtel hanté, les visiteurs se retrouvent plon-gés à la première personne dans une expérience où les bruits de respiration sont très présents. L'effet créé est saisissant car le site intègre toutes les options d'interaction disponibles, via la webcam, le microphone et le télé-phone portable. Aspect inédit, le site Hotel 626 est uniquement ouvert la nuit. Pour les plus im-patients ou ceux qui ont peur du noir toutefois, il est possible de changer l'heure de l'ordinateur afin d'y accéder en dehors des horaires d'ouverture nocturnes.

2008/

—

<u>Vermeersch</u>

—

The first human-sized website

By creating this life-sized website, Canadian Jeff Vermeersch gave his personal portfolio about as big an impact as was possible. It was certainly a simple, perhaps even obvious idea, yet was a success not just for being the first of its kind but because of its perfect presentation.

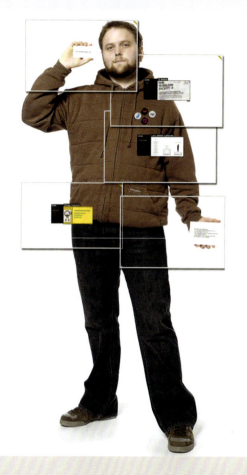

"I launched vermeersch.ca as a bit of an experiment. I decided to see what I could do with my own idea and proceeded to build the site over a couple of weekends. The day I was featured on the FWA my inbox exploded. Within a week I had job offers from three countries. The site went on to win several other awards that year and got me named the FITC Best Canadian Developer in 2008. It also secured me my first slice of creative cred."

Jeff Vermeersch
vermeersch.ca

Durch die Erstellung dieser lebensgroßen Website hat der Kanadier Jeff Vermeersch seinem persönlichen Portfolio eine möglichst große Wirkung verliehen. Es war sicherlich eine einfache, vielleicht sogar naheliegende Idee, doch es war ein Erfolg, nicht nur, weil sie die erste ihrer Art war, sondern auch wegen ihrer perfekten Präsentation.

En créant un site grandeur nature, le Canadien Jeff Vermeersch donne à son portfolio une importante projection. Le concept est très simple en soi, mais il triomphe pour être le premier du genre et grâce à une présentation impeccable.

—

Red Bull Flugtag
Flight Lab

—

A flying-machine creator right
from the drawing-board

MacBook Air

Building on its Easter egg treat for 2005, Red Bull here made a present of a fully functional interface for users to build and try out their own flying machines. The DIY approach let hand-drawn outlines be transformed automatically into a 3D model which could then make a test flight in an authentic simulator, backed by real physics.

"Launching Flugtag felt pretty good. The LessRain Berlin team was working for almost a year on it — painstakingly ironing out every little detail so we could offer a seamless browser experience in 3D. We had been trying to do an ambitious game for Red Bull for years, with an early version of Flugtag done back in 2001 as a 2D scroller. Finally, we could show Red Bull that investing in a proper game works — and it did."

Vassilios Alexiou
LessRain

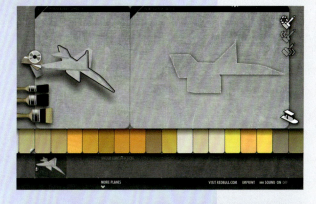

Sie bauten hier auf dem Osterei-er-Spaß aus dem Jahr 2005 auf. Red Bull präsentierte hier ein voll funktionsfähiges Interface, mit dem die Benutzer ihre eigenen Fluggeräte bauen und ausprobieren konnten. Mit dem DIY-Ansatz ließen sich handgezeichnete Konturen automatisch in ein 3D-Modell umwandeln, das dann in einem authentischen Simulator, unterstützt von realer Physik, einen Testflug machen konnte.

Reprenant l'idée de son œuf de Pâques de 2005, Red Bull offre ici une interface complète dans laquelle les utilisateurs construisent et testent leurs propres machines volantes. L'approche bricolage permet de transformer automatique-ment des ébauches tracées à la main en modèles 3D et de faire un essai de vol dans un authentique simulateur soumis aux lois de la physique.

—

The Alfa Romeo 159 Experience

—

Pushing the limits of a high-end website

One of the most impressive productions I had ever seen, with its slick splash-page that launched into a full-screen experience, this site showcased the Alfa Romeo 159 and fully achieved its goal. The imagery, subtle use of motion graphics, and special effects were world-class, and combined with high-resolution video and sophisticated sound showed how far web design could be pushed with the available technology.

"I remember how [we were] loaned a brand-new car for a week — so we could film it from every angle — and how we were so afraid of scratching it. I remember the day when it was impossible to do anything technically and the next day, when everything worked better than in our wildest dreams. I remember our discussions with Thibault Imbert and the Adobe technical teams on how to correct blocking points in Flash or work around them."

Benjamin Laugel
Soleil Noir; WooT

Eine der eindrucksvollsten Produktionen, die ich jemals gesehen habe, mit ihrer glatten Splash-Seite, die in ein Vollbild-Erlebnis startete. Diese Seite präsentierte den Alfa Romeo 159 und erreichte ihr Ziel voll und ganz. Die Bilder, der subtile Einsatz von Motion Graphics und Spezialeffekten waren Weltklasse und zeigten in Verbindung mit hochauflösendem Video und ausgefeiltem Sound, wie weit Webdesign mit der verfügbaren Technologie vorangetrieben werden konnte.

L'une des productions les plus sensationnelles à mon sens est cette page de démarrage débouchant sur une expérience plein écran. Conçu pour présenter l'Alfa Romeo 159 (et le résultat est probant), ce site est rempli d'images aux animations subtiles et d'effets exceptionnels, le tout assorti de vidéos haute résolution et de sons élaborés. Il montre ainsi jusqu'où les limites du Web peuvent être repoussées avec la technologie existante.

—

Spectra Visual Newsreader

—

An innovative 3D visualizer
for information

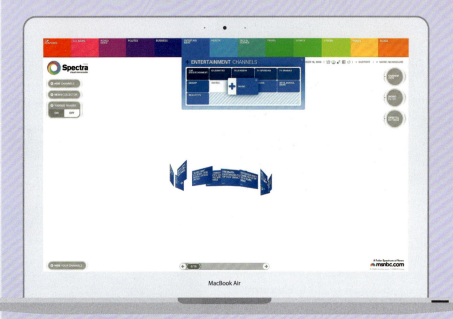

While the internet brought access to information at the click of a mouse, from real-time news websites to burgeoning online resources, few places were using this content cleverly. Spectra here allowed users to browse and interact with information in a 3D visualizer, featuring a webcam color sensor and the ability to filter and store favorite stories, videos, and blogs.

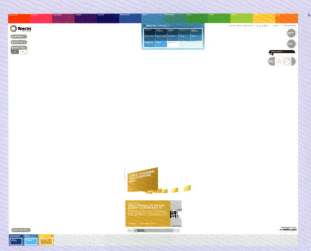

"Consuming and organizing your news on a daily basis was possible because Spectra was essentially also a web application. The reactions to the innovative and dynamic way to navigate, view, and read news were overwhelmingly strong. Spectra changed the perception of what was previously conceived as a 'news reader' [and] was part of the need to bring the world of functional software and interactive content-driven experiences closer together."

Remon Tijssen
Fluid; Kinetic Aesthetic

Während das Internet per Maus-klick Zugang zu Informationen verschaffte, von Echtzeit-Nach-richtenwebsites bis zu aufkei-menden Online-Ressourcen, nutzten nur wenige Orte diese Inhalte geschickt. Spectra ermöglichte es hier den Usern Informationen in einem 3D-Visualizer zu durchsuchen und mit ihnen zu interagieren. Sie verfügten über einen Webcam-Farbsensor und die Möglichkeit, Lieblingsgeschichten, -videos und -blogs zu filtern und zu speichern.

Internet fournit l'accès aux informations d'un clic de souris, qu'il s'agisse de sites d'actualités en temps réel ou de ressources en ligne, mais il est rare que le contenu soit savamment utilisé. Ici, Spectra permet aux utilisa-teurs de consulter des infor-mations et d'interagir avec dans un visualiseur 3D. Ils disposent d'une webcam avec capteur de couleurs, et ils peuvent filtrer et enregistrer leurs histoires, vidéos et blogs favoris.

—

Pencil Rebel

—

The website made of cardboard

One of the most original web games since Samorost (2003), users here had to rescue Dr. Esculap, who had been missing for five years. It was a point, click, and interact adventure that was habit-forming as well as charming, which abundantly demonstrated its creators' dedication to their idea and would gain them worldwide attention and acclaim.

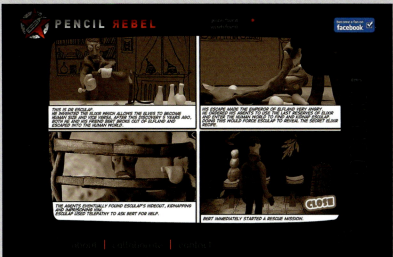

"Pencil Rebel was a personal project created in spare time with a huge amount of love. The first few months after launch in the May 1 Reboot 2008 were fairly quiet, but after it won the FWA visits sky-rocketed. This triggered a series of amazing events. I met lots of great people and was invited to conferences. Disney USA got in touch to put it on their XD portal and in the next quarter I received news that PR was one of the top 10 performing games."

Greg Hoyna
Pencil Rebel

Eines der originellsten Webspiele seit Samorost (2003). Die User mussten hier Dr. Esculap retten, der seit fünf Jahren vermisst wurde. Es war ein Point-, Click- und Interact-Abenteuer, das süchtig machend und charmant war und eindrucksvoll die Hingabe seiner Schöpfer an ihre Idee demonstrierte und ihnen weltweite Aufmerksamkeit und Anerkennung verschaffen sollte.

Dans l'un des jeux les plus originaux circulant sur le Web depuis Samorost (2003), les joueurs doivent secourir le Dr. Esculap, disparu depuis cinq ans. D'une belle esthétique, cette aventure par pointer-cliquer et par interaction crée une forte dépendance, résultat du savoir-faire de ses créateurs qui leur a valu une reconnaissance mondiale.

2008/
—

Red Issue

—

The first to involve drawing
shapes to navigate

In an unusual departure, the intro page for this
site actually required visitors to interact and
use their mouse to draw a shape in order to
enter. Once inside, different shapes could be
drawn to make the site work in certain ways.

Some people loved it, others thought this type
of navigation was risky for a target audience,
but either way the navigation was original and
clever and inspired many to think in different
ways for website accessibility.

"When we launched Red Issue we weren't really sure what people would think of this gesture-based navigation, instead of the more traditional 'arrow right' and 'arrow left' approach for moving to the next and previous image. But it was really well received and got a lot of recognition for at least trying something new and interesting. It showed us some of the interesting things that can happen when you choose to do something differently."

Anders Sønderby Jessen
Hello Monday

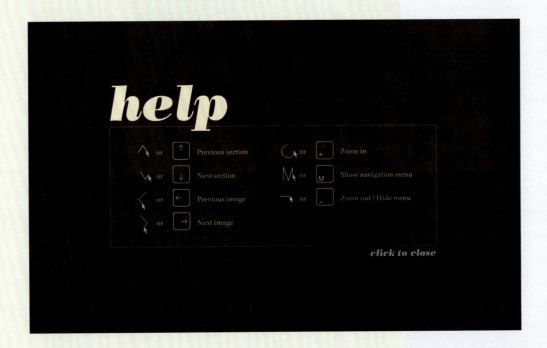

In einem ungewöhnlichen Beginn nötigte die Intro-Seite dieser Website die Besucher zu interagieren und ihre Maus zu benutzen, um eine Form zu zeichnen, um eintreten zu können. Einmal drinnen, konnten verschiedene Formen gezeichnet werden, um die Website auf bestimmte Weise funktionieren zu lassen. Einige

Leute liebten es, andere dachten, dass diese Art der Navigation für eine Zielgruppe riskant sei, aber so oder so war die Navigation originell und clever und inspirierte viele dazu, auf unterschiedliche Weise an die Zugänglichkeit der Website zu denken.

Les visiteurs sont surpris dès la page d'introduction car ils doivent interagir et dessiner une forme à l'aide de la souris pour entrer dans le site. Une fois à l'intérieur, ils peuvent tracer d'autres formes afin d'en altérer le fonctionnement. Certains aiment, d'autres considèrent ce type de navigation trop risqué :

dans tous les cas, la dynamique est originale et astucieuse, et elle en inspire plus d'un en matière d'accessibilité des sites Web.

The Outbreak

—

A streaming movie where user decisions determined the outcome

MacBook Air

This interactive horror movie, rated 18+, allowed viewers to make their own choices, but a wrong one could be the last. At certain points in the film alternatives were offered for how it might continue, and although a grisly ending awaited the wrong decision users could pick up where they left off with the chapter menu. This was another site plagued with bandwidth problems in its early days because of popularity.

"Upon launch, we truly understood the term 'overnight success'. We did absolutely nothing to promote it, other than tell our own handful of friends and colleagues. Pretty much went to sleep, and by the next day it was just off and running. Day after day brought in more craziness; it was everywhere. It was unlike anything we've experienced, but it was pretty amazing to create something that so many people got some joy from."

Chris Lund
SilkTricky

Dieser interaktive Horrorfilm ab 18+ erlaubte den Zuschauern, ihre eigenen Entscheidungen zu treffen, aber eine falsche konnte die letzte sein. An bestimmten Stellen des Films wurden Alternativen angeboten, wie es weitergehen könnte und obwohl ein grausiges Ende auf die falsche Entscheidung wartete, konnten die Benutzer dort weitermachen, wo sie mit dem Kapitelmenü aufgehört hatten. Dies war wieder eine Seite, die in ihrer Anfangszeit wegen ihrer Popularität von Bandbreitenproblemen geplagt wurde.

Réservé aux plus de 18 ans, ce film d'horreur interactif permet aux spectateurs de faire leurs propres choix, sauf qu'une erreur peut s'avérer fatale. À certains passages du film, des options sont en effet proposées quant à la suite de l'intrigue. Même si une mauvaise décision se solde par une fin sinistre, il est possible de reprendre là où l'histoire s'est arrêtée dans la liste de chapitres. Comme bien d'autres, ce site est victime de sa popularité et connaît à ses débuts des soucis de bande passante.

—

The Eco Zoo

—

An environmentally important
project run by powerful 3D engine

MacBook Air

Driven by Roxik's 3D engine, Sharikura, the Eco Zoo invited visitors to explore its environment and take a close look at the animals, and in doing so, numerous tips were offered on how to live in a more environmentally friendly way.

Users could click, hold, and drag, moving the mouse up, down, and from side to side, to explore this special zoo and appreciate both the content and the super-smooth 3D tower.

"The trigger that led to the development of this idea was that information about global environmental issues is frequently too difficult to grasp. It can also seem as if nations and companies are responding out of obligation or driven by some unspecified force instead of acting naturally and spontaneously, and the same applies to individuals. Unless we speak in language and in a manner that can easily be understood even by children, nothing will ever improve."

Seiichi Nishikawa & Masayuki Kido
Enjin & Roxik

Angetrieben von der 3D-Engine von Roxik, Sharikura, lud der Eco Zoo Besucher dazu ein, seine Umgebung zu erkunden und die Tiere genau zu betrachten. Dabei wurden zahlreiche Tipps gegeben, wie man umweltfreundlicher leben kann. Die User konnten klicken, halten und ziehen, indem sie die Maus nach oben, unten und von einer Seite zur anderen Seite bewegten, um diesen speziellen Zoo zu erkunden und um sowohl den Inhalt als auch den super gemachten 3D-Turm zu genießen.

Animé par le moteur 3D Shari-kura développé par Roxik, le site Eco Zoo invite les visiteurs à explorer les installations et à observer les animaux. Il donne de nombreux conseils pour vivre d'une façon plus respectueuse de l'environnement, et les utilisa-teurs peuvent cliquer et glisser dans les quatre directions pour découvrir ce zoo particulier, son contenu et une tour en 3D bien conçue.

—

Tracy Chapman

—

The first painting-by-numbers website

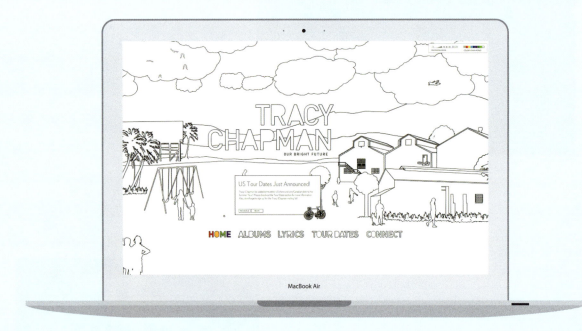

MacBook Air

By using a grid of colors located at the top-right of this site and the mouse cursor as a brush, visitors could paint their own landscape. Such a simple idea, but one that hadn't been implemented across a whole website before, while the fact that it was created to promote a globally recognized music artist made it even more notable.

"The Tracy Chapman website was a simple concept that sprang from some long conversations about the album, the future, and how our perspectives shape those futures. The coloring scenes were full of utopian images of birds and deer juxtaposed against more subversive images of industry and modern life. It was up to the user to engage with the world presented and fill it with color. The success of the experience was based not on conversions and analytics but on crafting compelling experiences driven by innovative concepts."

Jason Herring
OrdinaryKids; KQED

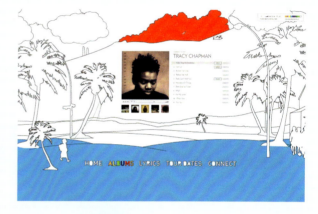

Mit einem Farbraster oben rechts auf dieser Seite und dem Mauszeiger als Pinsel, konnten Besucher ihre eigene Landschaft malen. Eine ganz einfache Idee, aber eine, die vorher nicht auf einer ganzen Website umgesetzt wurde. Die Tatsache, dass sie geschaffen wurde, um einen weltweit anerkannten Musik-künstler zu promoten, machte sie noch bemerkenswerter.

À l'aide d'une palette de couleurs en haut à droite et d'un curseur pour pinceau, les visiteurs peuvent peindre le paysage à leur guise, une idée simple mais qui n'a pourtant encore jamais été réalisée pour un site Web. Elle est d'autant plus saluée qu'elle est conçue pour la promotion d'une musicienne de renommée mondiale.

NOTABLE WEBSITE
LAUNCH
Dropbox

GOOGLE
FACTS

T-Mobile's G1 phone is the
first to use the Android OS

Searching by voice is added
to the Google iOS app

Google Chrome browser launches

First iOS Google app becomes
downloadable

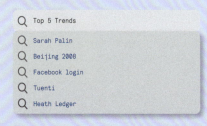

Top 5 Trends

The first Google I/O developer
conference is held

INTERNET COMMUNITY
Facebook tribute page
Pray for Northern Illinois
University Students and Families

One of the first Facebook tribute pages, created by Jim Combs to honor the students who had been shot, which had over 55,000 Facebook members within 48 hours.

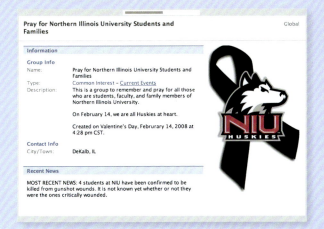

MOBILE EVOLUTION
iPhone 3G

Twice as fast as the first-generation iPhone and now with 3G networking, making it easier to multitask. Also featured push notifications for email.

2009/

The Year of Social Media Integration

2009/

—

The Year of Social Media Integration

—

Eternal Moonwalk

Facebook and Twitter were now being used by agencies and brands to integrate campaigns and immerse people, and their friends, within an experience of whatever was being promoted. These connected sites required users to allow access to their Facebook (or Twitter) accounts, so that data could be pulled from these sources, and this made many users extremely wary as it seemed all of their personal data was thus exposed and even that posts could be made to their accounts without permission being asked. It took a while before people felt they could trust this situation and were happy to engage with these new connected sites.

The sudden death of Michael Jackson showed how news was now traveling via social channels much more quickly than by news agencies. Twitter's servers crashed with the posting of over 100,000 tweets per hour, and Google blocked searches for 30 minutes featuring the singer's name in the belief that they were under a DDoS attack. A surge of tributes flooded social media, soon followed by memorial websites amongst which the Michael Jackson Eternal Moonwalk became an immediate hit.

Viral videos were almost international news now, including such classics as "David After Dentist, Baby Dancing to Beyonce, and the JK Wedding Entrance Dance". The millions of views these videos attracted made ordinary people into web celebrities overnight, something many would later turn to in order to make a living.

As video became the dominant force on the web for delivering content, a site for John Galliano was the first to allow each 15 seconds of footage to be divided into images, enabling users to search for a specific point or style within the catwalk show.

The Lexus RX 350 site persuaded people who were interested in the car that they were traveling into the future, since users had to set their system clock ahead to be able to access the site.

The Digital Concert Hall was the first website to stream concerts in full-screen HD with CD-quality sound, on a platform fitting for the Berlin Philharmonic.

Online tourism was taken to new levels with the Virtual Tour of New York, where an amazing set of aerial panoramas was converted into a multi-resolution presentation that made for a breathtaking way to view the great city of New York (and later several other cities).

Xixi no Banho (Pee in the Shower) presented a simple but well-meaning request: "We are asking people to pee in the shower to save water and contribute to saving the Atlantic rainforest."

The Sprint – Now Network was the first widget website. Intended to demonstrate the power of Sprint's network capabilities it linked together a huge number of data streams that changed by the second, ranging from babies being born to a live cam at Niagara Falls.

Incredibox enabled users to become a human beatbox in a game involving drag-and-drop sound icons.

Flash intros were now a thing of the past, but preloaders for websites were still a big deal and becoming increasingly impressive, many of them being showcased and archived at Pretty Loaded.

"Viral videos were almost international news now."

Lexus RX 350

JK Wedding Entrance Dance

John Galliano

Virtual Tour of New York

Facebook und Twitter wurden nun von Agenturen und Marken genutzt, um Kampagnen zu integrieren und Menschen und ihre Freunde zu begeistern, was auch immer beworben wurde. Diese verbundenen Seiten verlangten vom User, Zugang zu seinem Facebook-Konto zu erlauben (oder Twitter), damit Daten aus diesen Quellen abgerufen werden konnten. Das machte viele Benutzer extrem vorsichtig, da es so aussah, als wären all ihre persönlichen Daten aufgedeckt worden und dass Posts ohne Erlaubnis auf ihren Konten veröffentlicht werden konnten. Es dauerte eine Weile, bis die Leute glaubten, dass sie dieser Situation vertrauen konnten und sich freuten, mit diesen neuen verbundenen Seiten zu interagieren.

Der plötzliche Tod von Michael Jackson zeigte, dass Nachrichten viel schneller über soziale Kanäle unterwegs waren als über Nachrichtenagenturen. Twitters Server brachen durch das Posten von über 100.000

Tweets pro Stunde zusammen und Google blockierte 30 Minuten lang Suchanfragen mit dem Namen des Sängers, da sie dachten, sie wären Opfer eines DDoS-Angriffs geworden. Eine Welle von Tributen überschwemmte die sozialen Medien, bald folgten Gedenk-Websites, unter denen der Michael Jackson Eternal Moonwalk ein sofortiger Hit wurde.

Virale Videos wurden jetzt fast zu internationalen Nachrichten. Auch solche Klassiker wie „David nach dem Zahnarzt", „Baby tanzt zu Beyonce" und der „JK Hochzeitseintrittstanz". Die Millionen von Aufrufen, die diese Videos anzogen, machten gewöhnliche Leute über Nacht zu Web-Prominenten. Eine Tatsache die dazu führte, dass viele später damit ihren Lebensunterhalt verdienen wollten.

Als Video die vorherrschende Kraft im Web für die Bereitstellung von Inhalten wurde, war die Website für John Galliano die erste, in der alle 15 Sekunden Filmmaterial in Bilder aufgeteilt

werden konnten, sodass die User nach einem bestimmten Punkt oder Stil in der Laufstegshow suchen konnten.

Die Lexus RX 350 Website überzeugte Leute, die an dem Auto interessiert waren. Sie bekamen den Eindruck, dass sie in die Zukunft reisten, da die User ihre Systemuhr vorstellen mussten, um auf die Site zugreifen zu können.

Die Digital Concert Hall war die erste Website, die Konzerte in Vollbild-HD in CD-Qualität für die Berliner Philharmoniker übertragen konnte.

Der Online-Tourismus wurde mit der Virtual Tour of New York auf ein neues Niveau gehoben. Hier wurde ein erstaunlicher Satz von Luftpanoramen in eine Multiresolution-Präsentation umgewandelt, die eine atemberaubende Sicht auf die großartige Stadt New York (und später auf einige andere Städte) ermöglichte.

Xixi no Banho (Pinkeln in der Dusche) hatte eine einfache aber wohlmeinende Bitte: „Wir

baten Leute, unter der Dusche zu pinkeln, um Wasser zu sparen und zur Rettung des atlantischen Regenwaldes beizutragen."

The Sprint – Now Network war die erste Widget-Website. Um die Leistungsfähigkeit der Netzwerkfähigkeiten von Sprint zu demonstrieren, verknüpften sie eine große Anzahl von Datenströmen, die sich von Sekunde zu Sekunde änderten. Von Babys, die geboren wurden, bis hin zu einer Live-Kamera an den Niagarafällen.

Incredibox ermöglichte es Benutzern, zu einer menschlichen Beatbox in einem Spiel mit Drag-and-Drop-Sound-Icons zu werden.

Flash-Intros gehörten nun der Vergangenheit an, aber Preloader für Websites waren immer noch eine große Sache und wurden immer beeindruckender. Viele von ihnen wurden bei Pretty Loaded präsentiert und archiviert.

2009/
—

The Year of Social Media Integration
—

Pretty Loaded

Sprint – Now Network

> "Flash intros were now a thing of the past, but preloaders for websites were still a big deal and becoming increasingly impressive."

Xixi no Banho (Pee in the Shower)

Les agences et les marques se servent à présent de Facebook et de Twitter pour diffuser des campagnes et faire auprès des internautes et leurs contacts la promotion de quoi que ce soit. Ces sites connectés demandent à leurs visiteurs d'autoriser l'accès à leurs comptes Facebook ou Twitter pour récupérer des données de ces sources. Nombres d'utilisateurs sont très réticents car ils ont l'impression que toutes leurs données personnelles vont se retrouver exposées et que des publications peuvent même être effectuées dans leur compte sans leur accord préalable. Ils mettent du temps à finalement se fier de ces sites.

La disparition soudaine de Michael Jackson montre à quel point les nouvelles circulent beaucoup plus vite sur les réseaux sociaux qu'à travers les agences de presse. Les serveurs de Twitter plantent avec la publication de plus de 100 000 tweets par heure, et Google bloque pendant 30 minutes les recherches incluant le nom du chanteur, pensant être la cible d'une attaque de déni de service. Les hommages inondent les réseaux, puis viennent les sites Web commémoratifs, parmi lesquels Michael Jackson Eternal Moonwalk qui remporte un succès immédiat.

Les vidéos virales se placent presque au rang d'actualités internationales, avec des classiques comme «David After Dentist», «Baby Dancing to Beyonce» et «JK Wedding Entrance Dance». Du jour au lendemain, les millions de visualisations que reçoivent ces vidéos rendent célèbre monsieur Tout-le-Monde, et bientôt beaucoup s'y dédieront pour gagner leur vie.

La vidéo s'impose comme principal vecteur de diffusion de contenu sur le Web. Un site conçu pour John Galliano est le premier à permettre l'extraction d'images de chaque séquence de 15 secondes du défilé afin d'y faire des recherches.

Le site pour la Lexus RX 350 donne la sensation aux visiteurs qu'ils voyagent dans le futur en leur demandant d'avancer l'horloge de leur système pour y accéder.

Conçu pour l'Orchestre philharmonique de Berlin, le site Digital Concert Hall est le premier du genre à diffuser des concerts en vidéo HD plein écran et avec un son de qualité CD.

Le tourisme en ligne prend une nouvelle dimension avec le Virtual Tour of New York. De magnifiques panoramas aériens assemblés dans un montage multi-résolution offrent une vision spectaculaire de cette ville (d'autres suivront plus tard).

Le site Xixi no Banho (pipi dans la douche, en portugais) fait part d'une requête pour la bonne cause: «Nous demandons aux gens de faire pipi dans la douche pour économiser de l'eau et contribuer à la sauvegarde de la forêt atlantique».

Le site Now Network pour Sprint est le premier à inclure des widgets. Pour démontrer toute la puissance des fonctions réseau de Sprint, il met en relation une quantité de flux de données actualisés en permanence, allant d'un compteur de naissances à une webcam aux chutes du Niagara.

Incredibox permet aux utilisateurs de se transformer en boîte à rythmes humaine dans un jeu où des icônes de son doivent être déplacées.

Les introductions en Flash relèvent désormais du passé, mais les animations de préchargement des sites jouent encore un rôle important. Elles gagnent en sophistication et beaucoup sont présentées et archivées sur le site Pretty Loaded.

08 Facts of the year

Number of internet users:
1.8 billion, 26.4% of
the world population

Number of websites:
238 million

World news:
Michael Jackson dies

Website with most traffic:
Google.com

Tech hardware:
USB 3.0 launches

Tech software:
Minecraft is launched

Other tech:
Google blocks all searches
on Michael Jackson
believing it was a DDoS
attack

Highest-grossing film:
Avatar

2009/
—

We Choose the Moon

—

Recreating one of history's
most important events

On July 20, 1969, a special event took place: my mother gave birth to me in Welwyn Garden City, England. At the time, the nurses were slightly distracted watching *Apollo 11* land on the Moon, and ever since I have always felt a special connection to the Moon landing – so of course I was very excited about its 40th anniversary.

We Choose the Moon featured a real-time re-creation of the mission and included round-the-clock audio transmissions, coupled with top-quality 3D animations representing every step of the journey. The way the site played out was very special, and felt like history repeating itself.

"The biggest creative opportunities tend to come into view along with equally sizable challenges. This was certainly the case with We Choose the Moon. Creatively we knew that recreating the *Apollo 11* mission in real time could be epic — people are obsessed with space travel and the idea that we could take people out of their work cubicles, dorm rooms, homes, etc. and place them in the '3, 2, 1 lift-off' moment that changed the world 40 years earlier was a special thing… But of course, building it was stressful. The site required that we sync rich animated 3D renderings with streaming audio we'd received from NASA spanning the entire four-day journey. The whole experience was live, matched to the second when it originally occurred 40 years earlier, which put a huge load on the servers — over four million unique visits in four days."

Jonathan Hills
Domani Studios

Am 20. Juli 1969 fand ein besonderes Ereignis statt: Meine Mutter brachte mich in Welwyn Garden City, England, zur Welt. Zu dieser Zeit waren die Krankenschwestern leicht abgelenkt und beobachteten, wie *Apollo 11* auf dem Mond landete und seitdem habe ich eine besondere Verbindung zur Mondlandung – ich war daher natürlich sehr aufgeregt wegen des 40-jährigen Jubiläums.

We Choose the Moon zeigte eine Echtzeit-Wiederherstellung der Mission und beinhaltete rund um die Uhr Audioübertragungen, gekoppelt mit hochwertigen 3D-Animationen, die jeden Schritt der Reise darstellten. Die Art und Weise, wie die Seite abgespielt wurde, war sehr speziell und fühlte sich an, als würde sich die Geschichte wiederholen.

Le 20 juillet 1969 se produit un événement de taille : ma mère me met au monde à Welwyn Garden City, en Angleterre. À ce moment-là, les infirmières sont quelque peu distraites par la retransmission de l'alunissage de la mission *Apollo 11*. J'ai depuis lors toujours ressenti une connexion spéciale avec cet événement et son 40ᵉ anniversaire m'intéresse forcément.

Le site We Choose the Moon montre une reproduction en temps réel de la mission, avec des transmissions audio à toute heure et des animations 3D d'excellente qualité pour illustrer chaque étape du voyage. La dynamique du site est très originale et donne l'impression de revivre l'histoire.

2009/
—

Labuat

—

A music video orchestrated
by mouse movement

Essentially an interactive music video that enabled users to draw the music, by moving their mouse cursor, this addictive site was governed by the beat of the music which dictated when certain experimental events occurred. Those who made it to the end were rewarded with a host of visual delights and surprises.

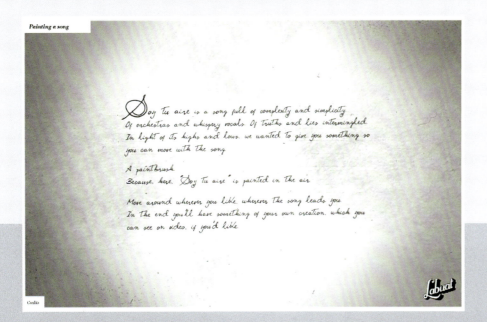

"Labuat was the beginning of the end of Flash for us. And it was, ironically, the most complex, useful, and beautiful use of Flash. Deeply coded, very well crafted, and very effective for the client. We got millions of views and the experiential music-video clip became a sort of new format in the industry and we got lots of new demands from different bands. I only have good memories about Flash and I actually miss it a lot."

Rafa Soto
Herraiz Soto

Es war im Wesentlichen ein interaktives Musikvideo, das es den Benutzern ermöglichte, die Musik zu zeichnen, indem der Mauszeiger bewegt wurde. Diese süchtig machende Seite wurde durch den Takt der Musik bestimmt, der diktierte, wann bestimmte experimentelle Ereignisse stattfanden. Diejenigen, die es bis zum Ende schafften, wurden mit einer Fülle von visuellen Freuden und Überraschungen belohnt.

Ce site addictif est avant tout un vidéoclip interactif. Les internautes dessinent à l'aide du curseur la musique qu'ils entendent, et le pinceau obéit au rythme frappé quand se produisent certains événements expérimentaux. Ceux qui arrivent au bout sont récompensés par une série de surprises visuelles.

Cinema 21:9
—

Dropping site visitors into a major crime incident

This impressive promotional site for the first TV with cinema-screen proportions was immediately intriguing as it plunged users right into the midst of a thrilling adventure.

With 'baddies' dressed as clowns and police everywhere, the deliberately slow-moving video experience was peppered with hotspots that took users to another level.

"Instead of putting a film in a website, we put a website in a film. Flash allowed us to blur the lines between web design and film direction and everything since the rise of the iPhone has felt like a step back in terms of interaction and immersion within stand-alone sites. Cinema 21:9, or *Carousel* as the film was known, did everything in one place, and gave people something worth talking about. And it's good to see people are still talking about it today."

Chris Baylis
Tribal DDB Amsterdam; Freelance

Diese beeindruckende Werbe-seite für den ersten Fernseher mit Kino-Proportionen faszinierte sofort, da der User mitten in ein aufregendes Abenteuer stürzte. Mit „Bösen", die überall als

Clowns verkleidet waren und Polizisten überall, war das absichtlich langsame Video-erlebnis gespickt mit Hotspots, die die Nutzer auf ein anderes Level brachten.

Ce site promotionnel pour la première télévision aux propor-tions d'un écran de cinéma est d'emblée intriguant. Les visiteurs sont transportés dans une aventure palpitante, avec des

méchants déguisés en clowns et des policiers dans tous les coins. L'expérience vidéo délibérément lente est remplie de points d'ac-cès à d'autres niveaux.

—

Because Clicking
Is So 90s!

—

Voice navigation arrives

Presenting his college thesis directly as an
experimental website, Andreas Lutz constructed
the first site where users could navigate by
using their voice. A brief guide was included too
so that visitors knew how to proceed.

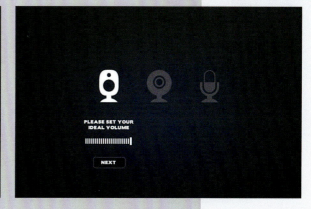

"When Because Clicking Is So 90s! was launched,
I think many visitors had their first experience
of touchless interaction, right in their own homes.
Project Natal, later better known as Kinect, was
introduced in the same year by Microsoft, while
Siri and Google's voice search launched two years
later, in 2011, so not many people had been able
to experience interacting with a desktop computer
(or more generally, with machines) other than by
using a mouse, keyboard, or some other touch device."

Andreas Lutz
andreaslutz.com

Andreas Lutz stellte seine
College-Arbeit direkt als experimentelle Website vor und baute
die erste Seite auf, auf der die
Nutzer mit ihrer Stimme navigieren konnten. Ein kurzer Leitfaden
wurde ebenfalls mitgeliefert,
damit die Besucher wussten,
wie es weiterging.

Andreas Lutz présente sa
thèse universitaire sous forme
de site expérimental, dont la
navigation se fait à travers la voix.
Un petit guide est inclus pour que
les visiteurs sachent comme
s'y prendre.

—

BooneOakley

—

The first YouTube website

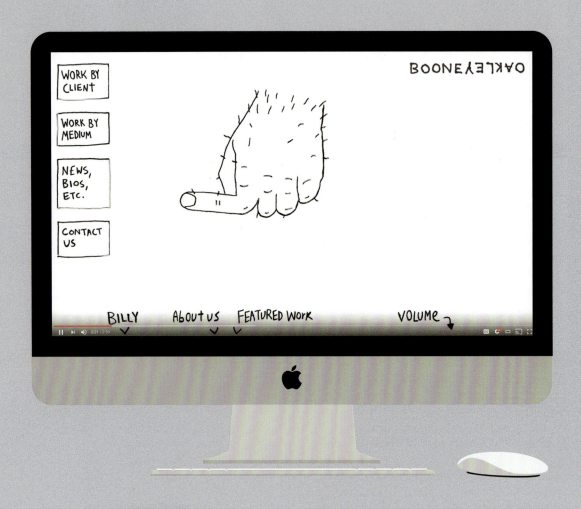

It might have seemed that making an agency's website entirely within YouTube was a foolish move, but the stats proved otherwise when more than a million views were clocked up in its first week. This site for BooneOakley consisted of several video clips hooked together by YouTube's framework, and made full use of the new ability to click on links within the actual videos.

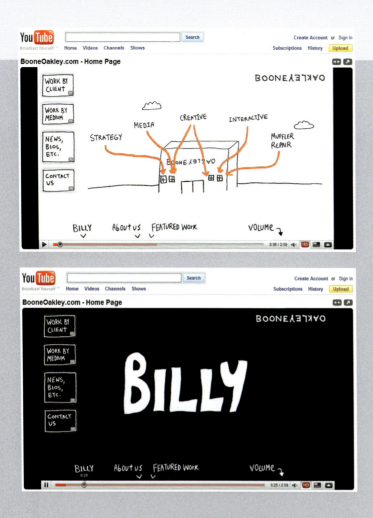

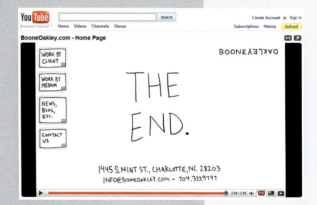

"We heard about a new technology that YouTube had just introduced called annotations that linked videos. Since most of the work that we were doing was video content for clients, it seemed like a no-brainer to get rid of our traditional website and use video on YouTube to tell our story. The tale of Billy the Marketing Director, whose wife had him murdered because he chose the wrong ad agency, really helped make the site a big hit."

David Oakley
BooneOakley

Es könnte so aussehen, als sei es völlig töricht, die Website einer Agentur komplett auf YouTube zu veröffentlichen. Aber die Statistiken sahen das anders, als mehr als eine Millionen Views allein in der ersten Woche verzeichnet wurden. Diese Seite für Boone-Oakley bestand aus mehreren Videoclips, die vom YouTube-Framework zusammengefügt wurden und nutzte die neue Möglichkeit, auf Links innerhalb der Videos zu klicken.

Il pouvait sembler insensé de mettre sur YouTube ce site Web d'une agence. Pourtant, les statistiques sont venues prouver le contraire, avec plus d'un million de visualisations rien que la première semaine. Ce site pour BooneOakley compte une série de vidéoclips assemblés dans le framework de YouTube et profite de la nouvelle fonction qui permet de cliquer sur des liens à l'intérieur de vidéos.

2009/
—

The Prototype
Experience

—

One of the first Facebook Connect sites

This year also marked the advent of sites that asked users to connect to Facebook, and in this early example, once users had connected they were treated to an impressive trailer for this Xbox video game where they featured in the trailer themselves. It was the first time content was taken from Facebook accounts and deployed as content for a third party.

"The Prototype Experience was built using Flash and Facebook Connect. The main idea of the experience was to make you believe we were stealing your memories. At the time, the web was really like a lab for crazy people. All you needed was a smart idea and good enough coding skills. The web was like a playground for a bunch of kids who'd just received new toys. After that, it became much more professionalized, and probably a bit too complex."

Lionel Cordier
1MD

In diesem Jahr wurden auch Websites aufgerufen, die Nutzer dazu auffordern, eine Verbindung zu Facebook herzustellen. In diesem frühen Beispiel wurden die Nutzer nach der Verbindung mit einem beeindruckenden Trailer für dieses Xbox-Videospiel belohnt, in dem sie selbst im Trailer zu sehen waren. Dies war das erste Mal, dass Inhalte von Facebook-Konten übernommen und als Inhalt für Dritte bereitgestellt wurden.

Cette année voit la naissance de sites demandant aux visiteurs de se connecter à Facebook. Pour accepter de le faire dans ce site d'un jeu vidéo sur Xbox, les internautes sont récompensés avec une remarquable bande-annonce dont ils sont les protagonistes. Pour la première fois, du contenu est récupéré de comptes Facebook et déployé dans un site tiers.

2009/

—

Hogwarts Wizarding Class

—

An early Twitter-connected website

The idea behind this site was to cast a spell on one of the user's Twitter followers. After signing in to the site via Twitter, users could select a potion, from a choice of four, and preview each one. After a potion had been selected, users would choose a message to go with it and a lucky recipient, who then received a personal tweet that would surprise them in a big way.

"The concept was simple, letting Twitter users cast spells from the *Harry Potter* movie on to their Twitter pages and their followers. We worked with a team of great animators and developers who brought the spells to life in fun and intriguing ways. The web app would scrape the user's Twitter feed and redeploy it on a unique URL, allowing them to cast spells over what looked like their feed. This was really progressive at the time."

Simon Spreckley
HelloComputer

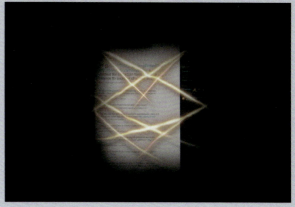

Die Idee hinter dieser Seite war es, einen der Twitter-Follower des Nutzers zu verzaubern. Nachdem sie sich auf der Website über Twitter angemeldet hatten, konnten die Benutzer einen Trank auswählen und sich eine Vorschau anzeigen lassen.

Nachdem ein Trank ausgewählt worden war, wählten die Benutzer eine entsprechende Nachricht und einen glücklichen Empfänger, der daraufhin einen persönlichen Tweet erhielt, der ihn im großen Stil überra-schen sollte.

L'objectif de ce site est de jeter un sort à l'un des followers dans Twitter des visiteurs. Après s'être connectés au site via Twitter, les utilisateurs choisissent une potion parmi quatre présentées, ainsi qu'un message l'accompa-gnant et l'heureux destinataire,

qui reçoit alors un tweet person-nel des plus surprenants.

Xbox
Beatles Rock Band
—

The first (and possibly only)
Silverlight website

In 2007, Microsoft launched Silverlight and it was immediately hailed in some quarters as a Flash-killer. However, it wasn't until 2009 that a whole website was made using Silverlight that would be worthy of a FWA award. Designed by AKQA, this promotional site for the Xbox title, The Beatles Rock Band, was the first and only site made entirely with Silverlight to scoop a FWA. In 2013, Silverlight was shelved by Microsoft.

"The challenge here was having to use Microsoft's Silverlight to deliver this experience, as we were working for Xbox. Nobody at that stage had a great deal of Silverlight experience, so it was a case of designer and developer working very closely together to get the maximum from it. The design of the site used the visual iconography of the songs themselves to trigger hidden experiences relating to the band and the music in surprising and entertaining ways."

Andy Hood
AKQA

Im Jahr 2007 startete Microsoft Silverlight und es wurde sofort in einigen Vierteln als Flash-Killer gefeiert. Allerdings wurde erst 2009 eine ganze Website mit Silverlight erstellt, die einen FWA-Award verdient hatte. Design von AKQA, war diese Werbeseite für die Xbox mit dem Titel: The Beatles Rock Band die erste und einzige Seite, die vollständig in Silverlight erstellt wurde und einen FWA einheimste. Im Jahr 2013 wurde Silverlight von Microsoft auf Eis gelegt.

En 2007, Microsoft lance Silverlight et certains s'en réjouissent, considérant qu'il signe la fin de Flash. Ce n'est toutefois pas avant 2009 qu'est créé le site promotionnel du jeu The Beatles Rock Band sur Xbox. Il s'agit du premier et unique site Web entièrement développé avec Silverlight à décrocher un prix FWA. En 2013, Microsoft met son plug-in au placard.

Radiotjänst:
The Hero

—

The personalized video that made viewers the hero

Here was another personalized movie that incorporated images from the user to make them the hero of a commercial, but what set it ahead of the rest was the fact that the developers created a web-based color-grading application to give the experience an even more authentic look and feel.

"Radiotjänst was one of those unexpected viral projects. We used Flash to build an interactive web-based commercial that was originally made for Swedish audiences. People could upload a picture of themselves which was then inserted into a personalized web film where you become the hero that paid your TV license. Pretty much overnight it became a global hit with 50 million unique visitors and we needed so much data to generate all of the films that Draft and Stopp had to help pay the streaming costs!"

Pasi Helin
Stopp; MediaMonks

Hier war ein weiterer personalisierter Film, der User-Bilder einbaute, um sie zum Helden eines Werbespots zu machen. Vor allem aber haben die Entwickler eine webbasierte Farbverlauf-Anwendung entwickelt, um das Erlebnis noch authentischer aussehen zu lassen.

C'est là un autre film personnalisé qui incorpore des images de l'utilisateur pour en faire le héros d'une annonce. Il se distingue du lot des sites de ce style grâce à une application d'étalonnage basée sur le Web qui dote le résultat de plus de réalisme.

AC/DC Rocks the Office

—

The first Excel website

AC/DC smashed through corporate firewalls with the first music video developed in Excel. It was a bewildering idea, and really made people stop and wonder what else could be done that was as unexpected as building a website using spreadsheet software, who would ever have thought of that! The project was a huge success, with over 1 million downloads of the Excel file and more than 2 million views of the site's video demo.

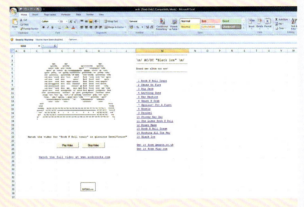

"Sony's consumer insight department had told us that most of AC/DC's fans were in office jobs and couldn't access sites like Facebook and YouTube, so we came up with a plan to reach them using Excel, a format allowed through every corporate firewall. We rendered the video for the single "Rock 'n' Roll Train" as ASCII art and animated it directly in the spreadsheet, creating a music video in Excel format."

Phil Clandillon
Sony Music Entertainment

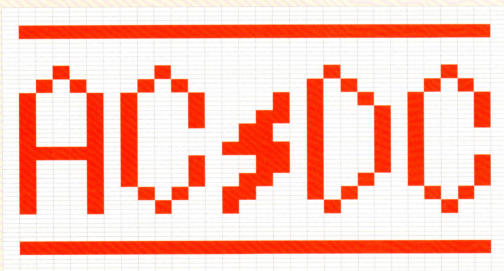

AC/DC durchbrach Unternehmens-Firewalls mit dem ersten Musikvideo, das in Excel entwickelt wurde. Es war eine verwirrende Idee und brachte die Leute dazu, innezuhalten und sich zu fragen, was sonst noch kommen sollte, was so unerwartet war, wie das Erstellen einer Website mit einer Tabellenkalkulations-software. Wer hätte das jemals gedacht! Das Projekt war ein großer Erfolg, mit über 1 Million Downloads der Excel-Datei und mehr als 2 Millionen Ansichten der Demoansicht des Videos der Website.

AC/DC passe à travers tous les pare-feux avec le premier vidéo-clip conçu dans Excel. L'idée déconcerte et tout le monde se demande ce qui peut encore se faire d'aussi inattendu et inimaginable que la conception d'un site Web à l'aide d'un tableur. Le projet remporte un énorme succès : plus d'1 million de téléchargements du fichier Excel et plus de 2 millions de visualisations de la démo du site.

NOTABLE WEBSITE LAUNCH
Kickstarter

Google Ventures announced

GOOGLE FACTS

Google Voice launches

Google
@google
Follow

I'm 01100110 01100101 01100101 01101100
01101001 01101110 01100111 00100000
01101100 01110101 01100011 01101011
01111001 00001010.

898 | 860

Google's first tweet, in binary

A series of doodles is released for the 40th anniversary of Sesame Street

Top 5 Trends
Michael Jackson
Facebook
Tuenti
Twitter
Sanalika

Top 5 Trends

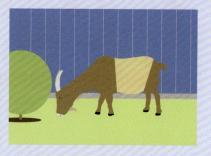

Google rents a herd of goats to clear fire-hazard brush around its HQ

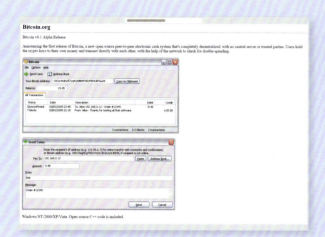

INTERNET COMMUNITY
Bitcoin

The global cryptocurrency is introduced
as internet currency by a person with
the fake name Satoshi Nakamoto.

MOBILE EVOLUTION
Nokia 5230

Nokia's smartphone reportedly
sold over 159 million units,
compared to 35 million for the
high-flying iPhone 3GS.

2010/

The Death of Flash

2010/

The Death of Flash

Verbatim

This was the biggest year for Flash, which is to say its worst. The launch of the iPad and growing popularity of the iPhone (neither of which supported Flash), combined with Steve Jobs's open letter in April, "Thoughts on Flash", resulted in a huge aftershock. Almost overnight, Flash became a bad word and was widely shunned.

In its hard-hitting conclusion, Jobs associated Flash with a bygone era of mouse interfaces and PCs, and, while acknowledging that Adobe would want to expand into mobile use as well, he stressed the shortcomings of Flash in terms of touch interfaces, low-power devices, and what he called open web standards.

The huge uptake on the part of media platforms in the rush to appear on mobile devices showed, for Jobs, that Apple's system had eclipsed Flash as a means of accessing web content or watching videos. In the same way, developers would no longer need to rely on Flash for developing graphics or games, if the quarter of a million apps already available to download from Apple was any indication.

The arrival of HTML5 as the new protocol for the mobile era was hailed at this stage already by Jobs as being the future for not only mobile devices but also PCs, and in a final riposte to Adobe he suggested this might be a better use of the company's creative energy than any complaints they might level against Apple.

Many people thought Adobe fell well short in responding to the threat concerning Flash's future, and some notable figures expressed their views in the article,

"The Industry – Thoughts on Flash", published on the FWA website.

Nevertheless, big brands and agencies continued to use it, and it was several years before it really disappeared from websites. Meanwhile, it was a defining year in the history of web design, with Google's The Wilderness Downtown being an HTML5 website that became the biggest game-changer in over a decade.

Verbatim's Championship kept the creative spirit alive with its online fighting game, where users could assemble a monster from various hardware components, all taken from Verbatim's removable media catalog, and then battle those built by other users.

In the run-up to the U.K. general election, 10downingtweets aggregated tweets from the various parties and leaders to allow people to read their political agendas and take part in an online poll.

Battle of the Cheetos let users command an army of Puffs or Crunchies and set out to conquer the web. Commanders could choose which website they wanted to battle across, such as mashable.com or even the user's own site.

The Perrier Mansion website starred world-famous burlesque dancer and seductress Dita Von Teese, and permitted visitors to observe her uninhibited enthusiasm for the bottled water.

Humor was the main force behind Tipp-Ex White and Rewrite, a project entirely derived from YouTube which featured over 50 mini-movies sewed together. Users could write, erase, and rewrite different titles for the film clip, thus deciding how the story of the hunter and the bear ended.

Fast Company's Influence Project set out to find the Most Influential Person Online, showcasing a graphical tier system for the 32,000+ submissions received whereby the greater a person's social media influence, the bigger their photo would be displayed.

Facebook now counted 500 million active users, its story being told with the release of the movie *The Social Network*,

while Lady Gaga became the first person to amass over 10 million Facebook friends.

Twitter was handling over 65 million tweets a day, and Instagram launched in October with over 25,000 sign-ups on its first day.

Angry Birds became a global sensation and the top-selling game on the App Store. Meanwhile, the iPhone 4 launched but was plagued with antenna problems and poor signal strength.

10downingtweets

Battle of the Cheetos

Dies war das größte Jahr für Flash, nämlich das Schlimmste. Der Launch des iPads und die wachsende Popularität des iPhones (die Flash nicht unterstützen), kombiniert mit dem offenen Brief von Steve Jobs im April „Thoughts on Flash" (Gedanken über Flash), führten zu einem riesigen Nachbeben. Fast über Nacht wurde Flash zu einem schlechten Wort und es wurde weitgehend gemieden.

In seiner vernichtenden Schlussfolgerung verglich Jobs Flash mit der alten Ära der mit der Maus verbunden Schnittstellen und PCs und als er bestätigte, dass auch Adobe in Mobilgeräte einsteigen würde, betonte er die Mängel von Flash in Bezug auf Touch-Schnittstellen, geringe Leistung der Geräte und was er Open Web-Standards nannte.

Die große Akzeptanz seitens der Medien-Plattformen in aller Eile, um auf den Mobiltelefonen zu erscheinen, zeigte Jobs nur, dass das Apple-System Flash als Mittel des Zugriffes auf Webinhalte oder um Videos anzusehen, in den Schatten gestellt hatte. So müssten sich die Entwickler nicht mehr bei der Entwicklung von Grafiken oder Spielen auf Flash verlassen. Ein Hinweis darauf waren die Viertelmillionen Apps, die bereits

verfügbar waren und bei Apple heruntergeladen werden konnten.

Das Erscheinen von HTML5 als das neue Protokoll für die mobile Ära wurde an dieser Stelle von Jobs begrüßt. Es sei die Zukunft für nicht nur der Mobilgeräte, sondern auch der PCs und in einer letzten Bemerkung zu Adobe meinte er, dass dabei die Kreativität des Unternehmens besser genutzt werden könnte, als bei all der Energie, die sie mit allen Beschwerden aufbringen würden, die sie gegen Apple vorbrachten.

Viele Leute waren der Meinung, dass Adobe auf die Bedrohung in Bezug auf die Zukunft von Flash zu vage reagierte und einige bemerkenswerte Zahlen brachten ihre Ansichten in dem Artikel „The Industry – Thoughts on Flash" zum Ausdruck.

Dennoch benutzten es große Marken und Agenturen weiterhin und es dauerte einige Jahre, bis es wirklich von den Websites verschwand. Inzwischen war es ein entscheidendes Jahr in der Geschichte des Webdesigns. Googles The Wilderness Downtown war eine HTML5-Website, die in mehr als einem Jahrzehnt zum größten Game-Changer wurde.

Verbatims Championship erhielt den kreativen Geist mit seinem Online-Kampfspiel,

bei dem die User ein Monster aus verschiedenen Hardwarekomponenten zusammenstellen konnten, die alle aus dem entfernbaren Medienkatalog von Verbatim entnommen werden konnten, um dann gegen die von anderen Benutzern erstellten Monster zu kämpfen.

Im Vorfeld der allgemeinen Wahlen in Großbritannien sammelte 10downingtweets Tweets der verschiedenen Parteien und Parteiführer, um es den Menschen zu ermöglichen, ihre politischen Programme zu lesen und an einer Online-Umfrage teilzunehmen.

Battle of the Cheetos lässt die User eine Armee von Puffs oder Crunchies befehligen und schickt sie auf den Weg, um das Internet zu erobern. Die Befehlshaber können wählen, auf welcher Website sie den Krieg führen wollen, wie zum Beispiel auf mashable.com oder sogar auf der eigenen Seite des Users.

Auf der Perrier Mansion Website wurde die weltberühmte Burlesque-Tänzerin und Verführerin Dita Von Teese vorgestellt und sie erlaubte den Besuchern, ihre ungehemmte Begeisterung für das Wasser in Flaschen zu beobachten.

Humor war die treibende Kraft hinter Tipp-Ex White and Rewrite, einem Projekt,

das ausschließlich auf YouTube basierte und über 50 zusammengesetzte Mini-Filme enthielt. Die Nutzer konnten verschiedene Titel für den Filmclip schreiben, löschen und neu schreiben und so entscheiden, wie die Geschichte des Jägers und des Bären endete.

Fast Company's Influence Project hatte sich vorgenommen, die einflussreichste Person online zu finden und präsentierte ein grafisches Einstufungssystem für die mehr als 32.000 erhaltenen Einsendungen, wobei das Foto einer Person umso größer angezeigt wurde, je größer ihr Einfluss in den sozialen Medien war.

Facebook zählte jetzt 500 Millionen aktive Nutzer, seine Geschichte wurde mit der Veröffentlichung des Films *The Social Network* erzählt, während Lady Gaga als erste Person über 10 Millionen Facebook-Freunde sammelte.

Twitter wickelte über 65 Millionen Tweets pro Tag ab und Instagram startete im Oktober mit über 25.000 Anmeldungen am ersten Tag.

Angry Birds wurde zu einer globalen Sensation und zum meistverkauften Spiel im App Store. Währenddessen startete das iPhone 4, hatte aber mit Antennenproblemen und schlechter Signalstärke zu kämpfen.

The Death
of Flash

—

Perrier Mansion

"This was the biggest year for Flash, which is to say its worst."

Tipp-Ex White and Rewrite

Influence Project

C'est l'année la plus noire pour Flash. Le lancement de l'iPad et le succès grandissant de l'iPhone, deux dispositifs qui ne prennent pas Flash en charge, puis en avril la lettre ouverte de Steve Jobs intitulée «Thoughts on Flash», viennent sonner le glas. Du jour au lendemain pratiquement, Flash est banni et tout le monde le boude.

Dans sa conclusion percutante, Jobs associe Flash à l'époque révolue des interfaces souris et des PC. Même s'il lui semble logique qu'Adobe veuille évoluer vers les dispositifs mobiles, il souligne les lacunes de Flash en matière d'interfaces tactiles, d'appareils de faible puissance et de ce qu'il nomme les standards ouverts du Web. L'afflux des plate-formes médiatiques pour être présentes sur des dispositifs mobiles prouve à Jobs que le système d'Apple a éclipsé Flash concernant l'accès au contenu Web et la visualisation de vidéos. De la même façon, les développeurs n'ont plus à compter sur Flash pour concevoir des graphismes ou des jeux, au vu des 250 000 applications pouvant déjà être téléchargées d'Apple.

L'apparition de HTML5 comme nouveau protocole à l'ère

mobile est déjà acclamée par Jobs, qui le voit comme le futur pour les appareils mobiles ainsi que les PC. Dans une riposte finale à Adobe, il suggère à la compagnie de dépenser davantage son énergie créative dans cette voie au lieu de se plaindre d'Apple.

Beaucoup jugent insuffisante la réponse d'Adobe à la menace concernant l'avenir de Flash, et de grosses pointures font part de leur opinion dans l'article «The Industry – Thoughts on Flash» qui est publié sur le site FWA.

Les grandes marques et agences continuent pourtant de l'utiliser, et sa disparition des sites Web prendra plusieurs années. Dans l'histoire de la conception Web, l'année 2010 reste déterminante, notamment quand Google publie le site The Wilderness Downtown. Codé en HTML5, il change la donne dans une mesure sans égale pendant une décennie.

Le site Championship de Verbatim défend l'esprit de créativité avec un jeu de combat en ligne. Les joueurs peuvent créer un monstre en assemblant des composants matériels issus du catalogue de supports amo-

vibles de la marque, puis le faire s'affronter à ceux construits par d'autres utilisateurs.

Lors de la campagne pour les élections générales britanniques, le site 10downingtweets compile des tweets de divers partis et dirigeants afin que les citoyens en consultent le programme et participent à un sondage en ligne.

Le site Battle of the Cheetos permet aux visiteurs de diriger une armée de Puffs ou de Crunchies et de partir à la conquête du Web. Les commandants peuvent choisir dans quel site Web combattre, comme mashable.com ou même leur propre site.

Le site Perrier Mansion met en vedette la célèbre et séduisante danseuse de cabaret Dita Von Teese. Les visiteurs y découvrent son enthousiasme sans retenue pour l'eau gazeuse.

L'humour est l'argument principal du site Tipp-Ex White and Rewrite, un projet entièrement publié sur YouTube avec plus de 50 mini-films enchaînés. Les utilisateurs peuvent écrire, effacer, puis réécrire différents titres pour chaque clip et ainsi déterminer comment finit l'his-

toire du chasseur et de l'ours.

L'initiative Influence Project lancée par Fast Company vise à trouver la personne la plus influente en ligne. Le site présente les plus de 32 000 propositions reçues sous forme de graphique à étages, et la taille de la photo de chaque personne est proportionnelle à l'influence qu'elle exerce sur les réseaux sociaux.

Facebook compte désormais plus de 500 millions d'utilisateurs actifs, et l'histoire de la firme arrive sur les écrans avec le film The Social Network. Pour sa part, Lady Gaga est la première personne à cumuler plus de 10 millions d'amis sur Facebook.

Twitter gère plus de 65 millions de tweets par jour, et Instagram est lancé en octobre avec plus de 25 000 inscriptions le premier jour.

Angry Birds remporte un succès mondial et devient le jeu le plus vendu sur l'App Store. La sortie de l'iPhone 4 est entachée par des problèmes d'antenne et une faible qualité du signal de l'appareil.

08 Facts of the year

Number of internet users:
2.05 billion, 29.7% of
world population

Number of websites:
206.9 million

World news:
a powerful earthquake
in Haiti kills over
100,000 people

Website with most traffic:
Yahoo.com

Tech hardware:
the iPad launches

Tech software:
Instagram launches

Other tech:
Apple becomes the most
valuable technology
company, overtaking
Microsoft

Highest-grossing film:
Toy Story 3

The Wilderness Downtown

—

The biggest, most influential website in over a decade

This was the first 100 percent HTML5 website that really shook Flash, tipping the balance in terms of innovation away from it. An interactive short film for the Arcade Fire track "We Used to Wait", it utilized Google Chrome's browser, Google Maps, and HTML5. Users entered their zip code and address (current, or from childhood) and watched as an incredible personalized music video played out right in their very own neighborhood. The site won the FWA SOTY and that in itself sent worrying tremors to die-hard Flashers around the world.

"The Wilderness Downtown was sparked by HTML5 support in Chrome. Chris Milk and I knew we wanted to make a music video which was meant for the web — something that was taking advantage of the internet, data, real-time interaction, etc. — not a music video meant for television. The key feature of the project was personally tailoring the experience for each person. By entering the address of the house you grew up in you were transported back to your home town through Google Maps and Street View images. It was all about creating an extremely precise trigger for empathy."

Aaron Koblin
Google; Within

Dies war die erste 100-prozentige HTML5-Website, die Flash wirklich erschütterte und damit seine Balance in Bezug auf Innovation wegnahm. Ein interaktiver Kurzfilm für den Arcade Fire Track „We Used to Wait" verwendete den Browser von Google Chrome, Google Maps und HTML5. Die User gaben ihre Postleitzahl und ihre Adresse (aktuell oder aus der Kindheit) ein und sahen sich ein unglaubliches personalisiertes Musikvideo an, das direkt in ihrer eigenen Nachbarschaft spielte. Die Seite gewann die FWA SOTY und erschütterte selbst hartgesottene Flasher auf der ganzen Welt.

Ce site codé à 100 % en HTML5 fait trembler Flash et s'impose à lui en termes d'innovation. La réalisation de cette vidéo interactive, qui a pour bande originale le titre «We Used to Wait» d'Arcade Fire, repose sur le navigateur Google Chrome, Google Maps et HTML5. Les visiteurs entrent leur code postal et leur adresse (actuelle ou de leur enfance) et découvrent un clip personnalisé qui se déroule dans leur quartier. Le site remporte le prix FWA SOTY, ce qui préoccupe les inconditionnels de Flash du monde entier.

Lexus Dark Ride

—

The latest technology pushes interactive films to the next level

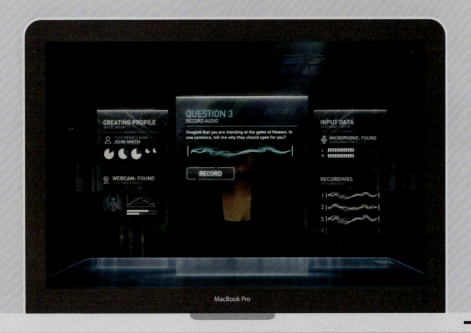

The Lexus Dark Ride experience invited users to play the role of navigator alongside driver Tony in a 12-minute interactive film. Pannable 180-degree sequences, user-recorded audio, Facebook/webcam integration, and an adaptive 3D soundtrack all blew me away, as did the production quality and levels of interaction available. The integration with Facebook and webcams really took this site to a whole new level.

"Dark Ride was easily our most ambitious project, and certainly our biggest ever Flash build. It's not every day you get a brief to create a 12-minute interactive film, so it was immensely gratifying to slowly see all the individual pieces congeal into a single piece of storytelling. I can't honestly say that I miss Flash as a programming language, but I certainly miss seeing more of the interactive film briefs that Flash was so ideal for."

Mark Pytlik
Stinkdigital

Die Lexus Dark Ride-Erfahrung lud Benutzer dazu ein, die Rolle des Navigators zusammen mit Fahrer Tony in einem 12-minütigen interaktiven Film zu spielen. Schwenkbare 180-Grad-Sequenzen, vom Benutzer aufgenommene Audiodateien, Facebook Webcam-Integration und ein adaptiver 3D-Soundtrack hauten mich ebenso um, wie die Produktionsqualität und das Niveau der verfügbaren Interaktion. Die Integration von Facebook und Webcams hat diese Seite wirklich auf ein neues Level gehoben.

La vidéo interactive de 12 minutes offerte dans l'expérience Lexus Dark Ride invite les utilisateurs à jouer le rôle de copilote aux côtés du conducteur Tony. Je suis bluffé par les séquences panoramiques de 180 degrés, l'audio que l'utilisateur peut enregistrer, une bande-son évolutive en 3D, sans parler de la qualité de la production et des niveaux d'interaction possibles. Mais c'est surtout grâce à l'intégration de Facebook et de webcams que ce site atteint de nouveaux sommets.

—

Coke Zero
Facial Profiler

—

The first Facebook Connect
experience with facial
recognition software

The idea here was to connect with Facebook and then, as the site declared, the Facial Profiler would check to see "If Coke Zero has Coke's taste, maybe someone has your face". The software then delivered an image of someone with a face similar to the user's, and while the results were often not a perfect match, it was quite exciting to play with just in case you really did have a double out there.

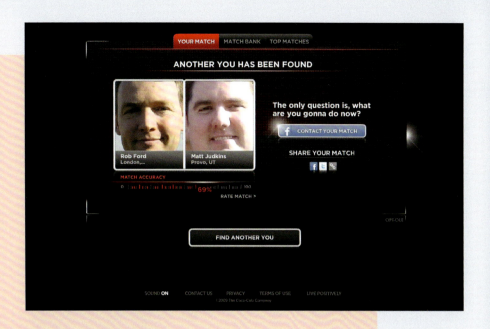

"Facial Profiler was a bit of a pipe dream. It challenged technology and was on the edge of what was possible. It had that appearance of magic factor that we so often look for with tech ideas. It broke through because it introduced you to new people in a shocking and surprising way. Who doesn't want to meet their doppelganger? It was around this time that we stopped thinking about microsites. Facebook up and killed them overnight."

Winston Binch
CP+B; Deutsch North America

Die Idee hier war, sich mit Facebook zu verbinden und dann, wie die Seite erklärte, sollte der Facial Profiler überprüfen: „Wenn Coke Zero den Geschmack von Coke hat, hat vielleicht auch jemand dein Gesicht". Die Software lieferte dann ein Bild von jemandem mit einem Gesicht, das dem des User ähnlich war und obwohl die Ergebnisse oft nicht perfekt zusammenpassten, war es ziemlich aufregend damit zu spielen, nur für den Fall, dass man wirklich eine/n Doppelgänger/in hat.

L'idée est que le visiteur se connecte à Facebook pour que ce système de reconnaissance faciale vérifie que, « si Coke Zero a le goût de Coke, quelqu'un peut avoir le même visage que vous ». Le logiciel affiche alors le portrait d'une personne ressemblant au visiteur. Même si la similitude n'est pas toujours exacte, il est amusant d'essayer au cas où un double soit vraiment trouvé.

—

Wrangler Blue Bell Spring Summer

—

The first interactive drag navigation

Visitors to this site could take control of the male model Tony Ward with their mouse and make him dance, simply by grabbing him and dragging him about. While this was going on, he would also take his clothes off and show the latest line from the jeans-maker's spring/summer collection for 2010.

CLICK & DRAG

1/6
DENIM: EDDY
DENIM TOP: CLAY WESTERN
JACKET: ROPE CLASSIC
ACCESSORIES: STRANDED LEATHER BELT

DOWNLOAD THIS FRAME
FACEBOOK | TWITTER

"The Wrangler Blue Bell campaign was
released at the same time as the iPad and
the click-and-drag concept really worked
out well. The user became the link between
music and picture. People got very emotional
about the imagination of controlling Tony
Ward, dragging him around, pushing him
off a chair, and so on. Everything during this
time was about awaking people's emotions,
to make people dream through interactivity."

Jimmy Herdberg
Kokokaka

Besucher auf dieser Site konnten die Kontrolle über das männliche Modell Tony Ward mit der Maus übernehmen und ließen ihn tanzen, indem sie ihn einfach packten und ihn hin und her zogen. Währenddessen zog er sich aus und zeigte die neueste Kollektion aus der Frühjahr/Sommer-Kollektion des Jeans-herstellers für 2010.

Les visiteurs de ce site peuvent faire danser le modèle Tony Ward en cliquant dessus et en le faisant glisser. Pendant qu'il bouge, il se déshabille et présente la dernière ligne de vêtements pour la collection printemps/été 2010 du fabricant de jeans.

—

Bank Run

—

The first web game that continued on users' smartphones

This was a very smart interactive movie which continued on the iPhone as an app, something that hadn't been seen before. Part one started online with "Run For It", where users took on the role of the main character as he was chased through a parking garage, while part two completed things on the user's iPhone. This interactive movie/game was a follow-up to the previously mentioned The Outbreak (2008).

"iPhones and iPhone apps were everywhere. The
idea was to allow users to advance to a certain
point in the movie and then let them download an
app to finish the rest. The app included cut scenes
that advanced the story along with various games
where the user took control of the hero character
and took down some bad guys. Instead of a simple
'choose your own adventure' narrative, interactive
mini-games were incorporated to give the user the
chance to advance through the movie."

Chris Lund
SilkTricky

Dies war ein sehr schlauer
interaktiver Film, der als App auf
dem iPhone fortgesetzt wurde.
Das hatte es noch nie gegeben.
Der erste Teil startete online mit
„Run For It", in dem die User
die Rolle des Hauptdarstellers
übernahmen, während man durch
ein Parkhaus gejagt wurde. Im
zweiten Teil wurden die Dinge auf
dem iPhone des Nutzers abge-
schlossen. Dieser(s) interaktive
Film/Spiel war ein Follow-up zu
dem zuvor erwähnten The
Outbreak (2008).

Grande première du genre, cet
astucieux film interactif possède
une suite dans une application
pour iPhone. Dans la première
partie diffusée en ligne et qui
s'intitule «Run For It», les internautes jouent le rôle du protagoniste poursuivi dans un parking
souterrain. Ils découvrent
ensuite la fin de l'intrigue sur leur
iPhone. Ce film-jeu interactif est
la suite de The Outbreak (2008)
mentionné auparavant.

Mexico Via Pacífico
—

The first website consisting
entirely of webcam footage

The whole of this site presented specially commissioned murals painted around Mexico and the United States, all relayed by webcams. Each wall corresponded to one section of the site, so as users navigated they were actually traveling between locations in real time. Naturally, the experience was dependent on local time, but with the timing right, users could enjoy a great experience.

"Mexico Via Pacífico was one of those projects you undesign to bring them closer to the magic world of live streaming. What really mattered was how you designed what happened in the stream, and what the branding looked like in this chilled-out destination… did it make you want to grab a cold bottle?"

Yates Buckley
Unit9

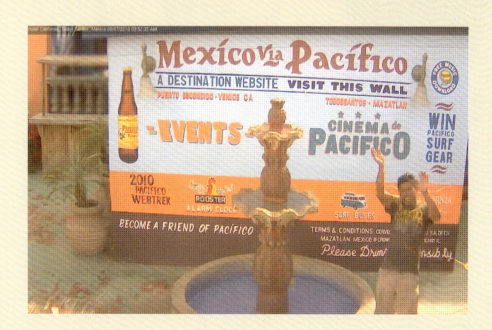

Die ganze Site präsentierte speziell beauftragte Wandmalereien, die in Mexiko und den Vereinigten Staaten gemalt und die alle von Webcams übertragen wurden. Jede Wand entsprach einem Abschnitt der Website, sodass die User während der Navigation zwischen den Standorten in Echtzeit unterwegs waren. Natürlich war die Erfahrung abhängig von der lokalen Zeit aber mit dem richtigen Timing konnten die User eine großartige Erfahrung genießen.

Par le biais de webcams, l'ensemble de ce site s'attache à montrer des peintures murales à travers le Mexique et les États-Unis. Chaque mur correspondant à une partie du site, les visiteurs voyagent en temps réel d'un endroit à un autre pendant leur navigation. L'expérience est évidemment liée à l'heure locale, ce qui ne suppose en rien un obstacle en choisissant le bon moment.

Juke Power-Up

—

The first smartphone app created in Flash

Juke Power-Up was only available for mobile phones running 'Froyo' (i.e. Android 2.2), but for those without a compatible device a demo link was provided in its place. The idea was to power up the phone by shaking it: simple but sure to put a smile on people's faces, and it worked perfectly. This was definitely an exciting first for Flash on mobile.

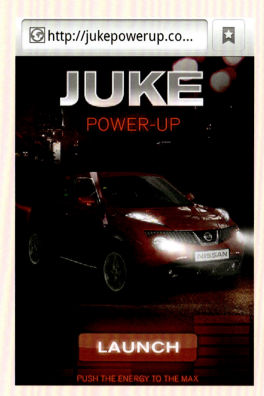

"Adobe was pushing hard to try to make Flash available on mobile and we had access to the pre-release info for Flash on Android directly from Adobe. I was then looking for an idea to create a 'game' for our client, Nissan, and while reading the API available I was interested by the gyroscope, which was something really new for me. This idea came for a PowerBall we had in the office and we decided to create a smartphone PowerBall."

Julien Terraz
DigitasLBi Paris

Juke Power-Up war nur für Mobiltelefone mit „Froyo" (d.h. Android 2.2) verfügbar, aber für diejenigen ohne kompatibles Gerät wurde stattdessen ein Demo-Link bereitgestellt. Die Idee war, das Telefon durch Schütteln anzutreiben: Einfach aber sicher, um ein Lächeln auf die Gesichter der Leute zu bringen und es funktionierte perfekt. Dies war definitiv eine aufregende Premiere für Flash auf dem Handy.

L'application Juke Power-Up est uniquement disponible pour les téléphones portables dotés du système Froyo (Android 2.2) ; les personnes qui n'ont pas de dispositif compatible peuvent cliquer sur un lien afin d'ouvrir une démo. L'idée est de donner de l'énergie au téléphone en le secouant, ce qui est simple, plaît forcément et fonctionne par-faitement. Le projet marque une première importante pour Flash sur des portables.

Nespresso Variations

—

A graphical beauty

This extremely high-end production, once again, from French agency Soleil Noir, was a deserved Site of the Month winner. Visitors entered the imaginary world of Nespresso's Variations to awaken the flavor-making machine, but the graphics involved were utterly awe-inspiring.

"We decided to create a surrealist capsule factory mixing precision mechanisms, small flying robots, clouds of cream, and even mountains of caramel to dive into. This fantasy universe also served as a pretext for entertainment to involve the visitor in the creation of virtual capsules through various activities. With the simple aim of putting the almonds in their receptacle, and finding the right melody to get the ingredients moving, each mission allowed content to be unblocked that was specific to each of the flavors."

Olivier Marchand
Soleil Noir; Linia Consulting

Diese extrem hochwertige Produktion, wieder einmal von der französischen Agentur Soleil Noir, war ein verdienter Gewinner der Site of the Month. Die

Besucher betraten die imaginäre Welt der Nespresso-Sorten, um die Geschmacksmaschinen aufzuwecken. Die Grafiken waren absolut beeindruckend.

Une fois de plus, l'agence française Soleil Noir signe une production haut de gamme qui mérite bien de remporter le prix Site of the Month. Les visiteurs

pénètrent dans le monde imaginaire des variations de Nespresso pour réveiller la machine à arômes. La qualité graphique est absolument sublime.

We're All Fans

—

A social media
aggregator first

Using real-time fan-generated videos, photos, and tweets, the social media aggregator for the Grammys created interactive portraits of its various different artists. Many of the portraits were incredible, and this really showcased a new level for social media and how it was the future.

"The hub of the campaign was a site which generated living portraits of the nominees using their fans' real-time social media – YouTube, Twitter, Flickr (this was pre-Instagram days). Fans could also create social media portraits of themselves by uploading a photo and choosing their favorite artists. A second feature of the site was the Fanbuzz Visualizer: a 3D data visualization comparing the nominees' daily social media presence. The social media portraits created by the site were used in TV, outdoor, and print ads."

Edward Mun
TBWA Chiat\Day; Freelance

The true voice of music. Visualized.
Click on any image to see what the fans are saying right now.

WE'RE ALL FANS

Der Social-Media-Aggregator für die Grammys erstellte in Echtzeit Fan-generierte Videos, Fotos und Tweets und erstellte interaktive Porträts der verschiedenen Künstler. Viele der Porträts waren unglaublich und dies zeigte wirklich ein neues Level für soziale Medien und wie die Zukunft aussehen könnte.

À partir de vidéos, de photos et de tweets en temps réel générés par les utilisateurs, cet agrégateur de réseaux sociaux conçu pour les Grammys élabore des portraits interactifs de divers artistes. Les résultats sont généralement incroyables et les réseaux sociaux prennent une nouvelle dimension, présage de ce que l'avenir sera.

2010/

—

Honeyway Train
Webcam Game

—

The first augmented
reality game using Unity

The game engine Unity made a big impact here
with this world-first augmented reality game.
By using an actual breakfast cereal box of
Honey Nut Cheerios as the game controller

users could maneuver and fly the character,
Buzz, to an ultimate showdown with the honey
bandit, known as Handsome Hector.

"We set off on an extensive RnD endeavor working with the then small 3D engine Unity3D, to develop a way to incorporate AR libraries into their development platform. The result was a hugely successful consumer experience with 3D graphics not previously seen in browsers at that time. We created an intuitive game with [the] physical product as the focal point of the experience and the actual game controller. We broke new ground and set the path for other leading-edge AR projects to follow."

Robert Stock & Stephen Van Elst
Boffswana

Die Game-Maschine Unity zeigte mit diesem weltweit ersten Augmented-Reality-Spiel große Wirkung. Durch die Verwendung einer echten Packung von Honey Nut Cheerios als Game Controller konnten die User den Charakter, Buzz, manövrieren und fliegen, zum ultimativen Showdown mit dem Honigbanditen, bekannt als der Handsome Hector.

Le moteur de jeu Unity crée l'événement avec ce tout premier jeu de réalité augmentée. Les joueurs se servent d'un vrai paquet de céréales Honey Nut Cheerios comme contrôleur de jeu pour faire voler le personnage Buzz jusqu'à sa confrontation finale avec le bandit Handsome Hector.

NOTABLE WEBSITE
LAUNCH
Pinterest

GOOGLE
FACTS

First playable doodle for
Pac-Man's 30th birthday

Google launches its Nexus One
smartphone

Google announces technology
for self-driving cars

Google Wave launches

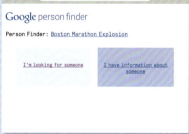

Top 5 Trends

Person Finder goes live,
in response to the Haiti
earthquake

MOBILE EVOLUTION
Nexus One

Google's first Nexus smartphone, with Android OS and made by HTC, was able to run Adobe Flash via the Froyo OS update.

Person Finder: Haiti Earthquake
English | Français | Kreyòl

What is your situation?

| I'm looking for someone | I have information about someone |

Currently tracking about 32500 records.

PLEASE NOTE: All data entered will be available to the public and viewable and usable by anyone. Google does not review or verify the accuracy of this data.

Embed this tool on your site · Developers · Terms of Service
powered by
Google

INTERNET COMMUNITY
Google Person Finder

In response to the devastating earthquake in Haiti, which affected more than 3 million people, Google engineers created Person Finder to help people connect with loved ones in the wake of disasters. The project was subsequently relaunched for a number of other crises.

2011/

The Dawning of a New Era: HTML5

2011/

—

The Dawning of a New Era: HTML5

—

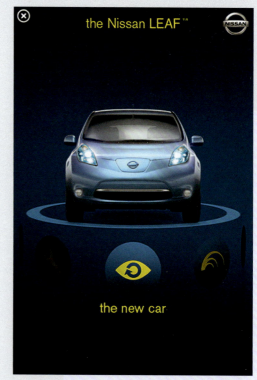

Nissan Leaf iAd

"HTML5 was now rapidly gaining pace, yet levels of creativity were lacking."

A decade of Flash web experiences was over. HTML5 was now rapidly gaining pace, yet levels of creativity were lacking in a big way. Since The Wilderness Downtown in 2010, only a handful of HTML5 experiences had surfaced.

The personal sense of character and fun that had become so familiar seemed all to have been stripped away. Even so, some of the early web design pioneers were at the forefront of this new era, developing innovative ideas for the immediate future.

The World's Biggest Pac-Man arrived, a community-based project for creating your own maze which even included a FWA maze.

The first 3D web game for iPhones appeared, and kijjaa! created a touch of irony too by presenting a Flash game that could be controlled by an iPhone.

Some impressive 3D interaction was enabled through WebGL for browsers without the need for any plug-ins, with HelloEnjoy's HelloRacer, a fully interactive Formula 1 car, being a perfect example.

One of the first LinkedIn-connected websites was Passat LinkedUit for Volkswagen, where users pitched their profile against others to find out who was the most full of themselves.

Apple had been pushing its iAd format since the previous year's launch as a new form of mobile advertising and several examples now emerged including one of the first, the Nissan Leaf iAd. The platform was discontinued in 2016.

Notruf Deutschland was a very dark and unexpected personalized Facebook Connect film, where the user was kidnapped and bundled inside a hessian bag while their abductor looked on.

The app industry continued to grow exponentially and with TASCHEN I published *The App & Mobile Case Study Book*, which showcased some of the most successful mobile apps and campaigns, including Angry Birds, Instagram, BBC News, and so on.

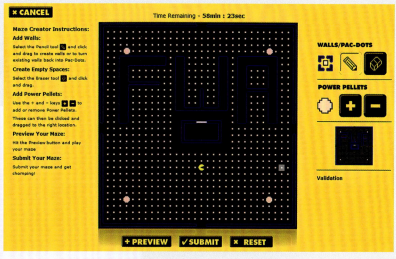

World's Biggest Pac-Man

HelloRacer

Ein Jahrzehnt Flash-Web-Erlebnisse war vorbei. HTML5 nahm nun rasant an Fahrt auf, doch es mangelte an Kreativität. Seit The Wilderness Downtown im Jahr 2010 tauchten nur eine Handvoll HTML5-Erfahrungen auf.

Das persönliche Gefühl für Charakter und Spaß, das so vertraut geworden war, schien verschwunden zu sein. Dennoch waren einige der Pioniere des Webdesigns an der Spitze dieser neuen Ära und entwickelten innovative Ideen für die unmittelbare Zukunft.

The World's Biggest Pac-Man kam, ein Gemeinschafts-

projekt, um sein eigenes Labyrinth zu erschaffen, das sogar ein FWA-Labyrinth enthielt.

Das erste 3D-Web-Spiel für iPhones erschien und kijjaa! brachte einen Hauch von Ironie hinein, indem ein Flash-Spiel vorgestellt wurde, das von einem iPhone gesteuert werden konnte.

Einige eindrucksvolle 3D-Interaktionen wurden durch WebGL für Browser ermöglicht, ohne dass Plug-ins benötigt wurden. HelloRacer, ein voll interaktives Formel-1-Auto von HelloEnjoy, ist hierfür ein perfektes Beispiel.

Eine der ersten mit LinkedIn verbundenen Websites war die Passat LinkedUit für Volkswagen, auf der User ihr Profil mit anderen verglichen, um herauszufinden, welches von ihnen voll mit ihnen selbst war.

Apple hatte sein iAd-Format seit der Einführung im vorherigen Jahr als eine neue Form der mobilen Werbung vorangetrieben und einige Beispiele, darunter eines der ersten, das Nissan Leaf iAd, entstanden. Die Plattform wurde 2016 eingestellt.

Notruf Deutschland war ein sehr dunkler und unerwarteter personalisierter Facebook

Connect Film, bei dem der User entführt und in einen Jutesack gestopft wurde, während der Entführer dabei zuschaute.

Die App-Branche wuchs weiterhin exponentiell und mit TASCHEN veröffentlichte ich das *App & Mobile Case Study Book*, in dem einige der erfolgreichsten mobilen Apps und Kampagnen vorgestellt wurden, darunter Angry Birds, Instagram, BBC News und viele andere.

2011/
—
The Dawning of a New Era: HTML5
—

kijjaa!

Passat LinkedUit

Notruf Deutschland

"The app industry continued to grow exponentially."

Une décennie de créations en Flash s'achève. HTML5 gagne rapidement du terrain mais la créativité reste assez pauvre. Depuis The Wilderness Downtown l'an passé, seule une poignée de créations en HTML5 se sont fait remarquer.

La dose de personnalité et de divertissement si habituelle jusqu'alors semble s'être envolée. Certains des précurseurs en conception Web sont tout de même à l'avant-garde de cette nouvelle ère et mettent au point des idées innovantes pour le futur immédiat.

Mené comme un projet collectif, le jeu World's Biggest Pac-Man fait son apparition et permet de créer son propre labyrinthe. Il en inclut même un formant les lettres FWA.

Le premier jeu Web en 3D pour iPhone fait ses débuts. Doté d'une touche d'ironie, kijjaa! est en Flash et peut être contrôlé depuis le téléphone.

La technologie WebGL pour les navigateurs permet d'impressionnantes interactions en 3D sans recourir à des plug-ins. La voiture de Formule 1 entièrement interactive HelloRacer de Hello-

Enjoy en illustre parfaitement le potentiel.

Le site Passat LinkedUit pour Volkswagen est l'un des premiers connectés à LinkedIn. Les visiteurs mettent leur profil en compétition avec d'autres pour voir qui a la plus grosse estime de soi.

Depuis sa sortie l'an passé, Apple fait la promotion de sa plate-forme iAd de publicité mobile. Plusieurs exemples voient le jour cette année, l'un des premiers étant l'iAd pour Nissan Leaf. La plate-forme sera abandonnée en 2016.

Notruf Deutschland est un film personnalisé via Facebook Connect, à l'histoire aussi dérangeante que sinistre. L'internaute est kidnappé et enfermé dans un sac de jute, sous la surveillance de son ravisseur.

Le monde des applications poursuit sa croissance exponentielle. Avec TASCHEN, je publie The App & Mobile Case Study Book, qui compile certaines des campagnes et applications mobiles les plus réussies, dont Angry Birds, Instagram et BBC News.

08 Facts of the year

Number of internet users:
2.27 billion, 32.2% of
the world population

Number of websites:
697 million

World news:
a 9.0 magnitude earthquake
causes a nuclear disaster
at Fukushima, Japan

Website with most traffic:
Google.com

Tech hardware:
Chromebooks start shipping

Tech software:
Adobe Creative Cloud is
announced

Other tech:
Steve Jobs dies on
October 5

Highest-grossing film:
Harry Potter and the
Deathly Hallows: Part 2

The Museum of Me

—

The ultimate Facebook
Connect website

This Facebook Connect site took data and photos from the user's Facebook profile and transformed them into a personalized museum which could then be toured. On winning the SOTY, Intel's Stephanie Gan said, "We're thrilled the Museum of Me has been named Site of the Year. First and foremost we wanted to create an experience people would love and want to share. The Museum of Me struck an emotional chord with people [and] we couldn't have achieved the result without the creative team at Projector."

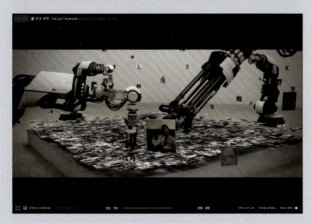

"During the production of the Museum of Me
a disastrous earthquake struck our country,
Japan. Many suffered as a result but this kind of
situation bonds people even more closely, and
motivated us, through a sense of responsibility, to
accomplish this Museum of Me which celebrates
every human life. We are honored to have worked
in a team with such tremendous talent, and
deeply appreciate every single person who took
a moment to visit and experience our website."

Eiji Tanigawa
Taiyo Kikaku

Diese Facebook Connect-
Website nahm Daten und Fotos
aus dem Facebook-Profil des
Nutzers und verwandelte sie in
ein personalisiertes Museum, das
dann besichtigt werden konnte.
Nach dem Gewinn des SOTY
sagte Intels Stephanie Gan:
„Wir sind begeistert, dass das
Museum of Me zur ‚Site of

the Year' ernannt wurde. In
erster Linie wollten wir eine
Erfahrung schaffen, die Menschen lieben und teilen möchten.
Das Museum of Me hat bei den
Menschen einen emotionalen
Nerv getroffen [und] ohne das
kreative Team von Projector
hätten wir das Ergebnis nicht
erreichen können."

Ce site Facebook Connect
extrait des données et des
photos du profil Facebook de
l'utilisateur pour créer un musée
virtuel personnalisé. Au sujet du
prix SOTY remporté, Stephanie
Gan d'Intel déclare : « Nous
sommes ravis que The Museum
of Me ait été élu Site of the Year.
Nous souhaitions avant tout

créer une expérience que les
personnes aimeraient et auraient
envie de partager. The Museum
of Me touche une corde sensible
[et] ce résultat n'aurait pas été
possible sans l'équipe créative
de Projector ».

—

Storming Juno

—

Recreating D-Day

This site was an online extension of History TV's docudrama *Storming Juno*, dedicated to Canadian soldiers. Site visitors were dropped on to Juno Beach, Normandy, amidst an impressive 360-degree rotating view of the surroundings on D-Day. The atmosphere created was truly incredible and was an absolute must-see experience. Throughout the site, users could expand content for more in-depth information, photos, and biographies.

"Storming Juno has long been a stand-out project in our company. In many ways it foreshadowed the industry of virtual reality as a unique storytelling medium. It was a mixture of powerful narrative enhanced by a unique user interface, a culmination of content and technology seeking to unfold through discovery. We wanted to encapsulate a war that had surrounded the WWII generation and bring a younger audience to the front lines of a story that the greatest generation had already known for many decades."

Ryan Andal
Secret Location

Diese Seite war eine Online-Erweiterung von History TVs Dokudrama *Storming Juno*, das kanadischen Soldaten gewidmet ist. Die Besucher der Website wurden am Juno Stand in der Normandie in einer eindrucksvollen 360-Grad-Ansicht der Umgebung am D-Day abgesetzt. Die geschaffene Atmosphäre war wirklich unglaublich und ein absolutes Muss. Überall auf der Website konnten die User die Inhalte um detailliertere Informationen, Fotos und Biografien erweitern.

Ce site est l'extension en ligne du docudrame *Storming Juno – À l'assaut de Juno* réalisé par History TV et qui rend hommage aux soldats canadiens. Les visiteurs se retrouvent en Normandie, sur Juno Beach, dans un panorama de 360 degrés de l'endroit où s'est passé le jour J. L'atmosphère rendue est remarquable et en fait une expérience incontournable. Dans tout le site, les internautes peuvent développer le contenu et accéder à davantage de détails, de photos et de biographies.

Lego Star Wars III

—

A real-time multi-player fan experience

The Red Universe site from 2007 took its own idea to a new level here for two of the world's best-known brands: Lego and *Star Wars*. Users got to play characters such as a Lego Yoda or Darth Vader in real time and could work collectively to solve puzzles, while discovering the latest Lego Star Wars video game. An idea like this needed a lot of people to be on the site at any one time, but this was easily achieved because the fanbase for both these brands was always huge.

"Due to COPPA rules, and the limiting fact that Lego Star Wars characters don't actually talk, we needed a way for the characters/users to connect with each other without the use of text-based chat. We ended up with a simple but really effective solution. Each character could emote in a variety of ways to communicate, encouraging users to work together as a community to solve challenges, unlock characters, and earn badges. At one point, the site consistently had 750,000 unique users per month spending hours on the site."

Jared Kroff
Red

Die Red-Universe-Site aus dem Jahr 2007 hat hier ihre eigene Idee für zwei der weltweit be-kanntesten Marken – Lego und *Star Wars* – auf ein neues Level gehoben. Die Spieler konnten Charaktere wie Lego Yoda oder Darth Vader in Echtzeit spielen und gemeinsam Rätsel lösen, während sie das neueste Lego Star Wars Videospiel entdeckten. Eine Idee wie diese brauchte viele Leute auf der Seite, aber das war leicht zu erreichen, weil die Fanbase für diese beiden Marken schon immer riesig war.

Le site Red Universe conçu en 2007 met son propre concept au goût du jour pour deux des plus célèbres marques au monde : Lego et *Star Wars*. Les joueurs entrent dans la peau de personnages comme un Yoda ou un Darth Vader Lego, explorent le dernier jeu vidéo Lego Star Wars et peuvent s'entraider pour résoudre des énigmes. Un projet de cette envergure requiert la présence constante de beau-coup de joueurs en ligne, ce qui ne suppose aucun souci vu les innombrables inconditionnels de ces deux marques.

Nike Better World

—

The parallax scrolling website that changed everything

Parallax scrolling, also known as asymmetrical scrolling, is a technique that allows background images to move more slowly than foreground images while scrolling, which gives the illusion of depth in a two-dimensional scene. Wieden+Kennedy applied the technique with incredible effect on this promotional site for Nike, at a time when most designers were still creating purely static scrolling web pages. Unheralded, it proved to be another huge game-changer.

"We were costing out the site and someone said: 'It'll be about 30 pages'. Then at some point we decided to make it one single page. But that meant all the traditional site architecture was getting in the way. I can't remember how the decision to build the site like this came about. It would have had something to do with the super-talented Duane King and Ian Coyle who we brought in to help design and build the thing."

Iain Tait
Wieden+Kennedy

Parallax Scrolling, auch bekannt als asymmetrisches Scrollen, ist eine Technik, bei der sich Hintergrundbilder beim Scrollen langsamer bewegen als die Bilder im Vordergrund, was in einer zweidimensionalen Szene die Illusion von Tiefe erzeugt. Wieden+Kennedy wendete die

Technik mit unglaublichem Effekt auf der Werbeseite für Nike an, zu einer Zeit, als die meisten Designer noch rein statische Scroll-Webseiten kreierten. Unvorhergesehen erwies es sich als ein weiterer großer Game-Changer.

Le défilement parallaxe, ou défilement asymétrique, est une technique permettant à des images en arrière-plan de se déplacer plus lentement que celles au premier plan, ce qui crée l'illusion d'une profondeur dans une scène en deux dimensions. Pour le site

promotionnel de Nike, l'agence Wieden+Kennedy obtient avec cette technique un effet incroyable, à une époque où la plupart des concepteurs en sont encore à créer des pages Web déroulantes essentiellement statiques. Sans prévenir, il vient changer lui aussi la donne.

2011/
—

5 Gum

—

A first to allow users to
create 3D projection mapping

One big trend this year was 3D projection mapping, but most, if not all results, were stand-alone offline videos. This launch campaign for Wrigley's 5 Gum was the first to enable users to create their own 3D-mapped building projection, to an electronic track by composer Étienne de Crécy.

"In a user-generated twist on the projection mapping trend at the time, we created the 5 Experience website for Wrigley's 5 Gum. Visitors could create their own projections at home that would later be projected on to buildings in either Cape Town or Johannesburg. We created 150+ animations that the user could choose between in a simple yet intuitive interface made in Flash. The projection blended animations seamlessly and made each session feel truly unique, empowering everyone to become a VJ."

Jakob Nylund
North Kingdom

Ein großer Trend in diesem Jahr war das 3D Projection Mapping aber die meisten, wenn nicht alle Ergebnisse, waren eigenständige Offline-Videos. Diese Markteinführungskampagne für Wrigley's 5 Gum war die erste, auf der die User ihre eigene 3D-mapped Gebäudeprojektion erstellen konnten, zu einem elektronischen Track des Komponisten Étienne de Crécy.

La grande tendance de l'année est le mapping vidéo en 3D, mais la plupart des créations, sinon toutes, sont des vidéos hors ligne indépendantes. Pour la première fois, cette campagne de lancement pour le chewing-gum 5 de Wrigley permet aux utilisateurs de créer leur propre mapping vidéo en 3D sur une façade, au son d'une musique électronique composée par Étienne de Crécy.

—

Greenpeace:
A New Warrior

—

Original crowdfunding to
create a ship for Greenpeace

The idea here was that visitors to the site, which took the form of an ocean-going vessel, would actually purchase a piece of the ship. These donations then helped Greenpeace to build the new *Rainbow Warrior*. The ship had been broken down so that there were thousands of pieces available to buy, and the amount of work that must have gone into this site was staggering.

"France has a long history with Greenpeace.
A complicated story. When DDB Paris wanted
to team up with 84.Paris to build the new
Rainbow Warrior, we thought it was time to
repair the past. Three websites in one: an
interactive 3D presentation of the new ship,
a digital map where users could interact with
different floors, and an integrated e-shop. What
was relevant? Every object, every piece, every
thing on the new *Rainbow Warrior* could be
bought to help the association build the new ship."

Jean-Vincent Roger
84.Paris

Die Idee hier war, dass die Besucher der Site, in Form eines Hochseeschiffs, tatsächlich ein Stück des Schiffes kauften. Diese Spenden haben dann Greenpeace geholfen, die neue *Rainbow Warrior* zu bauen. Das Schiff wurde auseinandergenommen, sodass es tausende von käuflich zu erwerbenden Stücken gab und die Menge an Arbeit, die dieser Seite vorausgegangen sein musste, war atemberaubend.

Présenté comme un navire, ce site cherche à ce que les visiteurs achètent une partie du bateau ; les dons sont ensuite reversés à Greenpeace pour construire leur nouveau *Rainbow Warrior*. Le navire a été frag- menté pour que des milliers de parties soient disponibles à la vente ; la quantité d'heures de travail nécessaires pour conce- voir ce site est sans conteste ahurissante.

—

Edding Wall of Fame

—

The social interactive
live-drawing wall

This interactive live-drawing board allowed users to meet other people online in different segments of the ongoing illustration. Each section was drawn with eight pens, each controlled by different users. Everything that appeared on the wall was in real time, making the site quite addictive, and there were some very impressive illustrations as well as the usual naughty or tongue-in-cheek drawings.

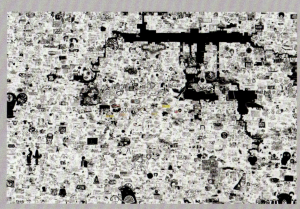

"For three months straight, the developers, Florian Wögerer, and I worked around the clock on the project. I was responsible for the Flash front-end as well as the real-time server. Florian worked on the back-end for efficiently processing the image data as well as the CMS, which allowed for editing and filtering the content. It was great fun to see the Wall develop and grow as the project's reach increased."

Alexander el-Meligi
Demodern

Dieses interaktive Live-Zeichen-brett ermöglichte es den Benut-zern, andere Menschen online in verschiedenen Segmenten der laufenden Illustration zu treffen. Jeder Abschnitt wurde mit acht Stiften gezeichnet, die jeweils von verschiedenen Benutzern kontrolliert wurden. Alles, was an der Wand erschien, war in Echtzeit, wodurch die Erfahrung ziemlich süchtig machte und es gab einige sehr beeindruckende Illustrationen sowie die üblichen ungezogenen oder ironischen Zeichnungen.

Cette planche interactive de dessin en direct permet aux internautes de se rencontrer en ligne dans différentes parties de l'illustration en cours de réalisa-tion. Chaque partie est tracée à l'aide de huit stylos que des utilisateurs distincts contrôlent.

Tout ce qui apparaît sur ce mur se fait en temps réel, d'où son côté addictif, sans compter la qualité de certaines illustrations et les inévitables dessins coquins ou humoristiques.

Pica Pic

—

Bringing old consoles
back to life

An amazing talent here revived so many old consoles and games, in what was a digitized collection of some of the best-known handheld electronic games from the past.

Not only was it impressive to look at, but users could even play the original games on animated consoles.

PicaPic
Hipopotam's digitalised collection of handheld electronic games
Created by Hipopotam

Gakken (1981)
made in Japan
Model No.: 81551

Search Light

High Scores

"We created Pica Pic because we wanted to document our LCD games collection. At first it was supposed to be just a Tumblr with HD photos, but we thought it'd be cool to play those games online. So after two years (it was just a side project) we launched Pica Pic with just eight games (it was the end of 2010). After a few months, we added the rest."

Daniel Mizieliński
Hipopotam Studio

Ein erstaunliches Talent hat hier so viele alte Konsolen und Spiele wiederbelebt, in einer digitalisierten Sammlung einiger der bekanntesten elektronischen Handheld-Spiele aus der Vergan-genheit. Es war nicht nur beein-druckend anzusehen, die User konnten sogar die Originalspiele auf animierten Konsolen spielen.

Cette collection numérisée de certains de plus célèbres jeux électroniques fait renaître avec talent d'anciennes consoles et des jeux d'avant. Le résultat est visuellement impressionnant, et les utilisateurs peuvent même jouer aux jeux originaux sur des consoles animées.

Take This Lollipop

—

The website that dared you to enter… at your own risk

When this site opened it dared visitors to take the lollipop, but looking closely a razor blade could be seen hidden inside it. After connecting to Facebook, users lost all control over what happened next as they were stalked by a lunatic, who seized their data, and then in the video could be seen getting into his car and driving… to the user's house. The project was liked over 15,000,000 times on Facebook alone and scooped an Emmy for director Jason Zada.

"Take This Lollipop was a project that really got under people's skin. In only a few days, the Facebook Connected film became the fastest-growing Facebook app of all time. Seeing your personal information on a strange man's computer, seamlessly integrated in a way that made it look so real that people never questioned its authenticity, Lollipop was a pop culture moment that made web audiences hungry for more personalized video. It was one of those magical moments in your career when everything went right — and it hit a cultural nerve that's still talked about today."

Jason Zada
Filmmaker & Multi-platform Storyteller

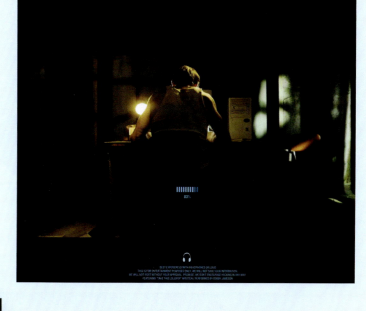

Beim Öffnen dieser Seite wurde der User verführt, den Lutscher zu nehmen aber wenn man ihn näher betrachtete, sah man eine darin versteckte Rasier- klinge. Nachdem der User sich mit Facebook verbunden hatte, verlor er die Kontrolle über das, was als Nächstes passierte, denn er wurde von einem Verrückten gestalkt, der seine Daten stahl und dann konnte man in einem Video sehen, wie er in ein Auto stieg und … zum Haus des Users fuhr. Das Projekt wurde über 15.000.000 Mal auf Facebook geliked und gewann einen Emmy für Regisseur Jason Zada.

À son ouverture, ce site défie les visiteurs de prendre la sucette mais en y regardant de plus près, on voit qu'elle renferme une lame de rasoir. Une fois connectés à Facebook, ils n'ont aucun contrôle sur les événements qui se produisent : un dingue les poursuit, s'empare de leurs données et apparaît dans la vidéo au volant d'une voiture pour se rendre… chez eux. Rien que sur Facebook, le projet reçoit plus de 15 millions de likes, et le réalisateur Jason Zada décroche un Emmy.

3 Dreams of Black

—

A pioneering website pushing
the boundaries beyond plug-ins

This lucid-dreaming narrative for Danger Mouse and composer Daniele Luppi's new album, *Rome*, used the relatively new WebGL and created a blend of 2D and 3D interactive animation whilst also showcasing the capabilities of Google's Chrome browser.

It was quite remarkable, and also comforting for many who'd been reliant on Flash for creating these types of experiences to see what could be achieved in a modern browser such as Chrome, without the need for any plug-ins.

"It was 2011 and Danger Mouse had made an amazing concept album with Daniele Luppi, Norah Jones, and Jack White. It was essentially a soundtrack without a film. I decided to make the film, as well as a weaving pre-narrative through a traditional music video, an interactive web-based music video, and a bunch of other stuff I forget now. 3 Dreams of Black was the lucid dream of the main character in the film. Aaron Koblin and the Google Creative Lab helped with that one. 2 Against 1 was the fever dream of the film's protagonist. I never ended up making the film."

Chris Milk
Within

Die Traum-Erzählung für Danger Mouse und das neue Album *Rome* von Daniele Luppi, verwendete das relativ neue WebGL und kreierte eine Mischung aus 2D und 3D interaktiver Animation und stellte gleichzeitig die Fähig-keiten des Chrome-Browsers von Google vor. Es war ziemlich bemerkenswert und tröstlich für viele, die auf Flash angewiesen waren, um diese Art von Erfah-rungen zu erstellen. Man sah, was in einem modernen Browser wie Chrome erreicht werden konnte, ohne irgendwelche Plug-ins verwenden zu müssen.

Conçue pour le nouvel album *Rome* de Danger Mouse et du compositeur Daniele Luppi, cette représentation d'un rêve lucide utilise la récente technologie WebGL et combine des anima-tions interactives 2D et 3D. Elle démontre toutes les fonction-nalités du navigateur Chrome de Google avec un résultat admirable. Elle encourage aussi tous les accros de Flash à voir le potentiel qu'offre un navigateur moderne comme Chrome pour ce type d'expérience, sans le besoin de plug-ins.

NOTABLE WEBSITE LAUNCH
Snapchat

GOOGLE FACTS

10,000,000,000

The Android Market passes 10 billion app downloads

Larry Page becomes CEO

Google introduces the +1 button and Google+

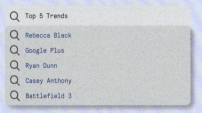

Top 5 Trends

The first wave of Chromebooks is announced

Google Wallet debuts

MOBILE EVOLUTION
Samsung Galaxy Note

Samsung set the stage with a
new direction for smartphones,
originally called phablets, which
had bigger displays (5.3 in.)
than the iPhone 4's 3.5 in.

INTERNET COMMUNITY
Egyptian revolution

The Egyptian government shut
off access to the internet in an
attempt to stop people organizing
protests which threatened to
overthrow President Hosni Mubarak,
but social networks such as
Twitter and Facebook enabled
activists to start an uprising.

2012/

The Year Google Chrome Redefined the Web-Design Landscape

2012/

—

The Year Google Chrome Redefined the Web-Design Landscape

—

HTML5 gathered pace with some really quite impressive experiences and the amount of Flash work being pushed online dropped rapidly, even though Flash Air was making headway for mobile apps and games.

Web design itself was taking an even bigger hit as agencies and brands switched to apps, which were really taking off. Brands were also turning away from microsites to Facebook Pages and it felt as if the web was disappearing into these and a wave of apps. It was understandable why people decided to move to Facebook as the site now had over a billion active users.

An interesting and one-of-a-kind project this year was BASE Persoton, which created a personalized ringtone from users' Facebook profile pictures.

The Gangnam Style video was released, and became the first to amass over a billion views on YouTube, and over 3.3 billion by 2019.

Mobile browsers were in their infancy and not up to handling boundary-pushing websites. There was still a flurry of new mobile websites but most were basic scrolling experiences with images and text, almost back to the early days of the web and as if someone had hit the reset button on what could be achieved.

Google Chrome for desktop became the driving force for web design and development, while many of the most groundbreaking projects required the use of Chrome. WebGL was the hot new prospect for creating impressive Flash-like experiences, Adidas – Adizero F50 being a prime example. This project had a fall-back page, so that if a browser couldn't handle WebGL, it would default to... a Flash version of the site!

More projects were being launched that started on the desktop and then had to be continued on the user's smartphone, such as the Take Them to School scheme for UNICEF, aimed at getting children into school.

Also concerned with the wellbeing of children was You Are Blind, from Russia, which put a blindfold on users so that they had to try and navigate around a city without their sense of sight.

Since the launch of Nike Better World in 2011, huge numbers of single-page scrolling websites had appeared. The Deepest Site took this new trend to its logical limit by becoming the deepest site of all, requiring users to scroll and keep scrolling to find out how a source of bottled water forms.

Overall, it was a time to pause, a time of reflection for web design.

Adidas – Adizero F50

"Brands were
turning away from
microsites to
Facebook Pages
and it felt as
if the web was
disappearing into
these and a wave
of apps."

The Deepest Site

HTML5 nahm an Fahrt auf, mit einigen wirklich beeindruckenden Erfahrungen und die Anzahl an Flash-Arbeiten, die online gestellt wurden, ging schnell zurück, obwohl Flash Air Fortschritte bei den mobilen Apps und Spielen machte.

Webdesign selbst war noch mehr betroffen, als Agenturen und Marken auf Apps umstellten, die immer mehr zunahmen. Auch die Marken gingen hin von Microsites zu Facebook Pages und es sah so aus, als würde das Web nun in einer Welle von Apps untergehen. Es war verständlich, warum sich die Leute dazu entschieden, zu Facebook zu wechseln, da die Seite nun über eine Milliarde aktive Nutzer hatte.

Ein interessantes und einzigartiges Projekt in diesem Jahr war BASE Persoton, das aus den Facebook-Profilbildern der User einen personalisierten Klingelton erstellte.

Das Gangnam Style Video kam heraus und wurde das erste, das über eine Milliarde Aufrufe bei YouTube hatte und über 3,3 Milliarden bis 2019 bekam.

Mobile Browser steckten noch in ihren Kinderschuhen und konnten noch nicht mit barrierefreien Websites umgehen. Es gab immer noch eine Flut von neuen mobilen Websites, aber die meisten waren im Grunde Scrolling-Erfahrungen mit Bildern und Text. Es war fast wie in den frühen Zeiten des Internets, als wenn jemand den Reset-Button gedrückt hätte, bei dem was erreicht werden konnte.

Google Chrome für Desktop wurde zur treibenden Kraft für Webdesign und -entwicklung, wobei viele der bahnbrechendsten Projekte die Verwendung von Chrome erforderten. WebGL war die heiße neue Perspektive für beeindruckende Flash-ähnliche Erfahrungen, wobei Adidas – Adizero F50 ein Paradebeispiel war. Dieses Projekt hatte eine Fall-Back-Seite, sodass, wenn ein Browser nicht mit WebGL umgehen konnte, standardmäßig ... eine Flash-Version der Site verwendet wurde!

Es wurden weitere Projekte gestartet, die auf dem Desktop begannen und dann auf dem Smartphone des Benutzers fortgesetzt werden mussten, wie das Projekt Take Them to School für UNICEF, das darauf abzielte, Kinder in die Schule zu bringen.

Mit dem Wohlergehen der Kinder befasste sich auch You Are Blind aus Russland, das den Usern die Augen verband, sodass sie versuchen mussten, in einer Stadt ohne ihren Sehsinn zu navigieren.

Seit dem Start von Nike Better World im Jahr 2011 sind eine große Anzahl von Single-Page-Scrolling-Websites erschienen. Die Deepest Site brachte diesen neuen Trend an seine logische Grenze, indem sie zur tiefsten Seite überhaupt wurde. Die User mussten scrollen und immer weiter scrollen, um herauszufinden, wie eine Wasser in Flaschen abgefüllt wird.

Insgesamt war es Zeit, eine Pause zu machen, eine Zeit des Nachdenkens für das Webdesign.

2012/

—

The Year Google Chrome Redefined the Web-Design Landscape

—

Take Them to School

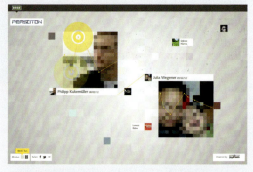

BASE Persoton

You Are Blind

"It was a time to pause, a time of reflection for web design."

L'expansion de HTML5 prend de la vitesse avec des expériences vraiment impressionnantes. En contrepartie, la quantité de créations Flash publiées en ligne chute rapidement malgré les progrès de Flash Air dans le domaine des applications mobiles et des jeux.

La conception Web à proprement parler est encore plus touchée car les agences et les marques se tournent vers les applications, en plein essor. Par ailleurs, les marques abandonnent les micro-sites au profit de pages Facebook : le Web semble alors se limiter de plus en plus à ces pages et à l'afflux d'applications. Rien d'étonnant à ce que le public s'inscrive sur Facebook maintenant que le site possède plus d'un milliard d'utilisateurs actifs.

Cette année, BASE Persoton est un projet unique et intéressant qui permet de créer une sonnerie personnalisée à partir de la photo de profil Facebook des internautes.

La vidéo Gangnam Style est diffusée et la première à obtenir plus d'un milliard de visualisations sur YouTube. Le chiffre dépassera la barre des 3,3 milliards en 2019.

Les navigateurs mobiles n'en sont qu'à leurs balbutiements et n'ont pas la carrure pour gérer des sites repoussant les limites connues. De nouveaux sites mobiles ne cessent d'apparaître, mais la plupart se cantonnent à des images et du texte dans des pages déroulantes, rappelant celles des débuts du Web. C'est un peu comme si quelqu'un avait appuyé

sur le bouton de réinitialisation en termes de potentiel.

La version de Google Chrome pour ordinateur s'impose chez les concepteurs et les développeurs Web, et elle est nécessaire pour accéder à nombre des projets les plus innovants. L'API WebGL est pour sa part la nouvelle tendance pour égaler la qualité des créations en Flash. Le site Adidas – Adizero F50 en est un exemple probant et si un navigateur ne prend pas en charge WebGL … une version Flash du site s'ouvre par défaut !

De nouveaux projets commencent sur un ordinateur mais doivent se poursuivre sur le smartphone de l'utilisateur. C'est le cas du projet Take Them to School pour UNICEF, dont l'objectif est de favoriser l'accès des enfants à l'éducation.

Autre projet en faveur de l'enfance, You Are Blind est un site russe qui bande les yeux des internautes pour qu'ils tentent de se déplacer dans une ville privés du sens de la vue.

Après le lancement de Nike Better World en 2011, une foule de sites d'une simple page déroulante ont suivi. The Deepest Site pousse cette tendance à sa limite logique et s'inscrit comme le site le plus profond jamais réalisé. Les visiteurs doivent en effet défiler longuement jusqu'à atteindre la source de l'eau qui est mise en bouteille.

Dans l'ensemble, la conception Web passe par un moment de pause et de réflexion.

Ø8 Facts of the year

35.4%

Number of internet users:
2.5 billion, 35.4% of
the world population

697 million

Number of websites:
697 million

World news:
NASA's Curiosity rover
lands on Mars

Website with most traffic:
Google.com

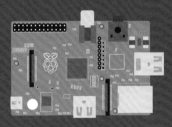

Tech hardware:
Raspberry Pi is released

Tech software:
Windows 8 is launched

Other tech:
Facebook acquires
Instagram for $1 billion

Highest-grossing film:
The Avengers

2012/
—

<u>Bear 71</u>
—

A multi-user, multi-platform,
20-minute interactive documentary

The National Film Board of Canada here presented a fully integrated web documentary that invited viewers to engage with an animal in the wild. The eventual Site of the Year winner for 2012, the film tracked the whole life of a grizzly bear that had been collared at the age of three, by editing together footage from trail cameras in Banff National Park.

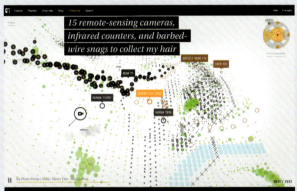

"Bear 71 was about the intersection of
humans, animals, and technology, so it was
interesting that it was also about challenging
the intersection of disciplines – documentary,
interactive, and data storytelling. The amazing
team that worked on this were pushed to
the limits of collaborating, and critics and
academics credited this project as defining the
form of the interactive documentary. It's pretty
awesome that in 2017 the project was reborn
as a VR experience – because the technology
finally caught up with what we had envisioned."

Loc Dao
National Film Board of Canada

Das National Film Board of
Canada präsentierte eine vollständig integrierte Webdoku-
mentation, die die Zuschauer
dazu einlud, sich mit einem Tier in
freier Wildbahn zu beschäftigen.
Sie wurde zur Gewinner-Site
of the Year im Jahr 2012. Der

Film verfolgte das Leben eines
Grizzlybären, der im Alter von
drei Jahren gefangen wurde
und ein Halsband bekam. Er
entstand durch die Bearbeitung
von Aufnahmen von Trail-Kameras
im Banff National Park.

L'office national du film du
Canada présente ici un documentaire Web interactif qui
permet aux visiteurs d'entrer en
contact avec un animal sauvage
dans son milieu. Lauréat du prix
Site of the Year en 2012, le film
montre la vie d'un grizzli muni

d'un collier depuis ses 3 ans à
partir d'images tournées par des
caméras installées dans le parc
national de Banff.

2012/
—

Only:
The Liberation

—

A new way to showcase fashion

This highly interactive film-like experience for the Danish fashion label set out to present their new collection. The video could be stopped at any stage and where hot spots lit up, users could have a closer look at the corresponding clothing. The site demonstrated very high levels of production and implementation throughout.

AMERICANA
CHECKED Shirt

"Only: The Liberation was an online interactive film experience bringing together the elements of a fashion catalog, movie, game, and music video. The experience was built around a story of rebellion, with three girls rolling into a sleepy town looking for trouble. This was actually one of North Kingdom's last Flash productions. We did consider HTML5 but it was not yet ready for this type of experience. At the time, people praised it for its simplicity and innovative navigation."

Jakob Nylund
North Kingdom

Diese hoch interaktive filmartige Erfahrung für das dänische Modelabel präsentierte ihre neue Kollektion. Das Video konnte zu jedem Zeitpunkt gestoppt werden und an den Stellen, an denen Hot Spots aufleuchte- ten, konnten sich die Nutzer die entsprechende Kleidung genauer ansehen. Die Website zeigte durchweg sehr hohe Produktions- und Implementie- rungsraten.

Cette expérience cinémato- graphique des plus interactives présente la nouvelle collection de la marque danoise de prêt- à-porter. La vidéo peut être arrêtée à tout moment et le visi- teur peut cliquer sur les textes à l'écran pour en savoir plus sur le vêtement concerné. Le site fait preuve d'un niveau très élevé de production et de mise en œuvre.

Old Spice, Terry Crews Muscle Music
—

One of the first interactive Vimeo videos

A project to make users smile and laugh, in which muscleman Terry Crews showed how to make hilarious music with his muscles. The fun really began though when the video stopped, and Terry could be controlled by using the keyboard to make the user's own muscle mix. This could then be recorded and shared to impress friends, and I think the only thing missing was the option for users to upload their own face.

Old Spice MUSCLE MUSIC

GUITAR — W
BIKE HORN — O

ORANGE BASS DRUM — E
METAL TUB — I

YELLOW DRUM — R
DUMBBELL — U

BLUE TOM-TOMS — Q
WOODBLOCK — P

KEYBOARD — S
KEYBOARD — J

KEYBOARD — D
KEYBOARD — K

KEYBOARD — F
KEYBOARD — L

TAMBOURINE — V
CYMBAL — M

How to Play

Hitting any of the colored keys to the left once triggers one note to play. Repeated keystrokes trigger repeated notes. Press and hold R, E, Q, I, O, P, V or M to activate instrument loops. Press again to deactivate.

Additional Functional Keys

1 2 3 4
PRE-SET MUSIC LOOPS

Z X C
FLAME SAX CONTROLS

T Y G H B N
TERRY YELLS

1 2 3 4

Q W E R T Y U I O P
S D F G H J K L
Z X C V B N M

"Our goal for Muscle Music was simple. Take an Old Spice personality that people love, Terry Crews, and let them interact with him in a new and surprising way. Working directly with Vimeo, we designed a web experience that was fun, intuitive, and most importantly custom-built within their native embeddable video player. Fans were able to watch the original music piece, experiment and create their own, then share it — all from wherever they came in contact with the experience across the internet."

Mike Davidson
Wieden+Kennedy

Ein Projekt, um den User zum Lächeln und Lachen zu bringen. Der Muskelmann Terry Crews zeigte, wie man mit seinen Muskeln urkomische Musik macht. Der Spaß begann jedoch erst richtig, wenn das Video angehalten wurde und Terry vom User über die Tastatur kontrolliert wurde und er so seine eigenen Muskel-Mix machen konnte. Das konnte dann aufgenommen und geteilt werden, um Freunde zu beeindrucken und ich denke, das einzige, was fehlte, war die Option für User, ihr eigenes Gesicht hochzuladen.

Le but de ce projet est d'amuser les visiteurs : le culturiste Terry Crews montre d'une façon désopilante comment faire de la musique avec ses muscles. Le plus drôle est quand la vidéo s'arrête et que l'internaute peut contrôler les mouvements de Terry à l'aide du clavier pour faire son propre mix. Il peut ensuite enregistrer et partager le résultat avec des amis. Je pense qu'il ne manque que l'option de pouvoir charger une photo de soi.

Google Ramayana

—

A traditional story becomes interactive

This site, with Indonesian text, took the timeless Hindu epic and adapted it into an interactive masterpiece. Using a number of pop-up windows, it exhibited levels of creativity previously only seen with Flash, so this was definitely a development for the future. Attention to detail was abundantly obvious, as was the love the team put into such an impressive project.

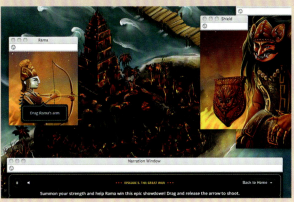

"Google Ramayana was probably one of the most fun projects I got to lead at Fantasy Interactive. This project represents pretty well that time in web design where the use of Flash was winding down and Google Chrome wanted to prove its capabilities and promote itself beyond Flash. Ramayana took something that was culturally relevant and very dear to a specific market, a wide range of users and ages, and associated it with a new type of interactive storytelling powered by the technology built in Google Chrome."

Claudio Guglieri
Fantasy Interactive; Microsoft

Diese Website, mit indonesischem Text, nahm das zeitlose Hindu-Epos auf und adaptierte es zu einem interaktiven Meisterwerk. Mit einer Reihe von Popup-Fenstern zeigten sie eine Kreativität, die zuvor nur bei Flash zu sehen war. Dies war definitiv eine Entwicklung für die Zukunft. Die Liebe zum Detail war ebenso offensichtlich wie die Liebe, die das Team in ein solch beeindruckendes Projekt gesteckt hatte.

Assorti d'un texte en indonésien, ce site offre une adaptation de l'épopée hindoue dans un chef-d'œuvre interactif. Avec sa série de fenêtres contextuelles et une créativité d'un niveau seulement égalé avec Flash, il s'agit sans conteste d'une conception avant-gardiste. Le soin du détail est flagrant, tout comme l'amour que l'équipe a mis dans ce remarquable projet.

2012/

—

Chrome Web Lab

—

A first to merge the boundaries of online and offline

This next-generation project was a prime example of what the future of digital could hold, by amalgamating real-life experiences with those on the web. Users could visit the Science Museum in London and interact with five experiments there, or compare this by integrating with the same experience but live via the browser, 24 hours per day.

Made by
Google

"Since its launch in 2008, Google's Chrome
browser has evolved and continues to push
the potential of what you can do on the web.
In collaboration with the London Science
Museum we created Web Lab – an exhibition
not bound to one geographical location, instead
a first-of-its-kind global museum experience
made accessible to the world online. Featuring
five physical interactive experiments designed
to bring to life the magic of the web, it could
be experienced physically, live from the
Science Museum in London, and digitally from
anywhere in the world at chromeweblab.com."

Steve Vranakis
Google Creative Lab

Dieses Projekt der nächsten
Generation war ein hervorragen-
des Beispiel dafür, was die digitale Zukunft bringen konnte, durch
die Verschmelzung von realen
Erfahrungen mit denen im
Internet. Die User konnten das

Science Museum in London
besuchen und dort mit fünf
Experimenten hantieren oder
sie durch die Integration der
gleichen Erfahrung live über
den Browser vergleichen,
24 Stunden am Tag.

Ce projet de nouvelle génération illustre parfaitement ce que
l'avenir du numérique réserve en
mariant des expériences de la
vie réelle à d'autres sur le Web.
Les internautes peuvent visiter le
Science Museum de Londres et

participer à cinq expériences, ou
réaliser les mêmes expériences
en live à toute heure du jour et
de la nuit dans leur navigateur.

Clouds Over Cuba

—

An immense historical
project that made users
think, "What if?"

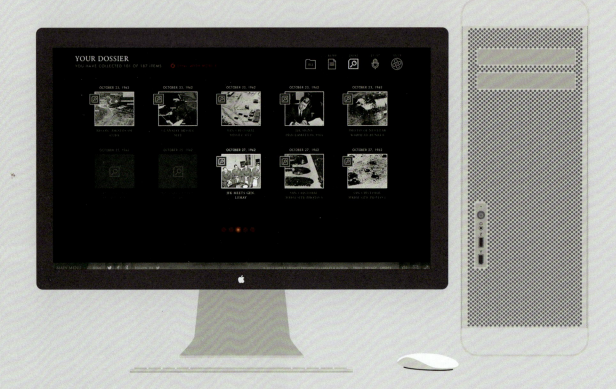

This monumental project was a great example of modern web design, in that it worked seamlessly over desktop, tablet, and mobile. The interactive multimedia documentary from the JFK Library marked the 50th anniversary of the Cuban Missile Crisis, and users were encouraged to navigate and examine all the detail, including a thought-provoking scenario based on an alternative timeline.

> "It was an exciting time. Every project was about doing something that hadn't been done before and Clouds Over Cuba was a great example of that. It was a project with a unique set of ingredients that doesn't come around very often. Despite all the tech innovation that went into the project, what made it really successful was the story. An incredible moment in history that is unfortunately still very relevant today."

Ben Tricklebank
Tool of North America; Smuggler

Dieses monumentale Projekt war ein großartiges Beispiel für modernes Webdesign, denn es funktionierte nahtlos auf dem Desktop, Tablet und Handy. Die interaktive Multimedia-Dokumentation aus der JFK-Bibliothek markierte den 50. Jahrestag der Kubakrise und die User wurden dazu ermutigt, durch alle Details zu navigieren und sie zu untersuchen, einschließlich eines zum Nachdenken anregenden Szenarios, das auf einer alternativen Zeitlinie basierte.

Ce projet d'envergure offre un excellent exemple de conception Web moderne, sachant qu'il fonctionne indifféremment sur ordinateur, tablette et téléphone portable. Le documentaire multimédia interactif de la JFK Library célèbre le 50e anniversaire de la crise des missiles de Cuba. Les internautes peuvent explorer le site en détail et découvrir une petite fiction dont le scénario inspirant est basé sur une chronologie différente.

Jam with Chrome

—

An original example
of social music creation

For anyone who's ever wished they could play an instrument, this interactive web application allowed various combinations of users to play and create music together. What was great was that each instrument had two modes, Easy and Pro, each controlled by the user's mouse and number keys. Users could also chat with other people online at the same time, or invite other users to join them on some music creation.

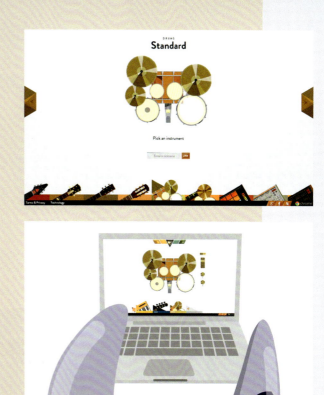

"Jam with Chrome started as a simple idea to get people to invite their friends to use Chrome. We imagined a place where everyone online could play music together. It was a very complex technical challenge that pushed the limit of what a website could do. I'll never forget when it launched and links to jam sessions popped up everywhere on social networks, the reception was incredible. Crafting 18 instruments based on iconic ones was also one of the best bits!"

Xavier Barrade
Google Creative Lab

Für alle, die jemals ein Instrument spielen wollten, ermöglichte diese interaktive Webanwendung verschiedene Kombinationen, damit die User gemeinsam Musik spielen und erstellen konnten. Großartig war, dass jedes Instrument zwei Modi hatte,

Easy und Pro, die jeweils durch die Maus des Benutzers und die Zifferntasten gesteuert wurden. Die User konnten auch online gleichzeitig mit anderen Personen chatten oder andere Benutzer einladen, sich an der Musikgestaltung zu beteiligen.

Pour tous ceux ayant toujours voulu savoir jouer d'un instrument, cette application Web interactive permet à divers groupes d'utilisateurs de jouer et de composer ensemble. Son point fort est que chaque instrument possède deux modes,

Easy et Pro, contrôlés à l'aide de la souris et du pavé numérique. Les internautes peuvent aussi converser en ligne ou inviter des personnes à participer à une création musicale.

Mind Scalextric

—

A first outing for mind controlling interaction

This experimental research and development project really gave a glimpse into the future. By embracing the latest technologies, participants could wear a headset and control the Scalextric slot cars through the power of their mind. As they concentrated they could control the cars' speed and even by blinking make them go faster as well.

"Mind Scalextric started as a personal project in 2011 with the desire of exploring new ways to interact with technology and blur the lines between physical and digital. With Mind Scalextric you could control a slot car and race with your friends using your mind. The more you concentrated, the quicker the car went. This was a new way of experiencing reality. Whilst EEG is not the best way of understanding human intent, this project gave people a first opportunity to experience what telekinesis might feel like one day."

Riccardo Giraldi
B-Reel; Microsoft

Dieses experimentelle Forschungs- und Entwicklungsprojekt gab wirklich einen Blick auf die Zukunft. Durch die Verwendung der neuesten Technologien konnten die Teilnehmer ein Headset tragen und die Scalextric Slot Cars durch die Kraft ihres Geistes steuern. Während sie sich konzentrierten, konnten sie die Geschwindigkeit der Autos kontrollieren und sie sogar durch Blinzeln schneller fahren lassen.

Ce projet expérimental de recherche et développement ouvre une fenêtre sur le futur. Comme il intègre les dernières technologies, les participants portent un casque et dirigent les voitures Scalextric par la pensée. En se concentrant, ils peuvent en contrôler la vitesse et même les faire accélérer en clignant des yeux.

Ponk

—

Interaction moving out of the browser

There had been several experimental ideas using Kinect motion detection, but this one really stood out. It was an experimental game installation that combined a touchless game-play device and reactive objects. Looking back to the original pong games, typically played on black-and-white TVs many years ago, and comparing them with this updated example, the wonder was what experimental minds might bring to the table next.

"Ponk was built in that particular and very experimental context. I was commissioned to create an installation for an office party, something fun and enjoyable, something anyone could play with. Microsoft had just launched their Kinect motion sensor and this was the perfect timing to experiment with it. After a few tweaks and tests with Flash, the concept of Ponk came up. The most popular tennis video game remixed, this time without controllers, only motion-detection over a huge tabletop-screen reacting with physical objects acting as obstacles or bonuses."

Jonathan da Costa
jonathandacosta.com

Es gab mehrere experimentelle Ideen, die Kinect-Bewegungserkennung verwendeten, aber diese war wirklich herausragend. Es war eine experimentelle Spielinstallation, die ein berührungsloses Spielgerät mit reaktiven Objekten kombinierte. Wenn man sich die ursprünglichen Pong-Spiele ansieht, die vor vielen Jahren auf Schwarz-Weiß-Fernsehern gespielt wurden und sie mit diesem aktualisierten Beispiel vergleicht, fragt man sich, was experimentelle Köpfe als nächstes auf den Tisch bringen.

Le système de détection de mouvements Kinect a déjà été employé pour plusieurs projets expérimentaux, mais celui-ci sort vraiment du lot. Cette installation combine un dispositif de jeu sans contact et des objets réactifs. Si on la compare au premier jeu Pong qui se jouait alors sur des télévisions en noir et blanc, on se demande ce que vont bien pouvoir s'inventer par la suite les créatifs.

2012/
—

Wrangler Europe: Get Your Edge Back

—

Innovative scene-breaking navigation

It was now a rare thing to discover a type of navigation that hadn't been experienced before, but this interactive movie won huge acclaim for doing just that: as users joined the story they got to move from scene to scene by way of dragging the cursor at 90 degrees. This made the person on screen literally break through into another scene, a simple idea, but perfectly executed.

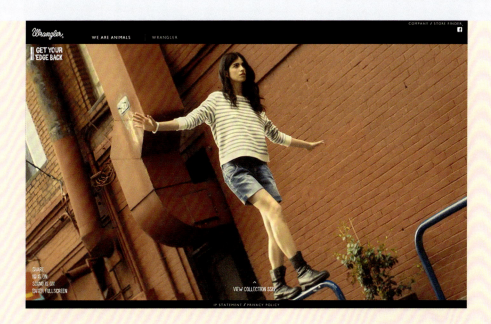

"Wrangler Europe wanted to make an interactive film to showcase their spring/summer collection whilst also playing off the campaign tagline 'Get Your Edge Back'. A couple of our creatives went to a nearby park to test out a few different transition techniques, and this one immediately stood out. During the shoot, our models fell on to mattresses which we then digitally removed; none the less, it still took some time for them to get comfortable with the idea of falling over in as straight a line as possible without bracing for impact at all."

Mark Pytlik
Stinkdigital

Es war jetzt selten geworden, eine Navigationsart zu entdecken, die es vorher noch nicht gegeben hatte, aber dieser interaktive Film erhielt große Anerkennung dafür, genau das getan zu haben: Wenn die User in die Geschichte eintraten, mussten sie von Szene zu Szene ziehen, indem sie den Cursor um 90 Grad zogen. Das brachte die Person auf dem Bildschirm buchstäblich in eine andere Szene, eine einfache Idee aber perfekt ausgeführt.

Il est à présent rare de ne pas avoir déjà vu un mode de navigation, mais ce film interactif obtient ses lettres de noblesse en créant justement la surprise. Les visiteurs doivent en effet passer de scène en scène en faisant glisser le curseur à 90 degrés. Ce geste projette alors littéralement la personne à l'écran dans une autre scène. Une idée aussi simple que parfaitement exécutée.

NOTABLE WEBSITE
LAUNCH
Medium

GOOGLE
FACTS

Google stands up against
SOPA and PIPA

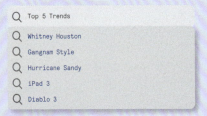

Top 5 Trends

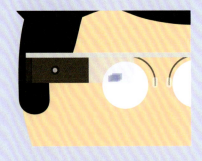

Project Glass is announced

Google Crisis Response
launches Public Alerts

Chrome launches on Android
and iOS

Google Drive launches

MOBILE EVOLUTION
iPhone 5

The world's fastest-selling smartphone

INTERNET COMMUNITY
Protests against
SOPA and PIPA

A series of globally coordinated protests were mounted on January 18 against two laws being proposed to Congress in the United States: the Stop Online Privacy Act and Protect IP Act. The internet protest involved over 115,000 websites, including Wikipedia, Reddit, Twitter, Craigslist, and Flickr. Google posted a special censor bar doodle and promoted a link to the petition, which was signed by over 7 million people. The next day, the bills were set aside.

2013/

The Year of Revival and Renewed Excitement

2013/

—

The Year of Revival and Renewed Excitement

—

#TreasureDance

The Chrome browser continued to gain users and established itself as the most popular browser, with around 36 percent uptake compared to the fading Internet Explorer at 20 percent and Firefox's 17 percent. This was because of the pioneering opportunities it had given back to web designers and developers who had found themselves abandoned by Adobe's lack of resistance to Flash being eclipsed.

The app gold-rush was beginning to wear off. It felt like a time of renewed focus on the web itself and that its original unchained opportunities were back.

In the year Yahoo! acquired Tumblr for $1.1 billion there was a surge of impressive Tumblr websites, including the one for Capitol Couture which used Tumblr's dynamic API and combined that with multi-touch using HTML5 Canvas, which showed modern thinking for desktop and mobile.

Bruno Mars's Instagram #Treasure-Dance used the hashtag to grab people's dance videos and insert the latest 100 in a random sequence alongside his own video.

As North Korea conducted its third underground nuclear test, The Defector emerged, a first-person interactive documentary where users had to try and escape from North Korea.

Tourism Victoria launched a live streaming experience, the Melbourne Remote Control Tourist, which allowed people to experience the state's capital in real time and also track and control a team of urban explorers.

Amidst the rapid increase in mobile phone use, Enjoy Your Privacy gave a glimpse of what might happen if a user's mobile device was left unprotected.

The Internet of Things also continued to evolve, keeping some people amazed at new developments whilst leaving others unmoved. The launch of KnitterStream presented an electronic knitting-machine, programmed to produce custom designs out of users' 140-character tweets.

KLM Space gave users the chance to win a ticket into space by predicting where a high-altitude balloon would burst in the outer atmosphere. The live broadcast enabled people to follow the balloon's ascent as it happened.

Melbourne Remote Control Tourist

The Defector

"The app gold-
rush was
beginning to
wear off."

Enjoy Your Privacy

Der Chrome-Browser gewann weiterhin User und etablierte sich als der beliebteste Browser, mit etwa 36 Prozent Aufnahme im Vergleich zum verblassenden Internet Explorer mit 20 Prozent und Firefox 17 Prozent. Dies lag an den bahnbrechenden Möglichkeiten, die Webdesignern und Entwicklern gegeben wurden, die sich von der mangelnden Widerstandsfähigkeit von Adobe gegenüber Flash in den Hintergrund gedrängt fühlten.

Der Goldrausch der Apps begann allmählich abzuschwächen. Es fühlte sich an, wie eine Zeit der erneuten Fokussierung auf das Internet selbst und dass seine ursprünglichen, ungeahnten Möglichkeiten zurück waren.

Im Jahr als Yahoo! Tumblr für 1,1 Milliarden US-Dollar kaufte, gab es eine Flut beeindruckender Tumblr-Websites, einschließlich der für Capitol Couture, die die dynamische API von Tumblr verwendete und diese mit Multi-Touch mit HTML5 Canvas kombinierte, was modernes Denken für Desktop und Mobile bezeugte.

Bruno Mars' Instagram #TreasureDance nutzte den Hashtag, um Tanzvideos der Leute zu erfassen und die letzten 100 in zufälliger Reihenfolge neben seinem eigenen Video einzufügen.

Als Nordkorea seinen dritten unterirdischen Atomtest durchführte, entstand

The Defector, eine interaktive Dokumentation, in der die Nutzer versuchen mussten, aus Nordkorea zu entkommen.

Tourism Victoria startete eine Live-Streaming-Erfahrung, die Melbourne Remote Control Tourist, die es den Menschen ermöglichte, die Hauptstadt des Bundesstaates in Echtzeit zu erleben und ein Team von urbanen Entdeckern zu verfolgen und zu kontrollieren.

Inmitten des rasanten Anstiegs der Nutzung von Mobiltelefonen zeigte Enjoy Your Privacy, was passiert, wenn das mobile Gerät eines Benutzers ungeschützt bleibt.

The Internet of Things entwickelte sich weiter und

verblüffte, während andere weiterhin nur mit den Schultern zuckten. KnitterStream brachte eine elektronische Strickmaschine auf den Markt, die so programmiert war, dass sie benutzerdefinierte Designs aus Ihren 140 Charakter Tweets stricken konnte.

KLM Space gab den Usern die Möglichkeit, ein Ticket für eine Reise in den Weltraum zu gewinnen, indem man vorhersagte, wo ein Ballon in großer Höhe in der äußeren Atmosphäre platzen würde. Die Live-Übertragung ermöglichte es dann, dem Aufstieg des Ballons live zu folgen.

2013/
—
The Year of Revival and Renewed Excitement
—

Capitol Couture

KnitterStream

KLM Space

"It felt like a time of renewed focus on the web itself and that its original unchained opportunities were back."

Chrome continue de se faire des adeptes et s'impose comme le navigateur le plus en vogue, comptant environ 36 % des utilisateurs contre 20 % pour un Internet Explorer en déclin et 17 % pour Firefox. Son succès s'explique par les fonctionnalités innovantes qu'il offre aux concepteurs comme aux développeurs, laissés pour compte après le manque de résistance d'Adobe pour sauver Flash.

La ruée vers l'or des applications commence à s'essouffler, et l'accent revient sur le Web à proprement parler et ses possibilités originales.

Suite à l'acquisition de Tumblr par Yahoo! pour 1,1 milliard de dollars, des sites Web Tumblr de qualité prolifèrent, comme celui de Capitol Couture : basé sur l'API dynamique de Tumblr et multi-tactile grâce à l'élément canvas de HTML5, il offre une approche moderne pour ordinateurs et dispositifs mobiles.

Le compte Instagram de Bruno Mars utilise le hashtag #TreasureDance pour récupérer des vidéos de personnes qui dansent et intégrer les 100 dernières dans une séquence aléatoire avec sa propre vidéo.

La Corée du Nord effectue son troisième essai nucléaire sous-terrain. Dans ce contexte apparaît The Defector, un documentaire interactif à la première personne dans lequel les utilisateurs doivent essayer d'échapper du pays.

Tourism Victoria lance Melbourne Remote Control Tourist, une expérience retransmise en direct qui permet de découvrir la capitale de l'état en temps réel et de suivre une équipe d'explorateurs urbains.

En plein essor des téléphones portables, Enjoy Your Privacy offre un aperçu des conséquences possibles si un dispositif mobile est laissé sans protection.

L'Internet des objets poursuit son évolution qui en fascine certains et en indiffère d'autres. KnitterStream lance une machine à tricoter électronique programmée pour créer des motifs personnalisés à partir de tweets de 140 caractères.

Dans le site KLM Space, les utilisateurs ont la chance de gagner un billet pour l'espace en devinant à quel moment un ballon à haute altitude éclatera dans l'exosphère. La retransmission en direct permet de suivre l'ascension du ballon en temps réel.

Ø8 Facts of the year

38,9%

Number of internet users:
2.8 billion, 38,9% of
the world population

673
million

Number of websites:
673 million

World news:
Nelson Mandela dies

Website with most traffic:
Yahoo.com

Tech hardware:
Microsoft launches
Xbox One

Tech software:
Apple releases iOS 7

Other tech:
Yahoo! acquires Tumblr
for $1.1 billion

Highest-grossing film:
Frozen

—

Pharrell Williams
24 Hours of Happy

—

The first 24-hour music video

Pharrell Williams's song "Happy" was written and performed by him for the *Despicable Me 2* soundtrack and was released in late 2013. The track was supported by a similarly addictive website that was touted as the first 24-hour music video: depending on when users checked in, they'd see the corresponding part of the footage, as performed by Pharrell and around 400 southern Californians. The video paid homage to neighborhoods in Los Angeles and their residents, many of whom participated in it and had only one take for their dance moves.

"When I wrote this song for *Despicable Me 2*, I never imagined it would have a 24-hour video, amazing interactive website, or win the FWA SOTY. This is an incredible honor. I am super grateful for the creative vision of the 'Happy' team — We Are From LA, Iconoclast, and i am OTHER — for creating a project that truly seems like it's inspiring happiness all over the world."

Pharrell Williams

Pharrell Williams' Lied „Happy" wurde von ihm für den *Ich – Einfach unverbesserlich 2* Soundtrack geschrieben und gespielt und kam Ende 2013 heraus. Der Track wurde von einer ähnlich süchtig machenden Website unterstützt, die als erstes 24-Stunden-Musikvideo angekündigt wurde: Je nachdem, wann die User eincheckten, sahen sie den entsprechenden Teil der Aufnahmen, wie sie von Pharrell und rund 400 Südkaliforniern gespielt wurden. Das Video war eine Hommage an die Stadtviertel von Los Angeles und ihre Bewohner, von denen viele an der Veranstaltung teilnahmen und eine eigene Einstellung für ihre Tanzbewegungen bekamen.

Pharrell Williams compose et interprète le titre «Happy» pour la bande-son de *Moi, moche et méchant 2* sorti fin 2013. En complément, un site Web tout aussi addictif se vante d'être le premier vidéoclip d'une durée de 24 heures : selon le moment auquel ils se connectent, les visiteurs voient la séquence correspondante avec les images de Pharrell et d'environ 400 habitants de Californie du Sud. Cette vidéo rend hommage aux quartiers de Los Angeles et à leurs résidents, dont beaucoup y apparaissant n'ont pu faire qu'une seule prise de leur chorégraphie.

Find Your Way to Oz

—

The chance for users to experience their own journey within a movie

MacBook Air

To bring the world of Disney's *Oz the Great and Powerful* to the web, Anrick Bregman created an interactive version of the start of the film, a circus scene users could explore which then led into the film itself, as per the site's name. The user's journey climaxed in the final dramatic experience where they were swept up in the storm, spinning out of control in a hot air balloon, and heading inside the vortex of the tornado.

"Firstly, we wanted to create a fairground experience that would allow you to put yourself into the world of Oz, meeting some of its characters and using your webcam to interact with them. And secondly, we wanted to make a storm that looked imposing, and beautiful. We wanted it to feel intense. The project was emblematic of web design around 2013, with exciting experiences that were immersive, and visually cinematic. It was essentially real-time rendering happening in the browser. And it allowed us to create websites that would surprise you, and took you on an adventure."

Anrick Bregman
Unit9; Director

Um die Welt von Disneys *Die fantastische Welt von Oz* in das Internet zu bringen, erschuf Anrick Bregman eine interaktive Version des Beginns des Films. Die User konnten eine Zirkus-Szene erkunden, was sie dann zum Film selbst brachte, gemäß des Namens der Site. Die Reise der User fand ihren Höhepunkt in der dramatischen Erfahrung, als sie im Sturm mitgerissen wurden, in einem Heißluftballon außer Kontrolle gerieten und in den Wirbel des Tornados stürzten.

Pour promouvoir sur le Web la dernière réalisation de Disney intitulée *Le monde fantastique d'Oz*, Anrick Bregman conçoit une version interactive des premières minutes, avec un cirque que les visiteurs peuvent explorer avant d'arriver au propre film, comme l'annonce le nom du site. Le voyage culmine avec une incroyable expérience finale, quand les internautes sont pris dans une tempête, perdent le contrôle d'une montgolfière et se dirigent tout droit vers une tornade.

—

Written in the Stars

—

A mobile browser experience with the power of an app

This special experience created by AKQA allowed users to send a message to friends or family who could then use their iOS device and hold it up to the night sky to find the North Star, and see the message actually written in the stars above. The project was a collaboration with Massive Attack who created an original soundtrack for it that would react to the orientation and location of each user's device. A unique experience every time, and working within the browser it was as simple as sending a text.

"Written in the Stars was developed to connect loved ones near and far during the holiday season. The aim was to create a personalized one-to-one mobile web experience which went beyond the traditional website experience and started to use the features and functionality of the mobile device. We used the iOS capabilities of the iPhone's gyroscope — so when you received a notification that a loved one had sent you a note, you would need to locate the North Star in the sky using your phone camera to reveal the personalized message."

Sam Kelly
AKQA

Diese besondere Erfahrung, die von AKQA erstellt wurde, erlaubte den Usern, eine Nachricht an Freunde oder Familie zu senden, die dann ihr iOS-Gerät verwenden und es in den Nachthimmel halten mussten, um den Polarstern zu finden und dann die Nachricht in den Sternen zu sehen. Das Projekt war eine Kollaboration mit Massive Attack, die einen originellen Soundtrack dafür kreierten, der auf die Ausrichtung und den Ort des jeweiligen Geräts des Nutzers reagierte. Jedes Mal eine einzigartige Erfahrung, und im Browser zu arbeiten war so einfach wie das Senden eines Textes.

Cette expérience unique créée par AKQA permet aux internautes d'envoyer un message à des amis ou des proches. De nuit, s'ils lèvent leur dispositif iOS au ciel, ils peuvent trouver l'étoile polaire et lire le message inscrit au milieu des étoiles. Ce projet a été mené en collaboration avec Massive Attack, auteur de la bande-son originale qui réagit à l'orientation et à l'emplacement du dispositif de chaque utilisateur. Cette expérience est chaque fois différente et l'emploi du navigateur est aussi simple qu'envoyer un message.

2013/

—

The Zoetrope

—

Recreating a 19th-century invention with WebGL

MacBook Air

For MTV's 19th annual European Music Awards a huge zoetrope was created by Berlin's Sehsucht, a fast-moving carousel based on the one originally invented in 1834 by William George Horner. This early moving-image projector was given a dose of the latest web technology, WebGL, and created the illusion of movement via a rapid succession of static mannequins coming to life under stroboscopic light.

The browser version took the form of a game and required users to drag and spin the zoetrope in time to the music, using the mouse or its scrollwheel. Advancing through the levels took some practice, but the visuals here were groundbreaking at a time when Flash had previously been the only way to create such experiences.

"While we are predominantly a design studio working in the field of 3D animation, we're naturally curious about interactive work as well. Especially things that push the technological limits. Using the high-quality render assets we had available from the MTV EMA project, we developed a pipeline to reuse them for the real-time 3D capabilities of WebGL at the time. The fact that the technology loads without any plug-ins, ubiquitous on any browser and now also on mobiles, still makes it one of the most exciting developments in the online space."

Mate Steinforth
Sehsucht

Für den jährlich stattfindenden, 19. MTVs European Music Awards wurde ein riesiges Zoetrope von der Berliner Agentur Sehsucht geschaffen, ein sich schnell bewegendes Karussell nach dem Original, das 1834 von William George Horner erfunden wurde. Dieser frühe Bewegt-bild-Projektor erhielt eine Dosis der neuesten Webtechnologie, WebGL und erzeugte die Illusion von Bewegung durch eine schnelle Abfolge von statischen Mannequins, die unter strobos-kopischem Licht zum Leben erwachten.

Die Browser-Version nahm die Form eines Games an und verlangte von den Usern, das Zoetrop rechtzeitig zur Musik zu ziehen und zu drehen, mit der Maus oder einem Scrollrad. Der Weg durch die Levels erforderte einige Übung, aber die Visuals hier waren wegweisend zu einer Zeit, als Flash bisher die einzige Möglichkeit war, solche Erfah-rungen zu machen.

Pour les 19ᵉ MTV European Music Awards, le studio berlinois Seh-sucht crée un énorme zootrope qui s'inspire du tout premier inventé en 1834 par William George Horner. Ce projecteur d'images animées est doté de la technologie WebGL et donne une illusion de mouvement grâce à la succession rapide de manne-quins statiques qui bougent sous une lumière stroboscopique.

La version pour navigateur prend une forme ludique en demandant aux internautes de faire tourner le zootrope en fonction de la musique, que ce soit en cliquant ou à l'aide de la molette. Il faut une certaine dose de pratique pour progresser dans les niveaux, mais le site suppose une révolution sur le plan visuel car jusqu'alors, seul Flash avait permis de créer ce type d'expériences.

Lincoln Presents
Hello, Again

—

The first interactive 360°
music experience

MacBook Air

In re-working the 1977 David Bowie song "Sound and Vision" for the Lincoln Motor Company's Hello Again campaign, American singer/songwriter Beck collaborated with director Chris Milk to film a single perform-ance of the song which experimented with possibilities of perspective and sound movement. The audience was seated around an orchestra of over 160 musicians, enabling a 360° environment to be created using multiple cameras that gave viewers of the website the feeling of actually being there. This virtual reality-style experience also allowed users to move within the interface and change the direction of the audio in real time via their webcam or their own head movements.

HELLO, AGAIN

THE STORY: BECK REIMAGINES DAVID BOWIE'S "SOUND AND VISION"

EXPERIENCE IT: CLICK HERE FOR THE FULLY IMMERSIVE PERFORMANCE.

"I took the opportunity that this project provided to test some of the audio-visual immersion theories I had been kicking around back in 2012. My thinking was that virtual reality was just over the horizon and this gave me a chance to see what a 'film' could be like in what I hoped could be a completely new medium. We had no VR headset at the time of shooting. It was all a bunch of guesses how it would work in VR. A few months after its completion my friends at Oculus got me an early DK1 and we ported it in. It worked quite well surprisingly and was really the catalyst for a lot of my explorations in VR since."

Chris Milk
Within

Bei der Überarbeitung des Songs von David Bowie „Sound and Vision" von 1977 für die Hello Again-Kampagne der Lincoln Motor Company, arbeitete der amerikanische Sänger und Songwriter Beck mit Regisseur Chris Milk zusammen, um eine einzige Performance des Songs zu filmen, wobei er mit den Möglichkeiten der Perspektive und Klangbewegung experimentierte. Das Publikum saß um ein Orchester von über 160 Musikern herum. Es wurde mit Hilfe von mehreren Kameras eine 360° Umgebung geschaffen, die den Besuchern der Website das Gefühl gab, tatsächlich dort zu sein. Diese Virtual-Reality-ähnliche Erfahrung ermöglichte es den Benutzern auch, sich innerhalb der Benutzeroberfläche zu bewegen und die Richtung der Audiodaten in Echtzeit über ihre Webcam oder ihre eigenen Kopfbewegungen zu ändern.

En vue de versionner la chanson de 1977 de David Bowie intitulée «Sound and Vision» pour la campagne Hello Again de la Lincoln Motor Company, le compositeur-interprète américain Beck a collaboré avec le réalisateur Chris Milk, qui l'a filmé en jouant avec la perspective et le mouvement du son. Le public a pris place autour d'un orchestre de 160 musiciens, et un environnement à 360° a été créé à l'aide de diverses caméras. Les visiteurs ont ainsi l'impression de se trouver parmi le public et, plongés dans une expérience de réalité virtuelle, ils peuvent se déplacer dans l'interface et changer la direction de l'audio en temps réel via leur webcam ou en bougeant la tête.

—

100 McDonald's Moments

—

Defining browser animation on
mobile devices without Flash

By asking McDonald's customers the question
"What's Your McDonald's Moment?", a wide
sample of responses was collected and
this website was created to showcase the
answers. What made the site so great was
that it was full of charm, thanks to all the
illustrations that had been animated for it and
which were presented in the gallery section
under the site's name.

"An experience inviting people to celebrate all the moments in their lives made more enjoyable with a McDonald's. Every illustration was hand drawn before being lovingly converted into bright and vibrant vector graphics. This was real-time marketing in practice. Seeding the question, collecting the responses, and crafting the Moments was an on-going process that produced a campaign that evolved from start to finish. Redoing this campaign today would take a very different form but a similar spirit."

Cyril Louis
Razorfish; R/GA

Als McDonald's Kunden gefragt wurden „Was ist dein besonderer McDonald's-Moment?", wurde eine breite Auswahl an Antworten gesammelt und diese Website wurde erstellt, um die Antworten zu präsentieren. Was die Seite so großartig machte war, dass sie voller charmanter Illustrationen war, die für sie animiert wurden und die in der Galerie unter dem Namen der Seite präsentiert wurden.

Une enquête menée auprès de clients de McDonald's avec la question «Quel est votre moment McDonald's ?» a permis de recueillir un grand échantillon de réponses. Elles sont présentées dans ce site Web dont l'attrait tient aux nombreuses illustrations animées et à une galerie sous le nom du site.

2013/

—

Just a Reflektor

—

When experimentation took
mobile/web interaction
to another dimension

MacBook Air

Visitors to this site were able to use their mobile phone or tablet to cast their reflection on a music video. This futuristic experience was the combined work of Vincent Morisset and Aaron Koblin (then Google Creative Lab), and resulted from experimenting with the GetUserMedia() web technology, which linked the browser to a user's webcam so that augmented data from a phone's gyroscope and accelerometer would allow the creation of a controller, the reflection. The project was designed for Arcade Fire's latest song, "Reflektor", and the interactivity and technological set-up became very much part of the story.

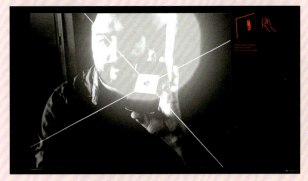

"For me, the song 'Reflektor' is a quest for truth.
It's a metaphor about representation and identity.
For the experience, a mobile becomes, in our
hand, an optical device that transforms what we
see on the computer. The interactivity is part of
the message. We create an invisible wall in the
physical space. The spectator on one side, the
protagonist trapped in the screen on the 'other
side'. Fiction, magic and reality colliding…"

Vincent Morisset
AATOAA

Besucher auf dieser Seite konnten ihre Mobiltelefone oder Tablet verwenden, um ihre Reflexion auf ein Musikvideo zu werfen. Diese futuristische Erfahrung war die gemeinsame Arbeit von Vincent Morisset und Aaron Koblin (Google Creative Lab), und resultierte aus dem Experimentieren mit der GetUserMedia() Web-Technologie, die den Browser mit der Webcam eines Benutzers verknüpfte, so dass erweiterte Daten von einem Gyroskop und einem Beschleunigungsmesser eines Telefons die Erstellung eines Controllers, der Reflexion, ermöglicht wurden. Das Projekt wurde für Arcade Fires neuestes Lied „Reflector" entworfen und die Interaktivität und das technologische Setup wurden Teil der Geschichte.

Les visiteurs de ce site peuvent utiliser leur téléphone portable ou leur tablette pour voir le reflet de leur image dans un clip vidéo. Cette expérience futuriste est le fruit d'une collaboration entre Vincent Morisset et Aaron Koblin (alors chez Google Creative Lab) et repose sur la fonction GetUserMedia(). Cette technologie Web connecte le navigateur à la webcam d'un internaute pour que les données augmentées du gyroscope et de l'accéléromètre d'un téléphone créent un contrôleur, à savoir le reflet. Le projet est conçu pour le dernier titre d'Arcade Fire intitulé «Reflektor», et l'interactivité comme la configuration technologique sont des composantes de l'histoire.

Cube Slam

—

A first to enable video
chat in the browser
without plug-ins

MacBook Air

Demonstrating seamless video chat, faultless game-play, and charm, this game was fun to play against the computer but when played with a friend, and both had webcams, the experience was elevated to a new level. A pong-like game that showed what was possible without the need for plug-ins and could run on a modern browser such as Chrome, Cube Slam in single-player mode added to the game by creating an imaginary visual world where animals such as Bob the Bear came to life to become the user's opponent. The main tech highlight here was WebRTC, which allowed the communication with sound and video directly through the browser.

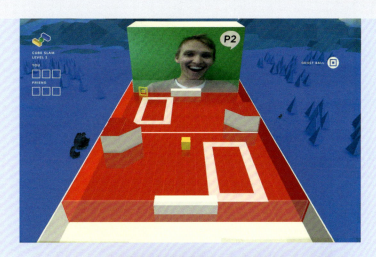

"The Cube Slam world was a woodland arena with giant jumbotrons where you and your opponent's faces appeared. To win, you smashed a cube against your opponent's screen and made it crumble to the ground, using all sorts of fun extras and multipliers along the way. Cube Slam's graphics were rendered in WebGL and CSS 3D, and its custom soundtrack was delivered dynamically through Web Audio. We built Cube Slam to celebrate all of those new technologies, and to have a little fun with our friends along the way."

Clem Wright
Google Creative Lab

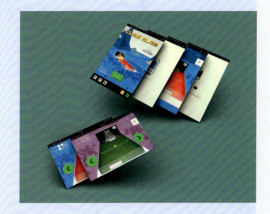

Mit dem nahtlosen Video-Chat, dem fehlerfreien Gameplay und dem großen Charme, hat es Spaß gemacht, gegen den Computer zu spielen, aber wenn es mit einem Freund gespielt wurde und beide Webcams hatten, wurde das Erlebnis auf ein neues Level gehoben. Ein Pong-ähnliches Spiel, das zeigte, was ohne Plug-ins möglich war und auf einem modernen Browser wie Chrome laufen konnte. Cube Slam im Einzelspieler-Modus ergänzte das Spiel durch die Schaffung einer imaginären visuellen Welt, in der Tiere wie Bob der Bär zum Leben erwachten, um zum Gegner des Users zu werden. Das wichtigste technische Highlight war hier WebRTC, was die Kommunikation mit Ton und Video direkt über den Browser ermöglichte.

Pour ce jeu combinant un chat vidéo intégré, une impeccable jouabilité et une dose d'élégance, il est amusant de jouer contre l'ordinateur, mais encore plus contre un ami équipé lui aussi d'une webcam. Sorte d'hybride de Pong, il montre tout le potentiel d'un navigateur moderne comme Chrome, et ce sans recourir à des plug-ins. En mode solo, Cube Slam enrichit encore l'expérience en créant un monde visuel imaginaire dans lequel des animaux comme Bob the Bear prennent vie pour s'opposer au joueur. Sur le plan technologique, son point fort est l'interface WebRTC, qui permet la communication audio et vidéo directement via le navigateur.

Roll It

—

The user's mobile phone becomes a controller without the need for plug-ins

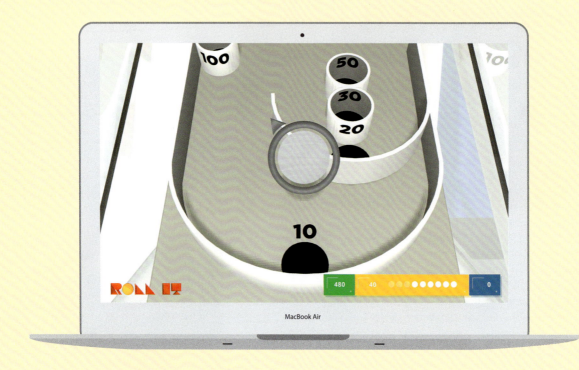

This modern-day version of the classic boardwalk game let users grab hold of their mobile phone and roll a ball right into their computer. Google's Chrome thus showed, by way of projects like this, what modern browsers could do and the powerful features they harnessed. The 'live accelerometer data' was collected here by getting users out of their seats and moving their bodies, while the ability to sync phones with computers meant that the motion data was linked with the power of desktop systems and all the capabilities that offered.

ROLL IT

"With Roll It, the idea of pairing your mobile browser to control something on your desktop browser was a new and emerging idea. We had to think of what Web Design, UX, and UI should be for an experience involving two devices with screens at the same time. Not just a stand-alone desktop site and stand-alone mobile site. Before this, the focus had been on responsive design and mobile touch interactions. Roll It sort of smashed the two together to show what was possible using the latest web technologies and having a little fun with a classic game."

Suzanne Chambers
Google Creative Lab

Mit dieser Version des klassischen Rummelplatzspiels konnten die Nutzer ihr Handy greifen und einen Ball direkt in ihren Computer rollen. Googles Chrome zeigte somit anhand solcher Projekte, was moderne Browser können und welche leistungsstarken Funktionen sie nutzen. Die Live-Beschleunigungsmess-

daten wurden hier gesammelt, indem Benutzer aus ihren Sitzen geholt und ihre Körper bewegt wurden, wobei die Möglichkeit, die Telefone mit den Computern zu synchronisieren, bedeutete, dass die Bewegungsdaten mit der Leistungsfähigkeit von Desktop-Systemen und allen Möglichkeiten verbunden waren.

Cette version moderne du traditionnel jeu d'adresse permet aux joueurs de saisir leur téléphone portable et de faire rouler une boule dans l'écran de leur ordinateur. Avec ce type de projet, Google Chrome montre le potentiel des navigateurs modernes et la puissance de leur fonctions. Les données en temps réel de

l'accéléromètre sont recueillies quand les internautes se lèvent et bougent. La synchronisation des deux appareils implique que les données des mouvements avec le téléphone sont liées à la puissance du processeur et autres fonctionnalités de l'ordinateur.

2013/
—

Lifesaver

—

A live-action interactive
film that helped save lives
by teaching CPR

This project worked across desktop and mobile to educate people about cardiopulmonary resuscitation (chest compressions), bringing this lifesaving technique to a new audience via a live-action interactive film that dropped the user into one of a number of scenarios where they encountered someone suffering a heart attack. Users were guided through three CPR situations and quickly realized they were expected to react within certain time limits if they were to save a life.

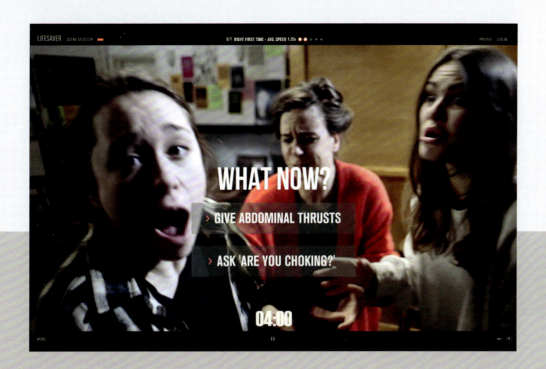

"One aim of Lifesaver was to prove that by fusing live-action film and interactivity, we could engage and teach people better than with text-based web pages or simple linear videos. And Lifesaver did indeed prove this. It has saved multiple lives. Recent medical research has shown that adding Lifesaver to traditional CPR training more than doubles learners' CPR score (compared to learners who only do traditional CPR training). It improves players' confidence and willingness to get involved in an emergency. And the site/app has won many passionate users and awards."

Martin Percy
Unit9, Director

Dieses Projekt lief auf Desktop-Computern und Mobiltelefonen und sollte Menschen über die kardiopulmonale Reanimation (Herzdruckmassage) aufklären. Diese lebensrettende Technik sollte einem neuen Publikum durch einen interaktiven Live-Action-Film zugänglich gemacht werden, der die User in eine Reihe von Szenarien versetzte, in denen sie auf jemanden trafen, der an einem Herzinfarkt litt. Die User wurden durch drei CPR-Situationen geführt und merkten schnell, dass sie innerhalb bestimmter Zeitfenster reagieren mussten, wenn sie ein Leben retten wollten.

Conçu pour ordinateurs et dispositifs mobiles, ce projet vise à expliquer comment réaliser une réanimation cardio-respiratoire par le biais de compressions thoraciques. Il présente donc une technique de premiers secours à un nouveau public via un film interactif : les internautes se retrouvent face à une personne souffrant un arrêt cardiaque et sont guidés dans trois situations de RCR. Ils comprennent très vite qu'ils doivent réagir dans un temps donné s'ils veulent sauver une vie.

NOTABLE WEBSITE LAUNCH
New Myspace

GOOGLE FACTS

The first "Explorers" receive Google Glass

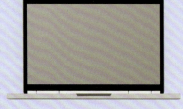

The Chromebook Pixel launches

Google acquires Waze

Chromecast is announced

Android passes 1 billion device activations

Top 5 Trends

- Top 5 Trends
- Nelson Mandela
- Paul Walker
- iPhone 5s
- Cory Monteith
- Harlem Shake

INTERNET COMMUNITY
Edward Snowden

Former CIA employee Edward Snowden reveals thousands of classified security documents to journalists.

MOBILE EVOLUTION
HTC One

Fashioned from a single piece of custom aluminum

2014/

The Year Mobile Browsers Became as Powerful as Desktops

2014/
—
The Year Mobile Browsers Became as Powerful as Desktops
—

Unnumbered Sparks

Active internet users passed the three-billion mark this year and the number of websites nudged one billion. WebGL reached the masses through mobile browsers with the release of Apple's iOS 8, while virtual reality was beginning to grace smartphones and giving a glimpse of WebVR via Oculus Rift, the South Park Oculus Experience being one of the first examples.

However, wider access to VR still seemed a long way off, that is until the entry-level hardware from Google changed everything this year, with the DIY VR headset launch of Google Cardboard.

Whilst VR, and especially its hype, was really beginning to take off, it was high time mobile browsers were able to support 3D. The timing couldn't have been more perfect with the launch of Retina HD displays on the iPhone 6 and 6+.

The Coca-Cola AHH campaign was responsible for many mobile-first experiences in this project that featured 61 independent URLs. Each one had a bite-sized game that was targeted at teens and how drinking their Coke was like a sip of "AHH". The URLs started at ahh.com and then added another H for each one after, up to ahhhhhhhhhhhhhhhhhhhhhhhhhhhhhhhhhhhh hhhhhhhhhhhhhhhhhhhhhhhhhhhhhhhhhh.com, with 62 Hs.

The web was now moving out of the web, as interactive work was taken into the physical world with real-time interaction. Unnumbered Sparks, a project by Aaron Koblin, allowed visitors to use the web on their smartphone to paint vibrant trails of light on a massive aerial sculpture.

Experimental work was also re-emerging from various individuals and small teams, who collectively helped propel HTML5, WebGL, and other tech fast-forward, similar to what happened in the late 1990s and early Noughties.

Pablo the Flamingo was a collaborative project that made good use of the latest tech (matter.js, three.js, and GSAP).

The careers of Louis Ansa, Florian Morel, and Corentin Bac were given a boost when they created the Omnisense Experience, which combined smartphone and desktop, and made people think about the different uses their social data could be put to.

It felt like a time when momentum was gathering but also of total freedom, something temporarily lost in the previous era of Apple apps and Facebook pages. The web was alive again.

"Google changed everything this year, with the DIY VR headset launch of Google Cardboard."

South Park Oculus Experience

Coca-Cola AHH

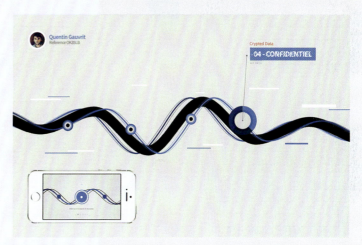

Omnisense Experience

Aktive Internetnutzer überschritten in diesem Jahr die Marke von drei Milliarden und die Zahl der Websites stieg um eine Milliarde. WebGL erreichte die Massen durch mobile Browser mit der Veröffentlichung von Apples iOS 8, während die virtuelle Realität damit begann, den Smartphones die Ehre zu geben und einen Einblick in WebVR über Oculus Rift gab. Die South Park Oculus Experience war eines der ersten Beispiele.

Ein breiterer Zugang zu VR schien jedoch noch in weiter Ferne zu liegen, bis die Einstiegs-Hardware von Google in diesem Jahr alles änderte, mit der Einführung von Google Cardboard bis zum DIY-VR-Headset.

Während VR und vor allem sein Hype langsam in Fahrt kamen, war es höchste Zeit, dass mobile Browser 3D unterstützen konnten. Das Timing hätte mit der Einführung der Retina HD Displays auf dem iPhone 6 und 6+ nicht perfekter sein können.

Die Coca-Cola AHH-Kampagne war verantwortlich für viele Mobil-Zuerst-Erfahrungen in diesem Projekt mit 61 unabhängigen URLs. Jede hatte ein Bite-sized-Game, das auf Teenager abzielte und wenn sie ihre Coke tranken, war es wie ein Schluck „AHH". Die URLs begannen mit ahh.com und fügten dann immer ein weiteres H hinzu, bis zu ahhhhhhhhhhh hhhhhhhhhhhhhhhhhhhhhhhhh hhhhhhhhhhhhhhhhhhhhhhhhh hh.com, mit 62 Hs wurde.

Das Web verlagerte sich nun aus dem Internet heraus, da interaktive Arbeit mit Echtzeit-Interaktion in der physischen Welt übernommen wurde. Unnumbered Sparks, ein Projekt von Aaron Koblin, ermöglichte es den Usern, das Netz auf ihrem Smartphone zu benutzen, um vibrierende Lichtspuren auf einer massiven Luftbildskulptur zu malen.

Experimentelle Arbeit tauchte auch durch verschiedenen Einzelpersonen und kleinen Teams wieder auf, die gemeinsam HTML5, WebGL und andere Technologien vorantrieben, ähnlich wie in den späten 1990er und frühen Nuller-Jahren.

Pablo the Flamingo war ein Gemeinschaftsprojekt, bei dem die neuesten Technologien (matter.js, three.js und GSAP) genutzt wurden.

Die Karrieren von Louis Ansa, Florian Morel und Corentin Bac kamen in Schwung, als sie die Omnisense Experience erschufen, die Smartphone und Desktop miteinander verband und die Leute dazu brachte, über die verschiedenen Nutzungsmöglichkeiten ihrer sozialen Daten nachzudenken.

Es fühlte sich an wie eine Zeit, in der sich das Momentum entwickelte, war aber auch die totale Freiheit, etwas, das in der vorherigen Ära der Apple-Apps und Facebook-Seiten vorübergehend verloren gegangen schien. Das Netz war wieder lebendig.

2014/

—

The Year Mobile Browsers Became as Powerful as Desktops

—

Pablo the Flamingo

"The web was alive again."

Le nombre d'internautes actifs franchit cette année la barre des trois milliards, celui de sites Web frôle le milliard. WebGL arrive au grand public via les navigateurs mobiles avec la sortie d'iOS 8 par Apple. Pour sa part, la réalité virtuelle pointe son nez sur les smartphones. L'un des premiers exemples, la South Park Oculus Experience, donne un aperçu de l'interface WebVR via le casque Oculus Rift.

L'horizon d'une RV plus accessible semble encore loin, jusqu'à ce que Google lance un dispositif d'entrée de gamme et crée ainsi la révolution : c'est la naissance du casque de RV à monter soi-même Google Cardboard.

La RV et le battage médiatique qui l'accompagne ne cessant de croître, il est grand temps que les navigateurs mobiles puissent prendre en charge le 3D. Le timing ne peut être plus parfait : les iPhone 6 et 6+ sortent et innovent avec un écran Retina HD.

La campagne AHH de Coca-Cola offre de nombreuses expériences « mobile first » avec les 61 URL indépendantes qui sont créées à cette occasion. Chacune présente un mini-jeu pensé pour les adolescents et transmet l'idée que boire un Coke, c'est prendre une gorgée de « AHH ». La première URL est ahh.com et en ajoutant un « h », on en obtient une autre, jusqu'à celle ahhhhhhhhhhhhhhhhhhhhhh hhhhhhhhhhhhhhhhhhhhhhhh hhhhhhhhhhhh.com qui en compte 62.

Le Web sort désormais du Web car les créations interactives se retrouvent dans le monde physique avec des interactions en temps réel. Conçu par Aaron Koblin, le projet Unnumbered Sparks permet aux visiteurs de peindre via leur smartphone des traînées lumineuses sur une énorme sculpture aérienne.

Des particuliers et de petites équipes se livrent aussi à des créations expérimentales, ce qui propulse HTML5, WebGL et d'autres technologies, un peu comme le phénomène ayant eu lieu à la fin des années 90 et au début des années 2000.

Pablo the Flamingo est un projet collaboratif qui sait tirer profit des dernières technologies disponibles (matter.js, three.js et GSAP).

La carrière de Louis Ansa, Florian Morel et Corentin Bac fait un véritable bond en avant quand ils lancent Omnisense Experience pour smartphones et ordinateurs. Elle fait réfléchir le public sur les diverses utilisations possibles de leurs données sociales.

Les choses semblent prendre de la vitesse, et une liberté absolue s'apprécie après avoir été perdue à l'ère des applications Apple et des pages Facebook. Le Web est de nouveau vivant.

Ø8 Facts of the year

Number of internet users:
3.08 billion, 42.3% of
the world population

Number of websites:
969 million

World news:
Ebola epidemic

Website with most traffic:
Google.com

Tech hardware:
iPhone 6+ launches

Tech software:
Apple Pay is introduced

Other tech:
Facebook buys WhatsApp
for $19 billion

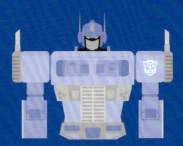

Highest-grossing film:
Transformers: Age of
Extinction

—

Sortie en mer
(A Trip to Sea)

—

The scrolling website that could save lives

WHAT A BEAUTIFUL DAY!

You're on a luxury yacht far out at sea when suddenly the boom swings round and knocks you overboard. As your life flashes before your eyes, you have to save yourself from drowning. As your friend calls you from the boat, you use your mouse scrollwheel to try and stay alive but have to keep scrolling or you'll drown. This promotional site for Guy Cotten gave a real sense of the panic experienced by people who have fallen overboard without a life jacket. The project itself showed how more than 14.5 million participants had already "drowned" on the website and encouraged people to think about safety, especially a life jacket, when out at sea.

"The sole objective we all kept in mind was to make the experience as realistic as possible. First-person POV was obvious right from the start. But then designing the right interface was more tricky. It had to convey the urge of scrolling to survive, without having to actually look at it. The result was tens of thousands of tweets and comments from people from all over the world saying they never thought they could experience the feeling of actually drowning from behind their computer screen!"

Romain Altain Aldea
Grouek

Du bist auf einer Luxusyacht weit draußen auf See, als plötzlich der Ausleger herumschwingt und dich über Bord wirft. Während dein Leben vor deinen Augen aufblitzt, musst du dich selbst vor dem Ertrinken retten. Wenn dein Freund dich vom Boot aus ruft, benutzt du dein Mausrad, um zu versuchen, am Leben zu bleiben, musst aber weiter scrollen oder du wirst ertrinken. Diese Werbeseite für Guy Cotten gab einen echten Eindruck von der Panik von Menschen, die ohne Schwimmweste über Bord gingen. Das Projekt selbst zeigte, dass mehr als 14,5 Millionen Teilnehmer bereits auf der Website „ertrunken" waren und ermutigte die Menschen, auf See über Sicherheit, insbesondere über eine Schwimmweste, nachzudenken.

Vous naviguez sur un voilier de luxe en haute mer quand soudain la bôme pivote, vous heurte et vous fait tomber par-dessus bord. Votre vie défile devant vos yeux et vous devez éviter la noyade. Alors que votre ami vous appelle depuis le bateau, vous devez faire rouler la molette pour rester en vie et ne pas couler. Ce site promotionnel pour Guy Cotten fait vraiment ressentir la panique qu'éprouvent les personnes tombées à la mer sans gilet de sauvetage. Le projet indique que 14,5 millions de participants se sont déjà «noyés» sur le site Web et encourage les visiteurs à penser à leur sécurité en mer, notamment à porter un gilet de sauvetage.

2014/

—

Orange #Futureself

—

Traveling 20 years into
the future to talk to
your future self

Using a combination of 3D animation, face detection via webcam, and intelligent API integrations, this site projected visitors into the future where they could ask about the news, their pets, and even their future love life. Amongst the latest technology involved were CLM Tracker for face-mapping, WebGL and three.js for rendering heads and faces, and the creation of hundreds of responses to simulate real conversations in various languages using an Xbox Kinect and a microphone. It was a huge viral success almost overnight.

"Before all the fancy Facebook and Snapchat face masks there was Futureself. While aging a person's face had been done before, it was always done as a simple static image. Our challenge was to up the ante by creating a real-time character in WebGL that not only looked like an aged version of yourself but one that could talk and that you could actually talk back to. (Take that Siri.) We positioned the whole experience as a 'video call to the future', effectively imagining what a video conference app might look like in 2034."

Adrian Belina
Jam3

Mit einer Kombination aus 3D-Animation, Gesichtserkennung per Webcam und intelligenten API-Integrationen schickte diese Seite ihre Besucher in die Zukunft, wo sie nach Neuigkeiten, ihren Haustieren und sogar ihrem zukünftigen Liebesleben fragen konnten. Zu den neuesten Technologien gehörten CLM Tracker für Face-Mapping, WebGL und three.js für das Rendern von Köpfen und Flächen und die Erstellung von Hunderten von Antworten, um echte Unterhaltungen in verschiedenen Sprachen mit einer Xbox Kinect und einem Mikrofon zu simulieren. Es wurde fast über Nacht ein riesiger Erfolg.

En combinant des animations en 3D, la détection faciale via la webcam et des intégrations d'API intelligentes, ce site transporte les visiteurs dans le futur, où ils peuvent poser des questions sur l'actualité, leur animal domestique ou leur vie sentimentale à venir. Entre autres technologies récentes, il repose sur CLM Tracker pour le mapping facial, WebGL et three.js pour le rendu des visages, ainsi que la création de centaines de réponses pour simuler de véritables conversations dans différentes langues à l'aide de Xbox Kinect et d'un microphone. Le succès est gigantesque, viral et quasiment du jour au lendemain.

Honda:
The Other Side

—

The website with minimal functionality, just the R button

This project was created to showcase the two sides of the Honda Civic Type R, a family vehicle with a special, high-performance 'Type R' mode. Through an interactive film with two storylines (a suburban school-run and an art heist), viewers could switch between plots immediately by hitting the R button on their keyboards. Despite this extreme simplicity, it was seen as a seriously clever way of promoting Honda's race-mode button.

"The Civic Type R was the Civic's alter ego. Built into the Type R was the 'R' button which set the car to 'race mode'. Rather than tell people how exhilarating it was to drive the Type R, we wanted them to feel it. We created a dual-narrative film on YouTube, where users could switch between two stories by pressing 'R'. The Civic story showed a father picking up his kids from school, while the Type R story showed the same man driving in a high-speed heist. Both stories were shot as a 'moving match cut', so narratives lined up seamlessly."

Scott Dungate
Wieden+Kennedy

Dieses Projekt wurde entwickelt, um die beiden Seiten des Honda Civic Type R zu präsentieren, ein Familienfahrzeug mit einem speziellen, leistungsstarken „Typ R"-Modus. Durch einen interaktiven Film mit zwei Handlungssträngen (Fahrt zu einer Schule und ein Kunstraub) konnten die Zuschauer sofort zwischen den Plots wechseln, indem sie die R-Taste ihrer Tastatur drückten. Trotz dieser extremen Einfachheit wurde es als eine sehr clevere Art empfunden, den Rennmodus-Button von Honda zu bewerben.

Ce projet est conçu pour présenter les deux facettes de la Honda Civic Type R, un véhicule familial doté d'un mode «Type R» haute performance. Dans un film interactif avec deux scénarios (le trajet jusqu'à une école de banlieue et un braquage), les spectateurs peuvent passer d'une intrigue à l'autre en appuyant sur la touche R du clavier. Bien que d'une très grande simplicité, c'est une façon astucieuse de promouvoir le bouton du mode course de cette Honda.

World Under Water

—

A website that demonstrated the catastrophic effects of climate change

On entering this site users could input their own location or click on the name of a city, for example, New York, which then transported them to a scene showing the location submerged as if in the finale of *Planet of the Apes*. The use of WebGL and Google Street View enabled the site's creators to show the consequences of climate change and to raise awareness concerning this vital issue, while the greatest impact was achieved by making the location specific to each user.

"We wanted to make the threat of climate change more personal for people around the world. From an advertising perspective, there was a shift happening from focusing on what brands say, to what they do. So we brought together a tiny creative and tech team and found a way to use WebGL to drive the climate change message home on a more direct level. World Under Water didn't just talk about climate change, it delivered the threat of climate change directly to the public's doorstep – quite literally."

Melanie Clancy
BBDO Proximity; Zeno Group

Beim Betreten dieser Seite konnten die Benutzer ihren eigenen Standort eingeben oder auf den Namen einer Stadt klicken, zum Beispiel New York, was sie dann zu einer Szene transportierte, wo der Ort wie im Finale von *Planet der Affen* aussah. Der Gebrauch von WebGL und Google Street View ermöglichte den Erstellern der Website, die Folgen des Klimawandels aufzuzeigen und das Bewusstsein für dieses wichtige Thema zu schärfen, wobei jeweils die größte Wirkung erzielt wurde, da der Standort für jeden Nutzer spezifisch gestaltet wurde.

En entrant dans ce site, les visiteurs peuvent indiquer leur emplacement ou cliquer sur le nom d'une ville comme New York pour être transporté à cet endroit, dont le décor rappelle la scène finale de *La Planète des singes*. En recourant à WebGL et à Google Street View, les concepteurs montrent les conséquences du changement climatique et sensibilisent à cette question vitale. Le résultat est très frappant car le lieu est spécifique à chaque visiteur.

2014/
—

Croacia Audio
—

The website with no website,
only sound

Over the years many different methods for navigating websites had been developed, but Croacia Audio presented something completely new with a website that could be navigated by the power of voice alone.

Taking the idea to its limit, the site featured no images, videos, or text, only sound responses, and was a clever way to gain a lot of attention for an audio production company.

A SOUND-ONLY WEBSITE

ONLY VOICE

"When we started thinking about the website for Croacia, a sound production company, we figured it would be a cool concept to avoid any visual interface and only use sound. With HTML5 audio and mic input, we managed to build a completely blank website where the content was only sound and the navigation was only through voice commands. Now these features are becoming more common than ever with smart speakers."

Raphael Franzini
Loducca; the community

Im Laufe der Jahre wurden viele verschiedene Methoden zum Navigieren auf Websites entwickelt aber Croacia Audio präsentierte etwas völlig Neues mit einer Website, die allein durch die Kraft der Stimme navigiert werden konnte. Um die Idee an ihre Grenzen zu bringen, wurden auf der Website keine Bilder, Videos oder Texte gezeigt, sondern nur akustische Antworten und somit war sie eine clevere Möglichkeit, eine Menge Aufmerksamkeit für eine Audioproduktionsfirma zu erregen.

Avec les années, diverses méthodes de navigation ont vu le jour mais Croacia Audio innove complètement avec un site Web pouvant être exploré exclusivement avec la voix. Le concept est poussé à la limite, et le résultat n'inclut aucune image ou vidéo, aucun texte non plus, seulement des réponses sonores. Une façon habile de promouvoir une société de production audiovisuelle.

Winterlands

—

One of the first mobile browser experiences to push 3D with WebGL

Winterlands enabled users to send a holiday greeting card via its interactive 3D and 360° mobile browser experience. By utilizing the latest mobile browser capabilities with WebGL, AKQA created 14 different interactive snow-scapes, representing each of their global offices (plus one generic one). As users moved their phone around they could explore each of these scenes and, as in a real snow globe, shaking the phone would make more snow fall. Within one month of launch 139 countries had been reached, with a fifth of all users coming from China.

"Winterlands was born out of the frustration caused by the limitations of mobile browser interfaces at the time. With the rise of responsive and adaptive design, the mobile browser interface was getting more and more confined and uniform. With WebGL, an opportunity arose to break that cycle and we set out to push the capabilities of 3D in the mobile browser to the limit. By combining art and technology, we wanted to build a rich virtual environment that the user could explore in full 360 and interact with, without having to download additional software."

Peter Lund
AKQA

Winterlands ermöglichte Usern, eine Ferien-Grußkarte über ihre interaktive 3D und 360° mobile Browser Experience zu senden. Durch die Nutzung der neuesten mobilen Browserfunktionen mit WebGL, erstellte AKQA 14 unterschiedliche interaktive Schneelandschaften, wodurch sie jedes ihrer globalen Büros zeigten (plus ein generisches).

Während die Nutzer ihr Telefon bewegten, konnten sie jede dieser Szenen erkunden. Wie in einer echten Schneekugel, bewirkte das Schütteln des Telefons, das mehr Schnee fiel. Innerhalb eines Monats nach der Einführung wurden 139 Länder erreicht, wobei ein Fünftel aller Nutzer aus China kam.

Winterlands permet aux internautes d'envoyer une carte de vœux par le biais d'une expérience interactive dans un navigateur mobile en 3D et à 360°. En s'appuyant sur les dernières fonctions des navigateurs mobiles avec WebGL, AKQA crée 14 paysages enneigés interactifs, un pour chacun de ses bureaux répartis dans le monde, et un autre générique. En bougeant leur téléphone, les visiteurs peuvent explorer toutes les scènes et s'ils le secouent, tel une boule à neige, des flocons tombent. Moins d'un mois après le lancement, des cartes sont envoyées dans 139 pays, avec un cinquième des utilisateurs provenant de Chine.

—

Build with Chrome

—

One of the largest Lego
community builds of all time

This site had the mission of encouraging people to build whatever they wanted with Lego and wherever they wanted to do it. The evolving project allowed the site's visitors to explore these constructions by clicking on the ones highlighted on the world map in Google Maps, while users could also try the build mode and create their own Lego masterpiece. For the more proficient builders, the academy mode offered a series of challenges of increasing difficulty.

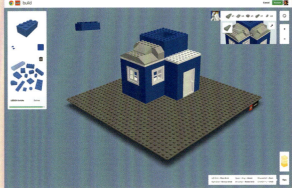

"Build with Chrome was incredibly satisfying to work on since the target group of the project was enormously huge – every kid loves to play with Lego, and every parent can relate to Lego in a nostalgic way from back when they were kids themselves. Since we knew lots of young kids would take part in the experience we had to keep it minimal, easy to use, and thereby strip down the variety of different bricks but still make it fun to play with based on the Lego brick limitation."

Jonas Eriksson
North Kingdom

Diese Seite hatte sich die Aufgabe gestellt, die Leute zu ermutigen, mit Lego zu bauen, wo immer sie es wollten, was immer sie wünschten. Das sich entwickelnde Projekt ermöglichte es den Besuchern der Website, diese Konstruktionen zu erkunden, indem sie auf jene klickten, die auf der Weltkarte in Google Maps hervorgehoben wurden, während die User auch den Bau-Modus ausprobieren und ihr eigenes Meisterwerk schaffen konnten. Für die geübteren Baumeister bot der Akademie-Modus eine Reihe von Herausforderungen mit zunehmenden Schwierigkeitsgraden.

Ce site avait pour objectif de motiver les internautes à construire ce qu'ils voulaient avec des pièces de Lego, où qu'ils se trouvent. Le projet évolutif permet d'explorer les constructions réalisées en cliquant sur celles activées dans Google Maps. Les visiteurs peuvent aussi tester les constructions et créer leur propre chef-d'œuvre en Lego. Pour les plus habiles, le mode «academy» offre une série de défis de difficulté croissante.

SWIP3

—

The first game built for Android Wear

Created by Unit9 Games, this was the first game ever built specifically for Android Wear, and featured a 5x5 grid puzzle where users had to match the blocks according to color in combinations of three or more. The design was clean and simple, with minimal controls, and only required the user to swipe in any direction, which was a great way of using a wearable device. SWIP3 was automatically installed on Android Wear devices, once they were connected to an Android phone.

"SWIP3 was designed around a dynamic gesture-based interaction that we felt would work well for a watch. A simple directional swipe moves colored squares across the screen to create combinations of Connect 5 or 2048 game-like scoring mechanics. For the style, we took direction from the Google material design approach, where motion gives meaning to the action, so that the first Android Wear would feel seamless with the operating system interface and so that you could learn to play without any instruction."

Yates Buckley
Unit9

Dieses Spiel wurde von Unit9 Games erstellt und war das erste Spiel, das speziell für Android Wear entwickelt wurde. Es wurde ein 5x5-Raster-Puzzle gezeigt, bei dem die User die Blöcke gemäß der Farbe in Dreierkombi-nationen oder mehr kombinieren und sie dabei übereinstimmen mussten. Das Design war sauber und einfach mit minimalen Steuerungen. Der User musste nur in alle Richtungen wischen, wodurch ganz einfach ein tragbares Gerät verwendet werden konnte. SWIP3 wurde automatisch auf Android Wear-Geräten installiert, sobald sie mit einem Android-Telefon verbunden waren.

Développé par Unit9 Games, il s'agit du premier jeu spéciale-ment conçu pour Android Wear. Dans un puzzle de 5x5, les joueurs doivent associer les blocs par couleur pour créer des combinaisons de trois ou plus. La conception est simple et épurée, les commandes minimales, et le seul geste nécessaire est un glissement dans n'importe quelle direction, ce qui est parfait pour les dispo-sitifs prêts-à-porter. SWIP3 s'installe automatiquement sur les dispositifs Android Wear connec-tés à un téléphone Android.

Five Minutes

—

The ultimate zombie countdown

This live-action experience blurred the line between a zombie game and an interactive film and gave users only five minutes to stop the main character from turning into a zombie by keeping him focused on his memories. The project had me on the edge of my seat, not wanting to look at times but pumped on adrenaline and knowing I had to focus and save lives. It was a fantastic project, with incredible production and interactivity that immersed users right into the story.

"Coming from a classical film background, our approach on Five Minutes was to deliver an interactive movie experience that wasn't a gimmick but rather more an additional emotional layer to the story. The idea was to create a hassle-free interactive experience that immersed the audience right from the beginning. To reach a broad audience and establish the emotional connection with the viewers, we tried to keep it as simple as possible. The whole process taught us an important lesson — if you can dream it, you can build it."

Maximilian Niemann
Director

Dieses Live-Action-Erlebnis verwischte die Grenze zwischen einem Zombie-Spiel und einem interaktiven Film und gab den Usern nur fünf Minuten Zeit, um den Hauptcharakter davon abzuhalten, sich in einen Zombie zu verwandeln, indem er sich auf seine Erinnerungen konzentrierte. Das Projekt hatte mich so ergriffen, dass ich auf der Stuhlkante saß. Ich wollte nicht mal mehr auf die Zeit schauen, sondern war vollgepumpt mit Adrenalin, da ich wusste, dass ich mich konzentrieren und Leben retten musste. Es war ein fantastisches Projekt mit einer unglaublichen Produktion und Interaktivität, das die Nutzer direkt in die Geschichte miteinbezog.

Cette expérience de fiction brouille la frontière entre jeu de zombies et film interactif. Les joueurs ont seulement cinq minutes pour empêcher le protagoniste de se transformer en zombie en le faisant se concentrer sur ses souvenirs. Ce projet m'a tenu rivé à ma chaise : je ne voulais parfois pas regarder, mais j'avais des poussées d'adrénaline et savais que je devais sauver des vies. Une réalisation remarquable, une production de qualité et une interactivité qui plongent les utilisateurs au cœur de l'histoire.

Chrome Experiments
for Cardboard

—

The first VR experience
designed for the mobile web

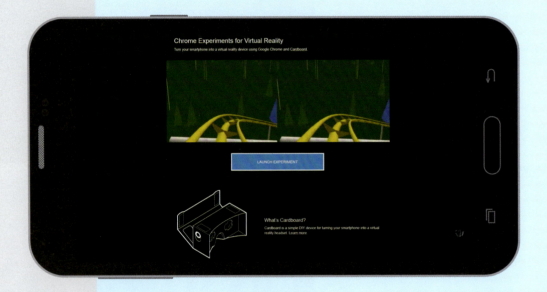

In June, Google announced Cardboard, a no-frills DIY enclosure that transformed a mobile phone into a basic VR headset. To accompany the launch a gallery of virtual reality Chrome Experiments was released and gave a new generation the opportunity to experience VR without the need for expensive new hardware. This ongoing gallery was open to submissions from anyone who had created a VR experiment, with the first exhibit being a VR experience created by the Google Data Arts Team themselves.

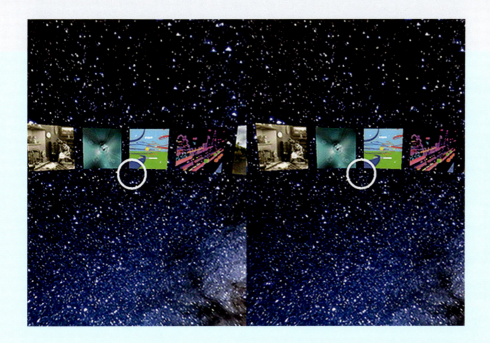

"Chrome Experiments for Cardboard showed that the
VR revolution won't be limited to downloaded content
but will be accessible to anyone with a smartphone
and a web browser. The site was the world's first VR
experience built for the mobile web. The project
featured seven experiments – games, 360° films, and
more – that all ran on Chrome for Android and iOS
and each explored unique interaction methods in VR.
We also released open-source code to enable anyone
to build upon our learnings and create their own
browser-based, interactive VR content."

Sabah Kosoy
Google

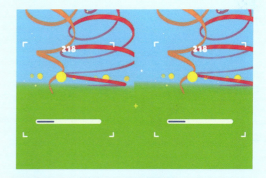

Im Juni kündigte Google Card-board ein No-Frills-DIY-Gehäuse, das ein Mobiltelefon in ein einfaches VR-Headset verwan-delte, an. Zum Start wurde eine Galerie von Virtual Reality Chrome Experimenten veröffent-licht und gab einer neuen Generation die Möglichkeit, VR ohne teure neue Hardware zu erleben. Diese fortlaufende Galerie war offen für Einsendun-gen von jedem, der ein VR-Expe-riment erstellt hatte. Das erste Exponat war eine VR-Erfahrung, die vom Google Data Arts Team selbst erstellt wurde.

En juin, Google annonce Cardboard, un boîtier sans fioritures à monter soi-même et qui transforme un téléphone portable en casque de RV. Pour accompagner ce lancement, une galerie de Chrome Experiments de réalité virtuelle est publiée et offre à la génération montante la chance de tester la RV sans investir dans un appareil onéreux. Cette galerie permanente est ouverte aux propositions de quiconque ayant créé une expérience de RV, et la première exposition est une création de la propre Google Data Arts Team.

NOTABLE WEBSITE LAUNCH
Ello

GOOGLE FACTS

The first 3D doodle appears, for Rubik's Cube

Google acquires Nest

The Made with Code initiative launches to inspire girls to code

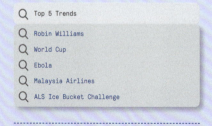

Top 5 Trends

Google Cardboard is announced

Inbox by Gmail launches by invitation only

MOBILE EVOLUTION
iPhone 6 and 6+

Retina HD displays are launched
with the new super-thin iPhone 6
(4.7 in) and 6+ (5.5 in)

INTERNET COMMUNITY
ALS Ice Bucket Challenge

In support of motor neuron disease,
this global phenomenon encouraged
people to film themselves as they
dumped a bucket of iced water over
their heads and share the videos
on social media.

2015/

The Year the Power of the Individual Led the Way

2015/

—

The Year the Power of the Individual Led the Way

—

Fashion Revolution: €2 T-shirts

Approaching half the world's population was now actively using the internet, but even though this figure was continuing to rise it was a rare year when the number of websites actually fell. This was a clear indicator that brands were turning away from traditional websites and promotional microsites and were throwing their budgets into social media.

Websites were far from dead though, and mobile browsers were becoming more powerful with the likes of Du Haihang showing this via an agency website created using WebGL.

Responsive websites that worked well across all devices were still the main focus for many agencies, while more projects in real-world settings were appearing, such as Fashion Revolution: €2 T-shirts.

Worthy causes were also prominent, such as The One Who Will End Cancer, which took users' uploaded faces and assembled them into a composite image that evolved in real time, to represent the support base for cancer research.

Superstars such as David Guetta were rediscovering their interest in web experiences, with his Dangerous project ("The world's first double-screen music video") enabling users to interact with his music video by using their phone.

Five years on from Steve Jobs's "Thoughts on Flash", experiences were finally appearing on the web that were made without any need for browser plug-ins, giving the feeling that things had now moved along.

The One Who Will End Cancer

David Guetta: Dangerous

"It was a rare year when the number of websites actually fell."

Annähernd die Hälfte der Weltbevölkerung nutzte nun aktiv das Internet, doch obwohl diese Zahl weiter anstieg, war es ein seltenes Jahr, in dem die Anzahl der Websites tatsächlich sank. Dies war ein deutlicher Hinweis darauf, dass sich Marken von traditionellen Websites und Werbe-Microsites abwandten und ihre Budgets in soziale Medien investierten.

Websites waren jedoch noch lange nicht tot und die mobilen Browser wurden immer leistungsfähiger. Du Haihang zeigte dies beispielsweise mit einer Agentur-Website, die mit WebGL erstellt wurde.

Responsive Websites, die auf allen Geräten gut funktionierten, standen für viele Agenturen immer noch im Mittelpunkt, während immer mehr Projekte in realen Umgebungen auftauchten, wie zum Beispiel Fashion Revolution: 2€ T-Shirts.

Caritative Anlässe waren ebenfalls prominent, wie zum Beispiel The One Who Will End Cancer. Die hochgeladenen Gesichter der Nutzer wurden zu einem Bild zusammengesetzt, das sich in Echtzeit entwickelte, um die Grundlage für die Krebsforschung zu zeigen.

Superstars wie zum Beispiel David Guetta mit seinem Dangerous-Projekt („Das erste Doppelbildschirm-Musikvideo der Welt") konnten den Usern ihr Interesse an Web-Erlebnissen wieder nahebringen.

Fünf Jahre nach Steve Jobs „Thoughts on Flash" (Gedanken über Flash) wurden wieder im Web Erfahrungen gemacht, die ohne die Notwendigkeit von Browser-Plug-ins entstanden und das Gefühl vermittelten, dass sich die Dinge nun bewegen würden.

2015/

—

The Year the Power of the Individual Led the Way

—

"Brands were turning away from traditional websites and throwing their budgets into social media."

Du Haihang

Près de la moitié de la population mondiale utilise à présent activement Internet. Pourtant, même si ce chiffre reste à la hausse, le nombre de sites Web diminue cette année, un clair indice que les marques tournent le dos aux sites traditionnels et aux micro-sites promotionnels pour investir dans les réseaux sociaux.

Les sites Web sont cependant loin d'être enterrés, et les navigateurs mobiles gagnent en puissance, comme le prouve Du Haihang avec le site d'une agence conçu à l'aide de WebGL.

La plupart des agences continuent de privilégier les sites Web adaptables qui fonctionnent sur tous les types de dispositifs. Par ailleurs, de plus en plus de projets se transportent dans le monde réel, comme le mouvement Fashion Revolution qui met en vente des T-shirts à 2 €.

Les grandes causes occupent aussi une place de choix. Dans le site The One Who Will End Cancer, des portraits d'internautes sont assemblés afin de composer un visage qui change en temps réel et illustre la base soutenant la recherche sur le cancer.

Certaines superstars ont un regain d'intérêt pour les expériences Web, comme David Guetta, dont le projet Dangerous («Le premier clip vidéo sur deux écrans») permet aux visiteurs d'interagir avec les images du clip à l'aide de leur téléphone.

Cinq ans après les «Thoughts on Flash» de Steve Jobs, le Web voit enfin apparaître des expériences créées sans recourir à des plug-ins, ce qui donne le sentiment que les choses progressent.

08 Facts of
the year

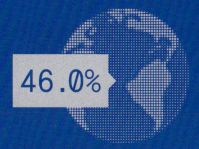

46.0%

Number of internet users:
3.4 billion, 46.0% of
the world population

863
million

Number of websites:
863 million

World News
1953–2015

World news:
Queen Elizabeth II becomes
the longest-reigning
British monarch

Google

Website with most traffic:
Google.com

Tech hardware:
Apple Watch launches

Tech software:
Windows 10 launches

BLIZZARD
ENTERTAINMENT

King

Other tech:
Blizzard Entertainment
acquires Candy Crush maker
King for $5.9 billion

Highest-grossing film:
Star Wars: The Force
Awakens

Inside Abbey Road

—

An invitation to visit the world-famous recording studios

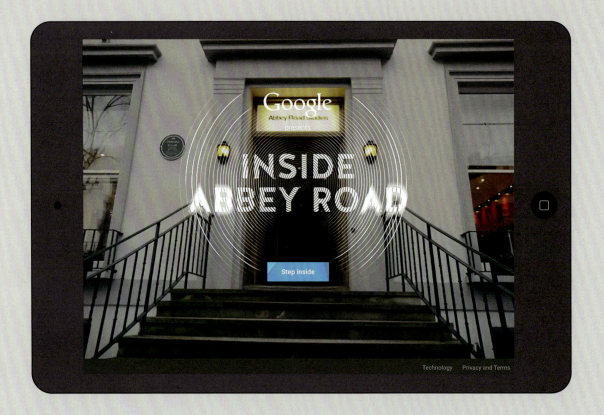

Google joined up with Abbey Road Studios to provide the first online opportunity for fans to go through the famous gates and follow in the footsteps of music legends. Visitors to the site could explore every part of the three recording studios and sample music spanning the decades. They could also learn more about famous stories that unfolded here, supported by images and videos, and even play with interactive versions of the impressive equipment.

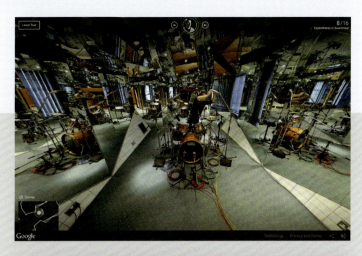

"Inside Abbey Road took 10 months to create. We wanted to make an enhanced Street View experience, so we captured the studios with over 150 panoramas, and 3D-scanned each room. We incorporated archival video positioned in the exact spot they were originally filmed, 80 years of anecdotes and history, playable versions of Abbey Road equipment, three audio tours, and over three hours of content. From the sound design all the way down to seeing the bits of tape on the floor, it was important that people really felt like they were inside the studios."

Tom Seymour and Graeme Hall
Google Creative Lab

Google schloss sich mit den Abbey Road Studios zusammen, um Fans erstmals die Möglichkeit zu bieten, durch die berühmten Tore zu gehen und in die Fuß-stapfen von Musiklegenden zu treten. Die Besucher der Seite konnten jeden Teil der drei Aufnahmestudios erkunden und Musik aus allen Jahrzehnten sampeln. Sie konnten auch mehr über die berühmten Geschichten erfahren, die sich hier abgespielt hatten, unterstützt von Bildern und Videos und sogar mit den interaktiven Versionen der beein-druckenden Ausrüstung spielen.

En s'associant à Abbey Road Studios, Google permet aux fans de franchir en ligne ses célèbres portes et de marcher sur les traces des légendes de la musique. Les visiteurs du site peuvent explorer tous les recoins des trois studios d'enregistre-ment et écouter des extraits de morceaux sur plusieurs décen-nies. Ils peuvent également découvrir des anecdotes qui s'affichent à l'écran, assorties de photos et de vidéos, ainsi que jouer avec des versions interac-tives de l'imposant équipement.

—

In Pieces

—

The epitome of stunning web design with an emotive subject

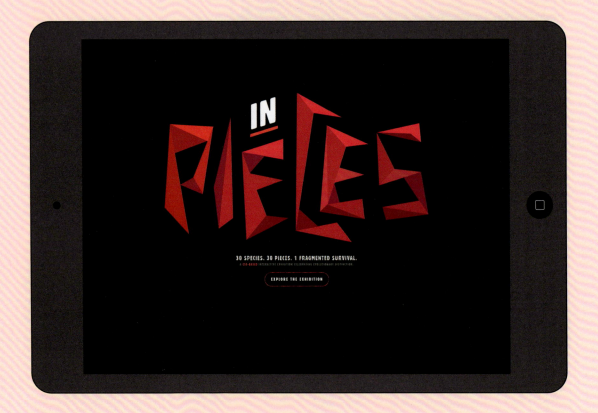

This CSS-based interactive exhibition, a project by Bryan James, celebrated evolutionary distinction by focusing on 30 endangered species from around the world. Each of these examples was constructed from 30 individual pieces, which animated beautifully to create a stunning visualization. The website also had an emotive atmosphere, heightened by the haunting background music, while each species was presented with its own detailed information, statistics, and video.

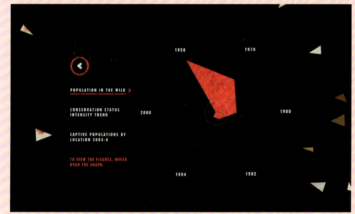

✝ HELMETED HORNBILL ◐◐

✝ GOLDEN POISON FROG ◐◐

"In Pieces was a personal project which started as
fooling about with a new CSS technology and ended
as a five-month-long investment to showcase the
plight of 30 incredible but sadly endangered species.
I saw a huge opportunity in mixing a new line of
CSS which worked beautifully in the browser when
using transitions – an often-used art directional
style, animals using shapes – and a story of species
endangerment through this art direction using a
language simile anchor: In Pieces."

Bryan James
bryanjamesdesign.co.uk

Diese CSS-basierte interaktive
Ausstellung, ein Projekt von
Bryan James, zeigt die evolutio-
nären Unterschiede durch
Konzentration auf 30 gefährdete
Arten aus der ganzen Welt. Jedes
dieser Beispiele wurde aus 30
Einzelteilen konstruiert, die
wunderschön animiert wurden,

um eine atemberaubende
Visualisierung zu erstellen.
Die Website hatte auch eine
emotionale Atmosphäre, ver-
stärkt durch die eindringliche
Hintergrundmusik, während jede
Spezies mit eigenen detaillierten
Informationen, Statistiken und
Videos präsentiert wurde.

Réalisée par Bryan James, cette
exposition interactive basée sur
des CSS illustre les différences
d'évolution de 30 espèces
menacées du monde entier.
Chaque exemple a été fabriqué à
partir de 30 éléments individuels
et s'anime avec grâce pour
donner un rendu exceptionnel.

Le site Web crée par ailleurs une
ambiance douce grâce à la
musique de fond, et il apporte
sur les espèces des informations
détaillées, des statistiques et
des vidéos.

2015/
—

Because Recollection

—

A global superstar website

In celebration of its 10th anniversary the record label Because Music created a website showcasing its history, with 10 years of video and 10 years of "bringing the public massively talented and successful new artists". Starting from the idea that music was for playing with as well as listening to, an easy-to-explore experience was developed where users just had to press and hold the spacebar and release it to enter the next section. Each new section was an experimental interactive art piece dedicated to one of Because Music's artists, and while the spacebar was held to load each new piece, flashback video showed glimpses of past glories.

"The Because label's brief was very simple:
'We celebrate our 10th anniversary this year,
so we want to do the coolest website ever
made!' One question kept being asked during
the creation process: what if, instead of just
listening to music, you could play with it? I
think Because Recollection was our masterpiece.
It combined 10 years of expertise, from Flash
to next-generation HTML. Entertainment is
the key to keeping interactive websites alive.
With the success of Because Recollection, one
thing was sure: desktop was not dead."

Olivier Bienaimé
84.Paris

Zum 10-jährigen Jubiläum
präsentiert Since Music seine
Geschichte auf einer Website:
10 Jahre in Videos, 10 Jahre, um
„die Öffentlichkeit mit neuen
Künstlern von immensem Talent
bekannt zu machen". Ausgehend
von der Idee, dass Musik sowohl
zum Spielen als auch zum Zuhören
gedacht war, wurde ein leicht
zu erforschendes Erlebnis
entwickelt, bei dem die Benutzer
einfach die Leertaste gedrückt

halten und loslassen mussten,
um in den nächsten Abschnitt zu
gelangen. Jeder neue Abschnitt
war ein experimentelles, interaktives Kunstwerk, das einem
Künstler von Because Music
gewidmet war und während die
Leertaste gehalten wurde, um
das neue Stück zu laden, zeigte
ein Flashback-Video Einblicke
in vergangene Herrlichkeiten.

Pour fêter son 10e anniversaire, la
maison de disques Because Music
présente son histoire dans un
site Web : 10 ans en vidéos, 10 ans
à « faire découvrir au public de
nouveaux artistes d'un immense
talent ». Cette expérience part
de l'idée que la musique se joue
tout autant qu'elle s'écoute.
L'exploration est simple grâce à
la barre d'espace : si celle-ci est
maintenue enfoncée, une vidéo
flashback de succès passés

défile et une création se charge ;
si elle est relâchée, la section
suivante s'ouvre et montre une
œuvre interactive expérimentale
consacrée à l'un des artistes de
Because Music.

Old Spice: Muscle Surprise

—

The last Flash site
ever made?!

There was still a trickle of Flash websites being made and this project for Old Spice was later claimed, tongue in cheek, to be the last Flash site ever made. It was certainly one of the last Flash websites ever awarded on FWA, and was a fitting example, full of the crucial ingredients that had made Flash so important for web design and development for many years: the experience was seamless, loaded with personality, and unforgettable. Users were invited to touch Terry Crews's muscles and discover the secrets behind his powerful body in what was called an "explosive interactive experience that continues to surprise".

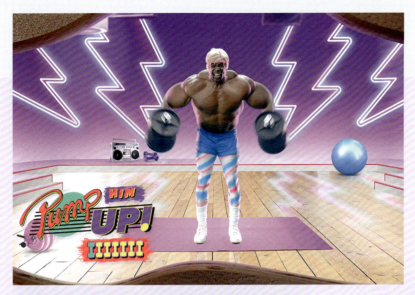

"Muscle Surprise was one of those projects that had all our departments coming together, from film, animation, and post-production, to games, design, and music composition. From the shoot with the endlessly energetic Terry Crews to delivery it was an insane cocktail of hard work, a ridiculous six weeks' production time and the most fun I've ever had on a project. And all of that coming together in the last Flash project we (or anyone else really) ever did. It was our first collaboration with the wonderful Wieden+Kennedy Portland, but turned out to be the first in many weird and wonderful campaigns together."

Tom Rijpert
MediaMonks

Es gab immer noch ein paar Flash-Websites und später wurde ironisch behauptet, dass dieses Projekt für Old Spice die letzte Flash-Seite gewesen sei, die jemals gemacht wurde. Es war sicherlich eine der letzten Flash-Websites, die einen FWA bekamen und ist ein passendes Beispiel dafür, dass sie voller wichtiger Zutaten war, die Flash seit vielen Jahren für Webdesign und -entwicklung so wichtig gemacht haben: Die Erfahrung war nahtlos, voller Persönlichkeit und unvergesslich. Die User wurden dazu eingeladen, Terry Crews Muskeln zu berühren und die Geheimnisse hinter seinem kraftvollen Körper in einer „explosiven interaktiven Erfahrung zu entdecken, die immer wieder überrascht".

Une poignée de sites Web sont encore codés en Flash, dont ce projet pour Old Spice, plus tard déclaré être, pour plaisanter, le dernier site conçu en Flash. C'est en tous cas certainement l'un des derniers du genre récompensé d'un FWA, sachant qu'il inclut tous les ingrédients clés qui ont fait la gloire de Flash pendant bien des années en matière de conception et de développement Web : l'expérience est fluide, pleine de personnalité et inoubliable. Les visiteurs peuvent toucher les muscles de Terry Crews et découvrir les secrets de son corps sculpté grâce à une « expérience interactive explosive qui ne cesse de surprendre ».

2015/

—

Way to Go

—

An early example of a
first-person 360°
interactive experience

An interactive walk in the woods, which was
a mixture of hand-made animation and 360°
video, Way to Go could be enjoyed through the
web browser or the VR version via Oculus Rift.
The project was created by Vincent Morisset,
Caroline Robert, Édouard Lanctôt-Benoit, and
the AATOAA studio, and was for "human beings
between 5 and 105 years old". Site visitors
could follow the defined track, for as long as
they desired, and move and interact with their
surroundings just like they would be able to in
the real world.

"Using hand-made animation, music, 360° capture technology, and WebGL sorcery, Way to Go imagines a dream-world of journeys. Walk, run, fly; crouch in the grass and remember what's hidden all around. Are you alone? Are you not alone? Are you dreaming or awake? Can you ever reach the mountains? Can you see what's here before you? Set out through woods and fields, sunlight and aurora, gray and colors. Set out, in deliberate lucid looking and you'll find, perhaps, the present."

Vincent Morisset
AATOAA

Ein interaktiver Spaziergang im Wald, eine Mischung aus hand-gemachter Animation und 360° Video. Way to Go konnte über den Webbrowser oder die VR-Version über Oculus Rift genossen werden. Das Projekt wurde von Vincent Morisset, Caroline Robert, Edouard Lanctôt-Benoit und dem Studio AATOAA erstellt und war für „Menschen zwischen 5 und 105 Jahren". Die Besucher der Seite konnten, solange sie wollten, dem festgelegten Pfad folgen und sich in der Umgebung bewegen und interagieren, so wie sie es in der realen Welt können.

Promenade interactive dans les bois combinant animations faites à la main et vidéo à 360°, le site Way to Go fonctionne dans un navigateur Web, et sa version RV s'apprécie avec Oculus Rift. Signé par Vincent Morisset, Caroline Robert, Édouard Lanctôt-Benoit et le studio AATOAA, ce projet s'adresse aux « êtres humains âgés de 5 à 105 ans ». Les visiteurs peuvent suivre le sentier autant de temps qu'ils le souhaitent, ainsi qu'interagir avec le milieu environnant comme ils le feraient dans le monde réel.

Boda-Ride

—

When the human body became a race-track

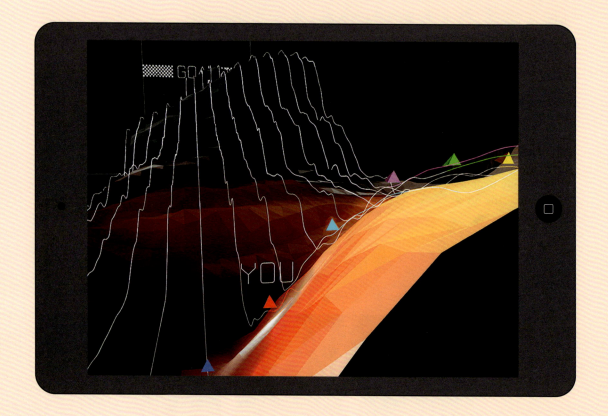

Created by Japan's Bascule, this promotional site for the Nippon Television Network featured a recumbent body on which users could select a lane and race against each other. Once it started, the racers zoomed over the contours of the female body which seemed like an extraordinary, almost mountainous terrain. The race could be viewed from all angles and the bodies used as race-tracks were those of Japanese TV celebrities.

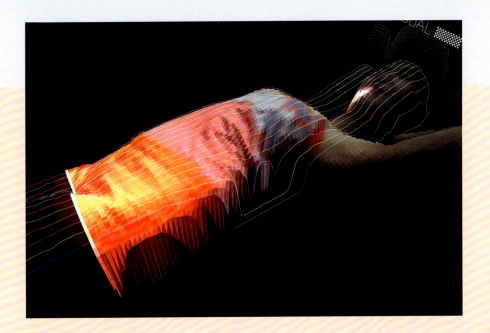

"Boda was a data archive project to record human motion and a sense of existence to posterity. The body data was acquired by Kinect and archived on the website, and body motion data can be played as entertainment contents. Irregular motion data led to an unpredictable race development. Boda-Ride was made in collaboration with a TV network and created a course using the motion data of famous Japanese female TV talents. Millions of TV viewers joined this race together at the same time using smartphones, and enjoyed the event together."

Megumu Kasuga
Bascule

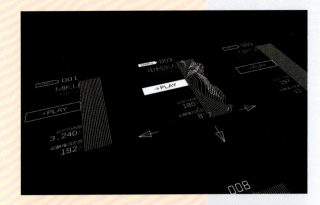

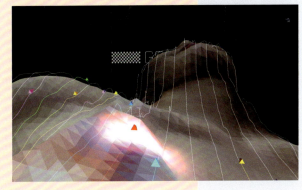

Erstellt vom japanischen Bascule. Diese Werbeseite für Nippon Television Network zeigte einen liegenden Körper, auf dem die User eine Spur auswählen und gegeneinander ein Rennen bestreiten konnten. Sobald es begann, zoomten die Rennfahrer über die Konturen des weiblichen Körpers, der wie ein außergewöhnliches, fast bergiges Gelände schien. Das Rennen konnte von allen Seiten betrachtet werden und die Körper, die als Rennstrecken verwendet wurden, waren die von japanischen TV-Stars.

Conçu par l'agence japonaise Bascule, ce site promotionnel pour la Nippon Television Network montre un corps féminin allongé sur lequel les internautes peuvent choisir une piste et faire la course entre eux. Après le départ, les coureurs font des zooms sur les courbes du corps, qui s'apparente alors à un formidable terrain légèrement montagneux. La course peut se suivre depuis tous les angles et les corps servant de support aux pistes appartiennent à des personnalités du monde de la télévision nippone.

2015/
—

<u>Nike</u>
<u>Sneaker Slam</u>

—

Bringing Nike to
Chinese children

This promotional 'sneakerverse' for Nike,
focusing on the Air Force 1, was an example
of mobile websites reaching the levels of
technology and performance of their desktop
equivalents. The site was created specifically
for the Chinese market, where younger

children were less informed about the Nike
shoes they were wearing, and made full use
of WeChat, one of the largest social networks
in China, so that users could share and chat
about the experience easily.

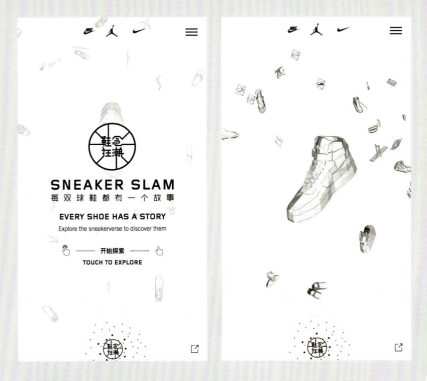

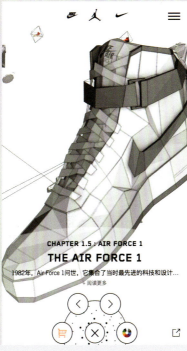

"Design-wise, we decided to use low-poly graphics. This allowed us to craft a sleek-looking 3D experience. We wanted the user to navigate completely free in this digital universe, so good renderings became crucial for the project. We achieved this through designing the 3D models with as few vertices and polygons as possible. This meant the technology and design teams had to collaborate closely. No matter the technical limitations, our goal was to find a way to deliver the best design possible for a mobile experience."

Julien Renau
AKQA; Huge.

Diese Werbeseite für „Sneaker-verse" für Nike, mit Fokussierung auf die Air Force 1, war ein Beispiel für mobile Websites, die das Niveau von Technologie und Leistung ihrer Desktop-Entsprechungen erreichen. Die Website wurde speziell für den chinesischen Markt entwickelt, wo jüngere Kinder wenig über die Nike Schuhe Bescheid wussten, die sie trugen. Sie nutzte WeChat, eines der größten sozialen Netzwerke in China, vollständig aus, sodass die Benutzer die Erfahrungen problemlos teilen und austauschen konnten.

Ce «sneakerverse» promotionnel pour le modèle Nike Air Force 1 prouve que les sites Web mobiles peuvent, en termes de technologie et de performances, égaler leurs homologues de bureau. Celui-ci a été spécialement conçu pour le marché chinois, dont les jeunes enfants en savent moins sur les chaussures Nike qu'ils portent. Il intègre WeChat, l'un des principaux réseaux sociaux en Chine, pour que les visiteurs puissent partager et commenter facilement leur expérience.

—

Assassin's Creed Unity

—

Where the fans became the website

In celebration of the action-adventure video game, fans of Assassin's Creed Unity were invited via this web experience to create their own avatars. Over 1,400 of these (out of 200,000 submitted) became part of the interactive trailer directed by John Kosinski, which was broadcast in cinemas and made into an interactive web experience where users could stop the video at any point to explore the avatars and try and locate their own. Some of the avatars were displayed on city walls and on the cover of a special edition of the game itself.

"To pay homage to this historic time, the team gave people the opportunity to take the power back in the campaign's TV spot. The spot showcased more than 1,400 unique assassins, created and selected by fans on the digital platform. Entirely interactive, it allowed any user to zoom in and find each personalized avatar. We gave life to the game's story in a way that echoed its origins: the French Revolution, the people uniting against royalty and laying the foundations of democracy."

Sylvain Thirache
Sid Lee Paris

Zur Feier des Action-Adventure-Videospiels wurden Fans von Assassin's Creed Unity über diese Web-Erfahrung eingeladen, ihre eigenen Avatare zu erstellen. Über 1.400 von diesen (von etwa 200.000 eingesendeten) wurden Teil eines interaktiven Trailers, unter der Regie von John Kosinski. Dieser wurde in Kinos gezeigt und zu einem interaktiven Web-Erlebnis gemacht, bei dem die Nutzer das Video an jedem Punkt stoppen konnten, um die Avatare zu erkunden und ihre eigenen zu finden. Einige der Avatare wurden auf Stadtmauern und auf dem Cover einer Sonderausgabe des Spiels selbst gezeigt.

Pour célébrer le jeu vidéo d'action et d'aventure Assassin's Creed Unity, ses fans ont l'occasion de créer leurs propres avatars. Plus de 1400 sur un total de 200 000 proposés sont intégrés dans la bande-annonce interactive réalisée par John Kosinski et diffusée dans les salles de cinéma. Elle devient ensuite une expérience Web interactive dans laquelle les internautes peuvent arrêter la vidéo et rechercher leur avatar à l'écran. Certains avatars sont même affichés dans les rues ou figurent en couverture de l'édition spéciale du jeu.

Enough

—

The web's epic picture-book

A deep experience with plenty to explore was presented here in Isaac Cohen's Enough project. Visitors could really lose themselves and the world around them and become completely immersed in Cohen's personal odyssey of procedural worlds, physical simulations, and hand-crafted audio. Cohen called it a picture-book but that doesn't begin to do justice to the extraordinary 20-30 minutes the user could spend in the company of Mani (a jellyfish).

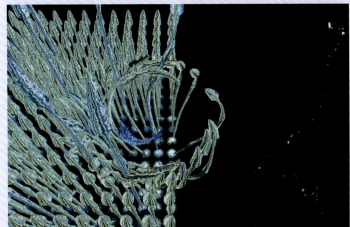

"It's difficult to describe the joy that I found from picking up a picture-book and reading it cover to cover. They let me explore galaxies, ride dinosaurs, slay dragons. They let me dig deep down into my own being as I wished upon a magic pebble, boarded a train bound for the north, or soared through the sky on a plane made from dough. I know I can never recreate the splendor, magnificence, or beauty that I found in these majestic works, but I hope that this project will still remind you of the wonder you found in these moments."

Isaac Cohen
Cabbibo

In Isaac Cohens Enough-Projekt wurde eine tiefgreifende Erfahrung vorgestellt, bei der es viel zu entdecken gab. Die Besucher konnten sich selbst und die Welt um sich herum verlieren und in Cohens persönliche Odyssee aus prozeduralen Welten, physischen Simulationen und handgefertigtem Audio vollkommen eintauchen. Cohen nannte es ein Bilderbuch aber das wird den außergewöhnlichen 20–30 Minuten, die der Benutzer in der Gesellschaft von Mani (einer Qualle) verbringen konnte, nicht gerecht.

Le projet Enough d'Isaac Cohen offre une grande expérience truffée de choses à explorer. Les visiteurs peuvent vraiment se perdre dans le monde qui les entoure et se laisser complète-ment absorber par cette odyssée personnelle combinant des mondes procéduraux, des simulations physiques et un audio artisanal. Cohen qualifie cette œuvre de livre de photos, ce qui est bien loin de rendre justice à ces 20 à 30 minutes extraordinaires que les visiteurs passent en compagnie de Mani, une méduse.

2015/
—

Mario Ballario
Instagram Portfolio

—

A new way of thinking
mobile first

The words 'mobile first' were on many people's lips now and there was much competition to stand out amongst the explosion of largely rather bland mobile websites. Mario Ballario showed something different by creating his portfolio within Instagram, through a mosaic of individual images, which enabled him to present his showcase in such a way that users would see the tiles in the exact way he wished, and in turn creating a website within Instagram itself.

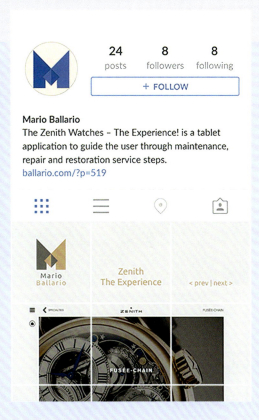

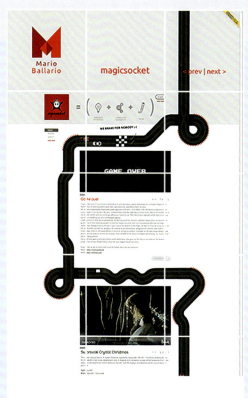

Mario Ballario
The Zenith Watches – The Experience! is a tablet application to guide the user through maintenance, repair and restoration service steps.
ballario.com/?p=519

"Mobile at the time was decisively becoming the norm, finally taking over from desktop as the primary channel to deliver experiences. I took an unconventional approach to Instagram, trying to use it creatively and in a way that was different from the original purpose of the platform. The idea to use it to drive content and to create my personal portfolio looked like a nice alternative so I made a mosaic-style design to be used in the tiles view of Instagram."

Mario Ballario
ballario.com

Die Worte „Mobile First" waren jetzt auf den Lippen vieler Menschen und es gab viel Konkurrenz, um sich bei der Explosion von größtenteils ziemlich matten mobilen Websites zu unterscheiden. Mario Ballario zeigte etwas Anderes, indem er sein Portfolio auf Instagram durch ein Mosaik von Einzelbildern erstellte. Dies ermöglichte es ihm, sein Showcase so zu präsentieren, dass die User die Kacheln genau so sahen, wie er es wünschte, und im Gegenzug selbst eine Website in Instagram erstellten.

L'expression «mobile first» est sur les lèvres de nombreuses personnes et la concurrence est rude pour se distinguer parmi les innombrables sites mobiles dans l'ensemble plutôt insipides. Mario Ballario présente une création différente en composant son portfolio dans Instagram à l'aide de mosaïques d'images. Il s'assure que les visiteurs voient les images exactement comme il le souhaite et crée par là même un site dans Instagram.

NOTABLE WEBSITE LAUNCH
Periscope

GOOGLE FACTS

Google Photos is announced

New version of Cardboard for larger smartphones is released

360°

Google Jump is announced for VR filmmaking

Google indicates it will favor mobile-friendly sites in search results

Offline Mode

Chrome and Maps get improved offline features

Top 5 Trends

INTERNET COMMUNITY
Facebook Safety Check and Solidarity filters

Following the Nepal earthquake in April, Facebook introduced Safety Check which enabled people to let their friends and family know they were safe. Then, following the Paris attacks in November, as people from all around the world were wanting to show their solidarity, Facebook provided an optional French flag filter which could be temporarily added to users' profile photos.

Alexandra Carr added a temporary profile picture.
15 hrs

Change your profile picture to support France and the people of Paris.

Try it

👍 Like   💬 Comment   ➜ Share

MOBILE EVOLUTION
Samsung Galaxy S6 Edge

Equipped with a wraparound display and wireless charging

2016/

The Year Artificial Intelligence Came to the Web

2016/

—

The Year Artificial Intelligence Came to the Web

—

WhackATrump

In a year of crazy politics and fake news, when the United Kingdom voted to leave the European Union and the United States voted in Donald Trump as the 45th President, it was perhaps no surprise that active web use now touched half the global population and the number of websites bounced back above the one-billion mark again. Certainly, many parody websites appeared in Trump's name, including WhackATrump, trumpdonald.org, trumpwith. love, Jrump, Political Punch 'Em, and The Poli-Graph, an online lie detector.

Microsoft launched its HoloLens Development Edition and was once again seen as a powerhouse for innovation. Google created its first phones that were produced entirely in-house, the Google Pixel and Pixel XL, while Pokémon Go stole the whole mobile show with the groundbreaking augmented reality game that actually got people outdoors and exercising without even realizing it.

It was also the year when FWA enjoyed its biggest evolution for many years and finally had a website that worked seamlessly over all devices. The new FWA came with a pioneering Live Judging feature, allowing users to see their own and other users' submissions in a live grid that moved up and down in line with how the judges voted, in real time.

A project that looked at the plight of dolphins kept in captivity, Resize My Home hit the mark by asking users to shrink their browser window. This resizing caused the sound of dolphins crying to be heard, but users were also able to learn about their natural behavior.

The IKEA Passport Challenge banner campaign aimed to stop Skype users in their tracks by challenging them to find and show their passport within 30 seconds. Anyone who managed it won a holiday.

Meet Graham became a global phenomenon as this road safety campaign invited people to examine the unfortunate character and discover what they would need to look like in order to survive a car crash.

As artificial intelligence and machine learning began to take off, the Giorgio Cam let users make music with their phone simply by taking a photo and turning the subject into the lyrics of a song, by way of image recognition.

The new era of AI, AR, and VR heralded great changes, although many people found the idea of such new technology daunting and confusing.

Resize My Home

IKEA Passport Challenge

"Active web use
now touched
half the global
population and
the number of
websites bounced
back above the
one-billion
mark again."

FWA

In einem Jahr voller verrückter Politik und Fake News, als das Vereinigte Königreich beschloss, die Europäische Union zu verlassen, und in den Vereinigten Staaten Donald Trump zum 45. Präsidenten gewählt wurde, war es vielleicht keine Überraschung, dass das Web wieder aktiver verwendet wurde und die Hälfte der Weltbevölkerung betraf und die Zahl der Websites wieder die Marke von einer Milliarde überschritt. Viele Parodie-Websites tauchten auf mit Trumps Namen, zum Beispiel WhackATrump, trumpdonald.org, trumpwith.love, Jrump, Political Punch 'Em, und The Poli-Graph, ein Online-Lügendetektor.

Microsoft brachte seine HoloLens Development Edition heraus und wurde erneut als

Motor für Innovationen gesehen. Google kreierte seine ersten Telefone, die komplett intern produziert wurden, das Google Pixel und Pixel XL, während Pokémon Go mit dem bahnbrechenden Augmented-Reality-Spiel allen auf dem Mobiltelefon die Show stahl, da es die Leute tatsächlich ins Freie brachte und trainierte, ohne dass sie es merkten.

Es war auch das Jahr, in dem FWA die größte Entwicklung seit vielen Jahren erlebte und schließlich eine Website hatte, die nahtlos über alle Geräte hinaus funktionierte. Die neue Seite der FWA bekam eine bahnbrechende Live-Judging-Funktion, die es den Benutzern ermöglichte, die Einsendungen ihrer eigenen und die anderer

Benutzer in einem Live-Raster zu sehen, das sich in Übereinstimmung mit der Abstimmung der Juroren in Echtzeit nach oben und unten bewegte.

Ein Projekt, das die Notlage der in Gefangenschaft gehaltenen Delfine untersuchte. Resize My Home, forderte die User auf, ihr Browserfenster zu verkleinern. Durch diese Größenanpassung wurde das Geräusch von weinenden Delfinen hörbar, aber die Benutzer konnten auch etwas über ihr natürliches Verhalten erfahren.

Die IKEA Passport Challenge Banner-Kampagne zielte darauf ab, Skype-Benutzer aufzuhalten, indem sie sie herausforderten, ihren Pass innerhalb von 30 Sekunden zu finden und zu zeigen. Wer es schaffte, hatte einen Urlaub gewonnen.

Meet Graham wurde zu einem globalen Phänomen. Diese Verkehrssicherheitskampagne lud die Menschen ein, den unglücklichen Darsteller zu untersuchen und herauszufinden, wie sie aussehen müssten, um einen Autounfall zu überstehen.

Als die künstliche Intelligenz und das maschinelle Lernen in Gang kamen, ließ Giorgio Cam den User mit seinem Handy Musik machen, indem er einfach ein Foto machte und das Thema durch Bilderkennung in den Text eines Liedes verwandelte.

Die neue Ära von AI, AR und VR kündigte große Veränderungen an, obwohl viele Menschen die Idee einer solchen neuen Technologie entmutigend und verwirrend fanden.

2016/

—

The Year
Artificial
Intelligence
Came to the Web

—

Meet Graham

"The new era
of AI, AR, and
VR heralded
great changes."

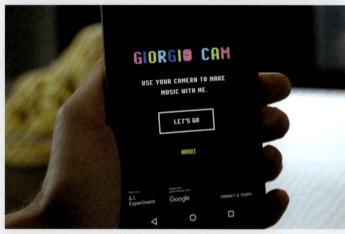

Giorgio Cam

Cette année est marquée par l'agitation politique et une série de fake news, avec le Royaume-Uni qui vote pour sortir de l'Union européenne et les États-Unis qui élisent Donald Trump 45ᵉ président du pays. La moitié de la population mondiale est maintenant active sur le Web et le nombre de sites repasse au-dessus de la barre du milliard. De nombreux sites parodiques sur Trump voient le jour, comme WhackATrump, trumpdonald.org, trumpwith.love, Jrump, Political Punch 'Em et The Poli-Graph, un détecteur de mensonges en ligne.

Microsoft lance ses lunettes HoloLens Development Edition et se gagne une fois de plus une reconnaissance en termes d'innovation. Pour sa part, Google commercialise ses premiers smartphones entièrement produits en interne, les modèles Google Pixel et Pixel XL, et Pokémon Go vole la vedette sur la scène mobile avec un jeu révolutionnaire de réalité augmentée qui motive les gens à sortir de chez eux et à faire de l'exercice sans s'en rendre compte.

Les FWA font leur plus grand bond en avant avec un site Web qui fonctionne sur tous les dispositifs et inclut désormais une innovante fonctionnalité « Live Judging ». Les internautes peuvent ainsi voir dans une grille leurs propositions et celles d'autrui qui se déplacent en temps réel vers le haut ou vers le bas selon le vote du jury.

Resize My Home est un projet s'intéressant à la détresse des dauphins retenus en captivité. Il touche les visiteurs en leur demandant de réduire la fenêtre du navigateur, ce qui émet le son de cris de dauphins. Il apporte aussi des informations sur le comportement naturel de l'animal.

La campagne de bannières IKEA Passport Challenge vise à interpeller les utilisateurs de Skype en les défiant de trouver leur passeport et de le montrer à la caméra en moins de 30 secondes. Ceux qui y parviennent gagnent un voyage.

La campagne sur la sécurité routière Meet Graham devient un phénomène mondial. Par le biais d'un malheureux personnage, elle montre ce à quoi les personnes dans une voiture devraient ressembler pour survivre en cas d'accident de la route.

L'intelligence artificielle et l'apprentissage automatique sont en plein essor. Dans ce contexte, Giorgio Cam permet de faire de la musique avec un téléphone en prenant simplement une photo et en générant les paroles de la chanson grâce à la reconnaissance d'images.

La nouvelle ère d'IA, RA et RV annonce des changements majeurs, même si beaucoup sont un peu intimidés par ces nouvelles technologies.

08 Facts of
the year

Number of internet users:
3.7 billion, 49.5% of
the world population

Number of websites:
1 billion

World news:
the United Kingdom votes
to leave the European Union

Website with most traffic:
Google.com

Tech hardware:
Microsoft HoloLens
Development Edition ships

Tech software:
Android 7.0 launches

Other tech:
Google's Alphabet becomes
the world's most valuable
company

Highest-grossing film:
Captain America:
Civil War

Google Play Music: Through the Dark

—

An emotional journey for father and son

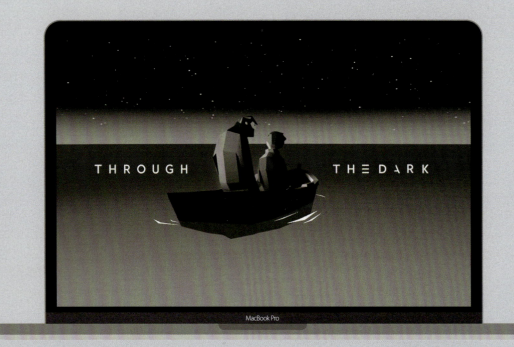

This interactive film, made for mobile but with an equally impressive desktop version, brought to screens a song written by Daniel Smith, aka MC Pressure, from Australian hip-hop group Hilltop Hoods as his son underwent treatment for leukemia. It told their story through two worlds, the light and the dark, and visitors to the site could turn their phones one way or the other to follow either the father's or the son's journey, with the dark representing fear and the light hope. It was a prime example of a world-class web experience and went on to international acclaim, including FWA of the Year and also the FWA People's Choice Award 2016, a double that has been only rarely achieved.

"Through the Dark wasn't just any track, it was the story of a father's experience of his son's battle with cancer. So everyone was incredibly focused on creating not just an immersive mobile experience, but taking the user on an emotional journey. Using 3D cameras mapped to the phone's accelerometer, the device could be tilted and rotated to reveal a father and son's journey through two animated worlds — the dark and the light. There was an incredible team on this project; it was a moment in time when the stars aligned."

Hamish Stewart
R/GA

Dieser interaktive Film war für Mobilgeräte gedacht, hatte aber auch eine ebenso beeindruckende Desktop-Version. Es brachte ein von Daniel Smith, aka MC Pressure, geschriebenes Lied auf den Bildschirm, mit der australischen Hip-Hop Gruppe Hilltop Hoods, da sein Sohn einer Behandlung für Leukämie unterzogen wurde. Es erzählte ihre Geschichte durch zwei Welten, durch das Licht und das Dunkel, und die Besucher der Seite konnten ihre Telefone entweder auf die eine oder die andere Weise drehen um entweder der Reise des Vaters oder der des Sohnes zu folgen, wobei die Dunkelheit die Angst und das Licht die Hoffnung repräsentierten. Es war ein Paradebeispiel für eine Web-Erfahrung von Weltrang und wurde international gefeiert, inklusive FWA of the Year und dem FWA People's Choice Award 2016, ein Double, das nur selten erreicht wurde.

Ce film interactif, conçu pour les dispositifs mobiles mais dont la version bureau est tout aussi remarquable, porte à l'écran une chanson écrite par Daniel Smith, alias MC Pressure, membre du groupe de hip-hop australien Hilltop Hoods, alors que son fils reçoit un traitement contre la leucémie. Le titre raconte leur histoire à travers deux univers, l'un sombre évoquant la peur et l'autre clair pour l'espoir : en orientant leur téléphone dans un sens ou un autre, les visiteurs suivent alors le voyage du père ou du fils. Cette sublime création offre une expérience d'une envergure et d'une reconnaissance internationales, dont les prix FWA of the Year et FWA People's Choice Award 2016, une double récompense rarement obtenue.

—

Star Wars: Lightsaber Escape

—

Turning a phone into a lightsaber

With the help of lightsaber training tutorials, users could battle with stormtroopers here as they tried to reach a hangar where a shuttle was waiting to transport them to safety. Competing to beat their friends' escape-times they could also share these on social media, while the music, provided by Lucasfilm, was mixed to sync with the user's mobile movement to create the most incredible atmosphere.

"Websites were already doing some amazing things. But we wanted to take it one step further with a real-time 3D Star Wars: Lightsaber Escape game — with cutting-edge visuals. Where you control a lightsaber using your smartphone and it can be played by hundreds of thousands of people simultaneously. I think it's fair to say that this was by far the most fun project that most of us had worked on to date."

Maciej Zasada
Unit9

Mithilfe von Lichtschwert-Trainingstutorials konnten Benutzer gegen Sturmtruppen kämpfen, wenn sie versuchten, einen Hangar zu erreichen, wo ein Shuttle wartete, um sie in Sicherheit zu bringen. Es war ein Wettbewerb, in dem es darum ging, die Fluchtzeiten ihrer Freunde zu schlagen. Dies konnte auch in sozialen Medien geteilt werden, während die Musik von Lucasfilm gemischt wurde, um sich mit der Handybewegung des Nutzers zu synchronisieren. So wurde eine wahnsinnige Atmosphäre geschaffen.

En suivant les instructions d'utilisation du sabre laser, les internautes peuvent s'affronter à des stormtroopers pour accéder à un hangar et se sauver à bord d'une navette. Ils essayent de battre le temps que leurs amis ont mis pour s'échapper et peuvent partager leurs résultats sur les réseaux sociaux. Composée par Lucasfilm, la musique a été mixée pour se synchroniser au mouvement du dispositif mobile et créer une atmosphère fantastique.

The Field Trip to Mars

—

The first-ever group virtual reality experience

In a future-thinking project that set out to inspire the first generation that might actually travel to Mars, the Red Planet was brought closer than ever before in this, the first group virtual reality experience. Lockheed Martin took a school bus and in six months transformed it, installing custom-built, switchable electric glass screens that shaded from transparent to opaque and were linked up with 4K transparent LCD displays, to create an incredible space journey. The bus had now become a virtual reality headset in effect and when it moved, the recreated Martian surface, which had been mapped on to the streets of Washington DC, moved too.

"Rarely does a single job require innovation in so many different areas at once. From the unique combination of tracking sensors, through the unusual use of Game-Engine tech and on to the custom screen configurations, nothing had been used in these ways before. I have rarely been more relieved and delighted than when we triggered the experience with the first busload of kids, and everything worked. The kids' shrieks of delight as the urban city streets outside the bus windows were replaced by the surface of Mars is something that I will remember for a very long time."

Theo Jones
Framestore

In einem zukunftsweisenden Projekt, das darauf abzielte, die erste Generation zu inspirieren, die tatsächlich zum Mars reisen könnte, wurde der Rote Planet näher als je zuvor zu uns gebracht. Es war die erste Virtual-Reality-Erfahrung in einer Gruppe. Lockheed Martin nahm einen Schulbus und in sechs Monaten baute er ihn um und installierte maßgeschneiderte, umschaltbare elektrische Glas-scheiben, die von durchsichtig bis undurchsichtig abgeschattet und mit 4K-transparenten LCD-Displays verbunden waren, um eine unglaubliche Welt-raumreise zu schaffen. Der Bus wurde nun zum Virtual-Reality-Headset, und wenn er sich bewegte, bewegte sich auch die neu gestaltete Marsober-fläche, die auf den Straßen von Washington DC gemapped war.

Avec ce projet visionnaire pensé pour inspirer la première génération qui aura peut-être l'occasion d'aller sur Mars, la planète rouge est plus proche que jamais via l'expérience inédite de réalité virtuelle collective. L'entreprise Lockheed Martin aménage en six mois un bus scolaire : les vitres sont remplacées par des écrans LCD transparents en verre actif, recouverts d'un film les rendant opaques grâce à un courant électrique intégré, et qui affichent une résolution en 4K afin de simuler un incroyable voyage dans l'espace. Le bus produit le même effet qu'un casque de réalité virtuelle et quand il roule, la surface de Mars recréée et mappée sur les rues de Washington DC change en conséquence.

Quick, Draw!

—

An early example of web-based machine learning, and AI

Taking the form of a game in which users drew an object and a neural network would try to guess what was being drawn, this site didn't aim to guess correctly every time as its focus was to learn, so the more drawings it was exposed to the more it developed. While the drawing was fun, it was amazing to see how accurate the interpretation could be, but users were also contributing to a huge doodling data set which was shared openly to help with machine-learning research. After six rounds of drawing the results were displayed to show what the machine had seen in the sketches it had failed to recognize correctly.

"When we first thought of Quick, Draw! there were already large projects focused on using AI. But there hadn't been a lot of attention given to exploring human interaction with AI on the web. Thing is, these AIs didn't always work well, but most projects at the time tried to hide those flaws. What if we could leverage the flaws in those APIs to play a game like Pictionary? Let the players explore the boundaries of AI to figure out what it could recognize and what it could not. The goal was to make AI accessible and playful, and something you could enjoy finding imperfections in."

Jonas Jongejan
Google Creative Lab

In Form eines Spiels sollten die User ein Objekt zeichnen und ein neurales Netzwerk sollte versuchen, zu erraten, was gezeichnet wurde. Diese Seite zielte nicht darauf ab, es jedes Mal richtig zu erraten, da der Fokus darauf lag, zu lernen. Je mehr Zeichnungen es ausgesetzt war, desto mehr entwickelte es sich. Während das Zeichnen Spaß machte, war es erstaunlich zu sehen, wie genau die Interpretation sein konnte, aber die Benutzer trugen auch zu einem riesigen Doodling-Datensatz bei, der offen geteilt wurde, um bei der Forschung für maschinelles Lernen zu helfen. Nach sechs Runden Zeichnen wurden die Ergebnisse angezeigt, um zu zeigen, was die Maschine in den Skizzen gesehen hatte und was sie nicht korrekt erkannt hatte.

Ce site prend les allures d'un jeu dans lequel les joueurs dessinent un objet qu'un réseau neuronal essaye de deviner, l'objectif n'étant pas une reconnaissance systématique mais un apprentissage : plus le système est exposé à des dessins différents, plus il s'améliore. L'activité de dessin en soi est amusante, mais il est surtout fascinant de voir avec quelle précision se font les interprétations. Les joueurs alimentent par ailleurs une gigantesque base de griffonnages qui est partagée librement pour faire avancer la recherche par apprentissage automatique. En cas d'échec de reconnaissance après six tours, les résultats sont présentés pour montrer ce que la machine a interprété.

2016/

—

Falter Inferno

—

A journey into a living hell

While this experience had a visual and atmospheric beauty, it was really brought to life by its interactions that affected both the scenery and the soundscape. On entering, users found themselves at street level amidst what looked like everyday life, but as they

descended through the different animation layers the interactive motion graphics kicked in to open up a seemingly bottomless abyss. In the final scene, a red hand was dangled above, for users to try and grab hold of so that they might be transported out of the nightmare.

THE MATRICIDE.

4

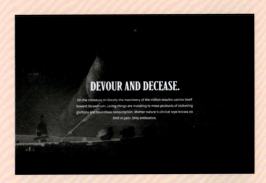

DEVOUR AND DECEASE.

On the conveyor of obesity the machinery of the million mouths carries itself toward its own ruin. Living things are mutating to mass products of sickening gluttony and boundless consumption. Mother nature's clinical rape knows no limit in pain. Only antibiotics.

FALTER   DOCTRINE 25/7.

9

"Falter Inferno was an interactive story through the eight layers of hell. Every layer was brought to life through different interactions affecting the scenery and the soundscape as well as combining the use of mouse and touch events and gyro input. The challenges were to keep loading-times low, to assure a smooth and seamless performance on desktop and mobile devices, to stay true to the original video by generating seamless image loops, and to get the most out of it. It was the perfect time to launch such a site, to push new technologies and to show what's possible with existing techniques."

Thomas Lichtblau
wild

Diese Erfahrung hatte eine visuelle und atmosphärische Schönheit. Hier wurde Etwas durch Interaktionen zum Leben erweckt, was sowohl die Landschaft, als auch die Klanglandschaft beeinflusste. Beim Betreten fanden sich die User auf Straßenebene mitten im Alltag wieder, doch wenn sie durch die verschiedenen Animationsschichten hindurch-fuhren, traten die interaktiven Bewegungsgrafiken ein, um einen scheinbar bodenlosen Abgrund zu öffnen. In der letzten Szene baumelte eine rote Hand herunter. Die User sollten versuchen, sie zu ergreifen, sodass sie aus dem Albtraum heraustransportiert werden konnten.

Outre l'esthétique visuelle et l'atmosphère de cette expé-rience, sa dynamique tient surtout aux interactions avec le décor et le paysage sonore. Une fois dedans, les visiteurs se retrouvent dans une scène de rue quotidienne ; s'ils descendent dans les couches d'animation toutefois, des graphismes interactifs les plongent dans les bas-fonds apparemment sans fin de la ville. Dans la scène finale, une main rouge apparaît en haut et peut être saisie pour sortir du cauchemar.

The VHS Retrominder

—

A responsive nostalgic experience

While many projects had struggled to work as well on mobile as desktop until the likes of Chrome and Safari came along, this example was equally successful on both and gave users 90 seconds to answer as many questions as possible on characters' and actors' names after watching a video clip. This was a nostalgic trip back to the time of VHS cassettes and the 1980s, an era that had come back in many ways and notably in advertising, where scoring three correct answers on the trot gave users a special bonus round.

"The VHS Retrominder was our homage to
the '80s and '90s culture which had rocked our
team's childhoods. We also wanted to anchor
our experiment in the Neoretro waves which had
been, and still are, a main trend in web design.
We loved to choose our favorite characters and
movies and use all the retro effects to create
a real old-school DNA on this project. To enjoy
this game every day, we decided to create a real
arcade machine, which was presented at the
Cannes Lions advertising festival in 2017."

Frédéric Paquet
Viens-la

Viele Projekte hatten Schwierigkeiten, sowohl auf Mobilgeräten als auch auf dem Desktop zu funktionieren, bis Chrome und Safari auf den Markt kamen. Dieses Beispiel war auf beiden gleichermaßen erfolgreich und gab den Nutzern 90 Sekunden Zeit, um nach dem Anschauen eines Videoclips so viele Fragen wie möglich zu den Namen der Charaktere und Schauspieler zu beantworten. Dies war eine nostalgische Reise zurück in die Zeit der VHS-Kassetten und der 1980er Jahre, eine Ära, die in vielerlei Hinsicht und vor allem in der Werbung zurückgekehrt war. Bei drei richtigen Antworten wurde den Usern eine besondere Bonusrunde gewährt.

Jusqu'à l'arrivée de Chrome et de Safari, le défi pour de nombreux projets a été de fonctionner aussi bien sur dispositifs mobiles que sur ordinateurs. Tout aussi performant sur les deux, ce site donne 90 secondes aux visiteurs pour répondre à un maximum de questions sur des noms de personnages et d'acteurs après avoir vu un vidéoclip. Il pose un regard nostalgique sur les cassettes VHS et les années 80 en général, une époque qui revient à la mode sous diverses formes, notamment dans la publicité. Trois réponses correctes d'affilée donnent droit à une partie bonus.

2016/
—

Mont Blanc VR Experience

—

Astonishingly realistic climb to the top of Europe's highest mountain

Visitors to this site were able to make the ascent of the highest peak in the Alps entirely within their mobile web browser, on Android and also iOS, with or without a VR headset. It was a hugely informative project that harnessed the power of Google Maps and the trip to the summit was amazingly lifelike, while the view from the top, via the 360-degree panoramic video, managed to be totally breathtaking and a little unnerving too.

"Climbing to the peak [of Mont Blanc] is a dream for many but the wild terrain and long, steep hike mean only mountaineers or intrepid explorers ever make it. We made a virtual-reality climb that let the viewer get up close and personal with the famous massif as they made their way up the Goûter Route. Leveraging Street View technology and audio narration by mountaineer Patrick Gabarrou, we built our version of Mont Blanc entirely in the web browser. Anyone with a smartphone can reach the peak in 360 degrees without having to leave home."

Mike Dorrance
Google Brand Studio

Die Besucher dieser Seite konnten den höchsten Gipfel der Alpen in ihrem mobilen Webbrowser auf Android und iOS, mit oder ohne VR-Headset, vollständig besteigen. iOS war ein sehr informatives Projekt, das die Macht von Google Maps nutzte und der Gipfelbesuch war unglaublich lebensecht, während die Aussicht von oben über das 360-Grad-Panorama-Video absolut atemberaubend war und auch ein wenig nerven-zermürbend.

Les visiteurs de ce site peuvent faire l'ascension du plus haut sommet des Alpes depuis leur navigateur Web mobile, tant sur Android que sur iOS, et qu'ils soient munis ou non d'un casque de RV. Regorgeant d'infos et exploitant toute la puissance de Google Maps, ce projet montre avec un réalisme incroyable l'ascension au sommet. La vue depuis la cime dans une vidéo panoramique à 360° s'avère époustouflante et quelque peu troublante.

2016/

—

Virtual Art Sessions

—

One of the first examples to use Tilt Brush

The new VR 3D painting app Tilt Brush enabled users to paint the 3D space around them via virtual reality, and in this experiment it was brought to the web so that the paintings of six famous artists could be examined in 3D and from any angle, and even as they were being painted. This ability to explore artworks in virtual reality was a first and was promptly adopted as a very powerful and exciting new tool, attracting artists and art-lovers from all areas and genres.

VIRTUAL ART SESSIONS

Andrea Blasich (Profile)

Speed: 1x   2x   4x   8x

4:28 / 5:12

"In Virtual Art Sessions, we wanted to share an aspect of virtual reality that we found most exciting, the potential to develop intuitive tools for making digital things. At the time of the project, position-tracked VR hardware wasn't widely available, and most of the hype around it promised passive immersion in static worlds. By showing both artists and their virtual creations, we hoped to help people imagine the possibilities. Standing in a room with your creation as it flows from your hands is a visceral and empowering experience."

Jeff Nusz
Google Data Arts

VIRTUAL ART SESSIONS

Katie Rogers (Profile)

Speed: 1x   2x   4x   8x

2:45 / 3:25

VIRTUAL ART SESSIONS

Die neue VR 3D-Malanwendung Tilt Brush ermöglichte es den Benutzern, den 3D-Raum um sie herum mittels virtueller Realität zu malen, und in diesem Experiment wurde es ins Netz gebracht, sodass die Gemälde von sechs berühmten Künstlern in 3D und aus jedem Blickwinkel untersucht werden konnten, sogar während sie gemalt wurden. Diese Fähigkeit, Kunstwerke in der virtuellen Realität zu erforschen, war eine Premiere und wurde prompt als ein sehr leistungsstarkes und aufregendes neues Werkzeug angenommen, das Künstler und Kunstliebhaber aus allen Bereichen und Genres anzog.

Tilt Brush est une application de peinture de RV en 3D qui permet aux utilisateurs de peindre virtuellement l'espace en 3D qui les entoure. Sur le Web, cette expérience est proposée pour observer en 3D et depuis tous les angles les peintures (parfois en cours de réalisation) de six artistes célèbres. La possibilité d'explorer des œuvres d'art en réalité virtuelle marque une première et devient vite un nouvel outil puissant attirant artistes et amateurs d'art de tous les styles.

Alice Wonder Mirror
D23 Installation

—

A breathtaking cutting-edge augmented reality installation

#DisneyAlice

Created for Disney's *Alice Through the Looking Glass*, this experience transformed users into a character from the film by using face-tracking combined with digital make-up and 3D assets. The installation, a 40 x 40 feet area, was an impressive space in itself with plush grass, cobblestoned pathways, mushrooms, topiary, and costumed characters, and was kitted out with four Wonder Mirror kiosks where visitors were transformed and then received a shareable video and photo of their experience.

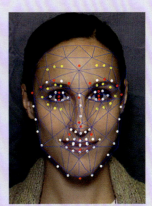

"We had a vision to magically transform users into beloved film characters right before their very eyes. Snapchat Lenses and the Masquerade app had not hit the marketplace yet. After several months in research and development we decided to build our own software to interface with raw facial-tracking data. This custom application allowed us to position our occluded 3D elements and pair them with our texture wrap make-up effects for a true first-to-market experience, and a revolutionary progression of the traditional 'photo booth', now truly allowing real-time augmented transformation."

Josh Golsen
Part IV

Für Disneys *Alice im Wunderland: Hinter den Spiegeln* erstellt, verwandelte die Anwendung den Nutzer mithilfe von Gesichtsverfolgung in Kombination mit digitalem Make-up und 3D-Elementen in eine Figur aus dem Film. Die Installation, ein 12 x 12 m großer Bereich, war ein eindrucksvoller Raum für sich, ausgestattet mit üppigem Gras, Kopfsteinpflaster, Pilzen, Formgehölzen und kostümierten Figuren und wurde mit vier „Wonder Mirror" Kiosks ausgestattet, wo die Besucher transformiert wurden und dann ein Video und ein Foto von ihren Erlebnissen erhielten.

Conçue pour le film de Disney *De l'autre côté du miroir*, cette expérience transforme les internautes en un personnage de l'histoire à l'aide du suivi du visage, d'un maquillage numérique et de ressources 3D. Dans un espace de 12 x 12 m, l'installation impressionne en soi avec un gazon artificiel, des chemins pavés, des champignons géants, des arbres formés et des personnages en costumes. Les visiteurs prennent place dans l'une des quatre cabines dotées d'un miroir magique et voient leur visage transformé. Ils reçoivent à la sortie une vidéo et une photo de leur expérience pour la partager.

Mmorph

—

An adventure into the future
of interactive music

This web-based audio experience invited users to explore new ways of delivering interactive music in the browser and beyond. After being greeted with a choice of interface, users could choose to continue with their mouse or sync their phone, and then begin mixing by choosing any of the samples and moving on from there, adding effects, delays, filters, and whatever else they wanted.

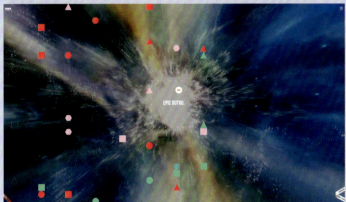

"Our team at MassiveMusic started looking into other workflows to accelerate the process of HTML5 catching up with Flash and we ended up going far beyond. We created a new methodology linking Pure Data, a compiler called Heavy, Web Audio, and javascript. mmorph was our self-funded proof of concept site. It combined a smartphone-controlled interactive music experience with real-time SVG animations. On launch, we had an overwhelmingly positive reception from the web and music comm-unities, and mmorph went on to win the FWA Site of the Month in 2016."

Roscoe Williamson
MassiveMusic

Dieses webbasierte Audio-Erlebnis lud die Nutzer dazu ein, neue Wege der Bereitstellung interaktiver Musik im Browser und darüber hinaus zu erkunden. Nach der Begrüßung mit einer Auswahl an Schnittstellen, konnten die User entscheiden, ob sie mit ihrer Maus oder mittels ihres Telefons weitermachen wollten. Dann konnten Sie mit dem Mixing beginnen, indem sie die Muster auswählten und von dort aus Effekte, Verzögerungen, Filter und was immer sie wollten hinzufügen konnten.

Cette expérience audio basée sur le Web invite les utilisateurs à découvrir comment produire de la musique interactive via un navigateur ou un téléphone. Après avoir choisi une interface, ils peuvent poursuivre avec la souris ou synchroniser leur téléphone, puis commencer à mixer un échantillon en ajoutant des effets, des décalages, des filtres et tout ce qui leur plaît.

INTERNET COMMUNITY
Pokémon Go

A location-based augmented reality game that took the world by storm was released on July 6 for Android and iOS and was downloaded more than 10 million times within the first week. It became the fastest-growing app in history, with an estimated 21 million active users at its peak.

GOOGLE FACTS

Google News introduces fact-checking feature

Google Assistant announced

Google Home unveiled

Google Allo announced

Google Duo released

Top 5 Trends

MOBILE EVOLUTION
Google Pixel
and Pixel XL

The first phone made entirely
by Google, inside and out

NOTABLE WEBSITE
LAUNCH
trumpdonald.org

2017/

The Year the Web Evolved out of the Web

2017/

—

The Year the Web Evolved out of the Web

—

"The power of
social media was
still a huge
focus for brands."

Game of Thrones HBO Fire & Ice Facebook Live Video

On July 25, Adobe announced the end of Flash, and that by the end of 2020 there would be no further updates or distribution for Flash Player. To many people, this news carried only a slight twinge as Flash had already begun to fade on the web in 2010, following the launch of the iPad and Steve Jobs's "Thoughts on Flash".

However, as with most things, there was still a sense of continuity and web projects proved they could still be innovative. A bigger concern perhaps was whether the slow death of websites themselves had begun, with more projects being created outside of browsers, although at the same time elements that had been external to browsers, such as VR, were now being incorporated into them, so evolution was continuing to find its path.

The power of social media was still a huge focus for brands, as could be seen with the *Game of Thrones* HBO Fire & Ice Facebook Live Video event, in which millions of fans from around the world, me included, tried to get a huge block of ice to melt by

commenting "Fire" or "Dracarys" to bring a flamethrower in closer.

More virtual reality experiences designed for children were now appearing, such as Into the Wild (a Google Tango experience), which transformed Singapore's ArtScience Museum into a virtual rainforest that could be physically explored by walking through the museum.

More surprisingly, a battalion of autonomous robots wrote fan messages in the snow for Swisscom's Snow Drawings at the Alpine World Ski Championships, which resulted in an artwork masterpiece the size of 16 soccer fields.

Simple innovations in navigation on the web also continued to emerge, with Nick Jones's portfolio being an example where he presented an interface based on the Fibonacci spiral.

Searching for Syria was a way for people to learn more about the Syrian refugee crisis by way of the five main questions being asked about the biggest humanitarian crisis in a generation.

Into the Wild

Nick Jones

Am 25. Juli verkündete Adobe das Ende von Flash und dass es ab dem Ende des Jahres 2020 keine weiteren Updates mehr dafür und keinen Vertrieb des Flash Players mehr geben wird. Für viele Leute war diese Nachricht nur ein kleiner Stich, da Flash bereits im Jahr 2010 im Web verblasst war, nach der Einführung des iPads und Steve Jobs „Thoughts on Flash".

Wie bei vielen Dingen gab es aber immer noch ein Gefühl der Kontinuität und einige Webprojekte bewiesen, dass sie immer noch innovativ sein konnten. Eine größere Sorge war

vielleicht, ob der langsame Tod von Websites selbst begonnen hatte. Immer mehr Projekt entstanden außerhalb von Browsern, obwohl gleichzeitig Elemente, die Browser-extern waren, wie VR, nun in sie integriert wurden, sodass die Evolution weiter fortschritt.

Die Macht der sozialen Medien war immer noch ein großer Fokus für die Marken, wie man es Live-Video von HBO Fire & Ice von *Game of Thrones* auf Facebook sehen konnte in dem Millionen von Fans aus der ganzen Welt, mich eingeschlossen, versuchten, einen riesigen Eisblock

zum Schmelzen zu bringen, indem sie „Fire" oder „Dracarys" kommentierten, um einen Flammenwerfer näher zu bringen.

Weitere Virtual-Reality-Erlebnisse für Kinder erschienen nun, wie zum Beispiel Into the Wild (eine Google Tango Experience), welche das Singapurs ArtScience Museum in einen virtuellen Regenwald verwandelte, den man im Museum erkunden konnte.

Überraschender war, dass ein Bataillon autonomer Roboter bei den Alpinen Ski-Weltmeisterschaften Fan-Botschaften im Schnee für die Snow Drawings von Swisscom

schrieb. Daraus entstand ein Kunst-Meisterwerk in der Größe von 16 Fußballfeldern.

Auch bei der Navigation im Web tauchen immer wieder neue Innovationen auf, wofür das Portfolio von Nick Jones ein Beispiel war, da er eine auf der Fibonacci-Spirale basierende Schnittstelle präsentierte.

Searching for Syria war für die Menschen eine Möglichkeit, mehr über die syrische Flüchtlingskrise zu erfahren, indem sie die fünf wichtigsten Fragen zur größten humanitären Krise einer Generation stellte.

The Year the Web Evolved out of the Web

—

Searching for Syria

"There was still a sense of continuity and web projects proved they could still be innovative."

Swisscom's Snow Drawings

Le 25 juillet, Adobe annonce la fin de Flash et qu'après 2020, elle cessera le développement et la mise à jour de Flash Player. Pour beaucoup, ces nouvelles ne provoquent pas plus qu'un léger pincement au cœur sachant que la disparition de Flash sur le Web a débuté en 2010 après la sortie de l'iPad et la publication des «Thoughts on Flash» de Steve Jobs.

Comme bien souvent toutefois, le sentiment de continuité est présent et les projets Web font toujours preuve d'innovation. La préoccupation concerne davantage la mort lente des propres sites Web, un grand nombre étant désormais créés en dehors des navigateurs. En parallèle, des éléments jusqu'alors externes aux navigateurs, comme la RV, s'y font une place. L'évolution trouve donc sa voie.

Le pouvoir des réseaux sociaux est toujours très prisé par les marques. Par exemple, lors de l'événement vidéo en direct Fire & Ice sur Facebook par HBO pour sa série *Game of Thrones*, des millions de fans de toute la planète, moi y compris, essayent de faire fondre un énorme bloc de glace en commentant «Fire» ou «Dracarys» pour approcher un lance-flammes.

Le nombre d'expériences virtuelles pour enfants va augmentant, comme celle Into the Wild (sur la plate-forme Tango de Google), qui transforme l'ArtScience Museum de Singapour en forêt tropicale virtuelle qu'il est possible d'explorer physiquement en se déplaçant dans le musée.

Pour l'initiative Snow Drawings de la marque Swisscom, un bataillon de robots autonomes crée la surprise en écrivant des messages aux fans dans la neige à l'occasion des championnats du monde de ski alpin. Le résultat est un véritable chef-d'œuvre de la taille de 16 terrains de foot.

Des innovations simples en matière de navigation sur le Web ne cessent de voir le jour. Le portfolio de Nick Jones par exemple propose une interface basée sur la spirale de Fibonacci.

Le site Searching for Syria permet aux internautes d'en savoir plus sur le drame des réfugiés syriens à travers cinq grandes questions qui se posent concernant la plus grande crise humanitaire en une génération.

08 Facts of the year

Number of internet users:
3.74 billion, 49.6% of
the world population

Number of websites:
1 billion

World news:
Hurricane Harvey causes
devastating flooding
in Texas

Website with most traffic:
Google.com

Tech hardware:
iPhone 8

Tech software:
Adobe announces Flash will
come to an end in 2020

Other tech:
About.com is renamed
Dotdash

Highest-grossing film:
Beauty and the Beast

For Honor:
Scars

—

New levels of design and 3D for desktop and mobile

French video-game maker Ubisoft here promoted its new franchise, For Honor, a third-person melee-fighting game which mixed speed, strategy, and team-play with close-range combat. The special Scars website featured an interactive story where users lived as a warrior from one of the factions in a way that was close to the actual game-play. The graphics, 3D, and animations demonstrated new levels in web design that immediately attracted a lot of praise on social media, although what was equally impressive was how this also worked so well on mobile.

"For Scars, the main idea was to create an interactive story where the gamers are invited to retrace the life of the For Honor warriors through the scars of their weapons. The big challenge was to create a beautiful and impressive experience while being easy to use so that it remains a game for the users. Within a full 3D and binaural-sound immersive experience and with only the help of scrolling, gamers were able to control and navigate around the weapons, see all the scars, and discover for each one an exclusive video where the narrator was none other than the weapon itself."

Mickaël Jacquemin
DDB

Der französische Videospiele-hersteller Ubisoft stellte hier seine neues Franchise-Projekt For Honor vor. Ein Kampf-Spiel in der dritten Person, das Geschwindigkeit, Strategie und Teamspiel mit Nahkampf kombinierte. Die spezielle Scars-Website erzählte eine interaktive Geschichte, in der die Nutzer als Krieger einer der Fraktionen auf eine Art und Weise lebten, die dem eigentlichen Spiel sehr nahe kam. Die Grafiken, 3D und Animationen demonstrierte neue Level im Webdesign, die in den sozialen Medien sofort viel Lob erhielten, obwohl es ebenso beeindruckend war, dass diese auch auf Mobilgeräten funktionierten.

L'entreprise française de déve-loppement de jeux vidéo Ubisoft fait ici la promotion de For Honor, son nouveau jeu de combat rapproché à la troisième per-sonne qui demande rapidité, stratégie et esprit d'équipe. Le site Scars créé spécialement présente une histoire interactive dans laquelle les internautes entrent dans la peau d'un guerrier de l'une des factions, selon une approche très sem-blable au jeu réel. Graphismes, 3D et animations dotent d'une nouvelle dimension la conception Web, immédiatement applaudie sur les réseaux sociaux. Il n'est pas moins impressionnant que le jeu fonctionne tout aussi bien sur des dispositifs mobiles.

2017/
—

Audi
Enter Sandbox

—

400 kilos of sand becomes
a VR test-drive

Developed as an in-store installation that let people test-drive the new Audi Q5 in virtual reality, this project took a real sandbox and let users design their own track in it. This was then turned into a virtual playground using a depth-sensing camera which converted the sandbox into a 3D environment that could be driven around in VR in the Q5. It proved so successful it went on to become a traveling installation for Audi.

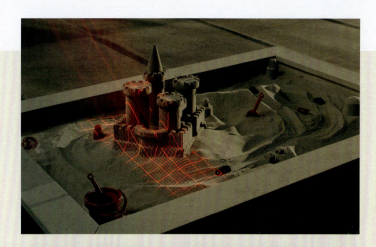

"I think Enter Sandbox was one of the first chances we really had to show people how real-time VR can be used. Up until that point a lot of 360° VR was being used, but audiences weren't that familiar with real-time VR. Enter Sandbox turned out to be the perfect opportunity to use the technology as it allowed us to create an experience that literally transforms a sandbox with real sand tracks into a virtual playground where users can test-drive the Audi Q5."

Pasi Helin
MediaMonks

Das Projekt wurde als Instore-Installation entwickelt, mit der der neue Audi Q5 in der virtuellen Realität erprobt werden konnte. Es wurde eine echte Sandkiste verwendet, in der der User seine eigene Spur anlegen konnte. Dies wurde dann zu einem virtuellen Spielplatz mit einer Tiefenkamera, die die Sandkiste in eine 3D-Umgebung verwandelte, in der in der Virtuellen Realität im Q5 herumgefahren werden konnte. Es erwies sich als so erfolgreich, dass es zu einer Reise-Installation für Audi wurde.

Conçu pour une installation en magasin afin que le public teste la nouvelle Audi Q5 en réalité virtuelle, ce projet part d'un bac à sable dans lequel les gens peuvent tracer des pistes. Une caméra équipée d'un détecteur de profondeur en fait ensuite un terrain de jeu virtuel et convertit le bac à sable en un environnement 3D dans lequel il est possible de piloter la Q5 en RV. Le succès remporté est tel qu'il devient une installation itinérante pour Audi.

—

Ouigo
Let's Play

—

Creating pinball for desktop, mobile, and the arcade

Created for the low-cost, high-speed French train service Ouigo, this project developed a pinball game for browsers but one that could also be played in an actual arcade cabinet. The game ran comfortably on smartphones, within the browser rather than as an app, and had everything a pinball game needed, including multi-ball and jackpot modes, all played out with highly realistic ball physics.

"We created, in collaboration with the Rosapark agency, the world's first pinball game that runs inside your web browser, on your smartphone! It took us about five months of titanic work, to do the research and build prototypes, try dozens of different types of pinball, design the game, the appearance, program the core and the interactions and then test it, refine it, again and again, until we reached the right level of achievement. Technically speaking we stretched the limits of web technologies to the maximum and it worked! I hope this project changed the game and inspired people."

Mathieu Domingues
Merci-Michel

Dieses Projekt wurde für den preiswerten, schnellen französischen Zugdienst Ouigo entwickelt. Es war ein Flipperspiel für Browser, das aber auch in einem echten Arcade-Gehäuse gespielt werden konnte. Das Spiel lief bequem auf Smartphones, im Browser statt als App, und hatte alles, was ein Flipperspiel benötigt, einschließlich Multiball- und Jackpot-Modi, die alle mit höchst realistischer Ballphysik gespielt wurden.

Créé pour l'offre de TGV à bas coûts Ouigo, ce projet est conçu comme un jeu de flipper pour navigateurs, mais il peut aussi se jouer dans une véritable borne d'arcade. Il fonctionne parfaitement sur les smartphones, dans le navigateur plutôt qu'en tant qu'application, et possède tout ce qui caractérise un flipper, y compris des modes multibilles et jackpot. Les déplacements des billes sont des plus réalistes.

AutoDraw

—

Collaboration between machine learning and the artist community

Visitors to this site were invited to start doodling and AutoDraw would then make suggestions about what was taking shape, for example, if a user started to draw a bicycle and drew the wheels first, AutoDraw would show possible finished drawings which might include bicycles, or even spectacles. The drawing tool worked across all devices and combined machine learning with drawings by a number of artists so that all users could learn to draw quickly. The project welcomed submissions to its drawings' database to broaden AutoDraw's competence.

"We wanted to help anyone create drawings or illustrations fast, without needing expensive professional tools. We realized there was an opportunity to use machine learning to enable people to quickly create complex artworks. After prototyping the feature we realized we were using the tool differently compared with before. I often selected artworks that had nothing to do with my original drawing and began to make stream of consciousness compositions of objects that were strange and interesting; it became a game between the team to see how strange an artwork we could make."

Kyle Phillips
Google Creative Lab

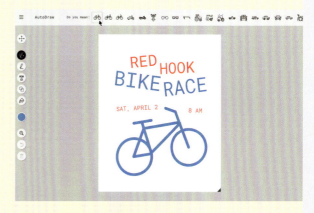

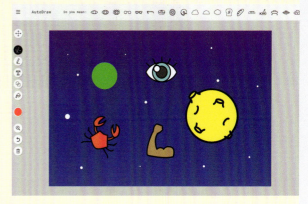

Besucher dieser Seite wurden dazu eingeladen, einfach Herumzukritzeln und AutoDraw machte dann Vorschläge, zu dem was gerade Gestalt annahm. Wenn ein Benutzer zum Beispiel ein Fahrrad zeichnete und zuerst die Räder malte, zeigte AutoDraw möglicherweise schon fertige Zeichnungen an, die Fahrräder oder sogar Brillen enthalten konnten. Das Zeichenwerkzeug funktionierte auf allen Geräten und kombinierte maschinelles Lernen mit Zeichnungen von mehreren Künstlern, sodass alle User schnell zeichnen lernen konnten. Das Projekt begrüßte Beiträge für seine Zeichnung-Datenbank, um die Kompetenz von AutoDraw zu erweitern.

Dans ce site, les visiteurs commencent à dessiner et AutoDraw leur suggère des formes possibles à partir de leurs premiers traits. Par exemple, s'ils veulent dessiner un vélo et tracent d'abord les roues, AutoDraw montre les dessins finalisés d'un vélo ou d'une paire de lunettes. L'outil fonctionne sur tous les dispositifs et repose sur un apprentissage automatique à partir de dessins de plusieurs artistes pour que les visiteurs s'améliorent rapidement. Le projet est ouvert aux propositions pour alimenter sa base de données et améliorer les performances d'AutoDraw.

2017/
—

Dunkirk WebVR

—

A co-play historical
experience in WebVR

This cooperative multi-player 360/WebVR experience was created to promote the movie *Dunkirk* by immersing people right in the battle from 1940. It was important to maintain a sense of respect for such a significant historical event while making sure the game-play was as engaging as possible, hence the idea of co-play with gamers from anywhere in the world which really brought home how the original soldiers had to rely on each other for survival.

"WebVR just started to become a thing and we wanted to be at the forefront of it. We all felt the inherent potential could make it spread like wildfire because we could reach the masses without heavy downloads, installs or fancy headsets. It could be enjoyed by anyone with a mobile phone. Our designer, Steven Mengin, was tasked to figure out new ways to interact without buttons and use only gaze-based interactions instead. This meant the user had to visually lock on to something to proceed. It was something of a unique challenge because everyone is so used to clicking on everything."

Dirk van Ginkel
Jam3

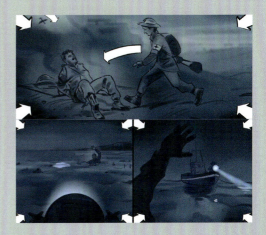

Diese kooperative Multiplayer-360 / WebVR-Erfahrung wurde erschaffen, um den Film *Dunkirk* zu bewerben, indem man die Leute direkt in die Schlacht von 1940 eintauchen ließ. Es war wichtig, den Respekt für solch ein bedeutendes historisches Ereignis zu bewahren und gleich-zeitig sicherzustellen, dass das Spiel so ansprechend wie möglich war. Daher kam die Idee, mit Spielern aus aller Welt zusam-menzuspielen. Es brachte wirklich rüber, wie sich damals die echten Soldaten aufeinander verlassen mussten, um zu überleben.

Cette expérience WebVR de 360°, multijoueur et coopérative, sert à la promotion du film *Dunkerque* et plonge le public au cœur de la bataille de 1940. L'idée était de préserver le respect d'un événement histo-rique de cette importance tout en créant un jeu aussi stimulant que possible, d'où le mode coopératif impliquant des joueurs du monde entier, à l'image des soldats de l'époque qui comp-taient les uns sur les autres pour leur survie.

G-Active Water: Made Active

—

A human figure made entirely from water

This project for Gatorade's new electrolyte water G-Active created a human figure from water, without using any CGI. This installation featured a custom-made 'rain rig' which released water in a sequence that could recreate the figure of a moving athlete.

Water pressure was controlled by 2,048 switches to trigger droplets at exact times, and this was combined with flash-lighting so that the droplets would appear illuminated and suspended in mid-air.

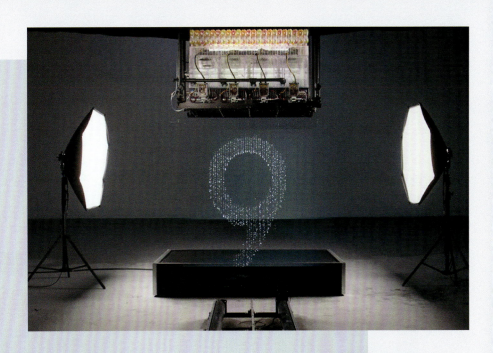

"We initially looked at building a machine that could produce a 2D human form using a single row of water nozzles, but I had a vision of a living, breathing, fully 3D woman, made entirely of water that could physically interact with her surroundings. I realized that our key R&D discoveries — like whether we could achieve a clear 3D figure — would only emerge dangerously close to the shoot. And every time we upgraded or dismantled the rig, our understanding of the pressures and quantities would reset so there was a danger of not knowing what we would be turning over on."

Cole Paviour
Unit9; Director

Dieses Projekt für Gatorades neues Elektrolyt-Wasser G-Active schuf aus Wasser eine menschliche Figur, ohne CGI zu verwenden. Diese Installation beinhaltete eine speziell angefertigte „Regenanlage", die Wasser in einer Sequenz freisetzte, die die Figur eines sich bewegenden Athleten nachbilden konnte. Der Wasserdruck wurde von 2.048 Schaltern gesteuert, um die Tröpfchen zu exakten Zeiten auszulösen und dies wurde mit Blitzlicht kombiniert, sodass die Tröpfchen beleuchtet wurden und in der Luft schwebend erschienen.

Ce projet pour la nouvelle boisson énergétique G-Active de Gatorade montre une figure humaine faite de gouttes d'eau, et ce sans recourir à une interface CGI. L'installation emploie une douche spéciale qui coule selon une séquence programmée pour recréer et animer un athlète. La pression de l'eau est contrôlée par 2048 commutateurs afin de libérer des gouttelettes à la microseconde près, le tout assorti d'un éclairage par flash pour que les gouttes semblent lumineuses et en suspens.

—

<u>Interland</u>
<u>Be Internet Awesome</u>

—

Teaching young people about digital safety

In an age when more and more young people start using the web, Google and North Kingdom worked together to create this site with the aim of making knowledge about digital safety as accessible as possible. Visitors were invited to embark on a quest to become a fearless explorer of an online world whose visuals pulled them into the experience and its various scenarios, such as Reality River which taught how not to 'fall for fake', and Mindful Mountain, which explained about 'sharing with care'.

"Interland was a fun online game designed to teach kids about phishing, internet harassment, passwords, and other internet safety topics that otherwise might seem boring or irrelevant. The immersive experience comprised four distinct worlds where children tackled challenges, puzzles, and games that would prepare them to be on guard against internet threats. Kids could play their way to Internet Awesome and become confident explorers of the online world."

Sarah Wilson
Google Brand Studio

In einer Zeit, in der immer mehr junge Leute das Internet nutzten, arbeiteten Google und North Kingdom zusammen, um diese Website mit dem Ziel zu erstellen, das Wissen über digitale Sicherheit so zugänglich wie möglich zu machen. Die Besucher wurden dazu eingeladen auf eine Suche zu gehen und furchtlose Entdecker einer Online-Welt zu werden, deren Bilder sie in das Erlebnis und dessen verschiedenen Szenarien hineinzogen, wie zum Beispiel „Reality River", wo man lernte, nicht auf „Fake" hereinzufallen und „Mindful Mountain", was erklärte, wie man mit Vorsicht teilt.

Alors que de plus en plus de jeunes font leurs premiers pas sur le Web, Google et North Kingdom s'associent pour créer ce site et apporter des informations sur la sécurité numérique. Les visiteurs ont pour mission de s'affirmer comme les explorateurs courageux d'un monde en ligne. L'esthétique choisie les plonge dans l'aventure et différents scénarios, comme «Reality River», qui apprend à détecter les infos bidons, ou encore «Mindful Mountain», qui explique comment partager des données avec précaution.

Konterball

—

One of the early wave of WebVR games

Here was a WebVR mini-game that was based on the mechanics of table tennis, which users could play on their own, against a wall, or by hooking up with anyone else online for a head-to-head game. This new generation of virtual-reality games, built for the web, very much brought VR to the masses since previously it was more of a niche area that required big VR experiences to be downloaded and then explored with what were often expensive headsets.

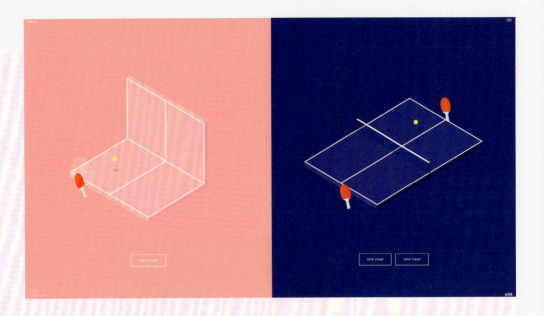

"Konterball started out as a simple experiment to demonstrate WebVR as a technology that easily allowed friends and strangers to join together in virtual space and enjoy an immersive ping-pong game. We even composed a custom soundtrack and added a rainbow mode to get across as much of the Konterball vibe as possible. Konterball is definitely one of our all-time favorite projects at wild because it allowed us to do what we do best: take a simple, strong idea, pair it up with technology, and polish the project until we're ready to share it with the world."

Thomas Ragger
wild

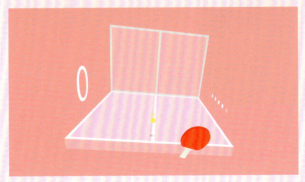

Hier war ein WebVR-Minispiel, das auf der Mechanik des Tischtennis basierte. Der User konnte alleine gegen eine Wand spielen oder sich mit anderen Personen ein Kopf-an-Kopf-Spiel liefern. Diese neue Generation von Virtual-Reality-Spielen, die für das Web entwickelt wurde, brachte VR zu den Massen, da es früher eher ein Nischenbereich war, in dem große VR-Experiences heruntergeladen und dann mit oft teuren Headsets erkundet werden mussten.

Ce mini-jeu WebVR se base sur le principe du ping-pong et peut être joué en solo contre un mur, ou à deux avec quiconque également en ligne. Cette nouvelle génération de jeux de réalité virtuelle conçus pour le Web démocratise la RV et en fait profiter le grand public, alors qu'elle était jusqu'alors plutôt élitiste et obligeait le téléchargement et la pratique des expériences RV avec des casques souvent onéreux.

2017/
—

Bacardi
InstantDJ

—

An early example of hacking
Instagram Stories

Following the launch of Instagram Stories in August 2016, it didn't take long for someone to create a hack that would transform the social platform into a DJ Simulator. The official Bacardi Instagram account was an early example, and could be transformed into a set of turntables by simply clicking on the Bacardi logo; controlling the turntables was then as simple as skipping back and forth within the story to jump between different clips of scratches, beats, and samples.

"People skip ads on social media every time they can, so we decided to embrace that behavior. By making skipping part of the idea and turning Instagram Stories into a fun interactive experience, we accomplished what should be everyone's goal: to make ads that don't feel like ads and entertain people along the way. BBDO's desire is to hack social platforms as soon as they launch any new functionality. And when Instagram launched the Skip Back option, we wasted no time and created, produced, and launched the idea in two weeks."

Danilo Boer & Marcos Kotlhar
BBDO

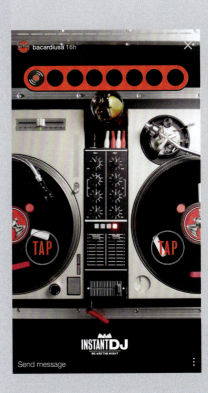

Nach dem Start von Instagram Stories im August 2016 dauerte es nicht lange, bis jemand einen Hack kreierte, der die soziale Plattform in einen DJ-Simulator verwandelte. Das offizielle Bacardi Instagram Konto war dafür ein frühes Beispiel und konnte durch einfaches Klicken auf das Bacardi-Logo in eine Reihe von Plattenspielern verwandelt werden. Die Steuerung der Plattenspieler war dann ganz einfach. Man konnte vor und zurück springen und zwischen verschiedenen Clips aus Scratches, Beats und Samples herumspringen.

Après le lancement d'Instagram Stories en août 2016, le piratage de la plate-forme sociale en un simulateur de DJ ne s'est pas fait attendre. Le compte Instagram officiel de Bacardi est l'un des premiers du genre : il suffit de cliquer sur le logo Bacardi pour faire apparaître un jeu de platines, facilement contrôlables en avançant et en reculant dans l'histoire pour changer les effets de scratches, de rythmes et de samples.

Smurfs:
The Lost Village
—

The future of digital?

With the launch of HoloLens in 2016 it was great to see one of the first-ever branded experiences, for the smurf film franchise, turning the real world into an augmented smurf playground. Users were immersed in the world of the smurfs in ways that hadn't been seen before, such as when the little characters sprouted up out of the floor and around the user so that a game ensued in which players were encouraged to use as many of the surfaces as they could. All this could only be achieved via Microsoft's HoloLens, and if the web now seemed to be moving out of the web, this was an example of where things could be heading for the next generation.

"VR is a new medium, but when you come from making virtual worlds in video games the challenges of not being able to control the camera and player's attention are nothing new. However, when you need to start making experiences that have to adapt to the player's environment then it's a whole new challenge and form. For us it was about stripping the design back to the core 'second-to-second' experience: controlling a smurf and directing him around the world. Working with smurfs was magical as we could breathe life into the form factor we remember from the Schleich Toys but with the animation of the films."

Alexander Horton
Unit9; Experiential Director

Die Veröffentlichung der Holo-Lens-Brille im 2016 machte es möglich, eine der ersten Erfahrungen damit im Zusammenhang mit einer Marke zu machen. Entwickelt für das Medien-Franchise der Schlümpfe, verwandelte sie die reale Welt in das Universum der kleinen Kreaturen. Die User konnten auf eine Weise in die Welt der Schlümpfe eintauchen, wie man sie noch nie zuvor gesehen hatte. Zum Beispiel wenn die kleinen Figuren aus dem Boden kamen und um den Benutzer herum sprangen. So wurden die Spieler ermutigt, so viele Oberflächen wie möglich zu benutzen. Dies konnte nur über die Holo-Lens erreicht werden. Da sich das Web nun aus dem Netz heraus zu bewegen schien, ist dies ein Beispiel dafür, wohin es in Zukunft gehen könnte.

La sortie en 2016 des lunettes HoloLens permet de découvrir l'une des toutes premières expériences liées à une marque. Conçue pour la franchise médiatique Les Schtroumpfs, elle transforme le monde réel en l'univers augmenté des petites créatures. Les utilisateurs se retrouvent ainsi plongés dans leur monde d'une façon inédite : par exemple, des Schtroumpfs surgissent du sol et autour du joueur pour l'encourager à utiliser le plus de surfaces possible. Fonctionnant seulement avec les lunettes Microsoft HoloLens, cette création laisse entrevoir le potentiel pour la génération à venir, sachant que le Web est en train de dépasser ses propres limites.

NOTABLE WEBSITE LAUNCH
WebVR Experiments

GOOGLE FACTS

Smart reply in Gmail launches

Google Lens announced

Android passes 2 billion active devices

Google Assistant becomes available for iOS

Google VR announces upcoming headsets that won't require a smartphone

Top 5 Trends

MOBILE EVOLUTION
iPhone X

With 5.8 in. OLED Super
Retina display and Face ID
(facial recognition)

INTERNET COMMUNITY
WannaCry ransomware attack

Over a quarter of a million PCs were
held to ransom in the WannaCry attack,
with demands of between $300 and $1,200
in bitcoin to unlock the machines.
The United Kingdom's National Health
Service was briefly crippled, though
a kill switch was eventually found by
22-year-old Marcus Hutchins.

2018/

Web Design, The Next Generation...

2018/

—

Web Design, The Next Generation...

—

FWA18

With smartphones having now overtaken all other ways of going online combined (accounting for over 52 percent of access), the CRT web of two decades ago seemed a distant relic, while more mobile-based digital experiences had appeared alongside real-world examples, i.e. as physical installations in everyday locations, such as bus stops, train stations, and in-store experiences.

Many of the digital pioneers of the Flash era, who had since founded their own agencies, were now turning their attention to experiences that affected the real lives of individuals.

The timeline of web design as presented in this book culminates in the need to consider what it actually means in 2019. A huge majority of websites employ a template style, as befits a needs-driven world where people expect access to information in quick and recognizable formats. This has led innovators in many different directions, as can be seen even from the FWA's showcase, which marked 18 years of existence with a special graphic illustrating how the web has developed via a collaboration with the seven leading interactive agencies since the Millennium (B-Reel, Google Creative Lab, Hello Monday, MediaMonks, Resn, Stink Studios, and Unit9) and summarizing web design's history in developmental stages: the CRT web; smartphones; tablets; virtual reality; augmented reality; installations; and artificial intelligence.

While some still hankered for the heady experimental work of the early 2000s, innovation had now moved far from basic template websites into realms of physical and augmented realities.

One constant since the web's inception has been websites for certain occasions, particularly Christmas. Every year, special festive micro-experiences are created, by individuals, agencies, and brands, including the interactive example from New Zealand, Resn's Little Helper, with the latest in click-and-hold and click-and-drag effects.

A similar trend occurs with the micro-sites created by agencies to show off their latest design and development skills, as with makemepulse's 2018 Wishes, a multi-level game experience that demonstrated the capabilities of their 3D engine.

The start of a year also evokes new life, a theme explored by Samsung in its revolutionary app for premature babies. Voices of Life recorded the mother's voice and heartbeat directly on to her smartphone and then 'wombified' these recordings for the baby's ears for playing inside the incubator holding the premature baby, in an effort to simulate a nurturing environment through sound.

The increasing popularity of phone camera lenses that let users change their appearance and setting prompted the U.S. Navy to create augmented reality masks for its Sea Stadium project. Via the latest Facebook Camera Effects, users could become a Navy officer or change their surroundings into a sea of ships and aircraft, or an entire naval base viewed in 360°.

The rise of AR as a means of interacting with the real world via a smartphone led Germany's Demodern Digital Agency to develop an app that helped people to build flat-packs with more visual assistance than the usual black and white image instructions.

This modern way of thinking almost made a game out of something that has become synonymous with head-scratching.

PopCorn TV celebrated a past web using the latest technology in a website that mixed challenges with a digital quiz for fans of pop-culture and TV series. The site's decor featured 66 hidden TV references, while the set was built in 4K with a zoom function, causing the detail to pop. With bonuses throughout and cult-quote trophies to share on social media, this experience tapped into the wider nostalgic trend for the 1980s.

Outrider Bomb Blast was an interactive tool that personalized the impact of nuclear weapons by enabling the site's users to enter their home or another address and see what would happen in the event of a missile strike. At a time of heightened nuclear tension, this was a sobering experience and encouraged people to become better informed.

Resn's Little Helper

2018 Wishes

The Voices of Life

Mit den Smartphones wurden jetzt alle anderen Möglichkeiten online zu gehen übertroffen (mit mehr als 52 Prozent Zugriff). Das CRT-Netz von vor zwei Jahrzehnten schien ein weit entferntes Relikt zu sein, während immer mehr mobile digitale Erlebnisse neben realen Beispielen erschienen, d. h. als physische Installationen an alltäglichen Orten, wie Bushaltestellen, Bahnhöfen und Geschäften im Laden.

Viele der digitalen Pioniere der Flash-Ära, die inzwischen eigene Agenturen gegründet hatten, widmeten sich nun den Erfahrungen, die das reale Leben von Individuen beeinflussten.

Der Zeitstrahl des Webdesigns, wie er in diesem Buch vorgestellt wird, gipfelt in der Notwendigkeit, zu überlegen, was Webdesign eigentlich im Jahr 2019 bedeutet. Eine große Mehrheit von Websites verwendet einen Vorlagenstil, wie es sich für eine bedürfnisorientierte Welt gehört, in der die Menschen Zugang zu Informationen in schnellen und erkennbaren Formaten erwarten. Dies hat Innovatoren in viele verschiedene Richtungen geführt, wie man im Showcase des FWA sehen kann. Dieser markierte das 18-jährige Bestehen mit einer speziellen Grafik, die zeigt, wie sich das Internet in Zusammenarbeit mit den sieben führenden interaktiven Agenturen seit dem Millennium entwickelt hat (B-Reel, Google Creative Lab, Hello Monday, MediaMonks, Resn, Stink Studios und Unit9) und fasst die Geschichte des Webdesigns in seinen Entwicklungsstadien zusammen: das CRT Web, Smartphones, Tablets, Virtual Reality, Augmented Reality, Installationen und künstliche Intelligenz.

Während sich einige immer noch nach der berauschenden experimentellen Arbeit der frühen 2000er Jahre zurücksehnten, war die Innovation von den grundlegenden Vorlagenwebseiten nun in Bereiche physischer und erweiterter Wirklichkeiten übergegangen.

Eine Konstante seit der Gründung des Webs waren Websites für bestimmte Anlässe, insbesondere zu Weihnachten. Jedes Jahr werden spezielle festliche Mikroerfahrungen von Einzelpersonen, Agenturen und Marken erstellt, darunter dieses interaktive Beispiel aus Neuseeland, Resns Little Helper, mit den neuesten Klick- und Halte- und Klick- und Zieheffekten.

Ein ähnlicher Trend tritt bei den Micro-Sites auf, die von Agenturen erstellt wurden, um ihre neuesten Design- und Entwicklungsfähigkeiten zu zeigen, zum Beispiel mit Wishes 2018 von Makemepulse, eine Multi-Level-Game Experience, welche die Fähigkeiten einer 3D-Engine demonstrierte.

Der Beginn eines Jahres erweckt auch immer neues Leben. Ein Thema, das Samsung in dieser revolutionären App für Frühchen erforscht hat. Voices of Life nahm die Stimme und den Herzschlag der Mutter direkt auf ihr Smartphone auf und „wombified" diese Aufnahmen dann passend für die Ohren des Babys, um sie im Inkubator mit dem Frühchen abzuspielen. Es sollte durch den Klang eine fördernde Umgebung simuliert werden.

Die zunehmende Popularität von Telefon-Kameraobjektiven, die es den Benutzern erlauben, ihr Aussehen und ihre Einstellung zu ändern, veranlasste die US Navy, Augmented-Reality-Masken für ihr Sea-Stadium-Projekt zu schaffen. Über die neuesten Facebook-Kamera-Effekte können Benutzer zum Marineoffizier werden oder ihre Umgebung in ein Meer von Schiffen und Flugzeugen verwandeln oder eine ganze Marinebasis in 360° sehen.

Der Aufstieg von Augmented Reality (AR) als Mittel zur Interaktion mit der realen Welt über ein Smartphone führte dazu, dass die deutsche Demodern Digital Agency eine App entwickelte, die Leuten dabei half, Flatpacks mit stärkerer visueller Unterstützung als die üblichen Schwarz-Weiß-Bildanweisungen zu bauen. Diese moderne Art zu denken hat aus etwas, das zum Synonym für das Kopfkratzen geworden ist, fast ein Spiel gemacht.

PopCorn TV feierte die vergangene Ära des Internets mit der neuesten Technologie auf dieser Website, welche die Herausforderungen mit einem digitalen Quiz für Fans von Popkultur und TV-Serien vermischte. Das Dekor der Website enthielt 66 versteckte TV-Referenzen, während das Set in 4K mit einer Zoom-Funktion gebaut wurde, wodurch Details aufgepoppt wurden. Mit Bonussen überall und die ganze Zeit und Kult-Zitat-Trophäen, die in den sozialen Medien geteilt wurden, griff diese Experience den allgemeinen Nostalgietrend der 1980er Jahre auf.

Outrider Bomb Blast war ein interaktives Tool, das die Auswirkungen von Atomwaffen personalisierte, indem sie den Nutzern der Website ermöglichte, ihre Heimat- oder eine andere Adresse einzugeben und zu sehen, was im Fall eines Raketenangriffs passieren würde. In einer Zeit erhöhter nuklearer Spannungen war dies eine ernüchternde Erfahrung und forderte die Menschen dazu auf, sich besser zu informieren.

2018/

—

Web Design,
The Next
Generation…

—

Sea Stadium

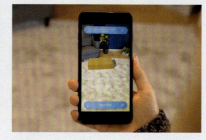

AR Build Assist

PopCorn TV

Outrider Bomb Blast

"For the first
time smartphones
had now overtaken
all other ways
of going online."

Pour la première fois, les smartphones deviennent le support par excellence pour naviguer (plus de 52 % des accès). Le Web que l'on voyait sur des écrans CRT il y a deux décennies a aujourd'hui des allures de relique comparé à toutes les expériences numériques pour dispositifs mobiles qui voient le jour, ainsi qu'aux installations physiques qui se montent dans l'espace public (arrêts de bus, gares, magasins).

De nombreux pionniers numériques à l'ère Flash, et qui ont depuis fondé leurs propres agences, s'intéressent maintenant aux expériences touchant la vie réelle du public.

La chronologie de la conception Web retracée dans cet ouvrage culmine avec la nécessité de s'interroger sur la signification l'année 2019 de ce concept. Une énorme majorité de sites affichent un modèle de style adapté à un monde où les utilisateurs veulent accéder à l'information d'une façon rapide et directe. Les esprits innovateurs partent dans plusieurs directions, comme l'illustre la propre évolution des sélections des FWA. Ces prix fêtent leurs 18 années d'existence avec un graphisme montrant le développement du Web grâce à la collaboration des sept plus

grandes agences interactives depuis le nouveau millénaire : B-Reel, Google Creative Lab, Hello Monday, MediaMonks, Resn, Stink Studios et Unit9. Il résume visuellement les étapes de la croissance du Web : CRT, smartphones, tablettes, réalité virtuelle, réalité augmentée, installations et intelligence artificielle.

Alors que certains rêvent encore du travail expérimental du début des années 2000, l'innovation prend désormais ses distances avec les sites qui obéissent à un modèle basique et privilégie la réalité physique et la réalité augmentée.

Depuis les origines du Web, les sites célébrant des occasions spéciales sont une constante, notamment pour Noël. Chaque année, des micro-expériences voient le jour au moment des fêtes de la main de particuliers, d'agences et de marques. Tel est le cas de Little Helper signé par l'agence néo-zélandaise Resn, qui fait appel aux derniers effets par clic sans relâcher et par cliquer-glisser.

On remarque une tendance comparable avec les micro-sites que créent les agences pour exhiber leurs compétences en conception et développement. Par exemple, l'expérience de jeu multi-niveau 2018 Wishes de la

société makemepulse illustre les performances de son moteur 3D.

Un début d'année peut aussi être synonyme de naissance. Samsung part de cette idée et développe une application révolutionnaire pour les nourrissons prématurés. Sur un smartphone, Voices of Life enregistre la voix et les battements de cœur de la mère, puis les traite pour qu'ils s'apparentent aux sons que le fœtus entend à l'intérieur du ventre. Les enregistrements sont diffusés dans la couveuse pour créer une ambiance sonore simulant celle du ventre maternel.

Les caméras des téléphones permettant aux utilisateurs de changer leur apparence et le décor qui les entoure bénéficient d'une popularité croissante. Dans cet esprit, pour son projet Sea Stadium, la US Navy met au point des masques de réalité augmentée. Grâce à la plate-forme Camera Effects de Facebook, l'utilisateur peut alors devenir un officier de marine ou voir autour de lui des navires, des avions ou toute une base navale sur 360°.

Le succès de la réalité augmentée comme moyen d'interaction avec le monde réel via un smartphone inspire l'agence numérique allemande Demodern.

Elle développe une application pour aider les gens à monter des meubles en kit grâce à une assistance visuelle plus explicite que les habituelles instructions et leurs images en noir et blanc. Cette approche moderne simplifie à l'extrême ce qui s'avère généralement un casse-tête.

PopCorn TV s'inspire d'un ancien site Web et grâce aux dernières technologies, propose des défis et des quiz numériques aux fans de culture pop et de séries télé. Pas moins de 66 indices sont cachés dans le décor, conçu en 4K avec une fonction de zoom qui fait surgir les infos. Avec des bonus et des trophées incluant des citations cultes à partager sur les réseaux sociaux, cette expérience exploite la nostalgie des années 80.

Le site Outrider Bomb Blast est un outil interactif qui simule l'effet meurtrier des armes nucléaires. Les visiteurs entrent leur propre adresse ou une autre de leur choix et observent les conséquences d'une bombe lâchée à cet endroit. Avec une tension nucléaire mondiale qui s'intensifie, cette expérience sensibilise et donne à réfléchir.

08 Facts of the year

52.9%

Number of internet users:
4.02 billion, 52.9% of
the world population

1.3 billion

Number of websites:
1.3 billion

세계 뉴스

World news:
the leaders of North and
South Korea meet and agree
to work for peace

Google

Website with most traffic:
Google.com

Tech hardware:
a Tesla Roadster is
launched into space

Hello

Tech software:
Google Duplex is announced

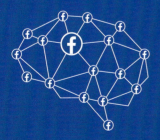

Other tech:
Cambridge Analytica
harvests 50 million
Facebook profiles

Highest-grossing film:
Black Panther

—

History of
the Internet

—

1,474 events create a
'3D sculpture tower'

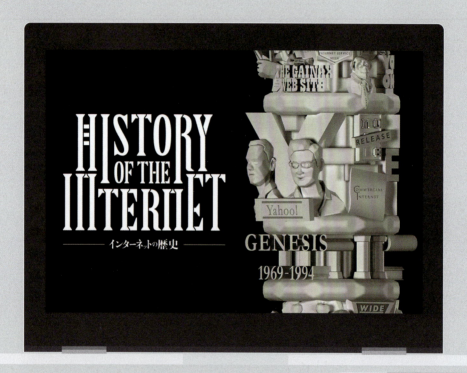

Few internet companies have a history as long and established as Yahoo!, so they were ideally placed to present this website on The History of the Internet from their Japan office, with snapshots of nearly 1,500 historical internet events dating back to 1995, as well as an even earlier summary for the years 1969–1994. Each event was individually visualized in 3D and together they were assembled into a special 3D Sculpture Tower. The WebGL-powered tower was fully interactive and could be explored in any direction or searched by year, internet event, or other criteria to locate a specific position. This was a visual feast and a fascinating and original way to present so much data and so many staging-posts in the timeline of the internet.

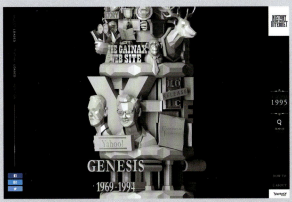

"Based on the idea 'Learn your history, so the next generation can shape the internet of the future', 1,474 international events that contributed to the internet's history were researched and selected. From there, 3D models of each event were designed and created, and the models were placed in a tower using WebGL. We challenged ourselves to create a website that pushed the limits of what smartphones in 2018 were able to handle."

Takayuki Nagai
Birdman

Nur wenige Internetfirmen haben eine so lange und etablierte Geschichte wie Yahoo! Daher waren sie ideal positioniert, um diese Website über die Geschichte des Internets in ihrem japanischen Büro zu präsentieren, mit Momentaufnahmen von fast 1.500 historischen Internet-Veranstaltungen bis zum Jahr 1995, sowie eine noch frühere Zusammenfassung für die Jahre 1969-1994. Jede Veranstaltung wurde einzeln in 3D visualisiert und dann zu einem speziellen 3D-Skulpturenturm zusammengesetzt. Der WebGL-betriebene Turm war vollständig interaktiv und konnte in jede Richtung erkundet oder nach Jahren, Internet Event oder anderen Kriterien durchsucht werden, um eine spezielle Position auszumachen. Dies war ein visuelles Festmahl und eine faszinierende und originale Art, so viele Daten und Etappen in der Zeitleiste des Internets zu präsentieren.

Rares sont les sociétés Internet de si longue date comme Yahoo! La firme est donc parfaitement en mesure de présenter ce site Web sur l'histoire d'Internet conçu par ses bureaux au Japon, avec un aperçu de près de 1500 événements Internet depuis 1995, ainsi qu'un résumé de la période entre 1969 et 1994. Chaque événement est représenté en 3D, et l'ensemble forme une tour sculpturale également en 3D. Cette dernière, reposant sur la technologie WebGL, est totalement interactive, visible sous tous les angles et permet des recherches par année, par événement ou selon d'autres critères. Véritable régal pour les yeux, il s'agit d'une façon originale et réussie de présenter une foule de données et de faits sur l'histoire d'Internet.

2018/
—

Audi Quattro Coaster AR

—

A car that burst out
of the TV screen

In 2005, Toyota's Aygo arrived through a letterbox, and 13 years later Audi crashed a car right out of the screen using the latest AR technology. The smartphone app presented an experience that was triggered by Audi's TV commercials, so that users could try out one of four Quattros which broke through their TV screen to appear beside them. The app also let the cars be shrunk to matchbox size and raced, as in Hot Wheels, around tracks laid down in their new surroundings.

Here you'll find a 100% realistic car to explore, inside and out.

Download quattro® coaster

"The Quattro Coaster app from Audi was the world's first AR experience to interact with a TV commercial. The app recognized the commercial and allowed the car to race out of the TV and into the user's living-room. Instead of watching the next commercial, viewers had an immersive experience, by building their own tracks using AR technology, and test-driving the Audi Quattro in all driving conditions, through the four seasons."

Petter Bryde
POL

Im Jahr 2005 kam Toyotas Aygo durch einen Briefkasten zu uns und 13 Jahre später ließ Audi ein Auto direkt aus dem Bildschirm stürzen, mit der neuesten AR-Technologie. Die Smartphone App präsentierte eine Erfahrung, die durch die TV-Werbefilme von Audi ausgelöst wurde, sodass User einen von vier Quattros ausprobieren konnten, die ihren Bildschirm durchbrachen und neben ihnen auftauchten. Die App ließ auch die Autos auf Streichholzschachtelgröße schrumpfen und wie bei Hot Wheels auf Strecken rasen, die in seinen neuen Umgebungen angelegt wurden.

En 2005, la Toyota Aygo sortait d'une boîte aux lettres et 13 ans plus tard, Audi fait surgir de l'écran une voiture grâce à la RA. L'application pour smartphones offre une expérience qui commence dans les spots publicitaires d'Audi : les utilisateurs voient alors l'un des quatre modèles Quattro sortir de leur écran de télévision et apparaître à leurs côtés. Ils peuvent également réduire les voitures à la taille d'une boîte d'allumettes et les faire courir, comme dans le jeu Hot Wheels, sur des pistes sillonnant l'environnement augmenté.

One Last Beat

—

An interactive story made for under $100

With social media, trends and new developments can be witnessed as soon as they happen, but as many people's lives became dominated by such instant access, personal web projects were now very unlikely to make an impact in this way. However, social channels soon began to light up with One Last Beat, a personal project by Héctor Monerris created in collaboration with his parents and all for under $100. An interactive story about a man trying to give his life meaning in the last moments before dying, in some ways it felt like a bit of a throwback yet also gave people a sense of how great things could be achieved with limited resources but lots of passion.

"Making One Last Beat changed me in so many ways. Every day was stuffed with unexpected and crazy challenges that needed to be solved on the go. I even quit my job to be able to finish it! But it was totally worth it. I spent really good moments working with my parents, and I learned out of necessity some useful stuff about photography, video, design, music, coding, crafts, and storytelling. Mostly dos and don'ts. I know the project was naive and amateurish, but I felt like it told my truth."

Héctor Monerris
nerris.com

Mit den sozialen Medien lassen sich Trends und neue Entwicklungen sofort feststellen, sobald sie auftreten. So viele Menschenleben werden aber von einem solchen sofortigen Zugang beeinflusst und es ist sehr unwahrscheinlich, dass persönliche Webprojekte auf diese Weise Auswirkungen haben werden. Allerdings begannen soziale Kanäle mit One Last Beat beleuchtet zu werden, ein persönliches Projekt von Héctor Monerris, das in Zusammenarbeit mit seinen Eltern für nur 100 US-Dollar erstellt wurde. Eine interaktive Geschichte über einen Mann, der versucht, sein Leben in den letzten Augenblicken vor dem Sterben sinnvoll zu gestalten. In mancher Hinsicht fühlte es sich an wie eine Art Rückschritt, gab den Leuten aber auch ein Gefühl dafür, wie große Dinge mit begrenzten Mitteln aber mit viel Leidenschaft erreicht werden konnten.

Grâce aux réseaux sociaux, les tendances et nouveautés en développement sont connues dès qu'elles se produisent. L'accès immédiat aux informations étant devenu monnaie courante dans nos vies, les projets Web personnels ont toutefois peu de chance de se faire remarquer. Les réseaux s'enflamment pourtant très vite avec One Last Beat, un projet d'Héctor Monerris créé en collaboration avec ses parents pour moins de 100 dollars : il raconte l'histoire interactive d'un homme qui tente de donner un sens à sa vie juste avant de mourir. Bien qu'au look un peu désuet, il démontre que l'on peut arriver loin avec des ressources restreintes mais une bonne dose de passion.

Stinkmoji

—

An early face-recognition web experience

The launch of the iPhone X introduced facial-recognition processing to a much larger audience, for even though webcams had enabled such experiences for some years, Apple's Animojis let people share animated personal emojis with others and provided a new creative tool with many possibilities. Stinkmoji (a name mash-up from Stink Studios) was a charming example that incorporated 3D modeling to celebrate internet popular culture. The mobile or desktop experience worked via the user's webcam or phone camera to bring the characters to life and make all sorts of facial expressions as they opened Easter egg treats.

"Stinkmoji was an adorable face-recognition experience celebrating iconic characters in pop culture. It was designed and developed as an ode to Apple's Animoji. Available on mobile and desktop, the experience offered users the possibility to select and then play as one of the characters. Each part of the user's face (lips, eyelids, eyebrows, and cheeks) was tracked so the 3D characters perfectly mirrored the user's movements. This tracking was also used to unlock a hidden extra feature inside the experience, which was unveiled when users made a specific facial expression."

Benjamin Laugel
Stink Studios

Durch die Einführung des iPhone X wurde die Gesichtserkennungsverarbeitung einem viel größeren Publikum vorgestellt, denn obwohl Webcams schon seit einigen Jahren solche Erfahrungen ermöglichten, ließen Apples Animojis die Leute animierte persönliche Emojis mit anderen teilen und bot ein neues kreatives Werkzeug mit vielen Möglichkeiten. Stinkmoji (ein Name, der aus Stink Studios entstand), war ein charmantes Beispiel, das 3D-Modellierung einbezog, um die Internet-Populärkultur zu feiern. Die mobile oder Desktop-Experience funktionierte über die Webcam des Users oder die Kamera des Telefons, um die Charaktere zum Leben zu erwecken und alle möglichen Gesichtsausdrücke zu machen, wenn sie die Osterei-Leckereien öffneten.

La sortie de l'iPhone X démocratise la reconnaissance faciale, même si les webcams offrent depuis quelques années déjà ce type d'expérience. Les Animojis d'Apple permettent de partager des emojis animés et de laisser libre cours à la créativité. La jolie création Stinkmoji (nom créé à partir de Stink Studios) intègre une fonction de modélisation en 3D en l'honneur de la culture populaire d'Internet. L'expérience mobile ou bureau fonctionne via la webcam ou la caméra du téléphone : l'utilisateur anime les personnages grâce à une série d'expressions faciales quand il ouvre des œufs de Pâques.

Mario in Google Maps

—

A first for Google Maps, with animated 3D models

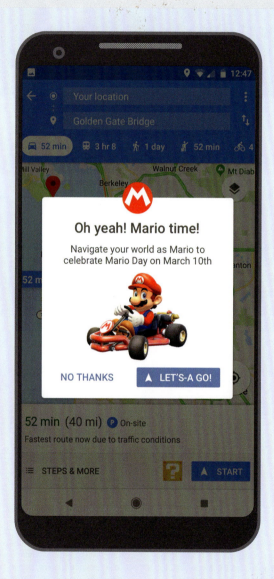

The world-famous animated plumber hosted a new experience here via Google Maps when users were invited to navigate around the mapping service as Mario, driving his Mario Kart in 3D. At one level a simple novelty, this combined effort between Nintendo and the Google Maps team was the first time an animated 3D model was used in this way. The experience was only live for one day but the collaboration opened the door to future innovation for navigation in general.

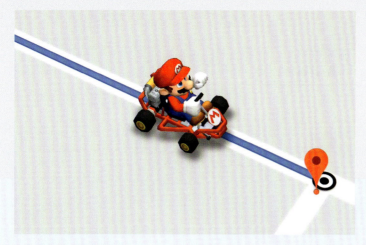

"To celebrate Mario Day (March 10), we wanted to let our users appear as Mario in Google Maps while navigating their world instead of the standard directional arrow. This was a 20% project initiated and led by a small team of passionate designers and engineers on Google Maps in close collaboration with Nintendo, and was the first time we introduced animated 3D models on our base-map which required a bit of experimenting to pull off in a way that would perform satisfactorily. The result was a delightful experience reminiscent of the beloved video game."

Munish Dabas
Google Maps

Der weltberühmte Zeichentrick-Klempner präsentierte hier eine neue Erfahrung mit Google Maps, bei der die User dazu eingeladen wurden, im Kartendienst als Mario zu navigieren und sein Mario Kart in 3D zu fahren. Einerseits war es eine einfache Neuheit, diese kombinierte Zusammenarbeit zwischen Nintendo und dem Google Maps-Team aber war das erste Mal, dass ein animiertes 3D-Modell auf diese Weise verwendet wurde. Die Erfahrung war nur für einen Tag live aber die Zusammenarbeit öffnete die Tür für zukünftige Innovationen der Navigation im Allgemeinen.

Le plombier le plus célèbre au monde nous fait vivre une nouvelle expérience via Google Maps : les utilisateurs se déplacent en 3D dans le site de cartographie en tant que Mario, à bord du Mario Kart. Cette réalisation est le fruit d'une collaboration entre Nintendo et l'équipe de Google Maps et utilise un modèle 3D animé d'une façon jusque-là inédite. L'expérience ne reste en ligne qu'un jour mais ce travail ouvre la porte à d'autres innovations en matière de navigation.

60th Annual Grammy Awards: Play the City

—

When a city became a musical instrument

To celebrate the 60th Annual Grammy Awards an Uber car was fitted with computer vision software that would play the city of New York as if it were a musical instrument. People and various objects, such as traffic lights, bicycle wheels, and even the helmets worn by horse-riding traffic police, acted as the triggers for different sounds and animation, allowing the car's passengers to experience a unique song being created around them in real time. One rear window doubled as a live video feed, to show the animations, via a camera rigged to the outside of the car.

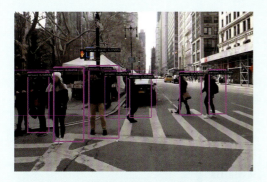

"The idea was to use AR to uncover the inherent musicality of New York City to celebrate the Grammy Awards returning for their 60th Anniversary. We created a software to run on two large machines in the trunk pulling a stream from a camera, processing, then sending back to display on the left back-seat window. The music was generated in real time with a software instrument converting the live computer vision data into triggers and modifiers for instruments and percussion."

Ben Priddy
Tool of North America

Um den 60. Grammy Awards zu feiern, wurde ein Uber-Auto mit einer Computer-Vision-Software ausgestattet. Die Stadt New York sollte damit wie ein Musikinstrument gespielt werden. Menschen und verschiedene Gegenstände wie Ampeln, Fahrraddräder und sogar die Helme der berittenen Polizei fungierten als Trigger für verschiedene Sounds und Animationen, damit die Passagiere im Auto in Echtzeit ein einzigartiges Lied um sich herum erleben konnten. Ein hinteres Fenster diente als Live-Video-Feed, um die Animationen über eine Kamera zu zeigen, die an der Außenseite des Autos angebracht war.

Pour la 60e cérémonie des Grammy Awards, un véhicule Uber équipé d'un logiciel de vision par ordinateur montre les rues de New York comme si elles étaient un instrument de musique. Les passants et des éléments, comme des feux de circulation, des roues de vélo, voire les casques d'agents de la police montée, déclenchent des sons et des animations : les passagers dans la voiture entendent ainsi une mélodie unique composée autour d'eux en temps réel. Grâce à une caméra fixée à l'extérieur du véhicule, une vitre arrière diffuse un flux vidéo en direct pour montrer les animations.

Digital Driving License

—

Completely re-imagining
how digital ID can work

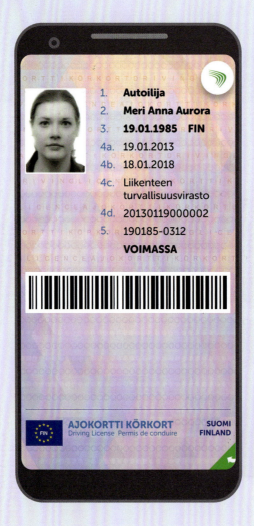

Whilst smartphones had effectively taken over from the need to carry cash or cards, as a form of digital identification they still didn't provide a safe and secure solution, especially for daily use. Finland's Digital Driving License tried to remedy this by using the smartphone's gyroscope and connecting it to a digital watermark that was a continuously animated dynamic OpenGL background, which supported interaction to prevent motion-capture fraud. The interactive touch layer added an extra level of proof that the ID was real and not a fake screen-grab of another person's ID.

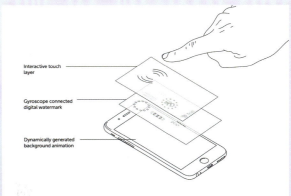

Interactive touch
layer

Gyroscope connected
digital watermark

Dynamically generated
background animation

"A pivotal moment in the project was when
we decided to approach the design from the
perspective of a counterfeiter. After that our
guiding principle was to build something that
was as difficult to counterfeit for a talented
developer as a bank-note would be to a talented
artist who works with offset printing. So we
never dismissed the fact that it could be done,
but made sure it would require unique talent
while remaining confident the back-end security
features would always provide a completely
different challenge for a different skill set making
the ID at least as secure as its analog counterpart."

Niko Sipilä
Great Apes

Zwar haben Smartphones die Bargeld- oder Kartennutzung praktisch überflüssig gemacht, doch für die digitale Identifikation bieten sie noch keine sichere Lösung, insbesondere für den täglichen Gebrauch. Finnlands digitaler Führerschein versuchte dies zu beheben, indem sie das Gyroskop des Smartphones benutzten und es mit einem digi-talen Wasserzeichen verbanden, das ein kontinuierlich animierter dynamischer OpenGL-Hinter-grund war. Dies unterstützte die Interaktion, um Betrug bei der Bewegungserfassung zu verhin-dern. Die interaktive Touch-Ebene sorgte für den zusätzlichen Beweis, dass die ID echt war und nicht ein falscher Screenshot der ID einer anderen Person.

Les smartphones ont éliminé le besoin d'avoir sur soi des espèces ou des cartes de crédit, mais ils n'offrent pas encore une solution sécurisée comme moyen d'iden-tification numérique dans la vie de tous les jours. En Finlande, le projet Digital Driving License tente d'y remédier en connec-tant le gyroscope du smartphone à un tatouage numérique, dont le fond OpenGL dynamique et animé prend en charge les interactions et empêche toute fraude par capture des mouvements. La couche tactile interactive ajoute un niveau d'authenticité supplé-mentaire de l'identité et prouve qu'il ne s'agit pas de la capture du document d'une autre personne.

Nike Reactland

—

A gaming installation where
players became characters
within the game

In 2016, Intel had mapped real people's faces on to historical characters in its History Comes Alive project, but people being turned into in-game characters in real time had not been seen before. For the launch of Nike's React shoes, a special retro-gaming installation was created which inserted players' faces into the action where they became part of the side-scrolling game and could be controlled via a real treadmill. The installation was set up in four major cities and players were able to emulate the Super Mario brothers and run through streets, jump over obstacles, and climb buildings.

"Reactland is a perfect example of where Unit9 excels, the meeting point of design and physical experiences, taking a client's raw, wild idea and turning it into something stylish that really works. We assembled an international team of specialists, from pixel artists to running machine hackers, game coders, and game designers, then created a complete interconnected system from account creation to delivery of a personalized shareable movie online. The functional and aesthetic design were constantly evolving until it all worked together, delivering brand messaging and awesome customer experience. To top it all off the experience was shipped and installed in four Chinese cities, then made a special appearance in Berlin. World Wide!"

Alexander Horton
Horton Design Works; Unit9

Im Jahr 2016 hatte Intel in seinem History-Comes-Alive-Projekt die Gesichter echter Menschen auf historischen Charakteren abgebildet, doch Menschen, die in Echtzeit in In-Game-Charaktere verwandelt wurden, gab es bislang noch nicht. Bei der Markteinführung von Nikes React Shoes wurde eine spezielle Retro-Gaming Installation erstellt, die die Gesichter der Spieler in die Handlung einfügten, wo sie Teil des Side-Scrolling-Spiels wurden und über ein echtes Laufband gesteuert werden konnten. Die Installation wurde in vier großen Städten durchgeführt und die Spieler konnten den Super Mario Brüdern nacheifern und durch Straßen laufen, über Hindernisse springen und Gebäude besteigen.

En 2016, Intel mappait le visage de personnes réelles sur des personnages historiques pour son projet History Comes Alive. Transformer des gens en temps réel en personnages d'un jeu n'avait en revanche encore pas été fait. Pour le lancement du modèle Nike React, une installation de rétrogaming intègre dans l'action le visage des joueurs, qui font alors partie de ce jeu à défilement horizontal et sont contrôlés via un vrai tapis roulant. L'installation est montée dans quatre grandes villes et les joueurs peuvent émuler le jeu Super Mario Bros., courir dans des rues, sauter des obstacles et escalader des immeubles.

—

Emoji Scavenger Hunt

—

A neural network tries to guess what your phone is seeing

Google's Emoji Scavenger Hunt was a browser-based game built with machine learning that used the smartphone's camera and a neural network to try and guess what it was seeing. The game asked players to find certain objects within a set time and then described what it thought it was looking at as the camera was moved around. After each emoji was found, such as a watch, more time would be allocated as the hunt for the next one began. A clever technical detail was the use of tensorflow.js, which meant that the game ran efficiently and quickly via the phone's web browser without the need to access back-end servers.

FIND

NICE, YOU SPOTTED A DOG.

"In 2018 tensorflow.js opened up the promise of machine learning for the web. We were excited to create an experiment that delivered on that potential and was also just a really fun game for people to play. Underlying the game was complicated image recognition made possible by ML, but the simplicity of the interface allowed anyone to experience this technology in a way that made them interact with their surroundings differently. We had a lot of fun with this and we're excited to see what others dream up and bring to life through tensorflow.js."

Jacques Bruwer, Jason Kafalas, and Takashi Kawashima
Google Brand Studio

FIND

in under 18 seconds.

Googles Emoji Scavenger Hunt war ein browserbasiertes Spiel mit maschinellem Lernen, bei dem die Smartphone-Kamera und ein neuronales Netzwerk versuchten zu erraten, was sie sahen. Das Spiel forderte die Spieler auf, bestimmte Objekte innerhalb einer bestimmten Zeit zu finden und beschrieb dann, was es dachte, worauf es blickte, wenn die Kamera herumgeschwenkt wurde.

Nachdem jedes Emoji, gefunden wurde, wie zum Beispiel eine Uhr, wurde mehr Zeit zugewiesen, und die Jagd nach dem nächsten begann. Ein cleveres technisches Detail war die Verwendung von tensorflow.js, was bedeutete, dass das Spiel effizient und schnell über den Webbrowser des Telefons ausgeführt werden konnte, ohne auf Back-End-Server zugreifen zu müssen.

Le nouveau jeu Emoji Scavenger Hunt de Google se joue dans un navigateur et repose sur l'apprentissage automatique à l'aide de la caméra d'un smartphone et d'un réseau neuronal devinant ce qu'il voit. Les joueurs doivent trouver des objets déterminés dans un temps imparti ; le jeu décrit ensuite ce qu'il croit être l'objet de la recherche quand la caméra bouge. Après qu'un emoji est trouvé, comme une montre, du temps est rajouté pour partir en quête du suivant. Sur le plan technique, l'emploi de tensorflow.js est astucieux car le jeu est plus performant dans un navigateur mobile sans devoir accéder à des serveurs dorsaux.

Prescribed to Death

—

An installation featuring thousands of pills carved with human faces

This public education campaign debuted in Chicago as an installation made up of banked arrays of pills each carved with faces to represent the 22,000 people who had died from prescription opioid addiction in 2017. It was a big success by making the issue so personal, while a new pill was engraved live every 24 minutes, matching the frequency of the opioid overdose deaths. With one in three Americans taking prescription opioids, this was a stark warning for people to protect themselves from the risk of addiction and overdose.

"It's a rare honor when you get to work on a project that saves lives. The National Safety Council gave us that opportunity when we developed Prescribed to Death, the first-ever memorial to the victims of the U.S. Opioid Epidemic. At a time when prescription opioid overdose was the fastest-growing cause of preventable death in the United States, we had to find a way to make the country face the issue. The memorial made the crisis personal, featuring 22,000 pill-shaped carvings of faces representing the lives lost each year. We illuminated their stories to raise awareness, and prevent future devastation of lives."

Andrés Ordóñez
Energy BBDO

Diese öffentliche Aufklärungs-kampagne hatte ihr Debüt in Chicago als eine Installation, die aus gestapelten Pillenfeldern be-stand, die jeweils mit Gesichtern verziert waren, um die 22.000 Menschen darzustellen, die 2017 durch die Abhängigkeit von ver-schreibungspflichtigen Opioiden gestorben waren. Es war ein gro-ßer Erfolg, das Thema so persön-lich zu machen, während alle 24 Minuten eine neue Pille live gra-viert wurde, was der Häufigkeit der Todesfälle durch Überdosie-rung von Opioiden entsprach. Bei einem von drei Amerikanern, die verschreibungspflichtige Opioide einnahmen, war dies eine deut-liche Warnung an die Menschen, sich vor dem Risiko von Sucht und Überdosierung zu schützen.

Cette campagne pédagogique publique commence à Chicago sous la forme d'une installation où sont alignés des comprimés sur lesquels sont gravés des visages pour représenter les 22 000 personnes décédées en 2017 d'une addiction aux opioïdes. Elle remporte un grand succès car elle rend le problème très personnel : un nouveau com-primé est gravé en direct toutes les 24 minutes, soit la fréquence à laquelle se produisent les morts par overdose d'opioïdes. Un Amé-ricain sur trois consomme des opioïdes sur ordonnance : il s'agit donc d'un avertissement sévère pour que les patients se pro-tègent contre les risques d'ad-diction et d'overdose.

NOTABLE WEBSITE LAUNCH
World Draw

GOOGLE FACTS

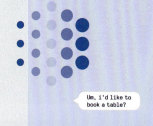

Google Duplex, an AI assistant, is announced

Hi James,

Please can we agree a time to meet? [tab]

Amy Thomas
Line Manager

Google announces Smart Compose for Gmail, the ability to auto-complete entire emails

Hello

R&B star John Legend to become the new voice of Google Assistant

10 hr 32 min

Other — YouTube
Gmail — Netflix
Chrome
Instagram
WhatsApp — Facebook

Android P is announced and focuses on digital well-being

BOOK COVER
by A

Google Lens can now highlight the text from a book and copy it to the user's phone

Top 5 Trends
World Cup
Avicii
Mac Miller
Stan Lee
Black Panther

Top 5 Trends

MOBILE EVOLUTION
Huawei P20 Pro

The first smartphone to
come with an AI-powered
triple camera

INTERNET COMMUNITY
#DeleteFacebook

The hashtag #DeleteFacebook trended
worldwide after news that Cambridge
Analytica had been harvesting data
from 50 million Facebook users'
profiles. Some well-known industry
figures, including Elon Musk,
publicly announced via the hashtag
that they were deleting their
Facebook accounts.

Index

Index/

Index/

Acknowledgements

Acknowledgements/

—

I have to pay tribute to the global design community portals
of the late 1990s and early 2000s whom I feel influenced the
early internet generation and gave them the stage to reach
all corners of the world with their pioneering work:

A List Apart	db-db	isolate
All Maple	de Lijst	Kaliber 10000
Archinect	Design Collector	Kiiroi
Australian INFront	Design is Kinky	Linkdup
BD4D	Design made in Germany	Lounge72
CBCnet	Domestika	Media Inspiration
Chaoticroots	Favourite Website Awards (FWA)	mi3dot
Computer Arts	Flash Kit	Moluv
Computer Love	Half Project	Motionographer
Coudal	Holodeck73	Nervousroom
Cre@te Online	HOWdesign	Netdiver
Crossmind	Infourm	Newstoday

pixel.ee	Three.Oh	Archive.org for filling many blanks, especially visually.
Pixelsurgeon	Uailab	KoolLondon.com for keeping my mind in a great nostalgic place when writing.
Projectneo	Ultrashock	
RES72	Ventilate	
Scene 360	visualOrgasm	
Shift Magazine	Webesteem	
Stylegala	Well Vetted	
Substitud	Wow Web Designs	
Surfstation		
Swedezine		
Swikiri		
thespot		

And, of course, the dream team for creating amazing books: Julius Wiedemann for guiding this book in the right direction. Without him, you would not have been able to hold this book in one hand. Daniel Siciliano Bretas for being the impeccable manager of the book at all times. Jon Cefai and his team for going the extra mile with another great book design and for the wonderful illustrations throughout. Chris Allen for his eagle eye, once again, on the manuscript.

Rob Ford, 2019

© 2019 TASCHEN GmbH
Hohenzollernring 53, D-50672 Köln
www.taschen.com

To stay informed about TASCHEN and our
upcoming titles, please subscribe to
our free magazine at www.taschen.com/
magazine, follow us on Twitter, Instagram,
and Facebook, or e-mail your questions to
contact@taschen.com.

EACH AND EVERY TASCHEN BOOK PLANTS A SEED!
TASCHEN is a carbon neutral publisher.
Each year, we offset our annual carbon
emissions with carbon credits at the
Instituto Terra, a reforestation program
in Minas Gerais, Brazil, founded by
Lélia and Sebastião Salgado. To find out
more about this ecological partnership,
please check: www.taschen.com/zerocarbon
INSPIRATION: UNLIMITED.
CARBON FOOTPRINT: ZERO.

Printed in Italy
ISBN 978-3-8365-7267-5

EDITOR
Julius Wiedemann

EDITORIAL COORDINATION
Daniel Siciliano Bretas, Cologne

DESIGN
Collaborate, www.collaborate-london.com

PRODUCTION
Stefan Klatte, Cologne

ENGLISH COPY-EDITING
Chris Allen, London

GERMAN TRANSLATION
Andrea Wiethoff for Delivering iBooks
& Design, Barcelona

FRENCH TRANSLATION
Valérie Lavoyer for Delivering iBooks
& Design, Barcelona